IMRAN KHAN

ALSO BY CHRISTOPHER SANDFORD

FICTION

Feasting with Panthers

Arcadian

We Don't Do Dogs

SPORT

The Cornhill Centenary Test

Godfrey Evans

Tom Graveney

FILM

Steve McQueen

Roman Polanski

MUSIC

Mick Jagger

Eric Clapton

Kurt Cobain

David Bowie

Sting

Bruce Springsteen

Keith Richards

Paul McCartney

THE CRICKETER, THE CELEBRITY, THE POLITICIAN

IMRAN KHAN

THE BIOGRAPHY

CHRISTOPHER SANDFORD

HarperCollins*Publishers*

HarperCollins*Publishers*
77–85 Fulham Palace Road,
Hammersmith, London W6 8JB

www.harpercollins.co.uk

First published by HarperCollins*Publishers* 2009

1

Christopher Sandford asserts the moral right to
be identified as the author of this work

A catalogue record of this book is
available from the British Library

HB ISBN 978-0-00-726285-4
PB ISBN 978-0-00-731888-9

Printed and bound in Great Britain by
Clays Ltd, St Ives plc

FOR K.W.

1953–2006

Contents

List of Illustrations

PAGE 4

Tyrian Khan White (both Getty Images)
Imran's London home (Mirror Syndication)
As famous in the tabloids for his social life (Press Association and Mirror Syndication)

PAGE 5

The Princess of Wales (Getty Images)
On David Frost's television show (Mirror Syndication)
Dar, seen here adjusting his client's hair (courtesy of Dar/ Christopher Sandford)
Nothing came to obsess Imran quite as much (Press Association)

PAGE 6

'Don't bring back a foreign wife' (Mirror Syndication)
The military-backed President Musharraf (Getty Images)
Ian Botham and Allan Lamb's 1996 libel action (Getty Images)

PAGE 7

Despite a number of personal distractions (Getty Images)
In 2007, Imran's anti-government stance (Getty Images)

PAGE 8

With sons Qasim and Sulaiman (Getty Images)
Still campaigning in 2009 (Getty Images)

Acknowledgements

First, Imran Khan. Although trying to pin him down proved nearly as challenging as was descending into the briar patch of Pakistani politics, he turned out to be a patient and generous interviewee. Reflecting the rather mobile nature of his life, we spoke by phone over a nine-month period when Imran was variously in London, Brussels, Lahore, Islamabad and aboard an Amtrak sleeper train somewhere on America's eastern seaboard. He made no conditions and did not ask for advance approval of the manuscript, for which I'm grateful. Although one or two of his long-time opponents declined the offer to speak, occasionally after venting at me, the research process generally was productive and tantrum-free. Writing this book after one on Roman Polanski was like drinking a glass of sparkling mineral water after gorging on heavily salted nuts. I only wish I could blame someone listed below for the shortcomings of the text. They are mine alone.

For recollections, input or advice I should thank, institutionally: Abacus, Aitchison College, *Atlantic Monthly*, Bookcase, Bookends, the British Library, British Newspaper Library, *Chronicles*, CIA, the Complete Line, CricInfo, CricketArchive, the Cricketers Club of London, *Cricket Lore*, *Daily Mail*, *Dawn*, FBI – Freedom of Information Division, Focus Fine Arts, General Register Office, Golem, Palgrave Macmillan, MCC, MultiMap, Office of the President, Islamic Republic of Pakistan, Orbis, Oxford University Cricket Club, Public Record Office, Renton Public Library, Seattle Cricket Club, Seattle Public Library, *Slate*, the *Spectator*, Sussex CCC, *The Times*, *Vanity Fair*, Vital Records, Worcestershire CCC.

* * *

Professionally: Qamar Ahmed, the late Les Ames, Aslam Anwar, Jeffrey Archer, Fareshteh Aslam, Trevor Bailey, Johnny Barclay, the late Ken Barrington, Alec Bedser, Daphne Benaud, Richie Benaud, Dickie Bird, Rob Boddie, Ian Botham, Kathy Botham, Geoff Boycott, Mike Brearley, Rodney Cass, the late Denis Compton, Melinda Cooksey, Dar, Dave Davies, Ted Dexter, Basil D'Oliveira, Sally Donaghue, the late Godfrey Evans, Gus Farley, Judy Flanders, George Galloway, Alix Gibb, Tony Gill, Jim Gillespie, David Gower, Tom Graveney, Jackie Graveney, Hugh Griffiths, Richard Hadlee, Naeem ul-Haque, Debbie Harris, Janet Harris, Antao Hassan, the late Reg Hayter, Alastair Hignell, the late Len Hutton, Asif Iqbal, Mick Jagger, Sarah Jones, Chris Kelly, Javed Kureishi, the late Omar Kureishi, Allan Lamb, the late Chris Lander, Neil Lenham, the late Tony Lock, John Major, Vic Marks, Jonathan Mermagen, Abdul Mirza, Mohammad Akram Mirza, Linda Morris, Jock Mullard, Colleen Murray, John Murray, Tahir Nawaz, Liz Neto, Mark Newton, Mark Nicholas, Barry Norman, the late Kerry Packer, Paul Parker, Peter Perchard, Tony Pigott, the late Harold Pinter, Nigel Popplewell, Dr. Simon Porter, Alison Prince, Derek Pringle, Abdul Qadeer, Abdul Qadir, the late Wasim Raja, Derek Randall, Haroun Rashid, Tim Rice, the late Graham Roope, Dicky Rutnagur, Yusuf Salahudin, Mike Selvey, Waris Sharif, Dennis Silk, Diana Silk, the late Peter Smith, Alex Stacey, Anne Stenson, Jack Surendranath, Angela Lue Taim, Jonathan Taylor, Ivo Tennant, Fred Titmus, the late Fred Trueman, Tony Vinter, Rev. Mike Vockins, Tom Whiting, Karen Wishart, Ali Zaidi.

Personally: Adis, Air Canada, Arvid Anderson, Rev. Maynard Atik, the Attic, Pete Barnes, the late Terry Bland, Bob Bridge, Hilary and Robert Bruce, Cocina, Common Ground, Ken Crabtrey, Roz Cranstoun-Corby, Celia Culpan, Deb K. Das, the Davenport, Mark Demos, Monty Dennison, the Dowdall family, John and Barbara Dungee, Jennifer Evans, Mary Evans, Fairmont Waterfront Hotel, Farmers, Malcolm Galfe, Audrey Godwin, Colleen Graffy, the Grafton on Sunset, James Graham, the Gay Hussar, the Gees, Grumbles, Richard Hill, Charles Hillman, the late Amy Hostetter, Hotel Vancouver, Hyde Park Hilton, Sarah Horn, JCC, Jo Jacobius, Lincoln Kamell, the late Alan Kennington, Tom and Joan Keylock, Terry Lambert, Belinda Lawson, Barbara Levy, Cindy Link, Vince Lorimer, the late Jackie McBride, Les McBride, Ruth and Angie McCartney, the Macris, Ron and Russell Mael, Lee Mattson, Teri Mayo, Uday Mehta, Jim and Rana Meyersahm, Missoula Doubletree, Sheila Mohn, the Morgans, National Gallery Sackler Room, Chuck

Ogmund, Valya Page, Robin Parish, Greg Phillips, Chris Pickrell, PNB, Roman Polanski, the Prins family, the late Navaal Ramdin, Keith Richards, Amanda Ripley, the late Malcolm Robinson, Debbie Saks, Sam, Delia Sandford, my father Sefton Sandford, Sue Sandford, Seattle International Film Festival, Peter Scaramanga, Rev. Kempton Segerhammar, the late Cat Sinclair, Skyway F.D., Fred and Cindy Smith, Rev. and Mrs Harry Smith, Spruce Street School, the Stanleys, Streamline Taxis, Airie Stuart, Thaddeus Stuart, Jack Surendranath, Chai Tarler, the Travel Team, Ben and Mary Tyvand, William Underhill, University of Montana, Syra Vahidy, Di Villar, the late Roger Villar, Lisbeth Vogl, John and Mary Wainwright, Walgreens, Chris West, Jim Wheal, Richard Wigmore, the Willis Fleming family.

And a doffed hat, as always, to Karen and Nicholas Sandford.

C.S.
2009

'True disputants are like true sportsmen, their whole delight is in the pursuit.'

ALEXANDER POPE

'It's not a question of aspirations. I know, God willing, one day I am going to succeed. And that's not very far away.'

IMRAN KHAN

speaking to the media about his chances of running Pakistan

ONE

Only a Game

Even in the 1950s, Pakistani representative cricket was popularly known at home and abroad as 'the cauldron', and for good reason. There were tribal conflicts, internecine feuds, intrigues, coups and denouncements, on-field theatrics and public tantrums, along with persistent allegations of match-rigging, intemperate betting and wholesale mob violence. That would be for starters. And if you wanted to replicate some of the uniquely vibrant drama of the national sport (which, it should be immediately said, has also included its moments of spectacular success) in another arena, Pakistani politics in the 30 years since the execution by hanging of former President Zulfikar Ali Bhutto in 1979 would have to be the place to start. In this largely male-dominated culture, the preservation of status and the all-important concept of revenge have sometimes tended to take precedence over complicated legal codes and sporting niceties imported from Britain. Imran Khan, then, links two particularly volatile and professionally highly precarious fields of activity. And while yet to achieve as a politician the sort of success he enjoyed as a Test captain and national father-figure, it may be only recently that his true paternalism has emerged in its purest form. One source close to the heart of the Pakistani government told me that when the young daughter of a man from a very different end of the political spectrum was diagnosed with bone cancer, Imran sprang into action. 'We'll get her in there,' he assured the girl's parents, referring to the Shaukat Khanum facility in Lahore, the leading hospital and research centre named after Imran's late mother, and for which he raised some $15 million in the six years before it opened to the public in December 1994. 'We've got this child up here, maybe dying,' Imran duly informed the head surgeon. 'A tumour's in her. Eating her up ... You've got to cure her.' When he went back to the girl's parents he told them that there would be no charge, and that 'My job is the easy one. I'm lucky. She has the hard job. She has to keep on living.'

It's worth dwelling on Pakistan's historic sporting tradition for a moment if only to show how much more than a player from England or Australia, say, Imran had his work cut out for him. For close on 25 years his daily routine took place against a backdrop of almost farcical administrative incompetence, fanatical public adulation or hostility, frequently swinging from one to the other and back again in the course of the same match, an equally heated national media, and, not least, a culture of dressing-room conspiracies, betrayals and figurative back-stabbings that would have raised eyebrows among the Borgia family. (Again, these were conditions Imran was to find instantly familiar in his post-retirement political career.) The operative words when describing the core atmosphere of modern Pakistani cricket are 'pride' and 'passion', which indeed happen to be the title of the journalist Omar Noman's definitive study of the subject. Two and a half decades' active involvement in the field argues a certain strength of character on anyone's part. There's perhaps little to be gained by seeking to analyse the peculiar essence of national hero-worship, as Imran experienced it. The 'pathology of fame' – a much debated topic – already has a long academic history, some of it quite reputable. But although, by all accounts, Imran enjoyed most aspects of being a celebrity, he was also aware early on that it had downsides he hadn't had to worry about when he was an anonymous schoolboy. One intrusive fan he encountered walking down the street in Worcester shortly after he went to live there in 1971 rapidly went from fawning on Imran to abusing him when he politely declined to join the man in the pub for a drink. 'Paki bastard!' he shouted. 'Get a real job!'

It would be fair to say that, over the years, Pakistan's whole perceived approach to the game, characterised as it is by not only internal strife but also a lack of fraternity with opposition players and fans alike, contributed to a siege mentality that perhaps had deeper cultural roots. Years before the 9/11 attacks and the subsequent hardening of opinion on the subject, Imran referred to this factor himself. 'Pakistan cricketers are treated like Islam in the West. Most of the time, [the] images are depicted by terrorists, fanaticism, veiled women and so on. Similarly, our cricketers are looked upon as an indisciplined, unruly mob who pressurise umpires, cheat, doctor cricket balls, whinge about umpiring decisions and are generally unsporting.' ('Well, yes,' some cynics might reply.)

For all that, the occasional misgivings between the Pakistan team and their English opponents may have had less to do with religous intolerance or lingering post-colonial animosity than with a specific incident that occurred at Peshawar on the North-West Frontier in February 1956. This was the tragicomic episode of the 'kidnapped' umpire, Idrees Beg. Its repercussions were felt for at least 20 years afterwards – well into Imran's own tenure in the Pakistan side.

The whole affair began when, in the course of a keenly anticipated Pakistan v. MCC 'unofficial Test', a number of the tourists' batsmen came to voice their concern at how receptive umpire Beg seemed to be to Abdul Kardar's repeated and highly animated appeals for lbw: there were five such decisions in the MCC first innings alone. Kardar's first victim, the young Ken Barrington, once told me that his dismissal had been the single worst injustice of a 15-year career not untouched by shadow. 'You've heard people say, "It would have missed a second set of stumps"? This one would have missed a third set,' Barrington recalled, still a shade rueful more than 20 years after the event. Another source assured me that Kardar, Pakistan's imperious Test captain, 'could [have] done no wrong in that match'. He had 'snapped out' his various appeals and umpire Beg, a former military man, had 'obeyed the orders unthinkingly, [in] the time-honoured way'. The strong MCC side were all out for 188, with Kardar taking six for 40 off 28.2 overs.

On the Sunday evening of the match, a number of the MCC players, led by their captain Donald Carr, had finished dinner at a local restaurant and then taken a taxi across town to the officials' hotel, where they went upstairs to Beg's room and invited him to accompany them. The details of what followed are unclear, but it seems fairly certain that the Englishmen hustled Beg into a tonga, or horse-drawn carriage, and drove him back to their own hotel, where a bucket of water was poured over him. The Peshawar daily *Mashriq* was later to claim that a number of the visitors had been wearing handkerchiefs over their faces, giving them the impression of 'brigands' and 'fiends', and that Beg himself had been clad throughout the ordeal only in his pyjamas. (A report that he had been debagged completely, leaving him to run 'stark bollock naked through the hotel corridors', has proved impossible to verify.) The 'dank and dishevelled' umpire was then released into the night amid 'sundry jeers and catcalls', and made his way home without further ado. Or that was at least one account; but the accounts are as varied and colourful as the events they claim to describe, and the only certainties are that the next evening's press ran a headline insisting that Beg had been the victim of a 'vile assault', that the tourists eventually lost the match by seven wickets, leaving the ground under a hail of abuse and with a police escort, and that the president of MCC subsequently offered a formal apology in response to an aggrieved telegram from the Pakistan board.

As the fall-out from the 'Beg affair' continued, an impression formed in some quarters that certain of the Pakistani players and officials were regrettably thin-skinned when it came to the sort of schoolboy prank that was routine, at least in those days, on the English county circuit. (It was perhaps unfortunate, even so, that the incident occurred in the politically sensitive city of Peshawar, home of the 'Red Shirt' movement which had played an active role in Pakistan's struggle for independence, and that there had allegedly been an attempt to persuade Beg, a Muslim, to take alcohol.) Whatever the rights and wrongs of the case, it set the scene for a mutually wary playing relationship between the two countries that, at least on the Pakistani side, lasted well into the 1970s. Somewhere along the way, a stereotype seemed to form of what one famous England player described to me as a 'little roly-poly guy with bags of natural talent and a massive chip on his shoulder' – the swarthy, hot-tempered 'Paki' of popular legend who, whether individually or collectively, seemed to positively court controversy. It's not the least of Imran Khan's achievements to have moulded the most mercurial of all Test sides into a cohesive unit as good as any in the world, and to have done so while actually playing much of his own cricket in England.

In fact, in the memories of his Pakistan players as well as the popular press, there sometimes seemed to be two Imrans, urbanely straddling East and West. Scores of team-mates knew him as the now imposing, now genial 'Skip' whose resonant voice and grandly laconic manner ('Abdul. Come. Bowl.') had the force of law, both on and off the pitch. Clearly, Imran wasn't the sort of captain content merely to make the bowling changes and move the field around. He also selected the team he wanted in the first place, often over the vocal objections of his board, and personally took responsibility while on tour for such matters as determining which player needed to be in bed by 10 p.m. and which one could be trusted to turn his own light out. 'Like God, he was everywhere,' one colleague recalls. 'Imran was a very intense person,' Kerry Packer said, high praise from that particular source, remembering him striding across the shaded outfield 'to fairly grab the ball out of the umpire's hand' before bowling the first session in a World

Series match at Sydney. 'He was a good listener,' another long-time team-mate thought, 'not the kind of guy who would ever monopolise a team talk or conversation.' Yet one or two of the junior Pakistan players found him impatiently cutting them off, and often peremptory. 'He was a benign dictator. He'd say, "Well shall we try 'X'?" and you'd say "Well, what about 'Y'?" and then in a few minutes it would be back to "X" ... You listened to him explain the decision, and that was collaboration.' Others saw him, off the field of play, as a bouffant-haired swinger and legendary Romeo, equally at home ushering a succession of sleek young women around various fashionable London nightspots as, years later, he would be campaigning among the slums of Lahore.

This combination of talent, good looks and a vibrant social life gave Imran a role in English public life and in tabloid newspapers both in western Europe and South Asia hitherto reserved for international footballers or film stars. The future cricket journalist Fareshteh Aslam, who was in her teens at about the time Imran came to prominence, recalls:

> Not only did everyone in Pakistan have his poster on the wall, he was the one person the whole country could be proud of. People forget that 30 years ago Pakistan was a bit like North Korea, this hermit kingdom that was cut off from the rest of the world and horribly claustrophobic to live in. There was one television channel, state run, and no internet. If there's such a thing as a national inferiority complex, we had one. And suddenly here was this exotic-looking guy doing battle around the world on our behalf. He was like Superman and Spiderman rolled into one.

A superhero, it should be added, who faced formidable home-grown obstacles as well as the external kind. When Imran inherited the captaincy of Pakistan in 1982, players from the different regions were often quite unfamiliar with one another and had typically never met off the field. The factional rivalries in the game as a whole were such that even Hanif Mohammad, the Karachi-based founding father of modern Pakistani cricket, had been barracked by the crowd when, in February 1969, he walked out to bat for his side against England at Lahore. Over the succeeding years, open verbal confrontations between various players of diverse social or geographical backgrounds did little for team morale. Imran himself recalls the case of Talat Ali, a promising young opening bat and occasional medium-pace bowler who was dropped first by Pakistan and then by his club side, PIA, officially because he was deemed 'too old' at 28. His place in the team was taken by the son of the PIA head of selectors. That same year, the successful Pakistan Test captain Mushtaq Mohammad was unseated in favour of Asif Iqbal. When Mushtaq then read in his local paper that he was no longer needed even as a player, he reportedly spent two days trying to phone the members of the board to discuss the matter. Not one of them was available to take his call. It was all somehow a representative case study of a culture whose leading practitioners tended to lack the gift of recognising their own limitations and compensating for them by drawing on the strengths of others. For some years, Imran would conduct a cold war by proxy with his illustrious colleague Javed Miandad over whether to include Iqbal Qasim or Abdul Qadir as Pakistan's first-choice spinner. Imran and Qadir hailed from the north of the country, Javed and Qasim from the south. Javed's and in turn Wasim Akram's leadership of the team both ended in tears, amid impassioned if unsubstantiated allegations of regional bias and cronyism.

As captain, Imran (who was proven right about Qadir) 'seem[ed] to care less about the individual player than about winning as a team', recalls a Karachi *Jang* editor, who often heard the private misgivings. His men were proud of the success he brought, but admired rather than liked him. Imran's entire tenure was characterised by a distinctly personal and hands-on approach to matters such as team selection, tactics and discipline of the kind conspicuously lacking both before and since, and whose results speak for themselves. Pakistan won 14, lost 8 and drew 26 of the 48 Tests they played under him, including three hotly contested tied series against the West Indies at their peak, before going on to win the 1992 World Cup.* Factional grudges and private intrigues were out, he made it abundantly clear, to be replaced by a steely professionalism which placed the premium on winning by any legitimate means. No detail was too small to escape Imran's notice in this new, centralised regime. When the Pakistan team came off the field at the end of the third day's play against India at Bangalore in March 1987, the same Karachi *Jang* journalist went up to Imran in the dressing-room and asked him why, out of interest, some of the Pakistan non-bowling fielders had played in as many as three sweaters, while

* For the statistically minded, 83.3 per cent of the Tests Pakistan played under Imran's captaincy thus ended in a win or a draw; Mike Brearley, widely regarded as the Freud of modern Test captains, scored 89.5 per cent, while for Imran's contemporary Ian Botham the figure falls to 66.6 per cent.

others had appeared in shirt sleeves. '"Oh, I decide all that," Imran answered casually. Apparently it was all part of some climate-control system impos[ed] from above, to keep each man fresh.'

Imran's elevation to the Test captaincy obscured for the moment the continuing frailties both of Pakistan cricket as a whole everywhere below international level, and more specifically of a Board of Control for whom nepotism and zonal 'quotas' had long been an integral part of the selection process. It also ushered in a period of sustained achievement in both the five- and the one-day game, and a commensurately increased, not to say rabid public support. While the new regime successfully replaced the air of unpredictable charm traditionally surrounding the Pakistan team with one of collective responsibility, it relied heavily (some thought excessively) on the undeniable charisma, all-round bravura performances and fanatical dedication of one man. Even his critics agreed that if greatness consists of the taking of infinite pains, then Imran was a great national leader. Paradoxically, as the Pakistan Test side grew more successful, certain individuals close to it grew more unhappy, apparently believing that a personality cult had been allowed to develop at the expense of a more communal team ethic. No doubt this explains why a former senior colleague of Imran's, while 'admir[ing] his talent to the skies', admitted to certain reservations when I asked him about his captain's unique leadership style. 'He was like Stalin,' he told me, with just a touch of hyperbole.

As we've seen, the particular Pakistani gift for self-destructive behaviour, both on and off the cricket field, preceded Imran's own playing days. In October 1969, to give just one example, the home board took the decision to appoint Intikhab Alam as captain in place of Saeed Ahmed. Saeed did not take the news well. After publicly threatening to brain the chairman of selectors he was suspended for the series and appeared again only sporadically (though with personally bitter consequences for Imran) before his early retirement.*

Imran's own tenure as captain got off to an unpromising start when, on the morning of his first Test in charge, against England at Edgbaston in July 1982, he left his senior professional Majid Khan, who was 35, out of the side. Majid had not only been Imran's mentor; he

---

* Reflecting on the incident, the veteran journalist Antao Hassan told me that 'It was really a question of what's now called ageism'; Saeed was already 31 when he was dropped – 'virtually senile' in a national cricket culture that puts an extreme premium on youth.

was also his first cousin. It would be hard to exaggerate the shock at the decision, both as expressed by Majid himself and in Pakistan as a whole. Anyone who remembers the circumstances of Margaret Thatcher's enforced departure from office in 1990 has only to think of that same level of drama, with an added touch of the Pathan tribal tradition of cousins hating each other, to get a bit of the flavour. By all accounts, Imran and Majid didn't speak for the next ten years, even when Pakistan won the World Cup, although peace broke out again between them later in the 1990s.

Before the tour of England there had been the home series with Sri Lanka in the spring of 1982, when the Pakistan team took the field for the first Test without eight of their senior men, including Imran. The same group had come to share certain private misgivings about Javed Miandad's leadership of the side, and shortly afterwards they released a public statement to that effect. Imran then unilaterally signalled his intention to return for the second Test, only for the other mutineers to prevent him from doing so. After further protracted negotiations, Pakistan eventually fielded a full-strength team for the third Test at Lahore. Imran took eight for 58 in the Sri Lanka first innings and six for 58 in the second. Pakistan won the match by an innings and 102 runs. Javed then diplomatically announced that he would be 'unavailable' to lead his country in England, leaving Imran himself to step in.

In January 1983 Pakistan played India in the fourth Test at Hyderabad, already 2–0 up in the six-match series. In the Pakistan first innings Javed and Mudassar put on 451 for the third wicket, tying the record for the most lucrative partnership in Test history. Javed finished the second day's play on 238 not out, 127 short of the then highest ever individual score in Tests, Garry Sobers's 365 not out for the West Indies against Pakistan in 1958. Javed notes that at that stage, 'there was no talk of a declaration. Imran never brought it up ... I took this to mean that I was actively being given a chance to go for all possible records.' He wasn't. Much to Javed's obvious displeasure, Imran declared midway through the following morning's session, leaving his predecessor as captain stranded on 280. A mutual colleague, reflecting on the two men's contrasting cricket philosophies, told me that 'Javed [was] a feisty little bugger, which I say in all affection. He wanted to score tons of runs, and in doing so he wanted to crush the opposition. It was a case of kill or be killed. By contrast, Imran took the view that you played your hardest, but that at the end of the day you shook your opponent's hand and went off to dinner. He wasn't demoralised by defeats. He wasn't aggrandised by victories.' Pakistan won that particular Test by an innings and 119 runs, with most of the last day to spare.

Zaheer Abbas, the bespectacled batting genius of Pakistan cricket, then led the team in Australia in the winter of 1983–84, when Imran suffered a recurrence of a serious shin injury. Zaheer's first act was to issue a statement saying that it was not the side he would have chosen and complaining that he was only a caretaker, with inadequate resources, which would appear to have been a tactical own goal on his part. Pakistan duly crumpled in the first two Tests. The third was only marginally more competitive, producing a draw. As a result, the home Board of Control in Lahore was toppled by a coup. Zaheer, meanwhile, took the opportunity of a local newspaper column to publicly castigate his predecessor for everything from his influence over team selection to his various alleged tactical foibles. Despite this rather muted welcome, Imran agreed to appear in the fourth Test at Melbourne as a specialist batsman. On a fast pitch against a still fiery Dennis Lillee, he scored 83 in the first innings and an unbeaten 72 in the second. After that tour Imran would be out of Test cricket for nearly two years, during which Javed Miandad and Zaheer assumed what was effectively a co-captaincy of the team. Against all the odds, Imran returned to international cricket in late 1985, promptly taking 17 wickets in three outings against Sri Lanka. In the course of the series, Javed let it be known that he would again be resigning as captain, and Zaheer announced his retirement. Imran himself then threatened not to play for Pakistan ever again following a dispute with the selectors, but returned to lead his country in the 1987 World Cup, where against expectations they managed to lose to Australia in the semi-final at Lahore. Following the match, a mob estimated at 10,000 roamed the streets, looted stores and demanded the wholesale sacking of the team. Imran's old fast-bowling partner Sarfraz Nawaz metaphorically fanned the flames by insisting that Pakistan had deliberately thrown the match as part of a betting scam. Evidently this was something of a fetish for Sarfraz, because he made the same allegation nine years later, when Pakistan equally unexpectedly lost a World Cup tie to India.

It would be a stretch, therefore, to claim that Imran's leadership was universally popular, or that he was always an easy man to get to know. 'He was constantly reinventing himself ... Had an inner wariness ... There was a kind of barrier between him and the rest of us, a film you couldn't get through ... Fanatically private' – phrases like these come up time and again in research. One colleague from his county cricket days in England told me that in his considered opinion there had been five or six Imrans, 'a veritable layer cake of contradictions'. There was Khan the Vengeful Warrior, Khan the Great Unifier, Khan the All-Knowing, Khan the Mild-Mannered, Khan the Dedicated Professional and Khan the Shagger. But whatever the various sides to the man, more or less everyone agrees that he was an outstandingly resilient Pakistan supremo, an office that traditionally enjoys the same degree of job security associated with that of the Italian government. Furthermore, Imran led from the front: five of his six Test centuries and 15 of his 18 Test half-centuries came when he was in office, and his bowling average improved from 25.53 to 20.26 over the same period. These were figures certain other all-rounders thrust into Test match captaincy could only dream of.

From Pakistan's arrival on the international cricket scene in 1952, the key piece of dressing-room wisdom handed down from player to player was 'Keep in with the board' – that remote and forbidding body of extravagantly mustachioed army officers which typically served at the pleasure of the head of state. It was good advice. Even at the best of times the board presided over a bewildering succession of abrupt resignations, embittered retirements and ill-advised comebacks, the direct result of their own long established habit of capriciously reversing themselves on most key decisions. Nowhere was this extreme administrative flexibility more keenly felt than in the Test captaincy. In a period of just 12 years, the national side was led by Saeed Ahmed, Intikhab Alam, Majid Khan, Asif Iqbal, Intikhab again, Mushtaq Mohammad, Wasim Bari, Javed Miandad, Zaheer Abbas and Imran. The bloody and sustained in-fighting would make even the shambolic England feud of early 2009 look like a trivial misunderstanding. There were certain Tests when up to half the Pakistan XI consisted of ex-captains. Imran's record, then, may not be unblemished, but merely to have survived for 48 matches in charge was itself a feat. To have done so while making it clear to the board that it was he, not they, who both chose the team in the first place and then ran it on the field of play makes it even more impressive. 'I came to admire his [Imran's] tactics and his principles ... how an organisation works and how you get things done,' General Muhammad Zia-ul-Haq, the former army chief of staff and state president, later said.

* * *

At the risk of hyperbole, or of sounding like an apologist, it could be said that there was no such thing as a dull Imran Khan performance in the dozen or so years that he was at his peak: weaker ones, certainly, county matches in front of a couple of hundred spectators where he failed to fire on all cylinders, or Tests where either the wicket or the umpires clearly favoured the opposition batsman (who could still expect a few irritated bouncers for his pains) – but never a truly boring spectacle, a match that was begging to be walked out on. At least part of the overall appeal was distinctly physical. Imran in his prime was a famously fine specimen of a man, with a gym-honed body, a leonine mane of shaggy dark hair and what was authoritatively described to me as a 'knee-trembler' of a voice. Men wanted to be like him and women wanted to go to bed with him, which a fair number of them duly did. Part was also technical, in that Imran was not only an accomplished bowler but a visually thrilling one. From a slow, crouching start he accelerated with a sprinter's poise and balance in his approach to the wicket, which culminated in a last-second propulsive leap and a virile, full-stretch whip of the body. The sheer energy of his bowling style was such that, even from the boundary, Ken Barrington 'fully expect[ed] to see dust and newspapers flying around in the air when he followed through, much like what happens when the Brighton Belle thunders past'. As a batsman, Imran was known as an improviser who liked to smash it around on occasion, but with an essentially sound, orthodox technique that included a full range of ground strokes. Along with the runs and the wickets he also provided a firm hand on the tiller and in general put the steel into his team. Imran himself modestly felt he did 'as well as [he] could' as a captain, given the available assets. Under him, Pakistan enjoyed 10 years of nearly unbroken success, all the more striking a record when measured against their ramshackle showings in the 1960s and early 1970s.

Imran, in short, changed the way Pakistan cricket was perceived around the world. The perennial cabaret turn of the international circuit was transformed into the hyper-aggressive fighting unit who lifted the World Cup. He was the figurehead of a sporting renaissance which had direct and dramatic results on national self-confidence. He personally turned in the performances with bat and ball that made most of this possible. And he did it while facing a continuing series of internecine feuds and self-inflicted crises which the Pakistan game unerringly managed to produce even amidst all the progress.

In fact, there's a theory, no doubt highly debatable and based on selective evidence, that Imran is one of only two professional athletes of the post-war era to have transcended his sport to the point of being a universal – or at least continental – icon, someone whom tens of millions of ordinary citizens instantly recognise. (The other one is Muhammad Ali.) Certainly his dazzling social life and long list of public causes were at least as well known as his bowling average. As more than one critic has remarked, Imran turned into a shout a voice that had hitherto hardly been heard, 'that [of] the developing world as a whole clamouring for respect'. No less an authority than Richard Nixon, a shrewd judge of geopolitics, whatever one makes of his own contribution to them (and, it emerged, something of a closet cricket fan), told me in 1992 that, in this sense, 'Khan [was] really on a par with a head of state'. Imran knew that, for many impoverished people, cricket was never a game. To millions, it was an escape from drab reality, while for the ruling elite it was a propaganda tool no less important than, say, Bollywood or the possession of nuclear weapons. Imran himself became the most potent visual symbol not just of Pakistan, but of an entire subcontinent coming to assert its identity in the aftermath of independence and partition, a role he played with characteristic, if not messianic self-belief. What's more, his appeal was always rather more earthy than that enjoyed by a Mahatma Gandhi. Imran's friend Naeem-ul-Haque told me of an occasion in the early 1980s when the two of them had been walking through Harrods department store in London and a young woman, seeing Imran, 'lost first her decorum and then her consciousness. She literally collapsed at his feet.'

Why did he do it? In his mid-forties, Imran abandoned the comfortable career of the recently retired sports superstar. Tempting as it is to see his decision to enter the unforgiving world of Pakistani politics as a clean break from his past, I think the precise opposite is the case. If anything, it was a straightforward, logical progression. After nearly three decades in Pakistani public life, he'd acclimatised to the country's peculiar political culture and was uniquely qualified to decry the practice of politics even as he prepared to embark on a political path. President Pervez Musharraf may well have been 'the most corrupt [and] vile ... the worst' petty dictator of Imran's acquaintance, but many of the cricket authorities with whom he came into contact every day of his playing career would have made a strong bid for second place. A few of the Pakistan board's internal memos and various other 'Eyes only' documents from the early 1980s have survived. They still exercise a morbid fascination. Taken as a whole, their bloated and sadly unwarranted complacency, and at times breathtaking disdain for their own team make the England authorities of the day seem like paragons of competence. At least one of the senior administrators concerned was to be ignominiously removed from office, an experience that did no discernible damage to his considerable self-esteem. Writing in his autobiography, Imran was to note, 'Too much is at the whim of powerful individuals. Nepotism and favouritism are rampant ... If only those at the top would sanction a radical shake-up of our system, [Pakistan] as a whole would benefit. Unfortunately, their reaction to constructive criticism has never been all that impressive.' He was speaking of the national cricket selectors, but it would be just as insightful and relevant an overview of his political career 25 years later.

The institutional turbulence of Pakistani public life, then, if anything merely perpetuated the hostile working environment of Imran's playing days. This extended right through his career, and managed to blight even some of his greatest triumphs. Fresh from winning the World Cup in March 1992, several of the Pakistan players expressed dissatisfaction with their captain (who top-scored in the final itself), or more specifically with his reported suggestion that certain funds go to his hospital rather than to themselves. The Board of Control conspicuously failed to back Imran, with the result that he declined to tour England that summer, signalling the end of his 21-year Test career. Any cricket team can have a falling-out when things are going badly. It takes self-destructive skills of a high order to do so when that team have just become world champions. Four years later, the cup final was staged in Lahore and, perhaps predictably, ended in organisational chaos. The prize-giving ceremony turned into a shoving match between supporters and opponents of Prime Minister Benazir Bhutto, who watched the melee with a frozen smile, and was eventually brought under control by police in full SWAT gear, against a backdrop of exploding smoke bombs and the widespread kindling of bonfires in the stands. This was not quite the 'simple, dignified [and] appropriate piece of ceremonial' the home board had promised in its pre-tournament literature.

Imran's first year in charge of Pakistan had revealed him as a tough, decisive, sometimes impulsive captain, not immune to occasional erratic streaks yet fortified by common sense. His third Test in office, against England at Headingley, saw what Imran calls some 'truly bizarre' decisions by the English umpires, notably one that arguably cost Pakistan both the match and series. This was David Constant's keenly debated lbw against the Pakistan batsman Sikander Bakht, a verdict which put those with long memories in mind of the Idrees Beg fiasco at Peshawar 26 years earlier. Of course, mistakes happen. But Imran was so stung by the incident that when Pakistan returned to England in 1987 he formally asked that Constant be appointed for only one Test, if even that, of the five-match series. At the time, Constant, still only 44, was widely regarded, at least by his employers, as being at the top of his game. The Test and County Cricket Board declined Imran's request and then leaked details of it to the press, resulting in ever more colourful variants of *Today*'s 'WHINGEING PAKIS' headline at intervals throughout the tour. (Imran and his board were to prove similarly unresponsive to England's concerns about the appointment of certain Pakistani umpires to officiate in the return series six months later.) By the time of the third one-day international, before the Tests had even begun, the tabloids were accusing Imran's team of out-and-out cheating – not a charge any fair-minded man of some integrity, let alone one descended from a long line of Pathan warriors, was apt to ignore. And he didn't. The repeated allegation was a blow Imran felt personally, if only because of its implied slur on his family honour – 'The carping never let up. It got to me,' he told a close English friend. Still, if the general intention of the headlines had been to undermine Pakistan's or more specifically Imran's confidence, they seem to have backfired spectacularly. If anything, they galvanised him. The tourists duly won their first ever rubber in England. Their captain, with 21 wickets, was the player of the series. As a rule, Imran wasn't a belligerent man, but his back went up when he was attacked or put on the defensive. From then on things were never quite the same between the English cricket authorities and the world's foremost all-rounder.*

Since the generally tempestuous atmosphere in which Imran operated for so long is such a significant part of the story, it's perhaps worth dwelling on this relationship just a moment longer. The folk memory of Pakistan's England tour of 1987 has it that the visitors were 'serial cheats', 'con artists' who had 'perfected the art of intimidation' by histrionic appealing, frequently accompanied by the fielders 'racing maniacally at the umpires [while their] English opponents could only watch in disbelief ... Imran's men were the most undisciplined team

* David Constant declined to comment on his feelings, if any, about Imran when I contacted him in 2008. However, Constant's sometime colleague Dickie Bird was happy to oblige. He told me that in his experience Imran had 'play[ed] within the spirit and the law' of the game, and that he had 'never had a problem with him'.

yet seen on these shores.' This account perhaps requires correction. It's true a certain petulance occasionally crept into the proceedings, and more than once Imran's direct intervention was required to prevent what threatened to become a full-scale evacuation of toys from the visitors' crib. But some background context might be in order. In trying to assess the barely concealed mutual hostility between the Pakistan team and most non-partisan observers, we have to acknowledge that both sides in the debate had 'form'. That the Pakistanis could be a touch excitable was no newsflash. But the roots of their particular problem with specifically *English* officialdom were almost certainly deeper and more intricate than the *Sun* or *Mirror* let on, and included a whole gamut of neuroses, ranging from rank paranoia to what psychologists call a 'morbid utterance of repressed infantilism' – or resentment – towards the former mother country. It's admittedly unlikely that many of the Pakistani bowlers decided to appeal quite as often as they did because of some sense of post-colonial, psychic frustration on their parts. But it would be fair to say that there was a mutual edge to the proceedings. Imran later reportedly remarked that the 'utterly unprincipled and vicious smear campaign' unleashed by his exposure of incompetent authority figures had been one of the hallmarks of his career.

The following list of incidents is by no means exhaustive.

The second Test, at Lord's, of the England–Pakistan series of 1974 ended in some disarray when the tourists' manager Omar Kureishi called a press conference to protest at the inadequate covering of the pitch, which had opened up a conveniently placed crack for the English bowler Derek Underwood to exploit. Kureishi's opening remark was, 'Gentlemen, I am not accusing you of cheating but of gross negligence.' Harsher words followed, in the privacy of the Pakistanis' hotel, over how such conditions could ever have existed at the 'so-called headquarters of cricket'. It would be true to say that there was a broad tendency among many of the tourists, Imran included, to interpret such incidents in a racist light.

Two years later, the touring Pakistani captain Mushtaq Mohammad made much of the 'absurd' umpiring that he believed had cost his side the series. This time the venue was the West Indies. Seeming to confirm the Pakistanis' impression of institutionalised bias against them from whatever quarter, the next major incident, in October 1978, came at Faisalabad. The final day's play in a generally ill-tempered encounter between Pakistan and India was delayed by 15 minutes to allow the umpire Shakoor Rana to harangue several of the players. This was not to be an entirely isolated incident in Rana's long career. Nine years later, standing at the same ground, he became embroiled in a discussion about gamesmanship with the England captain Mike Gatting. The language employed throughout the exchange was basic. Six hours of playing time were then lost while Gatting, to his very vocal displeasure, eventually composed a written apology acceptable to Rana. As a result of this and other perceived slights, the Pakistan board initially withheld a substantial slice of the guarantee money owed to their English counterparts. The England authorities replied by awarding £1,000 to each of their players by way of a 'hardship bonus', a move that did not visibly improve the host team's mood at the post-tour press conference.

In April 1984, the International Cricket Conference (ICC) gave its blessing to a triangular 50-over competition between Pakistan, India and Sri Lanka held in the Asian equivalent of Las Vegas, Sharjah. The venue was the newly opened 24,000-seat United Arab Emirates Association stadium, set in a vast tract of arid wasteland where Bedouin had roamed not long before. Alas, the cricket itself rarely lived up to the surroundings. But the tournament was significant nonetheless, because it was the first ICC-sanctioned series to employ exclusively 'neutral' umpires – umpires, that is, born and raised anywhere other than the three competing nations. From then on, this concept of non-aligned officials became something of a fetish for Imran. In October 1986, he persuaded the Pakistan board to appoint neutral umpires for the home series against the West Indies, to the evident satisfaction of both teams. Despite this initiative, the England authorities stubbornly resisted the temptation to assign two independent umpires to each Test for another 16 years. To Imran, for one, the delay was unconscionable, and could have only one explanation. 'It reeks of colonial arrogance,' he wrote. In the meantime his entire tenure as Test captain was punctuated by a series of umpiring controversies, often involving home officials such as Rana as well as English ones such as Constant. Highly debatable decisions, incredulous stares, on-field exchanges of pleasantries, calamitous press conferences, and spurious but widespread allegations of gambling, ball tampering and even food poisoning – these were the backdrop to the most successful career in Asian sports history.

The combustible world of Pakistan cricket was also frequently enlivened by charges of match-fixing, much of it reportedly centred on the ground at Sharjah. The ever voluble Sarfraz Nawaz would be neither the first nor the last player to go public with this particular allegation.

But whether Sarfraz's claim was deliberate or compulsive, there is no doubt the Pakistan team were affected by it. Although Imran himself was above reproach, he was made vividly aware of the rumours on a daily basis, chiefly by a Pakistani press never inclined to ignore or bury a good scandal. In fact some of the most lurid headlines on the subject came not in London but in Lahore and Karachi. It reached the point where in April 1990, at Sharjah, Imran felt compelled to gather his players together in the dressing-room before the start of play in a one-day international and have each of them swear on a copy of the Koran that none of them stood to gain by Pakistan losing.

The gladiatorial atmosphere in which Pakistan typically played their cricket also, perhaps not surprisingly, contained an element of crowd participation. In December 1980, Pakistan hosted a Test against the West Indies at Multan; Imran took five for 62 in the visitors' first innings. Late in the match the West Indies bowler Sylvester Clarke, apparently aggrieved at being struck by an orange peel while fielding on the third man boundary, retaliated by throwing a brick into the crowd. It was an incalculably cretinous thing to do, but, even so, the response was somehow peculiarly Pakistani. A press photographer's close-up of a victim of Clarke's assault bleeding from a head wound was blown up and became a popular poster in bus and train stations throughout the country. Some time later, disgruntled students invaded the pitch in the course of a one-day match between Pakistan and India at Karachi. Imran, who was bowling at the time, calmly assessed the situation, removed a stump, waved it under the nose of the lead demonstrator and reportedly offered to impale him with it. After that there was a loss of interest on the student's part in prolonging his stay on the field. Sometimes the source of the trouble was even closer to hand; at Perth, in November 1981, Javed Miandad became probably the first player to threaten to brain another one during a Test, after Dennis Lillee had kicked him. Lillee later admitted to having also given Javed some 'verbal', but insisted the Pakistani batsman had 'overreacted'; a not unheard-of development.

For Imran Khan, the perennially embattled cricket superstar, a career in politics must have seemed almost tranquil by comparison. It's rare for a player not only to operate at that level, in what he once called the 'toxic' atmosphere of Pakistan sport, but also to have graced the game in its every format around the world, chiefly in England. Although Imran took some time to find his feet in his adopted home, several good judges were left in no doubt, even then, that his arrival on the scene marked that of a major new talent. In July 1975, a 19-year-old Cambridge freshman named Alastair Hignell walked out to bat in the university match against Oxford at Lord's. Hignell had been away on an England rugby tour of Australia until the eve of the game, and 'therefore had no idea what to expect from the bowler ominously pawing at the ground before starting his run-up somewhere in the mid distance. Sure enough, it was a terrifying barrage ... At one point, I took the wrong option and ducked into a bouncer which hit the fleshy part of my ear and ricocheted past the wicketkeeper in the direction of the pavilion. I was hoping for a single to fine leg to get off strike, so set off immediately. As it happened, the ball hit the boundary wall before the fielder could intercept it, but for some reason the umpire, John Langridge, didn't bother tapping his leg for leg byes and instead signalled four runs ... As I was trotting by I pointed out that the ball hadn't hit my bat, but had bounced off my ear which by now was red, swollen and throbbing painfully. "Listen, sonny," he muttered out of the corner of his mouth, as Imran again limbered up in the distance. "You're not going to be here long, anyway. You might as well take all the runs you can get."'

TWO

Of Hospitality and Revenge

'Once, when I was 13,' Imran recalls, 'I was stopped by the police while I was driving my father's motor car. Of course, I didn't have a licence. So I did the only thing possible under the circumstances. I bribed the policeman. He took the money and I drove away again scot-free. But later that day the chauffeur, who'd been sitting next to me in the car, reported the incident to my mother. She was livid.' According to at least one reliable account of the ensuing five minutes of 'peak-volume drama' this was, if anything, to underestimate Mrs Khan's reaction. She 'literally turned purple'. Those who witnessed (or even heard of) the fury of this normally serene, well-bred lady would long marvel at the scene, speaking of it like old salts recalling a historic hurricane. The gist of her remarks was that by resorting to bribery Imran had brought a terrible shame both on himself and his family. No punishment was too severe for this uniquely heinous offence. Had she had anything to do with it, he would have been sent to gaol. Imran's spluttering attempt at a defence, in which he protested that other boys of his age had done the same thing – or would have done so, given the chance – was cut short by his mother's abrupt verdict on the matter. 'You're not other boys,' she reminded him, decisively. 'You are a Pathan.'

The story illuminates Imran's childhood, and perhaps his later life, on a number of levels. There's the fact that his family even owned a car (which one party insists was 'a sort of limousine – perhaps even a Mercedes') in the first place, at a time when most Pakistanis travelled exclusively by the country's notoriously congested train or bus network, if not on foot. At Partition in 1947 the entire Pakistan road system covered just 17,500 kilometres (10,900 miles), of which asphalt roads made up less than 20 per cent; as late as 1967, a couple of years after the bribery incident, the number of privately owned vehicles was estimated at only 240,000, more than half of which were motorcycles, out of a population of some 62 million. Then there's the matter of the chauffeur, one of four servants employed in the Khans' home in the exclusive Zaman Park suburb of Lahore, and the significant detail that the 13-year-old Imran had the sort of resources about him with which to bribe the policeman in the first place, let alone the *chutzpah* to pull it off. The hardship and rawness of the country as a whole, the family's striving to 'compete and contribute ... [their] utter disdain of sitting around by the pool', or of aristocratic languor of any sort, were real enough. But the five well-dressed Khan children, the car and the driver, the domestic help, the generous pocket money – all belied the later, well-publicised images of poverty certain Western political commentators would call on to promote Imran as a 'man of the people'.

Clearly the key message, though, lay in his mother's terse summation, 'You are a Pathan.' To her, as he later wrote, 'that was synonomous with pride and honesty'. Central to the tribal identity of the Pathans (or 'Pakhtuns') is strict adherence to the male-centred code of conduct, the *pakhtunwali*. Foremost in this is the notion of honour, or *nang*, followed in turn by the principle of revenge, or *badal*. It would be fair to say that the two concepts are closely linked, as the *pakhtunwali* makes clear that offences to one's honour must be avenged, or else there is no honour. Although minor problems may be settled by negotiation, murder demands blood revenge, and until recent times women caught in illicit sexual liaisons ran the risk of being severely beaten or killed by a male relative, part of a punishment ritual reserved for crimes of an 'immoral' nature known as *karo-kari*. Vendettas and feuds are also an endemic feature of Pathan social relations, and often handed down through the generations. There are said to be ongoing disputes today over land or women whose origins lie in the Middle Ages. On a more congenial note, the tribal code also stresses the importance of *melmastia*, or hospitality, and a complex etiquette surrounds the protection and entertainment of one's guests. A Pathan is required to give refuge to anyone, even one's enemy, for as long as that person chooses to remain under his roof. To fail to do so is a gross dereliction of *nang*. Although Imran was to adapt successfully to most aspects of the host culture while living in England, and certainly its more relaxed approach to *karo-kari*, the Pathan code as a whole remained integral both to the competitive cricketer and the man. His father Ikramullah Khan's tribe, the Niazis, could trace their ancestry back to 12th-century India, and were still waging a guerrilla war against the Mogul empire when the latter transferred authority to the British crown 700 years later. His mother Shaukat's, the Burkis, were a Turko-Afghan nomadic clan with a long commercial and military tradition, who turned to the Muslim faith; as Imran recalls, she was the devout one of the Khan family. Following Partition, a number of the Burkis migrated to Lahore, where they produced a remarkable sporting dynasty: no fewer than eight of Imran's maternal cousins went on to play first-class cricket, two of whom, besides himself, captained Pakistan. As a rule, the Khans were intensely loyal, if not fanatically so, to their adopted country. They invariably spoke Urdu, not English, and were openly contemptuous of the *kala sahibs* ('black masters'), the members of the Pakistani professional classes who shamelessly aped the mannerisms of the departed British. Taken as a whole, both the Niazis and the Burkis were formidable examples of the Pathan tribal ethic, whom training and instinct had taught to be tough, capable and self-sufficient even as they assimilated into modern urban life. The children of such people aren't apt to be weaklings.

He was born Imran Ahmed Khan Niazi on 5 October 1952, not, as recorded in *Wisden Cricketers' Almanack* and elsewhere, on 25 November. It was both traditional and somehow appropriate that there would be an 'administrative foul-up', Imran recalled, when he came to obtain his first passport, resulting in an official filling in the wrong date. Fitting, too, that he would be called Imran (which means 'construction', or 'prosperity'), and be known by his monosyllabic paternal surname, with its tersely assertive ring. In Pathan culture, each tribe has a 'khan', meaning 'lion' or 'chief', at its head. The word is thought to come from the Turkish *khaqan*, which has the specific connotation of being a conquering warlord. Since Imran himself has dabbled in astrology and isn't above consulting a clairvoyant before making a major decision, it might be added that he's a Libra, and thus said to be freedom-loving, refined, idealistic, sincere, broad-minded, truth-seeking, expansive, flirtatious and virile, among several other virtues. Being both precocious and male (one sister preceded him, and three followed), he seems to have been doted on as a small boy. Without wishing to descend too far into the abyss of psychiatry, biographers always seem to recall Sigmund Freud's line on these occasions: the dictum that 'a man who has been the indisputable favourite of his mother keeps for life the feeling of a conqueror' was undoubtedly true here. The young Imran was also something of a loner, by all accounts. At family gatherings his mother and others would sometimes notice him 'drift[ing] apart from the crowd' of relatives. Aged only three or four, a cousin told me, 'he would always be off stargazing by himself'.

Imran's birth preceded that of Pakistan's international cricket by just 11 days. The national team played its first ever Test, against India at Delhi, in October 1952. The Indians won by an innings. Pakistan had also just embarked on its long and continuing history of political turmoil. The founding father and Quaid-e-Azam ('great leader') of the modern state, Mohammad Ali Jinnah, had died in 1948, some 13 months after independence. His hand-picked successor, Liaquat Ali Khan, was fatally shot by a Pathan fanatic at a public rally in Municipal Park, Rawalpindi, in October 1951. (The former Pakistani prime minister Benazir Bhutto was assassinated just outside the same park 56 years later; the first medical worker on the scene was the son of the doctor who had tried to save Liaquat's life.) Elsewhere, it was the era of the Korean War, H-bomb tests and Stalinist show trials in Eastern Europe. In London the talk was of the perennial balance of payments crisis, as well as more pressing issues such as an electrical workers' strike, pickets and power cuts. Agatha Christie's stage adaptation of her radio play *The Mousetrap* made its West End debut in the week Imran was born half a world away.

Imran later told an English friend that he hadn't had a particularly happy, or unhappy, childhood. Instead he described it as secure and serious. One assumes he meant secure in the family sense, because he was born into a world of violent change. The state of Pakistan was just five years older than he was, brought into being after the end of British rule, when two new countries were created to form predominantly Muslim West and East Pakistan (now Bangladesh) with Hindu-majority India wedged in between. Even at the time, many observers had feared that the amputation of the subcontinent along religious lines would result in wholesale administrative chaos. It did. What ensued was some way short of a textbook example of smooth decolonisation. An estimated 700–800,000 people died in the riots that followed Partition, which also created some 14 million long-term refugees. It would be fair to say that, to many Indians, the very creation of Pakistan was seen as a violation of India's geographical, cultural and religious boundaries. The two nations would enjoy an at best strained relationship, not least in the disputed sub-Himalayan outpost of Kashmir, and pursued differing alliances around the world. While India looked to the Soviet Union as a strategic ally, the Pakistanis sought support from the Americans by portraying themselves as tough anti-Communists with a British-trained military, based only a cannon's shot away from the southern Russian border. In October 1952, President Truman spoke to a joint session of Congress of 'halt[ing] Red expansion by helping develop the resources of the third world', which he proposed to do by committing an initial $210 million-worth of military hardware and training, a somehow familiar-sounding gesture today.

By 1954 Pakistan had manoeuvred its way into both the Central Treaty Organisation (CENTO) and the South East Asian Treaty Organisation (SEATO), two US-sponsored consortiums designed to prevent 'Red expansion' in the region. (They were to prove of limited use in Vietnam.) Pakistan also soon adopted that unique combination of democratic procedures, military interference and Islamic ritual that still distinguishes the country. In April 1953 the state's governor-general Ghulam Mohammad dismissed the elected civilian government and replaced it with a military 'cabinet of talents'. A succession of governors-general, presidents and army chiefs were to remove a further nine civilian governments over the next 21 years. The 35 years since then have been characterised by direct military rule.

Nor is there any simple distinction between law and religion in Pakistan, and consequently, as the West has recently come to see, the clerics often perform a political role. In 1953, the Jamaat-i-Islami (JI), the largest and most articulate of the nation's religious parties, began a concerted campaign to purge the community of what it deemed blasphemous or 'fetid' behaviour, and to establish a fully Islamic state. The ensuing violence brought on the imposition of martial law and the first of Pakistan's recurrent constitutional crises. Although the details varied, the essential pattern of coups, military rule, violent deaths and ethnic strife came to characterise, if not define, the entire 62-year period from Partition to the present day. By the time Imran was old enough to take an interest in his surroundings, the struggle over the character and soul of Pakistan was well under way.

As we've seen, he had the good fortune to be born into a society which traditionally favours boys over girls, the latter of whom then rarely even bothered to attend school: an officially estimated 23 per cent of females over the age of 15 were classified as 'functionally literate' in 1952, compared to 47 per cent of males. In a patriarchal culture like Pakistan's, the birth of a son represents a potential source of income in old age, whereas a girl will eventually marry and leave. The Khan family were also well positioned in the Pakistani caste system, whose extremes were marked out by a small number of plantation-owning millionaires and morally flexible politicians at one end and the untouchables at the other. Of this latter category, rock bottom was represented by the humble domestic cleaner. There simply was no lowlier status in the Pakistan of the 1950s, and in those days no one would willingly marry a cleaner except another cleaner.

Imran, by contrast, grew up from an early age in a gated community of substantial redbrick houses with neatly manicured lawns that took its name from his own great-uncle, Zaman Khan. It was as if 'the most bourgeois part of Dulwich had been dumped down in Lahore', I was told. Immediately outside the gates was a setting more familiar to generations of ordinary Pakistanis. The town of Lahore spread out around a number of bustling squares in a haphazard jumble of shops, bazaars, tenements, bungalows and garishly painted billboards. Most people travelled by public transport, or if they were lucky by either rickshaw or bicycle. The distinctive item of male dress was the bright-red *ajrak*, a flowing shawl worn over a knee-length shirt and baggy trousers. To this ensemble many men added an embroidered cap decorated with tiny mirrors. The women were generally veiled. To relieve the monotony of daily life, there were frequent *melas*, or fairs, in which a merry-go-round was usually erected in the market square and a travelling circus displayed dancing bears and monkeys. The Basant festival, unique to Lahore, took place each spring and featured elaborate kite-flying competitions with an added touch of the hyper-gamesmanship so integral to much of Pakistani life. What brought drama to the event was that at least on occasion the kite strings would be coated with ground glass, with the idea of disabling rivals' kites by cutting through their strings in the air. Imran was 'extremely proficient' at kite-flying, I was told, though there is no evidence he was ever tied up in any unsportsmanlike conduct.

In addition to the class system, many Pakistanis were divided by their attitudes to the departed colonial masters. For every *kala sahib*, there was an individual like Imran's father, for whom Partition and independence had excited an almost religious zeal. By and large, both sides of the debate were broadly agreed on the supposed underlying racism of the West as a whole, and tended to be sensitive in cases where, to quote the *Mashriq*, 'the white man [had] set his backside on the black man'. This attitude perhaps helps to explain why the 'Beg affair' was still being keenly analysed by the Pakistani sporting press 20 years after the event.

In all, then, a political and cultural stew of a nation, a land with a violent hand and empathetic heart. Lahore, Pakistan's second city after Karachi, offers a particularly rich visual patisserie of ancient and modern: the medieval garrison town with its forts and mausoleums, the so-called 'Garden of the Moguls', and its gaudily futuristic 1960s facelift – all concrete slabs and municipal offices built out of giant glass eggshells – so symbolic of the two Pakistans. Following Partition, the word was 'clearance', the result acres of dead tramway lines and rubble dumped into the green, still hair-oil of Lahore's central canal. The town's ambient smell, at least in winter months, is remembered as a combination of 'coal fires, waste [and] the crisp tang of fatty foods'. In summer it was as if 'the whole place had decomposed'. In the words of the architectural writer Simon Jenkins, 'In no other world city have I seen so much magnificence so neglected ... All Pakistan's history is here, but disintegrating beneath encroaching shanties, cobwebs of wires and piles of rubbish.'

Imran, then, grew up not only in a state in transition, but in its most obviously changed town: he would have been as aware of Lahore's imperial past as he was of its squat, drab ghettoes and the abject poverty of tens of thousands of its inhabitants. For many, the hardship was institutionalised. Public assistance was rudimentary, at best; cancer, as Imran was to note sardonically, remained a rich man's disease; and most local schools were basic, in one graduate's words 'fail[ing] to satisfy the most minimal academic or even sanitary requirements'. In later years, this always potentially riotous city was to be the scene of regular outbreaks of political unrest and violent anti-government demonstrations. Indeed, Imran himself may have inadvertently played a role in a noted breakdown of municipal law and order when, in May 2005, he took the opportunity of a press conference in Islamabad to draw attention to a *Newsweek* article about a Koran being flushed down the toilet by American soldiers. Some 17 people died in the subsequent street protests that took place both in Lahore and across Pakistan.* There was a pattern of broadly similar civil or religious disturbances throughout Imran's youth, even if these tended to be less individually destructive. It was in Lahore that the Muslim League made the first formal demand for a separate Islamic homeland, and where the League

* At which point *Newsweek*'s editor apologised, remarking that his story had been based on an anonymous source who now 'wasn't sure whether it was true or not'.

subsequently conducted its vigilant campaign against the 'fetid' behaviour of non-believers. Several confrontations resulted, including a minor but well-publicised skirmish in May 1961 between local clerics and a group of provocatively dressed American tourists which ended ignominiously for the latter. I was told that the offending parties had 'turned and run'. On this occasion the only casualties were two Americans who in their haste slipped on wet cobblestones, and one cleric who collided with a bicycle.

Life in Zaman Park was less picturesque, perhaps, than in other parts of Lahore, but it differed little in terms of ritual. There was frequent obeisance to Mecca, as prescribed by the Prophet Muhammad. Although not excessively pious, on Thursday evenings Imran's family periodically gathered at one of the many local shrines for the chanting of religious songs, and Mr Khan and his son are said to have 'reasonably dutifully' attended a mosque on most Sundays and state holidays. (In 1977 the government of Zulfikar Ali Bhutto changed the 'day off' to Friday, among other innovations.) As noted, Imran was also keenly aware of his Pathan heritage, which he could trace back 700 years. Some of his earliest known ancestors exhibited the same refreshingly independent streak that prevails right to the present. The Niazis had first come to prominence in the sixteenth century, when Haibat Khan Niazi was the Governor of Punjab, and helped to build the massive Rohtas Fort near Lahore. Against family advice, Haibat subsequently backed the wrong side in one of the frequent Pathan civil wars. He, his wife and brother were all killed, and their heads displayed on poles by the enemy commander, a popular practice at the time.

Imran remarks that, despite their ensuing political eclipse, 'the Niazis continued to think of themselves as a ruling race, and were known for their strong physiques'. There are some colourful if, perhaps, occasionally also tall tales of the family's exploits over the years, particularly at the time of the Indian Mutiny. In the 1930s, a great-uncle of Imran's named Khan Beg Khan served as a police superintendent in the Salt Range, some 320 kilometres (200 miles) west of Lahore. One winter, Imran recounts, some villagers reported that a leopard had been seen making off with their livestock, and appealed to Supt. Khan for help. 'My uncle took three policemen with him,' Imran says, 'and rode off to see what he could do. They spotted the leopard on a ridge and my uncle began to approach, a pistol in his hand. By now the leopard, well used to terrorising the villagers, was quite fearless: it began to growl and hiss, warning my uncle not to come any closer. All of a sudden the leopard charged; my uncle fired and missed, and the next minute the leopard was on him. Two of the policemen ran away ... Luckily my uncle was wearing a thick winter overcoat, and he managed to ram his watch down the leopard's mouth as it tried to go for his jugular.' Imran concludes his account by noting that his great-uncle had subsequently spent six months in hospital with his injuries, but had recovered and lived to be 100.

Imran's maternal tribe, the Burkis, were of similarly hardy stock. Like the Niazis, it was in their nature to respond to a challenge. An affront to their friends or themselves, especially one that called into question their *nang*, uncapped their ample reserves of anger and righteous indignation. The Burkis were among the earliest followers of the 16th-century Pathan chief Pir Roshan, who led a revolt against the Mogul emperor Akbar after he had declined to destroy some Hindu temples when given the chance to do so. This, too, proved to be a principled but ultimately ill-advised alliance: Akbar crushed the uprising and resettled the Burkis in camps around the Indian fort town of Jullundur, some 150 kilometres (90 miles) east of Lahore. Several of the tribe known thereafter as Jullandari Pathans were later to migrate to the mountainous regions of northern Afghanistan and Persia, and as far west as Turkey. In time, Zaman Khan would become the first Muslim resident of the small Lahore neighbourhood that was settled by the government's Evacuee Property Board and effectively turned into a family compound in the years following Partition. By the mid-1980s there were 46 Khans and Burkis living side by side in the same development. Imran's childhood friend Haroun Rashid describes it as a 'very pleasant, upper-middle-class residential area [with] many large trees, old houses and a village feel to it'. In later years it earned the somewhat unkind nickname 'Jurassic Park' because of its inhabitants' physical size and alleged mental shortcomings. The uniting family theme, once again, appears to have been a healthy lack of respect for any form of central authority, coupled with a broad streak of individualism or, on occasion, eccentricity. As a boy, Imran had fond memories of his uncle Ahmad Raza Khan, who was known to enliven proceedings at Zaman Park by rolling around on the floor with his pet leopard – something of a Khan tradition. According to a source who asked for anonymity, there had been one 'heart-stopping' moment when the animal broke free and ran out on to the street, pursued by Ahmad Raza, where it eventually 'leapt through the window of a small house [and] chased an old lady off the lavatory'. Shortly after this incident, Mr Khan made a gift of the leopard to the Lahore zoo.

Intelligent, well-off, reverent, but no more so than many diligent Muslim families, Ikramullah, Shaukat and the five Khan children never took their life of comparative privilege for granted. According to a cousin, it was a 'paternalistic, unostentatious, self-effacing' household. Ikramullah, a London-trained civil engineer, was in the habit of quoting the Koran's teaching that 'no one [was] above or below anyone else', a principle he applied daily in his own life. To a junior colleague named Waris Sharif, 'He was the most gracious man, and always paid you the compliment of listening closely.' There were times when the family dinner table also included the domestic servants, hired hands, or even occasional passers-by seeking a handout, vivid instances of the tolerance and egalitarianism that stand out in the memories of friends and neighbours. The Khan children were positively encouraged to excel, if only because it was in their own interests to do so; there would be 'no subsequent trust funds [or] large inheritances'. In later years, Imran was at pains to stress that he couldn't possibly be a playboy, since 'playboys have plenty of time and money. I have never had either.'

For all that, he enjoyed a materially comfortable, urban – and, increasingly, urbane – childhood. No. 22 Zaman Park was a spacious, six-bedroomed brick home of 1950s-stockbroker decor. According to one visitor, there was a 'teak cabinet the size of a coffin, woven *farashi* rugs and doilied armchairs'. A water buffalo grazed in the back garden. The family also farmed several hundred acres of sugar cane outside Lahore. Every summer they escaped the heat by decamping either to Ghora Ghali, near Islamabad, or to a resort called Murree in the foothills of the Himalayas, where Imran acquired a love of the 'bright, crystal-clear climate' and exotic wildlife.

More important than material considerations, Imran grew up with a sense of inner authority that came from being the apple of his parents' eye: the lovingly indulged only son. He clearly inherited qualities from both sides of the clan, the spiritual instinct and sporting prowess of the Burkis, and the dour application of the Niazis. The boy Imran displayed a masterful self-confidence from an early age.

For the Khans, the summers also meant camping and shooting (game only) and ample scope for kite-flying, both solo and competitive. The last hobby seems to have become an increasing fetish, and I was told that as a six- or seven-year-old Imran had regularly run for more than 3 kilometres (2 miles) from one end of Zaman Park to the other, a contraption 'painted like the Pakistani national flag' fluttering above him. To add to the already punishing training regimen, he sometimes carried a pillowcase filled with rocks on his back. In later years when people asked Imran about his remarkable stamina, he always mentioned the kites: 'I would sprint, not just jog along,' he invariably pointed out. 'It would often be like an obstacle course – over walls, hedges, fields, roads and ploughed land ... My legs and knees got tougher and tougher.' On a more sedentary note, Imran enjoyed his food, particularly the heavily spiced curries (the typical Pakistani is not a vegetarian), and most forms of local music. He was known to attend extended performances of Qawwalis, the mystic songs traditionally played on a stringed instrument called the *sarangi* that can take up to half-an-hour to retune between numbers, a more leisurely pace than that set even at the Pink Floyd concerts Imran later enjoyed. As well as Lahore's spring festival he always looked forward to the *Eid ul-Fiter*, or Small Eid (as opposed to the more ascetic *Eid ul-Azha*, or Big Eid), a major religious celebration that marks the end of Ramadan, when families come together to share a meal broadly in the spirit of the American Thanksgiving. Lahore's Aitchison College, which he attended between the ages of seven and 16, was a sprawling, tree-lined campus whose curriculum perhaps over-emphasised Britain's former colonial glories. But compared to most local schools it was a bastion of learning, where Imran was once sent across the playing field into the 10-year-olds' classroom to recite what one of them describes admiringly as 'some long verse or some long poem', which he did in an 'already deep, mellifluous voice'. Other contemporary accounts recall Imran's 'inner poise' or 'seriousness'. A faded group photograph of the time shows a slightly chubby youngster with his dark hair combed neatly for the occasion, and a not entirely friendly expression on his face. Imran's older sister Robina considered the international sex symbol of later years an 'ugly little brute' as a boy.

What about cricket? Virtually from the moment Pakistan came into being, Imran's maternal family was busy turning out a galaxy of players who adorned the national sport. (The Niazis, by contrast, reportedly thought the whole thing 'boring' and 'uncompetitive ... Hardly anyone [was] ever physically struck.') Imran's first cousin Javed Burki was already playing professional cricket in 1955, aged 17, and went on to make 25 Test appearances throughout the 1960s. Another cousin, Majid Khan, didn't wait even that long; he made his first-class debut just a few days after his 15th birthday. Majid's father was Jahangir Khan, the Indian Test all-rounder who once managed to kill a sparrow when it came into the path of his delivery as he was bowling against the MCC at Lord's; the unfortunate bird is still on display in the ground's museum. In a tradition that was to be significant to Imran, all three of these men went to England to complete their education at either Oxford or Cambridge University. No fewer than six other Khan cousins played at least some form of competitive cricket for a variety of Pakistan clubs (one of whom, Asad Khan, appeared in a single match for Peshawar against Sargodha in November 1961 in which he didn't bowl, took no catches and was out for 1 – surely one of the shorter careers in professional sport). Literally dozens more, ranging in age from pre-school to the long-ago retired, performed on a less formal basis for teams on either side of the national border. Before partition, the Jullandari Pathans had sometimes turned out 22 men to play each other in family 'blood matches'. Imran's uncle Ahmad Raza Khan, of pet leopard fame, himself a useful bat, served on regional Punjab committees and later became a national selector. In March 1965, he took his 12-year-old nephew with him to Rawalpindi to see the Pakistani Test side, for which both Javed and Majid were lucky enough to have been chosen. Pakistan beat New Zealand by an innings. On the last day's play Ahmad Raza took Imran into the pavilion and told all his friends there that one day he would be 'our greatest living cricketer'.

Even then, everyone in Pakistan seemed to either play or watch the sport that was one of the few truly unifying national activities. Lahore's Iqbal Gardens, like many other municipal parks, would regularly host ten club matches at a time. Play typically started after breakfast, broke for a lengthy lunch, and continued right through the insistent call for *maghrib* prayers, signalling sunset. As Javed Miandad would recall, 'The light was often so bad [the spectators] couldn't follow the game, but still you kept making your shots.' There was a particularly vibrant cricket scene in Lahore, where club and even school matches, particularly those where any sort of feud existed, regularly attracted upwards of 5,000 spectators, and became a nursery for the national side. Nine out of the 11 names selected to represent Pakistan in the country's first ever Test played most or all of their cricket in Lahore. According to the fast bowler Mahmood Hussain, the long-running rivalry between the city's Government College and Islamia College 'was a good preparation for the competitive pressures of Test cricket. I always bowled better when the crowd was against me, as so often happened.' Rising right up in the historical centre of town, the Lahore (later 'Gaddafi') Stadium, modelled on the Mogul school of ornate brickwork and arches – reminding some of a clumsily iced cake – opened its doors in November 1959, providing a visually striking symbol of cricket's local importance. English readers need only to think of Lord's, painted bright red, soaring out of the middle of Piccadilly Circus rather than modestly tucked away behind a wall in St John's Wood, to get a bit of the feel. The sport was a prominent part of every young Lahorite's life and, in fact, a focus for the entire community. It's said by the Pakistan scholar and traveller Sean Sheehan that when the Test team was in action at Lahore 'five hundred miles away, near the Afghan border, tribal members [would] huddle around a radio, listening with bated breath and roaring with delight at every run scored'.

Speaking to the *Sunday Times* in 2006, Imran recalled that 'From when I was seven to when I was nine, I had dreams in which I would score 100 against England at Lord's, leading Pakistan to victory. I desperately wanted to be a Test cricketer. I remember clearly wanting that, never thinking I wouldn't make it.' It's a vivid and compelling story, told from the perspective of a fiercely patriotic, middle-aged Pakistani political leader. But some discrepancy exists between Imran's *Sunday Times* account and the one he gives in his 1983 autobiography, whose opening sentence is, 'The game of cricket and I travelled on distinctly separate paths for the first eleven years of my life ... quite frankly, I agreed with my father that it was a boring game with too much standing around.'

It's a small historical point, but one perhaps worth clarifying before we move on. In March 1959, when Imran was six (not seven, as he writes), his mother took him to see Pakistan play West Indies at Lahore's old Bagh-e-Jinnah ground. It was a generally unhappy occasion, at least from the home team's point of view. They were routed. The West Indies fast bowler Wes Hall tore through the Pakistan first innings, taking five for 87, and making life especially uncomfortable for the wicketkeeper-batsman Ijaz Butt. Butt was to be carried off with a broken nose 'as the blood gushed down his shirt', *Wisden* records. Pakistan lost the Test by an innings and 156 runs. Imran notes that he remained 'unenthusiastic' about cricket as a career option, particularly as angry crowds took to the streets that night to protest against their team's performance. This was to be a fairly frequent event in the history of the national side over the next 12 years or so. At about the same time as he watched his first Test, Imran and his parents moved to Zaman

Park. Not long after that he found himself taking part in family pick-up games, where he had the opportunity to measure himself against Majid, six years his senior, among others. Once again, the results weren't encouraging. 'I wasn't [even] as good as other boys of my age, and was always the last to be chosen,' Imran recalls.

The turning-point came when he was rising 13, and had moved into the upper school at Aitchison. As a result, when the new cricket season began in October, Imran found himself for the first time playing on a professionally prepared pitch. He also had access to a coach named Naseer Mohammad, a former club player with decided views about what a proper cricketer in the making should look like. 'Correct' was the operative word. Mr Mohammad took one look at Imran's repertoire of cross-batted slogs and went to work on him in the nets. An Aitchison contemporary and fellow Colt remembers that 'Naseer's interest and enthusiasm were just almost contagious ... He would practise with you – I remember hours of the forward defensive – literally until you dropped.' When the afternoon sessions did not go well, the coach often kept his pupil at it into the misty autumn dusk, bringing out an old white cricket ball and turning on the weak pavilion lights. Imran recalls that by the time the new season began in 1966, 'My attitude to the game had changed: all I wanted to do was play cricket ... I decided that I was going to play for Pakistan, and soon.' By this point Imran was just turning 14. He responded to maternal approval and appreciated applause. He participated enthusiastically in school Under-16 matches, impressing coaches because he took direction willingly and trained harder than anyone else did. And thanks to a sudden pubescent growth spurt, he possessed the classic fast bowler's physique long before he was a fast bowler. Imran had caught up with his illustrious cousins through hard work, natural talent and an utter unwillingness to fail at anything he put his mind to. The consensus at Aitchison was that he was an orthodox and hard-hitting batsman, as well as a safe pair of hands in the field. No one yet thought of him as a full all-rounder, least of all Imran himself.

The next three years saw the cricketing equivalent of the Great Leap Forward, even if they proved less distinguished academically. Although not studious, Imran was a quick learner and, with his mother's and older sister's assistance, proved an at least adequate pupil. The portrait of him that most often emerges from those who knew him at Aitchison is of a teenager who was long on graft and determination and less so on raw intellect. Even some of his later disciples had their doubts about his mental candlepower, although, as at school, no one who knew him ever questioned his perseverance. The curricular emphasis there was on English, maths, geography and history, the last two of which generally took a dim view of India and its territorial claims in Kashmir. Aitchison, originally known as Chiefs' College, had been founded in 1886, and was modelled strongly on the British public-school tradition. Delivering his inaugural address to the boys, the school's benefactor Sir Charles Umpherston Aitchison, Lieutenant-Governor of the Punjab, had remarked that '... much, very much, is expected of you. I trust you will use well the opportunities here afforded you both for your education and for the formation of your character ... This is an institution from which you will henceforth banish everything in thought and word and act that is mean, dishonourable or impure, and in which you will cultivate everything that is virtuous, true, manly and gentlemanly.' The school (motto: 'Perseverance commands success') was laid out along the lines of a Mogul fort, ambitiously crossed with a traditional English church – there were steeples, cloisters and stained glass windows – and set in a tree-ringed 200-acre estate. (One well-known American travel writer insists that Aitchison could have 'easily been found in the rolling Sussex countryside, were [it] not for its prominent central minaret', but this merely displays his ignorance of modern English rural life.) Several graduates I spoke to about the school referred to it as 'the Eton of Pakistan'. There was a house system, uniforms, an emphasis on organised sport and a daily routine 'as ritualised as Edwardian English behaviour'. By and large, Imran was in his element.

Both at Aitchison and its next-door neighbour Zaman Park, he was clearly moving in a more exalted world than most Lahorites. The student body included luminaries such as the princes Salahuddin and Falahuddin, the Nawab of Kalabagh's son and several future or present Pathan chiefs including Imran's friend Sardar Jaffer Khan Leghari, the strongman of the Leghari tribe. Even in this company Imran was considered quite combative. He seems to have been as adept at mind games as he was at the raw aggression that was such an integral part of his cricket. 'Imran was a merciless enemy on the sports field', whose great strength as a batsman 'was his ability to get his opponent off-balance', an Aitchison contemporary recalls.

> Even then, he was a crafty performer ... Imran would deceive the bowler into thinking he was weak against the short ball, for instance. He would hop and jump and generally carry on like a

> man standing on hot coals. You could see the fielders smiling to themselves ... The bowler would charge in and bowl probably the fastest bouncer of his life, and Imran would deposit it about twenty yards behind the tall trees on the square leg boundary.

Another Aitchison friend recalled an altogether gentler Imran away from the cricket field. 'There was a boy who sometimes begged at the school gates. He was about 16, like us, and he was crippled ... One evening he was dragging himself home [and] with his arms already full Imran leant down to speak to him and then picked him up. Off he staggered with the boy and crutches and books and cricket gear up the road and the steep steps to the boy's house, where he gently set him down again. No one else was around. To me, that was the real Imran as much as the cut-throat sportsman was.'

Imran sometimes used to say that his pleasure in playing cricket every available hour of the day was enhanced by the knowledge that, in at least one sense, it was a complete waste of time. So many hours ticking past, and it not mattering. So many afternoons when other boys were in the library or diligently writing essays or studying their Koran, while Imran, immaculately turned out in whites, practised his forward defensive in the nets or carted the opposing team's bowlers around the park. It's worth mentioning again just how fortunate he was in his choice of school. As Haroun Rashid, a year senior to Imran at Aitchison, recalls, 'The place prided itself on its sports, and certainly in [the 1960s] cricketing abilities were better appreciated by the powers-that-be than academic ones.' Imran was equally lucky to play on two such exquisite grounds as Aitchison and the Lahore Gymkhana (whose club was captained by another cousin, Javed Zaman) rather than the sparsely grassed mud tracks where most Pakistani cricketers honed their craft. As he was turning 16 Imran had duly become the youngest member of the Aitchison First XI. He modestly confirms, 'I was by far the best batsman [there]; I saw myself as the next Bradman.' In the course of a year and a half he had 'radically changed' his attitude to the game, if even that phrase conveys a process bordering on reincarnation. Imran now carried his cricket bat with him wherever he went, tucking it under his bed at night. He persuaded the domestic servants to bowl at him for hours on end in the garden at Zaman Park, moving proceedings to the front hall if it rained. When high summer came he stayed home in Lahore rather than join the traditional family holiday in the hills, in order to play for the local Wazir Ali league. This was cricket strictly for hard-core devotees of the game: the Wazir Ali matches were bruising encounters that typically began at 7 a.m. and continued in baking heat right through to sunset or beyond. In time even Mrs Khan, the scion of a fanatically keen cricketing family, was moved to ask Imran's older sister Robina if he was 'all right'.

The fighting spirit that Imran often credited to his Pathan ancestry wasn't just confined to cricket. In April 1965, when he was 12, Pakistan and India had gone to war in one of their periodic disputes over Kashmir. The whole family gathered at the Khans' house in Lahore, only 30 kilometres (18 miles) from the Indian border, and decided to form a home guard to repel a possible parachute landing by the enemy. Imran was vocally eager to go up the line nearer the battle, and had to be restrained from marching off with a knapsack in the general direction of the front. In the end he contented himself with doing sentry duty in Zaman Park with his 18-year-old cousin Majid. A year or so later he was running around the neighbourhood on one of his regular training exercises when a local boy with whom he'd exchanged words rashly shouted out, 'Look at that ponce!' Imran reportedly hit the boy so hard that he broke one of his own fingers. He was also known to play competitive soccer and hockey, could swim a length of a pool with seven or eight windmilling strokes, and once went trekking with a party of schoolfriends up into the Northern Areas close to the Chinese border. But when the cricket season began 'he was a man of such single-minded ambition … with such intensity,' says Haroun Rashid. 'In 1968 when we went to Lawrence College in Ghora Gali, our traditional rivals, for our annual sports meet, Imran opened the batting for us and, without losing his wicket, proceeded to decimate the hapless Gallians. It was a slaughter of the innocents … Due to Imran's sixes about half a dozen balls were lost in the forests surrounding their cricket ground. The match was over in half its allotted time.'

It was the watchword and comfort of the Pakistani Test selectors that their team 'got through the Sixties unscathed' as one of them said later. Unscathed, but hardly unbeaten; in the entire decade the Test side managed only two wins, both against New Zealand. The history of Pakistan cricket as a whole in the 1960s is one of corruption, dissent and consistent under-achievement. Hanif Mohammad remained the pioneering figure, but even he eventually outstayed his welcome, apparently wanting to finish his 17-year career with a then impressive-seeming 4,000 Test runs. He fell 85 short, after Abdul Kardar, the chairman of selectors, had remarked tetchily, 'I can't give him another five Tests.' Hanif went out to widespread barracking from crowds who had grown impatient with his kind of dour, bricklaying approach to batting, and after a power struggle with his successor as Test captain, Saeed Ahmed. Saeed was not a success in the job. On hearing the unsentimental announcement of his own replacement by Intikhab Alam, he threatened to punch (and reportedly did 'jostle') chairman Kardar, among others. Intikhab's first series in charge was at home to New Zealand, whose manager remembered his own side as being 'hopeless'. New Zealand won 1–0, with two Tests drawn. By 1969, around the time Imran was making the step up to first-class cricket, the Pakistan national team was anchored firmly at the bottom of the unofficial league table.

A public- and private-sector consortium had, it's true, raised funds for an Under-19 side to tour England in 1963, where they performed better against the counties than the senior team had a year earlier. As a result of this initiative, Pakistan went on to organise a number of youth teams to play both domestically and around the world. But set against this modest success, there was acrimony amid the acronyms – by 1966, the Board of Control for Cricket in Pakistan (BCCP) and the newly restructured Pakistan International Airlines (PIA) began a near-continuous clash, with the PIA chairman accusing the BCCP president of 'exploiting players' and being 'short-sighted'. In time, the major Pakistan banks, the national railway company and various government departments all fielded teams in the domestic first-class cricket tournaments, leading one BCCP administrator to fret that this could be a 'potential recipe for … disaster [in] providing competitive sport and a sound Test team'. It was. Imran himself was later to observe, 'Pakistan is the only country in the world where cricket is played between commercial organisations and not between regions, zones, cities or states. The result is abysmal … Most of the matches are meaningless and insignificant.' Added to the structural deficiencies were some of those unique qualities of Pakistani national life that were to continue to play such a vital part in their sporting fortunes. The 1965 war against India interrupted regularly scheduled Test cricket for two years, and the 1968–69 England tour of Pakistan was eventually abandoned when a crowd of some 4,000 students, unhappy with the current military regime, invaded the pitch at Karachi; the police responded by firing tear gas, most of which blew straight back over their shoulders and through the broken windows of the England dressing-room.

In the same week that the red-eyed MCC tourists caught a hurriedly booked return flight to London, the regional selectors summoned Imran to an Under-19s trial in Lahore. There were 200 other hopefuls present, each of whom batted for five minutes in two adjoining nets. Imran lasted only half as long as that before being given the hook – a rare failure for a self-assured 16-year-old whose school batting average was currently 67.50. 'As I stood watching the other triallists, reality slowly seeped in,' he later noted. 'I was a reject.'

The proceedings weren't quite over, however. Before he could slink off, Imran was told to go back to the nets and turn his arm over. Doing what any red-blooded teenager would do in the circumstances, he pulled up his collar, West Indies style, loped in and bowled a bouncer. According to the best available evidence, this was 'fast but somewhat deviant ... It nearly hit the man in the next net.' After his third or fourth ball, the chairman of selectors stopped Imran and announced to the group as a whole that he had 'the ideal seam bowler's action'. This was followed by something of a lull, I was told. Certainly Imran himself would remain, at best, ambivalent about his potential new role. By and large, batsmen were idolised in Pakistan, where the seamers typically sent down a desultory few overs before the captain summoned the first of his four or five spin bowlers. Often even this brief delay wasn't necessary, as there were competitive matches where the spinners opened the attack. To give the ball a good tweak was the instinctive response to the beach-like pitches, with cracks down which Geoff Boycott would remark he could stick not only his house key, but the house as well, that were prevalent at every level of the game in Pakistan. Men like Niaz Ahmed, Asif Iqbal and Majid himself, none of whom were exactly brisk, regularly took the new ball for the national Test team of the time. Nor did either the climate or the uniquely atrocious standard of most wickets around Lahore as a whole encourage the average aspiring cricketing prodigy to bowl fast. But there it was. The following week Imran was selected to play for the Lahore Under-19 team against a touring English side. He opened the attack, sending down four fiercely erratic overs in the England first innings, taking three for 7 in the second, and batting No. 10.

It was an only fitfully impressive debut, and Imran recalls that he was 'treated [with] a certain amount of hostility. My team-mates thought I didn't deserve a place in the side and was there on the basis of my connections.' This sense of perceived rejection, and an answering competitiveness on his part, was to be a theme right through his career. A day or so later Wasim Raja, the captain of the Under-19s and a future Test all-rounder, greeted a friend with an account of the wild antics of a 'posh kid' on the team named Imran. According to Wasim, Imran wanted to bowl a bouncer with every ball, threw in a generous quota of beamers, and generally sprayed it around in an arc from gully to leg slip. One particular delivery had come close to felling the square leg umpire. 'He's the craziest cricketer I've ever seen,' said Wasim.

Yet the Lahore selectors soon began to take the kid seriously. In the next two Under-19 games, Imran was to show an at least rudimentary grasp of line and length, taking three for 19 and five for 42 respectively. He wasn't, perhaps, as inherently gifted as some other up-and-coming bowlers around the world. He lacked the fluid hydraulics of even the teenaged Michael Holding. He wasn't as squarely built as Ian Botham, or quite as lithely fast as Dennis Lillee or Richard Hadlee. Yet no young cricketer ever brought together such an amalgam of carefully nurtured talents. Imran was relentless in his pursuit of excellence. At least one observer saw him in the light of the 20th century's approved canon for success, as 'literally a self-made man'. Wasim Raja would long remember that 'Imran was invariab[ly] the first on the ground every morning, where he would run circuits of the playing area' – a novelty in the cricket culture of those days – 'before repair[ing] to the nets to practise bowling at a single stump for an hour or more before the start of play.'

Fanatically determined as he was, Imran may also have enjoyed a certain degree of old-fashioned patronage in his early career. He made his full first-class debut for Lahore against Sargodha when he was just turning 17. The chairman of the Lahore selectors was Imran's uncle, and the captain and two of the senior players were his cousins. It was another only sporadically successful start. Bowling a lively mixture of bouncers and prodigously fast outswingers, Imran took two wickets at some 20 runs apiece. That was to be the highlight of his contribution to the match. During a subsequent rain delay, Imran wandered off to his nearby bedroom, fell asleep and returned to the ground to find he'd missed his turn in the batting order. When he did bat he was run out, and Lahore lost the match.

Wasim Raja remarked of Imran's bowling technique at the time that, while generally effective, 'it wasn't pretty ... He more or less just ran in and hurled it.' Other accounts of the young Imran recall that he had a slinging action much like that of the Australian Jeff Thomson. All parties agree that, in Wasim's words, 'It was awkward and unorthodox ... You wouldn't find it in the MCC manual.' Perhaps as a result Imran tore a back muscle in his next match and missed nearly a season's competitive cricket. He didn't waste the time, however. He was the 'most hard-working, the most focused student of cricket ever,' a man closely familiar with the game in Lahore told me. 'Everybody else would be gone at the close of play, and he would still be there. At that age, most of the kids in the team wanted to have fun. He wanted to be ... Imran Khan.' As soon as he was physically able to do so, he resumed his lengthy workouts, spending afternoons in the nets and evenings in indoor 'skull sessions' with men like Javed Burki and Majid, discussing the finer points of the game. In time he made a gradual comeback through the ranks of Lahore juniors and Lahore B, often coming on first change, before returning to the senior team. Wasim Raja saw an immediate difference in Imran's action. 'He was bowling chest-on, which looked even more awful. He'd also grown another inch and put on some muscle, and the whole effect [was] highly intimidating from the batsman's point of view.' Another Lahore colleague recalls Imran carefully smoothing down his hair on his brisk trot back to his mark, and his subsequent snorting approach to the bowling crease, 'like that of a well-groomed bull'. His repertoire now included a 'devastatingly fast' inswinger as well as his stock bouncer, which 'on average, he employed three times an over'.

Imran had, meanwhile, left Aitchison College, whose vaunted enthusiasm for sports seems not to have extended to sharing one of their own with a professional cricket team. He spent his sixth-form year at the nearby Cathedral School. Although founded and run by a Christian mission, and thus somewhat at odds with both Niazi and Burki family tradition, the school 'more or less indulged [Imran]', as one of the staff remembers. 'He was a special case, [someone] who just seemed to be in a hurry to get to somewhere else. He was always driving and pushing, even as a teenager.'

Besides cricket, that drive and push found expression in long-distance running, javelin- and discus-throwing, and various other demonstrations of adolescent physical prowess. Imran was a full-time member of the Lahore team in the 1970–71 season, where he was lucky enough to have his cousin Javed Burki as captain. Javed cannily used the 18-year-old tearaway in short bursts. In the BCCP Trophy against Rawalpindi Blues (surely a song title) Imran took two for 26 and one for 10, followed by the more impressive first innings figures of 18–3–54–6 against Pakistan Railways. In the cup semi-final against Karachi he scored 17 and 60 batting at No. 3, but was said to have served up a 'dog's dinner' with the new ball. Moving across to the three-day Quaid-e-Azam Trophy, Imran recorded figures of five for 75 off 16 overs against Rawalpindi, missed the grudge match against the government's Public Works Department, but returned to play in the losing semi-final against Punjab University, where he took two for 96 in the first innings and one for 10 in the second, while scoring 36 and 68 in the middle order. At the end of the season Imran had a first-class batting average of 31.69 and a bowling average of 21.60. His first full year in domestic cricket was also to be his last, because he was rarely seen again in Pakistan after that except at representative level.

As Imran played cricket, the situation in the country as a whole was 'desperate', he later recalled. The first ever fully democratic national elections were due to have been held on 5 October 1970, his 18th birthday, but had to be postponed by two months because of the cataclysmic damage caused by floods in East Pakistan, where 200,000 people died and some 12 million lost their homes. It was generally agreed the relief operations were not well handled by the government. The result of the election gave the Bengali militant Sheikh Mujibur Rahman (popularly known as Mujib) and his Awami League an absolute majority in the National Assembly and all but two of the 162 seats allotted to East Pakistan. Zulfikar Ali Bhutto, a champion of Islamic socialism, a strong army and 'a 1,000-year war with India', emerged as the leader in the West. The irreconcilable differences of the two men's programmes and the growing threat of secession by the Bengalis set in train the breakdown first of parliamentary government and eventually of all domestic law and order. President Yahya Khan, the hard-drinking, straight-talking former army chief, first refused to honour the election results and then sent 40,000 troops to arrest Mujib and suppress the rioting that erupted in Dhaka, the capital of East Pakistan. Unrelieved suffering from the cyclone, coupled with brutal suppression by Yahya's army, may have killed as many as 500,000 more men, women and children over the next month. The confrontation eventually led to the events that brought about Pakistan's dismemberment in December 1971. Even before that, Imran had seen 'AIR-RAID SHELTER' and 'CARELESS CHAT COSTS LIVES' notices being tacked up on public buildings, just as he had in 1965. More and more recruits signed up for

Yahya's, or Bhutto's, army; I was told that the Khan family had been 'rightly alarmed' they would be evicted from Zaman Park, either by invading Bengalis or the Indians, if not by government fiat, and forcibly resettled, much as had happened following Partition in 1947. In the end they kept their home, although in the most harrowing circumstances. India again went to war with Pakistan in 1971 just as the latter finally tore itself apart. In the ensuing 13-day bloodbath, some 300,000 Pakistani civilians died and the country's armed forces were crippled for a generation. As the author Tariq Ali says, in less than a fortnight the nation 'lost half [its] navy, a quarter of its air force and a third of its army'. India and its Soviet ally jointly declared the outcome of the war, and the emergence of Bangladesh from the ruins of East Pakistan, to be a triumph for socialist and democratic principles.

Under the circumstances, it's not surprising that Imran proved to be an aggressively patriotic sportsman, not least when it eventually came to playing against India. Already, by 1971, he's remembered as a 'fine adornment of Pakistani manhood', who was widely known for his 'impassioned if selective' monologues on his country's history. Physically, too, he was quite imposing, having coaxed his hair into a Beatle moptop and developed a particularly intense, piercing stare – 'that don't-fuck-with-me squint of his', as one ex-girlfriend characterises it. He spoke in an almost sepulchral tone, with the occasional incongruous 'Strewth!' or 'Gorblimey!' coming to intrude on his otherwise exemplary English. Even his dress code was distinctive, eventually flaunting a conflict of styles dominated on the one hand by traditional Pakistani garb, and on the other by a collection of hip-hugging velvet flares, garishly loud shirts splayed open to the chest and chunky jewellery such as might have been favoured by Gary Glitter in his 'Do You Wanna Touch Me?' era.

This was the self-admittedly 'bumptious' individual who, on 4 March 1971, strode out into the Lahore Stadium to play for the BCCP side against a touring International X1, marking his first representative appearance for his country. The short goodwill visit by the Internationals had not been entirely free of incident up until then. In fact, the team's previous match at Dhaka had come to an abrupt end shortly after England's John Murray, who was batting at the time, 'happened to notice the Pakistani who had been fielding at long leg edging up to the slips and furtively muttering to them, "There will be trouble" about a split second before someone set the main stand on fire. The next thing

I knew we were in the middle of an army escort screaming down a dark road towards the airport, where we caught the last plane out to Lahore.' Conditions there were 'marginally more tranquil', Murray says. Imran eventually took three wickets in the match and, coming in at No. 9, hit 51 not out after his team had collapsed to 80 for seven. The Internationals' Australian bowler Neil Hawke, the man who saw most of the batsman, recalled his 'not being aware [he] was in the presence of an obvious genius'. Another player I spoke to couldn't even remember that Imran had taken part in the match. But it was apparently enough of an all-round performance to impress the then 77-year-old Wing Commander William (or 'Harold') Shakespeare, the chairman of Worcestershire, and his outgoing county secretary Joe Lister, both of whom were accompanying the tour. According to the written minutes, they particularly admired the 18-year-old's 'attitude' and 'obvious passion' for the game. As a result, Worcestershire offered Imran a one-year contract, with an option to renew, at a basic salary of £35 a week along with a somewhat vague promise to secure his 'special registration' as the county's primary overseas player. The momentous deal was consummated with a simple handshake in the pavilion. Imran's parents initially withheld permission, but were eventually won over by the argument that he could finish his education at Oxford or Cambridge, as several Khans had before him.

Later in the spring Imran received a letter from the Pakistan national selectors, offering him a place in the party to tour England that summer. He was more than five months shy of his 19th birthday, and was still notionally studying for his A levels at Cathedral School. The country was just then embarking on the process of ripping itself apart. Displaying some of the same self-destructive qualities, the Test team had acquired the name of 'Panikstan' for its consistent ability to lose from a winning position. Impatient with the practice, the home crowds had increasingly taken to verbally or physically abusing their cricketers. After one Test at the National Stadium in Karachi, the Pakistanis' team bus had been set on fire. Even so, in a nation still struggling for its identity, playing representative sports remained the peak of most young male Pakistanis' ambitions. 'A cricketer then could be like a rock star today,' said Wasim Raja. The 'distinct [and] high honour' of the occasion was reflected in the board's printed invitation received by Imran, which one family member who saw it remembers as a 'really elaborate affair' bearing the signature of a 'government dignitary or minister', which may have helped soften Ikramullah Khan's disappointment that his only son had apparently shunned a technical career and instead taken up with so 'boring' a sport. It's possible that, like many fathers of his generation, he took a restrained approach to showing his emotions. I was told that Mr Khan had later been in a crowded shop in central Lahore when a radio news report announced that the Pakistan team had won a match in England. Everyone in the place had 'gone wild [and] started cheering'. He did not tell them that the young fast bowler who had helped bring about the victory was his son. When Mr Khan later told the story in private to a colleague at Republic Engineering, he was 'as proud as if Imran had been elected prime minister of Pakistan'.

No major team travelled overseas with less expectation than the Pakistanis did in late April 1971. Led by Intikhab Alam, who had finished on the winning side only once in his 26 Tests, the squad boasted the stylish but frail middle-order batting of Majid Khan, Asif Iqbal and an as yet only locally famous 23-year-old named Zaheer Abbas. The bowling resources, as Majid recalled, were 'thin, not to say gaunt' and focused on the young Lahore seamer Asif Masood, the man whose crouching approach to the wicket reminded John Arlott of 'Groucho Marx chasing a pretty waitress'. In the event Masood took nine wickets in his first Test against England, only to suffer a dramatic decline in form from then on, leading to his premature retirement from all cricket in 1976. The tour itself took place against the backdrop of the Pakistani civil war, which both split the party along ethnic lines and provoked mass demonstrations against its supposed regional bias even before the players left their home soil. Earlier in the spring, the national Under-25 side's visit to England had had to be cancelled when Bangladeshi separatists threatened to firebomb the team's hotel. Right up to the last moment, there was a lively debate about the propriety of 16 cricketers 'fly[ing] off to sun themselves in England', as one report put it, at that particular point in their nation's history. Hence, perhaps, the BCCP president's masterly understatement at the pre-tour press conference, when he admitted that his team was in 'a little bit of turmoil'.

For all that, Imran records that he was 'brimming with excitement' at the prospect not only of his first cricketing tour but of his first time out of Pakistan. Although not exactly a household name, he was beginning to acquire some of the trappings of being a local celebrity, a status he enjoyed. The Lahore newspaper ran a long if factually flawed profile of the schoolboy 'heavy hitter' who was sure to 'knock the spots [off] the English attack'. Family friends converged on Zaman Park with pre-tour congratulations and advice. Imran's father is said to have taken special pleasure in seeing his son kitted out for the first time in his navy blue Pakistan blazer. Shaukat Khan was 'beside herself' with maternal pride, I was told, although anxious that Imran should not return from his travels with an English wife; it was a 'long tradition of the Jullandari Pathans' – words Imran heard often as a boy – to marry inside the fold. The many cricketing Khan relatives can be presumed to have heartily joined in the celebrations. On the eve of the team's departure to London Imran came out on to the street in front of his family home and signed autographs for a small but vocal crowd who had gathered there, while some of the adolescent girls among them shouted endearments and threw rose petals at his feet.

Now all that remained was the tour, which did not go well.

Given the nature of Pakistani cricket, it's somehow inevitable that there would be various factors behind the scenes that contributed to a generally lacklustre performance on the field of play. The country's arrival on the Test-playing circuit in the 1950s and their periodic successes against all five of their international opponents had been one of the early bonds of nationhood. Less than 20 years later, that initial wave of optimism had given way to what Imran calls an 'inferiority complex ... The English team was thought to be invincible [and] I was told it would be impossible for me to take any wickets there.' An air of mild apology, or deference, seemed to attach to the blazered figure of Masud Salahuddin, the 56-year-old Pakistan manager (and another of Imran's cousins), whose self-professed lifelong ambition was to win honorary membership of the MCC. Early in the tour, Mr Salahuddin formally thanked his side's hosts by remarking in a speech that 'England [had] taught us Pakistanis much-needed discipline through the game of cricket', including the protocol of how to eat with a knife and fork. Imran reports that he had been too embarrassed to listen to the rest. To be fair, the manager was not conspicuously well served by his home board, whose most senior positions were now a sinecure of the Pakistan Water and Power Development Authority (WAPDA). Whatever their skills in managing a public utilities company, the WAPDA officials were not, for the most part, ideally suited to the job of supervising a national sports tour taking place thousands of miles away, whose day-to-day running at least one senior player thought 'a joke, even by our standards'. While in England Imran would receive just 150 rupees, or roughly £7.50, for every five-day Test he played. The fee for a three-day match against one of the counties was some 80–100 rupees, depending on attendances, and even this pittance was often slow in coming. The players' weekly stipend was an equally modest £3–7 each, based on seniority, not exactly a fortune even in the Britain of 1971. At the end of the 11½-week tour, Imran was awarded a bonus of £2. No wonder that Zaheer Abbas reports that 'one of the first English words I learnt when I switched from Urdu was "peanuts". Everyone in the Pakistan team told me it summed up our wages.' In another of those administrative lapses that characterised the tour, Imran was frequently called on to share a room with Saeed Ahmed, the deposed captain who had a 'persecution complex', Wasim Raja believed. Following his sacking, Saeed had developed an 'embittered disposition', I was told, and it was 'damn hard to be his friend'. According to the testimony of Wasim and others, he was not the ideal man to have as a mentor on your first overseas tour.

For all that, however, the real reason that Imran initially failed in England was simply that his ample self-confidence wasn't yet matched by his abilities. His team-mate Asif Iqbal told me that 'he had bags of determination, but only a fair amount of natural talent and, back then, hadn't learnt many of the tricks of the trade he acquired later'. Set against this measured description is the account of the former England captain who recalls that 'Imran bowled a lot of balls on his first tour: take that any way you want'. Another senior Pakistan player thought the 18-year-old to be at a 'critical point in his life ... I told him that he should strive to get some qualifications, in order [to] have something to fall back on if the cricket failed. Otherwise he stood a good chance to end up a mere ditch-digger in Pakistan.' Even if Imran made it, his colleague added, he should know that 'professional sport was filled with reprobates who gambled and drank and ran after lewd women'. The teenager couldn't argue, and merely kept saying, 'I know, I know ...'

Imran made his first appearance of the tour on a frosty early May morning, bulked up in three sweaters to play for the Pakistanis against Northamptonshire. Before that he'd restricted himself to bowling in the nets at Lord's, which proved to be an only partly successful introduction to English conditions. For one thing, he still had no formal run-up. He just tore in off anything up to 10 or 12 scything paces and let fly. Imran's first delivery in England duly reared up and spat past his colleague Aftab Gul's nose. This would have been promising, but for the fact that Gul was batting in the next-door net at the time. Imran's second ball ricocheted off the head of a spectator. His third was reported as being a vicious beamer that struck the iron cross-bar over the net and shot perpendicularly up into the air. 'I was bothered by the difference between the hard grounds of Pakistan and the soft, damp, English turf [and] couldn't get a foothold,' Imran later explained.

At Northampton he took just two wickets in the match, but partially redeemed himself by clouting 28 and 33 not out in a low-scoring game after coming in at No. 10. 'In the power and cleanness of his hitting, Khan gave as much pleasure as anyone,' opined that doyen of cricket correspondents, E.W. Swanton. Imran took three for 58 in his next outing, against Hampshire, failed dismally against Nottinghamshire and wasn't selected for the tourists' showpiece match against MCC at Lord's. In all, he was to have a distinctly mixed first impression of what soon became his adopted home. Some of the sledging in those pre-PC times tended to be blunter than today, and there was often a muttered 'Paki' or 'Curry breath' to be heard from the fielders as Imran came out to bat. The insults seem to have had the singular motivational effect of making him work even harder at his game. As Javed Miandad recalls, 'On [that] tour, Imran developed a strict routine of physical training that he adhered to without fail throughout his playing days ... Every day, he would bowl six to eight overs without fail. He wouldn't be bowling to any batsman, but would just be on his own, bowling at a single stump ... There was a popping crease, and 22 yards away there would be the solitary stump. It was just Imran and the craft of bowling, with the rest of the world completely blocked out.'

When the tour ended and Imran joined Worcestershire, he continued to practise in an indoor school with the county coach and former slow left-armer Henry Horton. The coach thought 'the lad bowl[ed] like a catapault', but recognised that there was talent there to be tapped.

One of Imran's Pakistan colleagues told me that, such were his shortcomings in England, there had even been talk of sending him home early 'to hone his skills with Lahore' – a fate not much better, for an ambitious young professional, than being sent down the salt mines. He probably survived as much by luck as by any sudden improvement in technique. Two of Pakistan's faster bowlers, Sarfraz Nawaz and Salim Altaf, were ruled out by injuries, so Imran found himself called up for the first Test against England at Edgbaston. For the record, he was 18 years and 240 days old on his debut: impressive, but almost a case of late development compared to other Pakistan internationals such as Mushtaq Mohammad, who had supposedly been just over 15 when he first played for his country. Imran would remember the pre-Test dinner as being a less than inspirational affair. Several of the senior players took the opportunity to remark that the England batsmen and bowlers were the best in the world; and as for their slip fielding, if you nicked the ball, there was no point in even looking round, as the catch would already have been taken. (They were obviously still unfamiliar with Keith Fletcher.) There were raucous celebrations when the news of Imran's selection reached Zaman Park, where Mrs Khan distributed a large tray of the enticingly-named *barfi*, a fudge-like confection traditionally reserved for holidays. As we've seen, Imran's father's response was generally more restrained. One English-based family friend told me that Mr Khan 'took great pride that Imran represented his country. He never missed his press cuttings and appearances on TV. But he followed them as though Imran had a permanent starring role in a school play. I don't think he ever fully grasped the size of the stage his son played on.'

At Edgbaston Pakistan won the toss, batted and were still there two days later. It was the Test in which Zaheer Abbas scored 274, Asif Iqbal 104 not out and Mushtaq 100, and England followed on for the first time against Pakistan. Imran's inaugural over in Test cricket was one he never forgot. It was bowled to Colin Cowdrey, who was then winning his 109th cap. Cowdrey failed to land a bat on the first four balls, if only because they were so wide. At the end of five overs Imran's analysis was none for 19. The figures would have been worse had the England batsmen not been content to stand back and watch the ball pass harmlessly by in the direction of long leg. In one account, the Pakistani wicket-keeper Wasim Bari was obliged to 'fling [him]self around like Gordon Banks'. At the end of Imran's spell his captain took him aside and gently explained that an inswinger should ideally pitch outside the off stump, not outside leg. England managed to hold out for a draw thanks to rain and an unbeaten century by Luckhurst. The former Australian captain Richie Benaud was commentating on the match and rather generously remarks that 'No one paid a great deal of attention to the tourists' young all-rounder. He was just one of 11 players.' Imran himself reports that as a result of the Test 'the reputation of our side rose, while mine sank without trace ... Dreadful ... I considered giv[ing] up serious cricket.' Clearly, a star wasn't born.

The rest of the tour can perhaps be quickly recalled. Imran was back to his old routine against Yorkshire at Bradford, using the scattergun approach to try to dismiss batsmen, if mostly favouring the leg side. He was dropped for the second and third Tests, which Pakistan drew and lost respectively. It rained almost constantly. At the end of June the tourists took the bus up to Selkirk to play Scotland, where Imran recalls that two of his colleagues 'sat talking about me, fully aware that I could hear them. They made no attempt to hide their scorn. Their verdict was that I would be lucky to get into the Second XI of an English club side, let alone a county team.' Imran adds that he was immediately fired up to prove his critics wrong, although with initially disappointing results: wicketless in both Scottish innings, he managed knocks of 14 and 0 with the bat. His primary challenge remained landing the ball on the cut part of the pitch. Against Surrey, Imran took off his sweater to start bowling and the umpire good-naturedly called down the wicket to the batsman, 'Right arm over, anywhere.' Everyone duly fell about laughing, including, to his credit, Imran. Or perhaps he had merely been gritting his teeth. In the 11 matches he played on the tour he took a total of 12 wickets at an average of 43.91 each.

Things didn't go that well off the field, either. Imran was fined £2, equivalent to his entire tour bonus, when he left the Pakistan hotel one night after stuffing a pillow down his bed, *Great Escape*-style, to make for the nearest disco. Another evening he enjoyed the heady atmosphere of the Top Rank, Swansea, only to find that his room-mate Saeed Ahmed had reported him for breaking the team curfew: fined £1.50. A day or two later a catch went down off Saeed's bowling, causing him to break into tears and Imran in turn to burst out laughing, resulting in another visit to the manager's office. One wet afternoon in the Pakistan dressing-room, Sadiq Mohammad, at 26 one of the senior members of the team, asked Imran to get him a cup of tea, whereupon Imran told him to do it himself. It was a characteristic response by a man whose hallmark was the untugged forelock. Sadiq had 'gone berserk,' I was told. 'He shouted at Imran, prodding his fingers towards his face, and said, "I'll finish you now!" and "You'll pay!"' Imran had calmly looked the older player in the eye and said, 'I'm not your servant.'

Even at this early stage, Imran attracted an entourage of flattering male followers who proved no threat to his ego and who acted as loyal buffers between him and the outside world. Or at least that was their role in later years, when a key duty was to restrain the more persistent of Imran's female admirers. The 1971 entourage was only the first in a series of royal courts, often made up of junior colleagues. Players like Talat Ali and Azmat Rana, neither of whom appeared in a Test on the tour, were typically part of the group. A then 20-year-old legal secretary named Judy Flanders well remembers Imran's activities at a popular Manchester nightspot: 'He sat around, smouldered, muttered a bit to his mates, didn't dance, drank only milk, and rested his hand affectionately on my thigh.'

There was something of a heroes' welcome waiting for the Pakistanis when they flew home in the middle of July. Losing an overseas series to England 1–0 was considered a rare achievement, given both the negative pre-tour publicity and the team's generally dismal track record over the past decade. The relative success on the field in turn fed into a renewed public enthusiasm for the national game. With hindsight, the centre of gravity of international cricket was already shifting towards South Asia, where most of the potential spectators, much of the wristy talent and a fair amount of the available gambling money all were. Imran himself was not on hand to hear the cheers and wolf-whistles of the crowd at Karachi airport. Later that week he treated himself to a final evening's entertainment at the Mecca dance-hall in London's Leicester Square, then caught the early train to Worcester, his principal English home for the next five years.

Had Imran gone back to Lahore and taken up engineering, as his father still periodically urged him to, he'd be remembered today as a talented underachiever. As it was, the odds were that he would go on to play perhaps one or two obscure seasons of county cricket. Then a professional career in Pakistan, possibly involving the civil service, along with an arranged marriage, and the occasional weekend appearance for the Gymkhana or a similar club; retirement; death; appreciative but not long obituaries, followed by a footnote recalling him as a 'one Test wonder' in the cricket reference books – that would have been it. The reason Imran succeeded where other, more naturally gifted, players failed was that he put his first year in England to such good effect, emerging from it fitter and faster than ever. More determined, too. Reflecting on Imran's self-belief, Wasim Raja (no martyr to false modesty himself) admiringly recalled that, as a 19-year-old, he had had 'a healthy ego [along] with the single-minded focus of a speeding bullet'.

Even so, it was a struggle. Imran would have been less than human if he hadn't taken time to adapt to single life in an English provincial town just as early autumn approached. Worcestershire initially accommodated their overseas signing in a rather spartan room in the market square's Star Hotel. Local folklore has it that, while staying at the Star, Imran put his mattress on the floor each night, and each morning the chambermaid, ignorant of the oriental custom, returned the mattress to the bed. He was not selected for the county side in the remaining part of the season, but played seven matches for the Second XI, and less formally in the Under-25 groups and assorted knock-ups. Once again these gave scant evidence of any latent genius, although the newcomer 'absorbed' everything, I was told, and was a 'quick study'. Imran was once seen to take a thick coaching book with him back to his digs. He had apparently combed through it overnight and mentally photographed what he needed, because the next morning 'he could quote the book's exact captions [and] whole chunks of the actual text,' an impressed colleague recalled.

On 9 August, Imran arrived at the unprepossesing County Ground, Derby, with his usual baggage: style. Clad in tailored whites and a Pakistan touring cap, a polka-dot handkerchief sticking out of a pocket, he treated the sparse Tuesday morning crowd to 110 of the best runs possible, out of a grand total of 222. Regrettably, this early-career promise wasn't to be entirely fulfilled. By the beginning of September, the Worcestershire Second XI had lost four of their last five games and were drifting near the bottom of the 14-team league. The county still seem to have thought of Imran, to the extent that they did so at all, as a middle-order belter who could bowl a bit. It wasn't an entirely illogical preconception, since they had engaged him in the first place after watching him hit the International XI's Neil Hawke around the park at Lahore. Although not exceptionally wristy, Imran had developed a series of taut, slightly robotic arm shots which could give the ball an almighty thump. Even so, one or two good judges including Henry Horton appeared to think he had the makings of an all-rounder, a natural replacement for the seemingly ageless but actually 40-year-old Basil D'Oliveira. Though not perhaps the most accurate, Imran's bowling was pretty spectacular by county, let alone Second XI or Club and Ground standards. He knew it. Beset though he often was at Worcester by nagging doubts about his overall prospects, his claims for himself weren't small – and weren't on the whole misguided.

On 1 September, Imran was selected to play for Worcestershire in a three-day match against the touring Indians. It seems somehow fitting that his opponents for his debut should be his nation's mortal enemies. Imran drew some attention to himself before play started by appearing in the net swinging three bats at once, a practice favoured by professional baseball players to make the bat they hit with feel lighter. To his bemused team-mates, though, it's possible it merely looked eccentric. He wasn't to follow up this preliminary flourish when in the middle, scoring 0 and 15 and failing to take a wicket. At least one of the Indian team thought him 'a hype'.

Imran hadn't forgotten his promise to his parents to finish his education in England, and shortly after the India game he entered Worcester Royal Grammar school as a boarder, with a view to taking A levels and going on to university. His ten months there don't appear to have been happy ones. Apart from the institutional food and the cold, he was miserably homesick, his one friend in England being his cousin Majid, who was far away at Cambridge. At half-term and on other holidays, Imran stayed behind and moved into an attic room in his headmaster's house. One retired staff member described him to me, perhaps not surprisingly, as 'a bit of a loner'. The English boarding school system was not then troubled, as it was later, by counsellors. Had it been, Imran would no doubt have been thought worthy of concern. In the event, he seems to have been somewhat of an object of satire to the other boys, to whom he had, in any case, little to talk about, preoccupied as they were with glam rock and soccer. Even so, the familiar determination and ambition were to the fore. Despite a still imperfect grasp of English, Imran passed Economics and Geography with an A and a C grade respectively. He completed the two-year course in the equivalent of just over two terms, or nine months.*

One winter Saturday afternoon Imran and Majid visited Mike Selvey, the future Surrey, Middlesex and England bowler (and *Guardian* cricket correspondent), at his flat in Cambridge. Selvey thought the nearly invisible teenager swathed in a heavy overcoat and a variety of scarves to be 'very quiet and shy. [Although] Imran said very little, years later he told me how much he appreciated it. I always got on well with him and called him Fred, as in Karno.'

It seems most people who met Imran during his first year or so in England had the same general impression Selvey did. Away from the cricket field, he was basically 'shy' and 'rather mousey – a bit of a mumbler,' two grammar school contemporaries recalled. Older and more sophisticated people reacted similarly, finding Imran a very different proposition from the later celebrity. 'He didn't treat himself like a statue of himself,' Basil D'Oliveira said after meeting him in 1971.

---

* Opening the bowling with Imran for the school's First XI was a Kenyan-born 18-year-old named Rabi Mehta, who in the 1980s went on to author several scholarly articles about the aerodynamics of a cricket ball in flight, and thus to 'explain' the theory of reverse swing.

He seems to have been commendably focused on his studies at Worcester Grammar (whose fees of about £200 a term were paid not by the club, as popularly rumoured, but by Imran's father). In the light of his future reputation as a sort of flannelled Austin Powers figure, it's worth quoting one final schoolfriend, now a lecturer in psychology, who saw him as a socially naive young man. 'He kept to himself, and didn't show any interest in girls or sex that I was aware of.' Sometime towards the end of the year, Imran apparently did write a well-received short story or essay, which he circulated to some of the senior boys, about a man who walks around London soliciting beautiful women. 'He certainly didn't do any fieldwork on it,' his friend insists. Imran also spent hours retooling his bowling action both in the school gym and in the indoor net at Edgbaston which Worcestershire then shared. Although Henry Horton worked doggedly to convert the 'catapault' bowler into the well-oiled machine of later legend, it was John Parker, the young New Zealand batsman also in his first year at Worcester, who looked at Imran one day and casually suggested he 'take a little jump' before delivering the ball. The idea was both to gain extra momentum and to get more side-on to the batsman, who, as an added bonus, would then have to deal with 'this crazy, vaulting Pakistani bowling at you at 90 miles an hour', as one distinguished former England opener puts it. The improvisations in Imran's bowling technique continued over the years. He could, and did, vary his run-up, steam in wide of the crease, move it both ways, or neither, and was apt to follow up a slower ball with a screaming bouncer that left batsmen wringing hands or standing transfixed. But what really set him apart was that 'little jump'. It was at once superbly efficient and shamelessly flamboyant, and as such could be readily appreciated by players and spectators alike. At Edgbaston in 1982 Imran took seven for 52 in the English first innings, and was paid the compliment of the home crowd applauding their own team's discomfiture as they savoured a bowling routine that was part athletics, part ballet and part tribal wardance. 'It was,' said the England captain, 'a privilege to be there.'

In July 1972 Imran won a place at Keble College, Oxford, after being brusquely rejected by Cambridge. Before going up he played some schools and Warwick Pool cricket, making use of his new action; although the exact number is hard to establish, I was told he had taken 'a minimum of 25 wickets' in the course of four single-innings matches. (He also played once for Worcestershire Seconds against Glamorgan, with the more modest if economical figures of none for 16 off eight.) In his autobiography, Imran notes a shade tartly, 'When I reported to the county in 1972 I found a few things entirely different from the terms we had agreed. For a start, my wages had been reduced' – supposedly from £35 to £25 a week – 'and secondly, John Parker was to be specially registered ahead of me.' Imran's account doesn't entirely square with that of the incoming county secretary, Mike Vockins, who, while not a party to the original deal struck in the pavilion at Lahore, had 'all the bumph' at his disposal. 'There would have been only limited opportunities to play [Imran] in that 1972 season, although under the rules he would have automatically become eligible and registered once he went up to Oxford. I can't recall any occasion during my 30 years as Secretary when any players' wages were reduced,' says Vockins.

Even at that stage, Imran seems to have had distinctly mixed views about the appeal of playing county cricket seven days a week. As he quickly recognised, the sheer repetitiveness of it, often cited as a weakness, can be a marked asset from the player's point of view; if you make a mistake, you get a chance to atone for it on an almost daily basis for five months. Set against that was the irksome routine of humping one's kit up and down the British motorway system, and lodging in a series of guest-houses or hotels with little pretension to luxury. The wages were unspectacular – £800 to £1,200 per annum was typical for an uncapped player. For reasons of both background and temperament, Imran never fully integrated into the general banter of the county dressing-room or indeed of the pub. He never drank alcohol, a major handicap in almost every aspect of life as a professional sportsman in the Britain of the early 1970s. 'We didn't know quite what to make of him,' one Worcestershire colleague recalls. 'He certainly wasn't one of the boys in the sense of going out on the pull, though I gather he did pretty well in that area by himself.' Basil D'Oliveira, the South African-born player then in his tenth year with Worcestershire, told me, 'I'm not surprised if there were misunderstandings, seeing most English county cricketers knew as much about Pakistan as they did about the dark side of the moon.' Imran came to think that the 'old pros' on the county circuit were hopelessly negative in their approach to the game, and 'slightly racist' to boot. D'Oliveira confirmed that he had once heard an opposition bowler greet the new recruit 'with a whole string of ethnic stereotypes, in which the word "chutney" somehow stood out', and that 'Immy's response was to hit the second or third ball he faced from the guy out of the park.' D'Oliveira added that it 'wasn't that unusual a scene'.

Imran eked out the balance of a forgettable season for Worcestershire Seconds, distinguishing himself only with a four-wicket haul against Leicestershire and their perhaps less than stellar middle order of Schepens, Stringer, Wenban and Stubbs. While on the road he roomed alone, generally ate alone, and found ways to kill time alone before and after games. In another departure from standard practice Imran spent long hours wandering through museums and art galleries, browsing in public libraries and visiting the historic sights in various provincial towns. He seems not to have bonded with any of his team-mates, or to have gone out of his way to make friends. Writing of his time at Worcestershire as a whole, Imran was to note, 'I just didn't enjoy myself ... Either the players were married and had their own lives, or they were unmarried and spent their evenings in pubs. Being a teetotaller, I was lonely and bored.' About the best that could be said of the experience was that it allowed him to play cricket at a marginally more competitive level than would have been the case in Pakistan, whose domestic contests between various state agencies, transportation conglomerates and banks proved of only limited appeal to players and spectators alike.

The crash course in culture served Imran well at Oxford, where he initially read Geography before switching to Politics and Economics. On the whole it seems to have been a more congenial atmosphere than that of the county Second XI circuit. One of his contemporaries told me that, at 20, Imran had been 'a bit green' and had stayed the course academically only through his own freelance efforts and the good grace of Paul Hayes, the senior tutor at Keble, who had evidently taken a shine to him. Imran had been 'socially agile', however – 'If it was female and had a pulse, he pursued it.' After a year living in college he moved out to a series of digs, getting around town on an ancient Bantam motorbike. It's remembered that he liked to ride this at top speed, often preferring a zigzag pattern to a straight line, and even in winter carried his cricket bat slung over the back wheel. One Saturday night Imran rasped up on the bike to a party in Oxford's Summertown area, accompanied by a 'ravishing looking' girlfriend. A certain amount of drinking and substance abuse had gone on among his fellow guests, I was told. Perhaps as a result, later in the evening a fresh-faced chemistry student reeled up to Imran and said, 'I'm Cassius Clay and I'm going to knock the shit out of you.' Imran, who was somewhat taller than his antagonist, put his hand on the man's right shoulder and held him patiently at arm's length while 'the little guy punched the air in between them'.

Imran was particularly fortunate to play his cricket at the Parks, a handsome, tree-lined ground that was only a short walk from Keble. In the summer term his practice was to go directly from his early morning tutorial to the playing field, returning home again for a late dinner. An Oxford team-mate named Simon Porter remembers him as 'more inherently gifted, obviously, [but] also more driven' than his colleagues. 'Imran spent hours trundling away in the nets, essentially in an effort to perfect his inswinger. He always wanted to know if you could "read" him, which I, for one, couldn't – and I had the bruises all over my leg to prove it.' It wasn't unknown for Imran to attract a 'small harem' of supporters to the ground for even the most insignificant fixture. Another colleague remembers that, on losing his wicket in one inter-college game, Imran 'strode straight through the front door of the pavilion, grabbed a bag, and strode straight out the back one, where a blonde in a sports car was waiting for him. He jumped in, and that was the last we saw of him for two days.' A subsequent Oxford girlfriend, another blonde now called Karen Wishart (not her name at the time), thought Imran a 'physically beautiful' man whose charm was nonetheless limited in its scope. One evening the two of them went off together to 'a little flat above a fruit and veg shop' in the Oxford suburbs. Looking back on the episode years later, Wishart was left to conclude that Imran was a 'music and roses at night, pat on the bum in the morning' type. It would be only fair to add that another woman found him an 'attentive, funny and charming' partner, who nonetheless struck her as the kind who would 'hug you politely and then just stroll away once you broke up'. The words proved prophetic.

One of Imran's earliest appearances for Oxford was against Worcestershire, where he clearly had something to prove. Over the years, some of these county versus university encounters could be the ultimate in boredom, and many of the old pros saw them as little more than an agreeable way to improve their averages. That wasn't to be the case here, at least in Oxford's second innings. A powerful Worcester attack of Holder, Pridgeon, D'Oliveira and Gifford appeared to be sending down half-volleys and long hops all afternoon. It wasn't so, but Imran's polished innings of 54 more than had the measure of the professionals' line-up. He followed it by scoring 47 and 51 against Sussex, a match I illicitly cycled over from my nearby boarding school to watch. Nothing seemed to better crystallise events than the straight six with which Imran greeted Sussex's highly regarded off-spinner Johnny Barclay; 2–0–4–2–6 followed, all in the direction of the River

Cherwell. After the over, Barclay took his sweater and came back to field at third man, still muttering to himself. Something similar happened a fortnight later against Gloucestershire. Imran scored 59 out of 106 in the Oxford second innings, peppering the old wooden score-box-cum-groundsman's hut with sixes. Others landed in the copse of trees behind square leg. Generally speaking Imran did rather less with the ball, but was still in a class of his own compared with his fellow undergraduates, a tall poppy among shrinking violets.

It was the same story against Cambridge in the varsity match. Imran top-scored with 51 in the Oxford first innings (caught off the bowling of Phil Edmonds), but took only a modest three wickets throughout. One or two of his Oxford colleagues wanted him to bowl faster, of which he was fully capable, rather than to concentrate on line and length as Worcestershire always insisted. Both Imran and his new bowling action were still works in progress. Although tall, he wasn't as well upholstered as he would be when he filled out two or three years later, and the 'little jump' was a formidable physical feat that wasn't yet invariably effective when it came to getting the ball on the wicket. In those days, the former England captain Ted Dexter told me, 'Imran used to come charging in [and] plant his left foot virtually parallel to the batting crease in the delivery stride. "Sooner or later, that young man will do himself an injury",' Dexter thought presciently. Oxford drew their match with Cambridge. A night or two later, Imran walked into the White Horse in Oxford's Broad Street, where he became one of the first men to successfully order a glass of milk in a British pub. As usual there was a small group of acolytes at his table, including the statutory blonde girlfriend. 'People were fawning on Imran because he was already a bit of a superstar,' one of the party recalls. 'But the English have always been fascinated with swarthy oriental mavericks. Or at least they were in those days. Imran would have turned heads even if he'd never picked up a cricket ball. I have a fond memory of him sitting there with his milk and his blonde, trying desperately to look unimpressed while somebody read out all the glowing references to him – how he was a tiger and a fighter and so on – in the morning press. He loved it. Who wouldn't have?' Imran may not have been the finished article, but good judges had begun to take serious note of him.

Fighting was what life was about. That was the reason Imran 'worked like a cur', to quote a Keble source, to support himself at Oxford. When he was later to claim that 'playboys have plenty of time and money –

I've never had either', he didn't exaggerate his case. In the wake of the civil war and the subsequent currency crisis, the Pakistani government had imposed strict exchange controls that made it illegal to send more than the equivalent of £15 out of the country annually, with the prospect of a lengthy gaol term for anyone breaking the law. As a result Imran had no trust fund and an only minimal allowance. To keep himself afloat in the off-season he took a series of menial jobs, including one washing dishes over the Christmas holiday at Littlewoods store in south London. It was no worse than the fate of thousands of other students over the years, but it does refute the idea that he swanned through his time at Oxford like one of the teddybear-carrying toffs in *Brideshead Revisited*.

Despite his claim to have been neglected by Worcestershire, Imran played for the county in 11 first-class matches in the second half of the 1973 season. The club found him new if rather basic digs in the town's Bromyard Road, and even went to war with the Test and County Cricket Board to keep him registered with them under the board's Rule 4, relating to 'temporary special players'. Imran came into the team in time to play Warwickshire in a fixture starting on 14 July, just three days after appearing for Oxford at Lord's. The more free-spirited, if not always effective, student approach to the game gave way to the trench warfare of the county championship, conducted behind the sandbag of broad pads – the main idea being for batsmen to obtain a reasonably good average each season at the minimum of risk and physical exertion to themselves. For a cricketer who abhorred the safety-first school epitomised by certain old pros, it was all mildly depressing. Imran took just 31 wickets in the 11 matches (one of them, admittedly, when he bowled Garry Sobers) at some 24 apiece. But even that modest achievement eclipsed his performance with the bat – 15 innings, 228 runs, average 16.28. Being Imran, though, what he lacked in mature ability he fully made up for in self-belief; the fact that he neither scored runs nor took wickets troubled him as little as did most of the criticism he received over the years, and had the same general effect. 'It taught me never to stop, that when you lose you fight harder the next time.'

Back in Oxford, Karen Wishart sometimes talked to Imran about his future – Imran apparently uncertain, Wishart positive that he would play cricket for only a year or two more and then go back to a steady job in Pakistan. Both the civil service and engineering were mentioned. Wishart often urged Imran to ignore the temptation to become a fully professional sportsman who presumably might just about eke out a living for another ten years or so while his contemporaries got on with their 'proper' careers. Down that road, she insisted, there was nothing to gain and everything to lose. Imran frequently said he didn't much like the idea either.

If Wishart took that for an answer, she knew less than she thought she did about a man who was born to perform.

THREE

The Swinger

In 1974 Imran was elected captain of Oxford. It was a somewhat surprising choice, considering his only mixed form with bat and ball, untried diplomatic skills and still limited command of English. According to those with whom he discussed the club's offer, he hesitated a day or two before agreeing, apparently concerned that 'the guys' might not accept him. There was also the question of whether the added responsibility would affect his own game, as has been known with cricket captains. Trying to bat, bowl, lead from the front *and* learn the language, one friend said bluntly, was at least one job too many.

The offer was nonetheless a heady one for a 21-year-old Pakistani who had a somewhat romantic view of the British university tradition as a whole, based as it was on the exploits of men like Majid's father Jahangir Khan, who had been up at Cambridge in the 1930s. Accepting it would give him a certain cachet, as well as the chance to bowl himself as he saw fit. After another winter of training and periodic trips to the indoor school at Edgbaston, Imran's action was now close to the real thing. 'I also knew I had the temperament for fast bowling,' he remarks. With five years of first-class cricket and one Test appearance to his credit, 'I was ready ... confident the job would [make] me a better player' – a judgement that events bore out to a quite astonishing extent.

Imran hit the ground running, taking five for 56 against a Warwickshire side including six current or former England Test players and the West Indies' Alvin Kallicharran. He then began to do the thing in style. Innings of 117 not out and 106 against a full-strength Nottinghamshire. Another five-wicket haul against Derbyshire. A cameo of 20 (Oxford's top score) against a Somerset who were giving a second match to a teenager named Botham. Imran seemed to be playing some of the counties by himself, fielding tigerishly to his own bowling and driving batsmen into errors and indecision where previously there had been only confidence. As one of his colleagues told me, 'You frequently had the feeling that he could have made up a team with just himself, a couple of serviceable all-rounders and maybe a wicketkeeper.'

At the Parks on the bitterly cold morning of 15 May, Imran went out to toss with the captain of Yorkshire, Geoff Boycott. At ten o'clock the entire playing area was covered with a sleet that had frozen in the night, and both the pavilion and the rows of deckchairs rather optimistically displayed in front of it seemed to have been varnished with ice. This gave the two men the opportunity to agree that conditions for early-season English cricket could be a bit on the crisp side. After these pleasantries were concluded, Boycott told Imran (whom he addressed as 'young man') that he didn't much care for the occasion as a whole. 'It's not worth getting out of bed for these fucking student games,' he complained. Someone in the sparse crowd then made an audible and rather racist remark in which he drew comparison between the ethnic make-up of the two teams. You could literally see the steam coming off Imran as he bounded back up the pavilion steps. Anyone at all familiar with him would have known what to expect next. Bowling at maximum revs for the next two hours he took four Yorkshire wickets, including that of Boycott with a late inswinger. A young boy's perhaps ill-timed request for the Yorkshireman's autograph a few minutes later was met in the negative. Back in the middle Imran was the most restless captain, pacing around with a frown when not actually bowling, making pantomime signals to his fielders. He took himself off at last after 39 overs, mentally perhaps, if not physically, exhausted.*

There followed a short and unremarkable match with Worcestershire, then the visit of the touring Indians, against whom Imran made 160 and 49. He began his first innings quietly enough, with just a clipping four or two against Madan Lal. But with the arrival of the spinners came one of the most ferocious onslaughts on any type of bowling which can ever have been inflicted at the Parks. The students put on 189 for the third wicket, 120 of them by Imran who, playing on the off-side at one end and on the on-side at the other, struck the ball relentlessly to the near boundary, at least once with such force that it

---

* Even 35 years later, Boycott could still vividly recall the ball with which Imran bowled him. 'It was bloody good,' he told me cheerfully, high praise coming from that particular source.

rebounded off the heavy roller half-way to the pitch. For good measure, he also took four wickets in the Indians' first innings. Imran's century was his highest score to date in first-class cricket. Eight days later, he broke his record with 170 against Northamptonshire. He then proceeded to dispatch the Northants middle order with three wickets in the first innings and four in the second. Imran was still bowling when Oxford won by 97 runs, having given one of the really great all-round performances.

Imran's well-developed sense of self-respect might go some way to explain why, time and again, he and his bowling seemed to step up a gear when he had something particular to prove. An associated element of revenge – the Pathan principle of *badal* – was also observable deep in the mix. Most sportsmen, of course, talk about 'pride', at least as an abstraction, and virtually no pre-match press conference at any level of the professional soccer world would be complete without repeated references to the concept. But Imran took it to an almost messianic degree, and an ill-advised remark such as Boycott's was apt to have roughly the same effect as lighting the touch-paper on a particularly spectacular firework. 'Ten of us were just students together, playing a game,' one of the Oxford team told me. Imran, by contrast, 'came up with an antagonistic attitude, which in his mind turned any little slight into a life-or-death struggle. I wouldn't say he always thought everyone was ganging up on him. That sounds a touch paranoid, whereas in my experience he saw things from a very clear cultural-historical perspective. From what I heard and saw of Imran, and charming as he often was, he had a definite thing about certain aspects of the mother country. As far as he was concerned, we were all essentially colonialist swine who had been screwing his people for centuries.'

Such was the general backdrop to Imran's first match as captain against Cambridge, the university which had seen fit to shun his services two years earlier. It scarcely needs adding that his bowling proved a shade brisk for the opposition. Imran took five for 44 off 20 overs in the Cambridge first innings and five for 69 off 38 overs in the second. As a rule he was very fast, variable both in length and direction, with a preference for the ballooning inswinger, and desperately hard to score from. When he was short and on line a number of the Cambridge batsmen elected to take the ball on the body anywhere between the top of the pads and the general area of the forehead, if more out of necessity than choice. Not that Imran's robust approach to the game precluded the odd moment of light relief, as when he saw fit to amble in once or twice and lob up a gentle leg break. One Cambridge batsman thought this to have been a prime example of reverse psychology on Imran's part. 'It bloody nearly worked, too, because one of our guys promptly lost his head and dollied up a catch, which was dropped.' This had been 'poorly received' by the bowler. Pantomime then stalked proceedings on the third day, when Oxford were chasing 205 to win. They eventually needed just 61 off the last 20 overs, with half their wickets in hand. Imran's 'crystal clear' instruction to go for runs was somehow missed by the Oxford No. 5, Edward Thackeray, who proceded serenely to 42 not out in just over three hours. Towards the end the general noise from the Tavern stand dissolved into an exasperated chant of 'Wake up, Oxford' and 'We want cricket'. The situation was apparently no less trying to Imran, who could be seen pacing restively from side to side on the players' balcony, occasionally pausing long enough to scowl or shake his fist towards the middle. After what was described as a 'strained' tea interval, he had resorted to thumbing through a copy of the laws to see whether Thackeray's innings could be involuntarily declared closed. It couldn't, and the match was drawn.

The team party, or post-mortem – there was no formal dinner – that evening was an equally stiff affair. For the most part, Imran (who left early to catch a train to Hove, where he was appearing for Worcestershire against Sussex) engaged only in uncomfortable small talk with his men, and chose not to dwell on the match at any length. Many silences resulted. At one point, apparently in an effort to warm things up, one of the less experienced members of the side reached over to the bar and offered his captain some champagne.

'Thank you,' Imran said. 'I drink milk.'

Since 1971 Pakistan had been gradually returning to cricketing health, if not without the occasional relapse or well-publicised temper tantrum. The national team had a new bowler in Sarfraz Nawaz and a well-remembered one in Mushtaq. Asif and Zaheer were batsmen fit to set before the world. In 1972–73, when Imran was bedding down at Oxford, his countrymen had toured Australia and acquitted themselves rather better, both on and off the field, than the 3–0 result suggests. No side including Saeed Ahmed could be entirely incident-free, even so, and the selectors had been forced to draft in the all-rounder Nasim-ul-Ghani for the Sydney Test after Saeed refused to open the batting against Dennis Lillee. Pakistan had gone on to win and draw series against New Zealand and England respectively. Along the way, Intikhab

Alam had been replaced as captain by Imran's cousin Majid, who was considered an only modest success in the job. After three consecutive draws against England, Majid stood down and Intikhab returned for his third time in charge. '[The captaincy] is out of control ... it's a circus,' the PIA president was heard to complain at a press conference in his office, throwing his pen so hard it bounced off the carpet.

The labyrinthine world of Pakistan politics, meanwhile, continued to be mirrored by that of its cricket administration. Abdul Kardar, the former captain of the national team, now combined his position as chairman of the BCCP with a cabinet office in the Bhutto government. In 1974, Bhutto and Kardar moved the headquarters of Pakistan cricket from Karachi to Lahore. They took the opportunity to rename the Lahore stadium after the self-styled 'Glorious Guide of the First of September Great Revolution of the Socialist Peoples Brotherly Libyan Army' (and supporter of both the eventual South-East Asian nuclear powers, if not their cricket), Muammar al-Gaddafi, along with a gushing tribute from the Pakistani prime minister: 'Today, to you, we say thank you ... thank you, thank you, Glorious Guide.'

For what? some journalists wondered, no doubt in keeping with many residents of Karachi. Most of Bhutto's government were involved in one way or another in the management of Pakistan cricket, although generally they restricted themselves to various pet schemes, such as their decision to honour the Libyan dictator, rather than the tedious business of day-to-day administration. Before and during Test series, therefore, when the BCCP should have been most active, its new office, a dim, green-carpeted room in the bowels of the Gaddafi stadium, was often utterly deserted – a condition which was only slightly improved even on the rare occasions when Kardar scheduled a meeting of the full 'committee', which consisted of a dozen or so Bhutto appointees based in Islamabad; more than once, the only people who bothered to show up were Kardar and a secretary.

It's not clear to what degree, if any, the BCCP officials balanced their misgivings about Imran's one Test performance to date with their apparent new-found preference for Lahore over Karachi, a bias which was to be reflected in a number of hotly debated selections over the next decade. Perhaps they simply felt that after three years he was ready to return. In either event Imran joined his colleagues midway through their 1974 tour of England. His first appearance, against Warwickshire, following just four days after the varsity match, came as a rude lesson in the comparative merits of student and representative cricket. Imran went for 126 runs off his 22 overs in the Warwickshire first innings. At one stage the opener John Jameson carted him for 50 in four overs. Rain then spared him any further indignity. The unimpressed tour manager, Omar Kureishi, promptly called the team together and read them the Riot Act, which 'in no way dented Imran's high spirits or self-confidence', according to Kureishi's then teenaged son Javed, who accompanied the side. 'I remember him as this supremely cocky, long-haired guy who was tremendous fun to be around. Imran thought nothing of marching up to a senior player and telling him, "Your grip's all wrong, chum", or advising everyone on their fitness and diet. I once watched, fascinated, as he dropped two raw eggs into a glass of milk in a London restaurant and drained it off in one gulp. Very specific about things like that, Imran. Always finished his day off with a carrot.'

The tour management took the view that Imran's jaded performance against Warwickshire must be due to a hectic nightlife, and as a result imposed a 10 p.m. curfew on the entire team. 'This brought some dirty looks in my direction,' he recalls.

Duly rested, Pakistan turned in a bravura performance against Nottinghamshire, whom they dismissed for 51 in their first innings. Sarfraz moved the ball about 'like a boomerang' in Derek Randall's phrase (the pitch having been 'a bog', he added), and finished with eight for 27. Imran took a single wicket. The following week he managed a modest one for 56 and two for 65 against the Minor Counties, and was sufficiently worried about his finances to write a 'Dear Mike' letter to the Worcestershire secretary, telling him that he had been 'made to understand by the other professionals in the touring team that their clubs keep on paying their basic wages throughout the duration of the tour. I wonder if that applies to me as well ... I hope it does' – all part of a 'miserable' first month back in Pakistani colours. (Javed Kureishi, even so, remembers accompanying Imran to the cinema around that same time, where the 21-year-old 'laughed like hell' throughout a Snow White cartoon. 'There really was a core enthusiasm and innocence to the guy.') As slumps go, this wasn't quite on the scale of, say, Denis Compton's famous bad patch of 1946, but it contained some pretty spectacular flops which inevitably caught the critics' attention. 'The student looked out of his depth at this level,' was the *Daily Mail*'s scathing assesment. Imran was distinctly lucky to play in the first Test, at Headingley, and even then he operated as a third seamer after Sarfraz and Asif Masood had taken the new ball. If anything, he shone more with the bat: appearing at No. 8, he lashed 23 and 31 in a low-scoring match which petered out in a draw. These weren't tail-end runs, either; Imran hit Old high and handsomely for a first-bounce four into the crowd in front of the press box, and when Arnold tried him likewise with a bouncer he found himself flat-batted down to the West Stand bookstall with, in one account, a stroke 'like a tracer bullet'.

Imran went back to the nets and worked on his action, sending down the daily equivalent of 10 overs to a batsman and another half-dozen with just himself and a stump. Another game he evolved was to bounce a cricket ball off the side of a bat, and then try to retrieve it again with either hand as it shot off at odd angles. Wasim Raja once watched Imran spend 20 or 30 minutes by himself throwing a ball against a small upended trampoline; he would then catch the rebound and, in the same action, try to return the ball to hit the target, and again field the rebound. The performance was 'all very impressive, because the [other] players just focused on their batting or bowling, while Imran also wanted to improve as an athlete.'

It worked, not right away in every case, but eventually in a series of improved bowling performances on the tour. The second Test, another draw, was notable chiefly for the incessant rain and the Pakistanis' subsequent complaint about the state of the Lord's pitch.* Little did they or the spectators know that this was to be a feast of entertainment compared with what followed. The third and final Test at The Oval – drawn again – 'tapered off into the type of meaningless sport which only cricket can produce', to quote the journalist Omar Noman. Imran then bowled a tidy 10 overs for 36 in his first ever one-day international, which Pakistan won, and took two for 16 in his second, with the same result. He ended with an 'immaculate exhibition' (*Wisden*) of fast bowling in the admittedly more relaxed atmosphere of a 50-over thrash against a Yorkshire League XI at Harrogate. Imran's figures for the tour – 249 runs at an average of 31.12, and 15 wickets at 41.66 – perhaps failed to do justice to what one critic described as an 'efficient but rather lugubrious' young all-rounder. *Wisden* was kinder: 'He should be a powerful figure in Pakistan cricket for years to come.'

---

* To cap a generally wretched occasion, Intikhab had somehow forgotten Imran's name when the time came to introduce him to the Queen on her annual visit to the ground. After a lengthy pause, Her Majesty had shaken his hand nonetheless, and moved on.

That 'efficient but lugubrious' might have given pause to anyone who knew Imran only as the priapic Oxford smoothie who charmed his way into a succession of beds. ('About thirty' over the three years, I was told – an impeccably moderate figure for the mid-1970s, although another well-placed source thought it had been more like one a week.) But spending any extended amount of time in close quarters with the Pakistan cricket team and its management would have tried the most equable of personalities. As Imran himself recalls, 'My overall performance on the tour had been adequate, yet snide remarks were still being made about my connections, and statements to the effect that better men had been left behind.' By all accounts there were one or two unflattering references behind his back to what one famous contemporary later dubbed his 'Olympic ego'. (When you talk to people who knew the young Imran professionally, the word 'humility' comes up a lot. They say he was extremely sparing with it.) The 21-year-old's self-confident manner occasionally chafed the other players, but in 1974 he encountered little overt hostility except from Asif Masood, who apparently disliked him almost on sight. Intikhab was fairly friendly, and Majid remained a firm ally. Mostly, though, Imran's colleagues just ignored him, which was the usual practice with the younger players. None of them seems to have known or cared much about his life in England. 'Imran was thought to have a superior attitude,' Wasim Raja recalled. 'People backed away and left him in his own castle.'

The demands of university and Test cricket, as well as of the Oxford examiners, left little time for Worcestershire, and as a result Imran made only a handful of one-day appearances for his county over the summer. He used most of the brief gap between the varsity game and the Pakistani tour to bowl in a Gillette Cup tie against Sussex that ran long, thanks to rain. That would have made his schedule over the course of one six-day period: Saturday, Monday and Tuesday, captaining Oxford at Lord's; Wednesday and Thursday, playing the knockout game at Hove; early Friday, reporting for international duty with Pakistan at Birmingham. On most of those days, Imran also had to give interviews, attend functions and generally roam around the country by British Rail. It was a full workload, even by his standards. The people who knew him best also knew how utterly unsparing of himself he was apt to be – how 'he gave 200 per cent, whatever the competition', as Wasim Raja put it. 'No matter what anyone said, we felt he had a chance, because we knew Imran would work harder than anyone else.' But even they didn't know *how* hard he would work.

Back in Oxford, Imran made a friend out of a fellow third-year student on his Politics and Economics course. Now a 55-year-old television pundit and author of various self-help books, he had heard that the 'famous Khan' could be a bit standoffish. He adds that when he met Imran for the first time he'd been expecting someone 'as warm as a December night on an ice floe', but in the event 'he turned out to be almost absurdly polite, in that rather courtly way some Asians have. Between the accent and the blazer, he was almost like a Terry-Thomas stereotype. Better-looking, though.' After banking his admittedly meagre appearance money from Pakistan and Worcestershire, Imran was able to rent a small flat close to Oxford town centre. There were framed hunting prints on the wall, a wolfskin rug and reportedly rather more in the way of furniture than the average student digs of the era. On several mornings in the autumn of 1974, a plump young woman with the word 'IMRAN' daubed on her forehead kept up a forlorn vigil outside the main gate at Keble (where, these days, her quarry rarely appeared), displaying a '*Fatal Attraction*' form of obsession, erotomania, of which Imran would come to see more over the next 20 years. The trappings of fame were starting to come fast.

The future Somerset and England bowler Vic Marks went up to Oxford in that same term. Thirty-five years on, he remains one of the game's more astute critics. I asked him if at that stage in his university career Imran had ever appeared the least bit shy around his English teammates. 'No,' Marks replied. 'More aloof.' He added that Imran had been 'hard on those he didn't know and didn't rate, declining to bowl them or encourage them … He knew he was better than the rest, [but] if he rated you he would try to help and advise.' Still, at least one other colleague in the Oxford side remained bemused by Imran's insecurity. 'The guy generally had bags of self-confidence, sure, but oddly enough not when it came to his bowling. I thought he was a natural. Thousands of fans thought he was a natural. Just about every batsman he ever played against thought he was a natural. Imran remained unconvinced.'

Perhaps Imran's qualms had something to do with the distinctly mixed signals he was still getting from his two principal teams. At Worcester, he notes, 'I [was] bullied into bowling medium pace line-and-length stuff which didn't suit my temperament.' The key message from Pakistan was very different. Imran was astonished and overjoyed when Intikhab had thrown him the ball early on in the Test series with

England and told him to do what came naturally – but, whatever happened, 'Make them jump around.' (He did.) Indeed, Imran occasionally seemed to be in two minds about his bowling even when he was his own captain. He rarely appeared for Oxford in the 1975 season, thanks to a commendable and possibly justified concern about passing his finals. In one of the games he did play prior to the varsity match, against Derbyshire at Burton-on-Trent, Imran surprised both the Derby batsmen and his own team by persisting in his attempts to bowl a leg break, an effect that was uneasily like that of a champion shot-putter who'd strayed inadvertently on to a badminton court. It was a curious strategic decision, or so the Oxford men thought. As it turned out, it was a repeat experiment and nothing more. After Imran's leg spin had gone for eight in two balls he turned around, muttered something to the non-striking batsman, and measured out his full international run. A few overs later, he had taken three of the first four Derbyshire wickets to fall.

If his cricket career was somewhat erratic in the summer of 1975, his love life was a constant. Imran generally brought a 'special' girl with him to his matches, or even to watch him practise in the Parks nets. One female undergraduate recalls having feigned an interest in the game, 'which I actually thought coma-inducing', just to be near him. Imran made it immediately clear to his companion that he was a man of no small ambition, displaying 'brass' which impressed her. She wasn't the only college girl who noticed the emerging star; a 21-year-old fellow politics student named Benazir Bhutto, the daughter of the former Pakistan president and serving prime minister, was 'much taken' by Imran's obvious talent. The elegantly shod Bhutto did not go unnoticed herself. Then in her second year of residence at Lady Margaret Hall, she was intensely outspoken both about Pakistan's place in the world and the role of women in society. Several of Bhutto's already quite vocal critics pointed to her Dior wardrobe and liberated lifestyle as a political symbol of conspicuous consumption, or worse, on her part. A mutual acquaintance who falls into this category told me that Bhutto had been 'visibly impressed' by, or 'infatuated' with, Imran, and that she may have been among the first to dub him affectionately the 'Lion of Lahore'. In any event it seems fairly clear that, for at least a month or two, the couple were close. There was a lot of 'giggling' and 'blushing' whenever they appeared together in public. It also seems fair to say that their relationship was 'sexual' in the sense that it could only have existed between a man and a woman. The reason some allowed themselves to suppose it went further was because, to quote one Oxford friend, 'Imran slept with everyone' – a gross calumny, but one takes the point – rather than because of any hard evidence of an affair. On balance, I rather doubt that Pakistan's future prime minister and future cricket captain were ever anything more than good friends, and only for a term or two at that. Even in the morally libertine days of the mid-1970s, Imran's Oxford love life soon attained legendary status. It was the beginning of a personal myth of sexuality that led some to credit him with literally scores of spurious 'conquests' in addition to the real, still quite impressive, total.

Cricket's first ever World Cup, staged in England, and in which Pakistan started among the favourites, probably wasn't the best of times for Imran to be concentrating on his finals. Although not originally selected, he was called up to play for his country in their opening fixture against Australia at Headingley, on 7 June. In Imran's account, he sat the first two of his five exams on the 6th, a Friday, took the evening train to Leeds and arrived at his team's hotel at four o'clock the following morning, the day of the match.* Australia won by 73 runs, the Pakistanis, like so many others, having been done for pace by Lillee and Thomson. After an epic road-rail return journey some friends finally dropped Imran off in the centre of Oxford where, after going down with flu, he sat his final three papers just as his team-mates were losing to the West Indies by one wicket, with two balls to spare, at Edgbaston. That concluded the Pakistanis' World Cup. Under the circumstances, Imran did well to get a 2.1 for Politics, if only a Third in Economics. 'I could have exceeded that,' he remarks. Two days later he was back playing for his country in a meaningless victory over Sri Lanka. The West Indies went on to win the cup. In stark contrast to the protracted seven-week ordeal of the 2007 tournament, the entire competition was completed in 14 days, Pakistan's campaign in just seven. Majid Khan, again back in charge of the team following an injury to Asif, had won himself a considerable reputation as a

* This may be an understandable and minor lapse of memory on Imran's part after an interval of more than 30 years. The last possible weekday train from Oxford to Leeds in 1975 would have left at around 9 p.m. and taken four hours or so to reach its destination. Even allowing for the vagaries of a typical British Rail journey of the time, a 4 a.m. arrival would seem to be a stretch – but one can accept Imran's point that he was 'totally knackered' throughout most of that fateful week.

specialist in English conditions, as well as being something of a thinker. His own run-a-ball innings of 65 against Australia was a classic of its kind. But Majid's tenure proved an only limited success, in part because up to half his men would be bickering with the other half at any given time. And even his fondest admirers have never maintained that he was a particularly charismatic or inspiring leader. Pakistan, then, returned home in June 1975 in some disarray. The board sacked Majid, and replaced him with Mushtaq.

Imran left Oxford with a flourish, driving up in his new World Cup blazer, accompanied by his latest blonde, to play in his third varsity match at Lord's. Several other admirers, both male and female, were seen to be waiting at the gate for a glimpse of their idol, at least one of them sporting a T-shirt customised with slogans indicating how positively she would react to any romantic overtures he might care to make to her. Inasmuch as most of the other students just walked into the ground unnoticed, it was an impressive entrance. The match itself was another draw, but a rather more distinguished one than its two predecessors. The chief honours went to Peter Roebuck and Alastair Hignell, who respectively hit 158 and 60 for Cambridge. Those items apart, Imran's bowling had all the virtues of a cool, calculated, well-executed assault. As Hignell says, it was a 'physically terrifying' and 'sickening' barrage; no small accolade from a man who had just come through several bruising encounters with the Australian rugby team.

Imran was to have a modestly successful fifth season at Worcestershire, finishing with 46 first-class wickets at 26, almost exactly the same figures as those for his up-and-coming rival Ian Botham. Still, it was an 'only fair' existence. A salary of £ 1,500, paid in six instalments of £250, with a munificent £10 for each county championship win, allowed for little lavish indulgence. But over and above the financial rewards, or lack of them, it had become clear even to Worcestershire that Imran had certain deep-seated misgivings about county cricket as a whole. 'The English professional just isn't hungry enough for success. There's too much cricket ... the players get stale,' he wrote of his experiences some years later. Apart from the 'essential tedium' of a system in which too many buckled when they should, perhaps, have swashed, Imran had a more specific objection to his working environment. As he says, 'I simply found it boring in Worcester', where he had moved out of the Star Hotel first into digs and then into an 'unsalubrious' short-term flat above a fish-and-chip shop in the town centre.

Almost from the first, Imran had vocal reservations about his English club, where he had initially played a series of 'grim' and 'dead-end' Second XI matches before being 'bullied' into bowling 'military medium' for the seniors, allegedly at a reduced salary than the one 'Harold' Shakespeare (who died in 1976) had promised him in the pavilion at Lahore. As we've seen, the eventual terms were on the slim side: as well as his basic salary, the club undertook to '... arrange accommodation for away games on a bed-and-breakfast, early-morning tea and one newspaper basis ... A meal allowance of £1 will be paid for an evening meal when away from home and for Sunday lunches when away from home', before adding the rather bleak assurance that 'a sum equivalent to the Second Class Rail Fare from Worcester to the venue of [an] away match will be paid to all players participating in the match'. Imran, though one of the least materially minded of professional sportsmen, was moved to send a two-page handwritten letter to Tony Greig, the captain of Sussex, in September 1975. 'Dear Tony, I wondered if you and [your] committee would consider the possibility of taking me on staff next year?' he enquired, citing 'the availability of overseas registration and the young age group of the team' as reasons for his interest. Four days later, Greig wrote back in more measured terms: 'In reply to your correspondence of 12 September 1975 I would suggest that you telephone our Secretary as soon as your position becomes clear. You will appreciate the implications of any approach prior to your official release from Worcester ... Yours sincerely, A.W. Greig, Captain of Sussex.'

I asked Mike Vockins, the long-serving Worcestershire secretary, about all this. Among other things, Vockins mentioned that he and his committee had fought a hitherto unreported running battle with the Test and County Cricket Board to retain Imran's services. There were various sub-plots involved, but the basic problem concerned the TCCB's rule, already the source of a skirmish with the club in 1973, restricting each affiliate side to a maximum of two overseas players. As Worcestershire already had New Zealand's Glenn Turner and the West Indian bowler Vanburn Holder on their books, the club had mobilised on their somewhat unappreciative young all-rounder's behalf.

'At the end of Imran Khan's time at Oxford, the TCCB decided, to my surprise, that his qualification for us lapsed,' Vockins recalls. As far as the board were concerned, Imran had effectively become a Pakistani again after graduating. 'It seemed totally illogical, and was also at odds with what both the club and more to the point Imran himself wanted. Not only did we appeal, but we were determined that we should present our case as well as we could and duly retained John Field-Evans QC, later to be a High Court judge, to fight our corner. It was quite an anxious time. I didn't want Imran to be unduly worried, and so sought to give him confidence that the appeal would be successful and otherwise didn't involve him directly.' Another source then on the Worcestershire committee told me that it had cost 'a lot of money, certainly in the several hundreds of pounds' to appeal against the TCCB's ruling, and that 'that should answer any questions about whether or not we were fully committed to Mr Khan and his welfare'. (Even so, there remained Imran's core point that 'all my Oxford friends had moved to London, and I was stuck in Worcester … I was bored to tears there,' he told me.) After several 'trying' months the club had prevailed and 'both we and the player in question were happy to continue our association together'. Imran omits the episode of the TCCB registration from both his autobiographies, but it does seem to refute the idea that he'd been utterly miserable at Worcestershire from the start, or that the club had ever been less than wholehearted about keeping him on their books.

Imran went back to Pakistan that autumn, for only his second visit home in four-and-a-half years. He marked the occasion by making a few low-key appearances in the BCCP Patron's Trophy on behalf of Dawood Industries, a 'manure and insurance combine' based in Karachi, as it intriguingly described itself. The same tournament hosted sides from the federal Water and Power Development Agency and a heavily fancied Income Tax (Collections) Department. In the second half of the season Imran represented Pakistan International Airlines (PIA) in the Quaid-e-Azam Cup. He took six for 68 and five for 79 against Punjab, gave a bravura all-round performance in the tie against National Bank by taking three for 53 and six for 48 as well as scoring a second-innings century, and followed up with another six-wicket haul against Sind. Imran finished his short involvement in the domestic season with 446 runs at a touch under 30, and 52 wickets at 19 apiece. PIA paid him the equivalent of some £75 a month for his services. Back in Worcester, Mike Vockins was sitting down to write to Imran: 'The committee has agreed that your basic salary for 1976 should be £2,000, on top of which you will receive appearance money, win money and team prize monies in the normal way … We shall also contribute £100 towards your air fare back to this country.' On 19 November Imran wrote back to thank Vockins for his offer. The financial terms were 'very satisfactory', although he evidently still had doubts about the quality and cost of his local digs, for which 'last summer I had to pay about £9.50 a week until John Inchmore moved in with me'. Imran's eventual contract for 1976 bears the handwritten codicil: 'I would like it to be noted that my accommodation should be subsidised if the rent is too high.'

Imran's devotion to the grail of constant self-improvement was again kindled during his winter in Pakistan. When not playing competitively in the domestic competitions he found time to practise at the Lahore Gymkhana, next to his family home in Zaman Park. Imran had greatly disappointed the citizens of that cricket-mad enclave by not showing up during any of his Oxford vacations over the previous three years. Now crowds of them came to the Gymkhana to watch him work out (he had a young net bowler throw bouncers at him from 15 yards to improve his hook shot) and mill around the pavilion door for autographs. 'Every young boy in Lahore wanted to shake Imran's hand,' one friend recalls, 'and many of their elder sisters also worshipped him in their own way.'

Relatively few who have grown up in Lahore, as Imran did, have willingly returned for any extended time after tasting the seductions of the West. (It would be fair to say, too, that a stint in the likes of Birmingham or Dallas has, conversely, led some to appreciate Pakistani life all the more.) And, perhaps unsurprisingly, the 23-year-old native son who spent the winter of 1976 there was 'virtually unrecognisable' from the 18-year-old tyro who had flown off with the Pakistani team in 1971. Imran's boyhood companion Yusuf Salahudin told me that his friend had led a 'somewhat cloistered life' growing up in Zaman Park, 'surrounded by his extended family almost as if it was a colony'. When Salahudin met Imran again after some five years' absence, 'I thought he was more obviously mature and outgoing ... A man of the world ... There was a certain familiar confidence there, but also a new sense of calm. As you grow older, you begin to realise more and more what works for you and what doesn't, and I think he'd settled into himself in his twenties more than as a fanatically ambitious teenager.' But for all his cosmopolitanism, Imran clearly remained a Pakistani to his core. 'London's most famous socialite', as *Today* called him in 1986, wasn't born in England and apparently preferred not to live there either, once his playing days were over, even if it meant being separated from his two young sons. Years later Imran was to refer to the 'sad spectacle' of 'timid and alienated Pakistanis losing their identity [in] Britain', a fate he conspicuously avoided.*

There's nothing quite like the gathering of players, officials and press on the first day of training before the beginning of a new English cricket season. The start-of-term atmosphere, with its ambient smell of embrocation and linseed oil, is often enlivened by tropical rain or even snow falling on the newly cut playing area. They still talk about having to swim for the pavilion in Worcester. By contrast, the spring and summer of 1976 were the hottest for 30 years, with outfields that were baked to a shade of burnt yellow and white. On the grass banks in front of the stands during Test matches, bare chests and floppy hats were in order. This was the series in which the England captain Tony Greig ill-advisedly spoke of making the West Indies 'grovel', only for the tourists to take the rubber 3–0, the beginning of some 15 years' domination of world cricket. Back at Worcester, Imran seems to have rapidly appraised the situation and concluded that these were conditions ideally suited to out-and-out fast bowling. The pitches were rock hard, and with the hook shot now in his repertoire he was able to bowl bouncers with the confidence that he could handle any return bombardment that happened to come his way. About the only cloud on the horizon was again the knotty and apparently insoluble matter of Imran's accommodation. There's a note in his file suggesting that Worcestershire had 'made arrangement for [Khan] to meet a local Estate Agent', but that even this had not fully resolved the long-running problem. 'On two occasions the player failed to take advantage of that arrangement,' the note concludes.

Imran announced his intention right from the start, when the county hosted Warwickshire at the end of April. This was one of those matches that begin in a downpour and end in a heatwave. After a briefly delayed start, Worcestershire scored 322. The visitors, for whom Amiss made 167, were able to see off the somewhat benign Worcester

---

* Even in the spring of 1976, Imran seemed able to restrain his enthusiasm for returning to live in the UK. 'Have just received your letter,' he wrote to the Worcestershire club on 26 March. 'I didn't realise that the first match is going to start on 24 April – and hence the need to return earlier than the 20th. Unfortunately Majid and Myself have booked tickets to come via the Far East – USA – London route – and this means that I cannot arrive soon[er] ... But please don't worry. I am at the peak of my fitness.'

new-ball attack of Inchmore and Pridgeon without undue difficulty. There was an opening stand of 146. Imran then appeared and proceeded to bowl a selection of inswingers and bouncers at speeds of around 90 miles an hour, hurling the ball down like a live coal. Wickets fell. At the other end, Paul Pridgeon continued to plug away on a line and length for most of the second afternoon session. After just a few overs of this contrasting attack, the senior Warwickshire batsman had called a midwicket conference with the junior one. 'I've assessed the situation, son,' he announced solemnly, 'and if you take the Pakistani, I can look after Pridgey.' A minute or two later, the junior batsman took the opportunity of the tea interval to slip off to hospital for a precautionary X-ray to his skull after Imran had dropped in another short one. (This was to be the last full English season before the introduction of helmets.) The Warwickshire bowlers, led by England's Bob Willis and David Brown, duly returned the favour on the third day, by which time the wicket appeared 'like concrete', with the addition of 'several deep cracks, off which the ball shot like a skipping rock', to quote the local paper. Coming in at No. 4, Imran scored 143 at slightly less than a run a minute.

Even in the John Player (or 'Sunday') League, Imran evidently decided that this was to be his year. He turned in some impressively consistent figures: three for 23 off his allotted eight overs against Glamorgan; another three for 23 against Yorkshire; three for 34 against Gloucestershire; three for 39 against Middlesex; and so on. If the match warranted, he generally added a brisk 30 or 40 runs with the bat. The message seemed to be that he would take an average of three wickets in each one-day outing, and bowl that much faster than anyone else. It was the same story in the Benson and Hedges trophy, where Worcestershire went all the way to the final against Kent, which they lost. If Imran's bowling was often, as one observer put it, 'fast to the point of dementia', it was also successful more times than not. He left everyone stunned in a Gillette Cup tie against Gloucestershire at Bristol when he began to bounce his friend Mike Procter, who was then widely regarded as not the best man to provoke. Sure enough, Procter retaliated when it was his turn to bowl. After a couple of hooked fours, Imran appeared to have won this particular duel, only for him to fall to the more innocuous seam of Tony Brown.

Imran's combative temperament helped make him the supreme bowler he now became. 'I've always hated taking a beating lying down – something essential to a medium-pacer,' he says. 'Sometimes [I] just saw blood in front of my eyes ... It was during those moments that an increase of adrenalin would add an extra yard or two to my pace.' People who played against him at the time generally agree that he was a difficult, extraordinarily driven opponent. Several of them described him as having been 'intense' or even 'manic' when he came 'hurtling in', his 'fiery brown eyes' with an 'electric glaze'. With his fist clenched and his knees pumping up and down 'he seem[ed] like a loose power line crackling around, and just as dangerous'. One Worcestershire colleague thought Imran's intensity on the field 'took a lot out of him as far as being a human being was concerned. You don't turn that kind of competitive drive on and off. He was always away by himself somewhere, and we didn't see him socially.' Mike Vockins, a professional acquaintance for six years, 'never got that close' to Imran, and remembers that he would 'disappear pretty frequently to London or Birmingham, presumably to visit Pakistani friends or family.' You hear a lot about this sense of him having been a man apart from the rest of the team. Imran had a 'persecution complex', one former colleague believes. 'One thing most cricketers have is a sense of humour – you need it – but he pretty well totally lacked the ability to laugh at himself.' Set against this is the testimony of a well-known former Test player and academic, who remarked that Imran was 'warmly accessible to all sorts of people on the periphery of the action like autograph collectors and dressing-room attendants and programme sellers, and a complete mystery to his team-mates. Without stretching it too far, you could see some of the elements of the classic cowboy type there in the way he did the business and then just silently walked off into the sunset. I always thought there was a touch of Clint Eastwood to the guy.'

So it seems fair to say that Imran wasn't regarded as the life and soul of the party among his English county team-mates. But even those who had doubts about him as a person admired the often thrilling and always robust quality of his all-round cricket as seen in 1976. It remained a moot point whether Imran would ever thaw out as a human being, but clearly he'd already made the leap from journeyman county professional to world-class entertainer.

In the three-day match against Somerset in early June, Imran scored a full-bodied 54 in the first innings and 81 in the second. There was a raw fury to some of his strokes that made his partner D'Oliveira's seem merely polite by comparison. Imran added an equally lusty 57 against Kent – and the pattern was set. He then beat Lancashire virtually single-handed, with bowling figures of seven for 53 and six for 46, as well as an unbeaten 111 in Worcestershire's only innings. Another century followed against Leicestershire. And another against a Northants attack led by Sarfraz. Fast bowlers didn't generally hope for glamorous figures against the Surrey of the mid-1970s, whose top order typically read: Edrich, Butcher, Howarth, Younis, Roope, Test players all. Imran took five for 80 against them. There were wickets or runs, and frequently both, right up to the game against Gloucestershire in the second week of September. Imran managed a single victim (ironically, his Test colleague Sadiq), having for once – exhausted, perhaps – forsaken pace for control. The local paper speaks of his 'almost robot accuracy' in the Gloucester first innings. Little did the reporter or anyone else know it at the time, but Imran had played his last match for Worcestershire.

In retrospect, his departure was logical enough. A fractious relationship with certain colleagues, occasional friction with the club authorities and that oft-quoted boredom with Worcester itself all added up to a strong case against Imran's returning for a seventh season at New Road. The reason his decision came as a shock to so many there was that they saw it in the context of his recent performances for the county. Imran finished the 1976 season with 1,092 runs at an average of 40 and 65 wickets at 23 apiece, earning him the Wetherall Award for English cricket's best all-rounder. Worcestershire had enjoyed record attendances and reached a cup final at Lord's. Some of his colleagues could only puzzle at the fact that, as one of them puts it, 'Imran chose to fix something that wasn't broken'.

Nonetheless, living abroad turned out to be an only mixed blessing for the 'fanatically patriotic' young star. On the positive side, it was liberating for him, as it was for so many other Test colleagues, from Asif to Zaheer, and more personally fulfilling, perhaps, than the likely alternative of a career in the middle reaches of the Pakistani civil service and an arranged marriage. Exposure to English county cricket, for all its flaws, also had the advantage of allowing him to develop as a bowler under the sharp eye of men like the Worcestershire coach Henry Horton and the evergreen D'Oliveira. Imran was doubly fortunate to play so much of his cricket at New Road, not only a picturesque ground in its own right, but in those days also a pitch that more often than not rewarded an attacking bowler like himself. Of his 65 first-class wickets in the 1976 season, 42 came on his home turf. Imran was an immeasurably better all-round cricketer when he left Worcester than when he joined them.

On the debit side, it's clear that in more than five years there he never really settled in his adopted home. 'Exile' may be too strong a word for it, but Imran's sense of isolation – not only from his English team-mates but from those 'timid and alienated' fellow expats – was something he repeatedly spoke of at the time. Instead of 'fawn[ing] over British institutions' the way so many displaced Pakistanis of his generation did, he seems to have regarded the host culture, personally gratifying though it was, as all too often wallowing in a mire of frivolity and decadence. Since Imran wasn't the sort of man to insert metal studs in his face or to stab someone after a bout of drinking, he was clearly always going to be out of step with a significant part of British society as it developed during his time there. Nor was he that impressed with the 'right-wing Tory regime' of Edward Heath or the equally feckless Labour government that succeeded it. One or two friends and colleagues in England saw the first stirrings of Imran's demotic, broadly speaking anti-West politics 20 years before he launched his Tehreek-e-Insaf ('Movement for Justice') party.

It's also easy to believe that Imran was simply homesick in Worcester in a way that he wasn't in the more collegial atmosphere of Oxford. Although most people in the club went out of their way to make him feel welcome, not every member of the local community was as obliging. These were still early days for the multicultural society, and many Britons avoided the shackles of excessive deference to what became known as political correctness. As it happened, there was one distressingly widespread illustration of the UK's still somewhat rudimentary concept of race relations as a whole: 'Paki-bashing', of which Worcester saw its fair share around pub closing time most Saturday nights. As far as is known, Imran was never directly targeted, but he attracted his quota of muttered asides both on and off the cricket field. For some reason, a disproportionately high number of these seem to have occurred while playing against Yorkshire. There was apparently one occasion when Imran went out to bat on an overcast evening at Leeds, to be greeted by the home team's bowler ostentatiously peering down the pitch at him and enquiring, 'Where are you, lad? Give us a clue. I can't see nowt' – all 'standard, knockabout stuff, [but] not appreciated by Khan', I was told by one of his team-mates, speaking of such antics in general. As we've seen, he tended not to fraternise with his own colleagues, though this seems to have been more out of choice than necessity. As Mike Vockins notes, 'Worcester had a good group of very personable young cricketers around then. I'm confident that there would have been enough sensitivities among them for one or other to have dropped a word if they felt that Imran was unsettled, [and] for it to be noted.' Seeming to refute the idea that Imran had complained about his life in Worcester virtually on a daily basis, Vockins adds, 'We were wholly unaware that he disliked living here. I have no recollection of his ever having spoken about it over the course of five years, or having talked about being unhappy to me or any senior officer of the club.'

There were, it's true, certain ongoing administrative difficulties when it came to the matter of Imran's lodgings. In his 1983 memoirs, written relatively soon after the events in question, he insists that he had arrived in Worcester for the start of the 1976 season, his *annus mirabilis*, to find that he was effectively homeless. 'I had to sleep on Glenn Turner's floor for the first five days, then the county put me up in what I thought was the lousiest hotel I've ever seen ... After six weeks, I managed to find a flat of my own and then the club made me pay half the hotel bill.' In time Imran solved the problem of his Worcester accommodation by rarely turning up there. After taking possession of a 'lively' second-hand Mazda, he preferred to bomb up and down the A44 to London at every opportunity. There appears to have been a familiar theme to Imran's restiveness. Speaking of monogamy, the Nobel Prize-winning author Saul Bellow would write in his novel *Dangling Man*, 'The soft blondes and the dark, aphrodisical women of our imaginations are set aside. Shall we leave life not knowing them? Must we?' For Imran, the answer was clearly no. Even when he was seeing one of his 'special girls', he made little pretence of fidelity. Imran's taste in women ignored all considerations of age and appearance, and also spanned the class structure. In the course of the Worcestershire years there was a 'succession of debs, dolly birds and shopgirls', I was told by one of his still impressed colleagues. To be fair to Imran, he also showed notable self-restraint, given that he was as often the pursued as he was the pursuer. One of his relatively few male English friends recalled an occasion when they had been sitting together on a 'perfectly decorous night out' in a London club, only for 'a siren' to walk over, sit down in Imran's lap and place his hand on her leg. 'Help yourself, sexy,' she'd announced, rather unnecessarily. Although Imran declined that particular offer, he can hardly have failed to reflect on the life he left behind in Pakistan, where the authorities had recently re-introduced public flogging for 'those who drink, gamble or sexually philander'.

Perhaps it's not surprising that Imran had reservations about Worcester, an undeniably lovely town but one which lacked any of the raw energy, vital nightlife and racy promise of neighbouring Birmingham, another of his frequent overnight haunts. His predominant sense of the place would remain its 'soulless' amenities, oddly enough with the sole exception of the public library, where he was a regular weekly patron. As well as the matter of his 'lousy' hotel and subsequent accommodations, Imran seems to have had two other particular issues with the Worcestershire club. They had waited until 1976 to award him his county cap, at which time his wages had risen from a basic £2,000 to a relatively munificient £2,500, with the prospect of various allowances and bonuses.

'Provided I make up my mind to return to Worcester next year,' Imran wrote to Mike Vockins in September 1976, 'I would like the following terms: a) £4,000 basic salary; b) free accommodation; c) full return airfare.' In time the club wrote back to offer £3,000. 'After giving myself two months to make up my mind,' Imran replied, 'I have finally decided [not to return]. I have realised that even if you had agreed to everything I had demanded in that note, that still would not compensate me for the dreary existence that Worcester has to offer me ... I honestly don't think I can spend another six months of my life in such a stagnant place.'

This general dissatisfaction was compounded by Imran's distaste for a specific ordeal he faced at Worcester, where, to a man, from the club chairman down to the lowliest programme vendor they addressed him as 'Immy'. It was no more than the standard dressing-room lingo, which turned D'Oliveira into 'Dolly', Pridgeon into 'Pridgey', Inchmore into 'Inchy' (though Hemsley remained Hemsley), and so on. Although he never seems to have openly complained about it, Imran 'absolutely loathed' the practice, which apparently struck him as patronising. One of his local girlfriends remarked that by the time he left Worcestershire, it had become a 'fixation' for him and 'definitely poisoned the atmosphere [with the club]'. He had pronounced the offending name as if he was 'smelling a dead fish'. Early in their own relationship, she had noticed that Imran seldom gave up on that sort of grudge. 'Once he took a dislike to someone or something, you could absolutely never get him back again.'

For their part, some at Worcestershire believed that Imran had effectively used the club as a sort of paid finishing school. According to this theory, he had joined the county as a promising but erratic young seamer and, thanks to men like Henry Horton, left again as a devastatingly hostile 'quick' of international class. This was perhaps to downplay the role the bowler himself played in the transformation. In the same vein, certain of the county membership remained stubbornly convinced that they had subsidised Imran's education at Worcester Royal Grammar School, whereas in fact the fees were paid in full by his father. (The members might have been on firmer ground had they raised the matter of the help given him in areas such as his work permit and TCCB registration.) There were equally persistent and unfounded rumours that he had been poached by another team with the promise of higher wages. As the whole dispute became noticeably more bitter in the autumn of 1976, a senior member of the Worcester committee summoned Imran and put it to him that he was leaving 'because there aren't enough girls in this town for you to roger'. This same general thesis was aired in the local press, and was eventually widely reproduced in Pakistan.

The opinions of most Pakistani news organisations are not noted for nuance, so the varying fortunes of their Test side tended to get the most graphic possible treatment. 'WORLD BEATERS!' the Karachi *Star* had insisted following a short, unofficial tour to Sri Lanka in January 1976 in which Imran participated. Taken as a whole, the media believed the appointment of Mushtaq Mohammad as national captain to be a major turning-point in the history of Pakistan cricket. 'We have seen some heated exchange of words between the Board and several of the players,' the main Lahore morning paper conceded. 'But those days are over. We can go to the extent of predicting our men will remain successful, peaceful and united for many decades to come.'

It lasted about nine months. Once back in Pakistan, Imran promptly joined his fellow members of the Test squad in protesting their rates of pay, which currently stood at 1,000 rupees (or £50) a man for each five-day match – substantially better than their 1971 levels, but still leaving them firmly at the foot of international cricket's financial league table. All hell again broke loose in the press. One imaginative and much-quoted report in Lahore insisted that the dispute was really about the players' hotel and travel arrangements, and that the entire squad would take strike action were their 'nine-point list of perks' not met in full. Had a request for a chauffeur-driven limousine apiece made it a round 10, there could not have been more public outrage. The whole matter came to a head in the middle of the three-Test series against New

Zealand in October 1976, when the Pakistan team wrote to the board to confirm that they would down tools unless their grievances were at least taken under consideration. The board responded in kind, with a telegram stating that anyone who didn't immediately accept the existing terms would be banned from Test cricket for life. Five of the team promptly dropped their demands. The remaining six, including Imran, were in negotiation with the board until 90 minutes before the start of play in the second Test, which Pakistan won by 10 wickets.

Not untypically, there appears to have been some misunderstanding between the two sides about the exact terms of the deal that had been thrashed out to allow the match to go forward. Imran recalls that the board chairman Abdul Kardar had 'admitted our demands were not that unreasonable' and 'agreed to a full dialogue'. A fortnight later, Kardar was quoted in the press calling the players 'unpatriotic bandits'. The board's subsequent threat to ban the so-called rebels from the winter tours of Australia and the West Indies made headlines even in England, where a 'distraught' Mushtaq Mohammad suggested that he would resign from the captaincy. At that stage the Pakistan head of state, Fazal Chaudhry, intervened. The board's selection committee (though not Kardar himself) were sacked, eventually to be replaced by a government-appointed sports authority, and the players were each awarded 5,000 rupees (£250) a Test, sufficient to ensure that the winter's itinerary went ahead as scheduled.

Meanwhile, Pakistan had overrun the New Zealanders, with Imran taking a respectable 14 wickets (including his best Test analysis to date, four for 59, at Hyderabad) over the three matches. It possibly says something for the Pathan revenge ethic that, years later, he was to speak of his particular satisfaction at dismissing Glenn Turner, 'who had said that I didn't have it in me to become a fast bowler'. Although one-sided, the series wasn't entirely free of incident. Early in the proceedings, Imran had occasion to speak to the umpire in Urdu to ask him to stand back from the stumps, whereupon the non-striking batsman had requested that he confine himself to English when addressing the match officials. Some choice Anglo-Saxon expletives had followed. In the third Test at Karachi, Imran was prohibited from completing his over against Richard Hadlee and temporarily removed from the bowling attack by another umpire, Shakoor Rana, who felt he had been over-generous in his use of the bouncer.

Six weeks later the Pakistanis arrived in Australia to find that the home press didn't much fancy their chances there. 'COBBLERS!' was the initial assessment of the *West Australian*, while the *Herald Sun* restricted itself to the only marginally more charitable 'PAK IT IN!' Dennis Lillee took the opportunity of his own newspaper column to remark that, though Pakistan had a few talented batsmen, their bowling attack (with Imran himself dismissed as 'a trundler') was rubbish. The first Test at Adelaide seemed to confirm the generally low opinion of the tourists. Australia got the better of a high-scoring draw, even though they lost their nerve when chasing a relatively modest 285 to win on the last day. The Melbourne Test, played over the New Year, followed a broadly similar pattern, at least up to the half-way point. Australia's Greg Chappell won the toss and batted. A day and a half later he was able to declare on 517 for eight, Imran having been 'tonked around', to again quote the *Herald Sun*, with figures of none for 115 off 22 overs. Pakistan, who had seemed to be cruising at 241 for one, were then dismissed for 333.

Under the circumstances, and now faced by a vocally derisive 60,000-strong crowd, certain other bowlers might have quietly given up the fight. But that was rarely to be an option that appealed to Imran. In the next two sessions he took five Australian wickets, including that of Dennis Lillee, whom he clean bowled. According to those who saw it (and Lillee himself, who didn't) it was very possibly the fastest ball ever sent down at the Melbourne ground. Richie Benaud told me that, on the basis of this performance, which proved to be in a losing cause, 'I promptly chalked Imran up as extremely interesting.' In Benaud's measured technical opinion, 'he was [quite] determined, and had markedly increased his pace and improved his balance in delivery'. Cricket, of course, is played as much with the brain as it is with the body. Here, too, Imran was quite well fixed. That same week, he had happened to meet his old sparring partner Geoff Boycott, who was spending the winter playing for an Australian club side rather than with England in India and Sri Lanka. Boycott remembers that he took Imran aside and advised him to bowl 'really quick', preferably aiming 'about four inches outside off stump' in short, controlled bursts to make the most of the conditions. The Pakistan tour management seemed to concur. Seven days after leaving Melbourne, Imran went on to take six for 102 and six for 63 in the course of the third and final Test at Sydney, which the tourists won by eight wickets. It was their first such victory in Australia, and only their fifth anywhere overseas, and a major turning-point both for the team and for the 'Orient Express', as the *Herald Sun* now hurriedly renamed him. Some of the hyperbole might have been a touch overdone, but after this match there was no longer any question that Imran was a fast bowler to be reckoned with. Both the Australian and, more particularly, Pakistani press were highly complimentary. When the reader wasn't swept along by the lively similes – 'like a rampant stallion', 'like a blistering typhoon', 'like a runaway truck' and so on – there was the statistical evidence to back the imagery up: in just three innings, Imran had taken 17 Australian wickets at slightly over 16 apiece. His departure from the field at Sydney, his shirt sleeve ripped off his arm from all the effort, had brought the house down; as he led his team into the pavilion, spectators of all ages pummelled the railings of the lower terraces, and jaded critics broke into wide grins up in the press box. The next minute saw a steady crescendo in the sort of rowdy whoops and high-pitched acclaim normally associated with a major rock star. Geoff Boycott was in the home dressing-room. 'Even the Aussie players were standing up applauding,' he recalls. 'They thought it was bloody fantastic.'

Imran was 24, and he was famous.

Back in England, Imran's representatives were engaged in an as yet quiet but ugly spat with the Worcestershire committee, his decision to quit the club seemingly only hardened by his triumphs of the past 12 months. Or perhaps it would be fairer to say that there were no obvious personal confrontations before that. But by late 1976 Imran was clearly impatient to move on. In retrospect, Mike Vockins believes that it was 'inevitable … the real reason for his departure was to be somewhere nearer London, and the party life that went with that'. Seeming to confirm this thesis, Imran's friend and occasional landlord, the journalist Qamar Ahmed, told me that it wasn't about 'cricket as such … he left to have a more exciting life and to enjoy the bright lights'. Worcester must have seemed even more dreary a prospect to Imran after his having tasted international fame, although the same problem never seems to have applied to Basil D'Oliveira, the best-known sportsman in the world for a time in 1968–69 following his controversial omission from an England tour of South Africa on allegedly racial grounds. 'I love it here,' D'Oliveira once told me as we enjoyed the hospitality of an after-hours club in central Worcester. 'Wouldn't live anywhere else in the world.'

In his own quiet way, Imran now measured himself against the modern giants: Lloyd, Richards, the Chappell brothers and Lillee. Though he didn't bluster about 'climbing in the ring' with Larwood and Voce in the way Fred Trueman occasionally had, he aspired to belong in their company; as Asif Iqbal recalls, he was 'always going to do more than the rest of us'. Some of the same self-assurance was evident in Imran's handling of the protracted judicial wranglings with Worcestershire. By all accounts, the county appears to have initially accepted the inevitable with some good grace. Dropping the club a note on a souvenir postcard while on an overseas tour, Imran wrote, 'I am sorry to inform you that I really do want to leave ... I genuinely feel guilty I'm letting [people] down, but I am afraid I have also to think whether I am happy living in a place I don't like. Moreover I was treated pretty poorly by the club as regards my accommodation.' 'I was distressed to read the contents of your note,' Mike Vockins wrote back, urging him only to 'keep an open mind' and 'achieve a truly objective decision'. On 1 January 1977, the day he was to tear out the heart of the Australian batting at Melbourne, Imran was formally released from his contract and thus able to negotiate with other counties. He chose Sussex, on account of his friendship with Tony Greig as well as the club's relative proximity to London. To his evident displeasure, Worcestershire then objected to the move, claiming to have a 'proprietary interest', to quote the subsequent legalese, in a player they might reasonably have felt they had discovered in the first place. Their creative solution to 'Mr Khan's withdrawal of labour', as the lawyers put it, was for him to serve a suspension for the entire 1977 season, after which he would be free to play for whomever he chose.* Later that winter the parties met before the TCCB registration committee at Lord's, where Worcestershire's barrister cross-examined Imran over the course of two 'intense' sessions about his 'capricious' motives for leaving the county. The judicial process as a whole had been 'almost like [a] criminal trial,' he later complained. At the end of the hearing, the TCCB formally found Imran's case 'not proven' and agreed to suspend his registration until January 1978. The curt, one-paragraph ruling made reference to 'the player hav[ing] put forward reasons ... deriving solely [from] his own personal enjoyment and social convenience to reside away from Worcestershire'. To the men in the committee room, this was 'not grounds for his [immediate] registration with Sussex', nor was it 'in the best interests of competitive County Cricket as a whole'.

---

* The TCCB also called for a concurrent 12-month 'qualification period', which was standard practice when a player moved from one county to another, although there were exceptions to the rule – such as Ray Illingworth's transfer from Yorkshire to Leicestershire, and Mike Denness's from Kent to Essex.

At that stage Imran and Sussex appealed to the 25-man Cricket Council, the sport's ultimate governing authority in the British Isles, and a body hardly less august than the medieval Star Chamber. In due course there was another all-day hearing at Lord's before the Council's independent tribunal, accompanied by an epistolary scrap between the various lawyers over who exactly would pay the estimated £7,000 bill for the two proceedings. The event was umpired by Oliver Popplewell, QC, aged 50, a distinguished Cambridge University and Free Foresters wicketkeeper in his day and more recently Recorder of the Crown Court. Each side arrived for the encounter with a full complement of barristers, solicitors and expert witnesses. Among those appearing for the appelate was the former Sussex and England captain Ted Dexter, who told me:

> I didn't know Imran. But I got a call from Tony Greig seeking my help in securing a 'free' transfer to Sussex. Next thing I found myself speaking in a panelled room at Lord's along these lines: 'Imran is a very unhappy young man. He has been unable to make friends. His natural habitat is the London area and though he would prefer to move to Middlesex, Sussex is willing to ensure his access to old haunts and a reconnection with old acquaintances, male or female ...' It's the only time in my life that I have knowingly committed perjury. I still get a cold shiver when I think back to the quizzical looks that came my way that day at Lord's. Just as well it was not a court of law or I might have spent time inside at Her Majesty's pleasure.

After only ten minutes' deliberation, the tribunal found for Imran, whose 'special registration' for Sussex would be completed on 30 July 1977. In his ruling Mr Justice Popplewell noted: 'We are impressed by the argument that Khan's unhappiness was a genuine one, and that there was no evidence of financial motivation in his movement ... The strict application of the requirement of 12 months prior residence [in Sussex] can be mitigated.'

It was not a universally popular decision. On 26 May, Worcestershire formally wrote to the TCCB secretary, Donald Carr (of Idrees Beg fame), to express their 'very considerable misgivings over the procedural arrangements adopted for the Appeal'. Carr volleyed back on 29 May that the matter was 'closed'. There was talk of some county pros refusing to play against the 'disloyal' Pakistani, who further earned the censure of the Cricketers Association for 'hasten[ing] the onset of a football-style transfer system'. Reading the correspondence now, one is struck by the quaint sense of outrage at the notion that a professional athlete should feel free to take his services wherever he chose. 'Cricket and its relationship between authority and players has suffered a grievous blow,' the Association's Jack Bannister thundered on 25 May. Bannister subsequently revealed that acting in his professional capacity he had 'contacted the 17 county sides with the question, "In your dressing-room, is there a totally unanimous view either for or against the decision allowing Imran Khan to play in August?"' The results showed nine sides 'totally opposed' and four sides 'largely opposed' to Imran, with only two in favour and one neutral. Curiously enough, according to Bannister 'No reply [had] yet been received from Sussex, for whom John Spencer says that the players want more time to consider the matter.'

In the end, the boycott never materialised. Bannister and the other parties dropped their protest. Imran was, however, subjected to some choice abuse on his later visits to play Worcestershire. Of this Mike Vockins says, 'I was so incensed with the crowd on more than one occasion that I felt minded to get on the PA and insist that spectators show the normal sporting courtesies, before swiftly recognising that this would just have goaded further those who behaved in that unacceptable way.' In time Vockins himself inherited Imran's locker in the Worcester dressing-room 'along with some abandoned cricket gear which was in pretty dire straits. "Festering" would just about sum it up. The boys believed that on occasion, rather than getting kit laundered he rang the sponsors for a new lot and threw the old stuff in the locker.' Despite this rather dubious personal legacy, Vockins, an eminently fair-minded man who went on to take holy orders, has 'delightful' memories of Imran, a view broadly shared by the current Worcestershire regime 30 years after the acrimonious events at Lord's.

In between dressing up in a dark suit and tie to go into the witness box, Imran had continued his scintillating run of form on Pakistan's tour of the West Indies. The first Test at Bridgetown featured some notably robust bowling from the home team's Roberts, Garner and Croft. But even they appeared sluggish in comparison with the 'Orient Express', who announced himself with three consecutive bouncers to the opener Gordon Greenidge. The former England wicketkeeper Godfrey Evans told me that he had watched this blitz while standing immediately in front of the pavilion with a 'strangely silent' Sir Garry

Sobers. While Godders himself had characteristically cheered and whistled in appreciation, his illustrious companion had merely followed proceedings with narrowed eyes. When the third ball in rapid succession 'nearly decapitated' the batsman, Sobers finally spoke: 'Bit brisk, this chap.' The words were uttered with a thin smile and seemed to Evans to be a sort of 'royal warrant' coming from the man who was arguably cricket's greatest ever all-rounder. That Test was drawn, and the West Indies won the second, at Trinidad, by six wickets. Imran reports that he had lost his temper and 'bowled appallingly' after being attacked (something of a role reversal) by Greenidge and Roy Fredericks in the latter match. There was then another draw at Georgetown.

Following this, Imran's tour, hitherto only intermittently dazzling, took much the same upward trajectory as it had at a comparable stage in Australia. Reviewing his performance in the series as a whole, one Jamaican paper wrote, in an only slight case of overstatement, that 'his fame soared like a rocket and hung high over Caribbean skies for weeks'. In more prosaic terms, in the fourth Test at Trinidad Imran took four for 64 off 21 of the most hostile overs imaginable in the West Indies' first innings. There was a moment in mid-afternoon when, with the ball flying round the batsmen's heads and some in the crowd calling their disapproval, the atmosphere threatened to grow 'iffy', to again quote Evans. But Imran and Pakistan had stuck to it, eventually winning by 266 runs. The West Indies then generally did Pakistan for pace at Kingston, to take the series 2–1. Imran took six for 90 in the first innings and two for 78 in the second, as well as contributing much-needed runs in the lower middle order. Short of staying behind to sweep up the pavilion, it was hard to see what more he could have done. Unfortunately, Pakistan's specialist batsmen failed to similarly rise to the occasion. Set 442 to win, they were soon 51 for four. At that stage, in a show of less than total confidence in the outcome, the tour management saw fit to change the date of the team's return flight to Pakistan from Wednesday, the last scheduled day of play, to Tuesday; an admission of 'a general lack of resolve', Imran notes ruefully.

In the five Tests Imran took 25 wickets at 31.60 apiece. He'd clearly taken his time to find his form early in the tour, as great players frequently do in unfamiliar conditions; only mediocrity being always at its best. Generally speaking, the series confirmed that Pakistan for all their occasional frailties deserved their place at cricket's top table. It also did no harm at all to Imran's reputation. 'I want to be known as a good bowler … My ambition is to dominate … What I'm always after is penetration,' he'd once remarked. Within a few short months his textbook technique, iron will and unshakable self-confidence had convinced even the most sceptical that his targets were well within his scope.

His fame was already secure in Pakistan, where satellite technology had allowed huge numbers to watch their team's two winter tours. As a result, cricket soon reached the plateau occupied only by soccer or rock music in Britain. This was the era in which the journalist Fareshteh Aslam refers to Imran as a combined Superman and Spiderman, 'this exotic-looking guy doing battle on our behalf'. Mobs now followed him about, and Imran, who a year earlier had been known to stop and chat with fans at his local Lahore milk bar, learnt to hurry out of the players' entrances of cricket grounds around the world and make his way to safety through side streets and roped-off alleyways.

As it happened, there was something of a precedent for this level of intense adulation of a Pakistani cricketer. A hard-hitting batsman named 'Merry Max' Maqsood had played for his country 16 times in the 1950s, while enjoying a particularly active social life. Equally famous for his strokeplay on and off the cricket field, he had soon acquired a substantial cult following. At the end of the 1954 tour of England, Merry Max had stayed behind to take a local bride. Since he was allegedly already married the news initially caused something of a splash in Pakistan, though even the *Star* eventually held this to be a 'largely private matter' between him and the lawful Mrs Maqsood. No such restraint greeted the news of Imran's various affairs 30 years later, for which the press deployed their full, 24-point size headlines. He was the first tabloid superstar of Asian sport.

On a bitingly cold morning in late May 1977, a shaggy-haired, tanned young man wearing a silk shirt splayed open to display a gold medallion walked through the gate of the municipal cricket ground on Pavilion Lane in Rotherham, South Yorkshire. His arrival was noted by a solitary reporter, who saw the man nod to one or two friends, then sit down in one of a sea of empty seats, essentially unrecognised by those few duffle-coated spectators in attendance. The reporter was intrigued to learn the man's identity. It was an 'almost comically mild-mannered' Imran, already one of the world's most famous sportsmen, who would spend the early part of the season playing a variety of modest Yorkshire league and club matches while waiting to qualify for Sussex. He seems to have enjoyed the substantially less formal atmosphere of rural northern grounds and all the familiar icons associated with the lower reaches of English cricket: deckchairs, long grass, tiny plastic cups of volcanic tea and a sparse but surprisingly loyal fan base. Imran took the opportunity to put in place some final refinements to his bowling action, running in closer to the stumps and occasionally going round the wicket in order to stand up straighter at the moment of delivery. By the end of his first season in Sussex, he reports, he felt 'more confident of putting the ball where I wanted it'.

That year Imran saw rather more of London than had been the case before, often staying at the Shepherd's Bush flat of the journalist Qamar Ahmed. Also there while passing through town was another young rising Pakistani star, Javed Miandad, a 'feisty little bugger' of a cricketer, to quote one good friend. Javed, too, was beginning a four-year playing association with Sussex. According to Qamar Ahmed, 'Imran was shy and not an extrovert, and remained so even after becoming an overnight star in that Sydney Test. He stayed with me off and on whenever he visited London. He was a lot younger person than me, basically quiet, and never any bother.' Ahmed insists that Imran's good nature extended toward his fellow house guest. 'Javed was also very young, and competitive, when he joined Sussex. But he and Imran never spoke against each other. Even on tour overseas they were quite good mates and Imran would listen to him agreeably – in some ways Javed possessed a sharper brain cricketwise.' For all that, the relationship would face a number of well-publicised snags in the years ahead. Imran would later be one of 10 players to issue a statement deploring Javed's leadership of the Test side, and subsequently to refuse to play under him. Although the crisis was defused and they were to remain international colleagues for another decade, Imran appears to have harboured certain long-term reservations about the younger man's character. 'Javed's man management was poor [and] he lacked the strength of will to drag the team along under his wing,' he notes. I was told that Imran gave particularly short shrift to Javed's 'highly vocal' complaints following the declaration that had left the batsman stranded on 280 in that 1983 Hyderabad Test against India. Coming across the 25-year-old Javed later that night in the Pakistan hotel, Imran reportedly remarked (in Urdu), 'This is a team game, son. I don't believe in playing for personal records.'

Wasim Raja considered Imran 'deeply sensuous' and 'somewhat cavalier' as a cricketer, whereas 'there wasn't much sensuousness' about the practical-minded Javed. 'In most cases, [Miandad] would have one eye on the scoreboard, while Imran didn't give a damn about averages – nor was he ever frightened to lose, if it came to that.' Imran was interior, self-referring; Javed was more up front and superficial, concerned with material rewards and acclaim. Another well-placed source told me that where Javed was 'obvious', meticulous and ambitious, Imran was laid back, affable and self-contained. 'You could buy most of what Javed had, if not his talent. You couldn't buy what Imran had. He had something that's inside.' The result, as Wasim Raja observed, was 'much detachment, some respect and a little distrust', all part of an occasionally dysfunctional but long-running working relationship that was to be the making of modern Pakistani cricket.

In his memoirs, Javed recalls a somewhat curious incident when he had acted as a peacekeeper between Imran and their mutual landlord Qamar Ahmed. Evidently miffed at something the journalist had written, Imran let loose one night with a whole series of complaints, including the observation that the Shepherd's Bush flat was 'a pigsty'. At that Ahmed rose to his and his home's defence. 'All of a sudden,' Javed writes, 'the two men were screaming four-letter words at each other and Qamar was sticking out his chest urging Imran to take a swing. I stepped in and put an end to it.' If so, the scene would seem to reveal hitherto under-reported diplomatic skills on the part of Javed. (Wasim Raja, when I once ran the story past him, glowered in a pained way and eventually said, 'Bit of a turnaround, isn't it?')

When Imran began to play for Sussex, the club found him a small ground-floor flat next to the gates of the county ground in Hove. As a result he could commute to work in a minute or two, while London was only an hour away by train. Imran initially spent much of his free time with Javed, but soon reactivated his old social life. By early in his second season at Hove, he had 'plugged himself in like an "Open" sign', to quote one of his county colleagues. Accounts of Imran's dating habits differ. According to his amused team-mate, 'Immy was on the pull in London or Brighton on average four or five nights a week.' He was allegedly vain of his appearance. The team-mate remembers Imran standing in front of the mirror grooming himself, smoothing down his thick hair, 'adjusting the chain round his neck so it hung just so', then happily padding off with his 'feline lope'. According to others, Imran was actually 'quite relaxed' or 'passive' with the opposite sex, and more inclined to the role of the hunted than the hunter. The Sussex and England bowler Tony Pigott told me he had once been in a nightclub in

Brighton with Imran and the county's South African star Garth le Roux. 'It was a mirrorball and Bee Gees sort of place; that whole thing … After a bit Le Roux and I chugged back from the dance-floor to the table where Imran was sitting alone with his glass of milk. "Come on and meet some girls," Garth said, only to hear Imran's superb reply, "No, thanks. If they want to meet me, they can bloody well come over here".'

On 9 May 1977, just as Imran was settling in to life in the Yorkshire leagues, the news broke that Kerry Packer and his Australian television network had signed some two dozen of the world's top players to appear in an exhibition round under the name of World Series Cricket. It would be hard to exaggerate the ensuing shock in certain quarters. Among several perceived villains of the piece, the press heaped special scorn on the Sussex and England captain Tony Greig, who had acted as Packer's recruiting agent. Greig appears to have convinced most of the players involved that a compromise would be swiftly reached whereby they would still be available for Test cricket. Imran was one of 14 non-Australians initially contracted to represent a WSC World XI in Packer's circus, as much of the cricket establishment and media came to know it. There would be particular repercussions for Pakistan, which lost five leading players, including their captain Mushtaq, to the enterprise. For his services, Imran was paid Aus $25,000, or roughly the equivalent of £10,500, for some ten weeks' cricket. At the time he was making a hard-earned £250 per Test, £3,000 a season for Sussex and a further £70–80 a month from PIA on the rare occasions he played in Pakistan – a total income of around £4,600 from all sources.

Although Abdul Kardar had eventually resigned as chairman of the Pakistan board after the feud about match fees, his successor Mohammad Hussain took a similarly hard line when confronted with the latest demonstration of player power. The dispute that broke out in May 1977 soon threatened to make that earlier row look like a 'little local difficulty' by comparison. In short order, Hussain announced that the five Pakistanis who had signed for Packer would be 'ostracised' from Test cricket, adding that they were 'unpatriotic … mercenaries [of] the worst stripe'. The board went on to assure the Pakistani public that there were 'ample quality reserves' available to cover for the defectors – a self-confidence not entirely borne out by events, in particular the 1978 Pakistan tour of England, which was a rout.

At 9.30 in the morning of 30 July 1977, Donald Carr of the TCCB sent a telex to the secretary of Sussex confirming that 'Imran Khan, the subject of our recent discussions' was now free to play for the county. Two hours later, the subject in question was in action in a championship match against Gloucestershire at the College Ground in Cheltenham. He took two for 52 in the first Gloucester innings and one for 15 in the second; a respectable if not electrifying debut. Opponents, press and public were soon struck by the raw pace of the now visibly stronger, broad-chested bowler – he again took the opportunity to pepper Mike Procter with bouncers – but also by his versatility. His elegance, power and stamina (he could, and often did bowl unchanged all morning) were noted. Nevertheless, some reservations were expressed. Imran was lucky, it was agreed, to play much of his English cricket on the seamer's paradise at Hove. Would the 'languid-looking playboy', as *The Times* called him, 'succeed on slower wickets [or] when a really top-class batsman – Barry Richards, for example – [got] after him?' One expert who didn't hedge his bets was Geoff Boycott, who told me that 'Sussex was the making of Imran. He'd had the talent but now he also had the brain and the spirit. A great competitor. Like me, he's a dragon in Chinese astrology.'

In the event, Imran, or 'Immy' as, much to his distaste, he continued to be almost universally known, mocked the doubters. He took four for 66 and hit a rapid 59 (a third of his side's total) against Glamorgan at Eastbourne. There were a further seven wickets in the win over Yorkshire at Hove, and commendably thrifty figures of 16–5–26–0 against a run-chasing Nottingham side, including Clive Rice, at Trent Bridge. Imran's batting and bowling averages were good enough, but they failed to tell the full story: the way his best attacking shots appeared to be both fast yet totally unhurried, for instance, or how, in that curious way it has when struck by a great timer, the ball always seemed to gather pace on its way to the rope. And until statistics can indicate such factors as pride and the love of a fight they won't adequately convey the mettle of such bowling performances as the one Imran gave in the county match against Hampshire at Hove. As mentioned, the Hove wicket often inclined to extravagant morning life, but it takes more than a helpful pitch to account for first-innings figures of five for 51 against arguably the county championship's strongest batting line-up. Among Imran's victims: Barry Richards.

As he climbed the ladder of sports success, Imran made good and repeated use of a variety of role-models and patrons. Indeed, he could almost qualify as a professional protégé; there were enough men who were 'like a father' to him to make Imran look like Abraham in reverse.

His cousin Javed Burki was one of the first. 'If Javed told Imran it was eleven o'clock at night, even now Imran would believe him,' Wasim Raja once remarked. At Worcester there had been the likes of Basil D'Oliveira, Henry Horton and Norman Gifford. The county secretary Mike Vockins, though too modest to say so, also appears to have been an avuncular presence in the young Imran's life, as witnessed by some of their correspondence. Despite the later acrimonious events at the Cricket Council and the independent tribunal, much of this reads like the exchanges between a benign Victorian employer and a favourite junior. 'I just wondered what my financial arrangement with the club might be this season, if any,' Imran enquires politely in July 1974, while on tour of England with Pakistan. The following month, Vockins is able to reply with good news. 'The Cricket Committee wish me to pass on this cheque for £200 [to] cover the difference between the remuneration you will receive from the BCCP and from us. Don't spend it all at once.' Fifteen months later, Imran writes to thank Vockins effusively for his help in re-registering him for Worcester and to assure him that 'the terms offered to me are very satisfactory and I am quite content with their financial aspects'. Even as the storm clouds gathered in February 1977, Imran would find time while on tour of the West Indies to write to Vockins and 'sincerely thank you for your many letters … [and] especially for your concern shown for my cricket career'.

At Sussex, Imran's chief benefactors were the county captain Tony Greig and their veteran fast bowler John Snow. The former recruited him to World Series Cricket. The latter helped mould him from a richly gifted, occasionally world-beating turn into one who could consistently deliver the goods on English wickets. Snow, then 35, was nearing the end of a colourful career that had brought him both 49 Test caps and a reputation as a somewhat enigmatic Jekyll and Hyde personality. Although a quiet man off the field with a taste for poetry, his aggressive playing style had seen its share of strife over the years, notably in the Test match at Lord's in 1971 when he flattened Sunil Gavaskar in an attempt at a run-out. The bowler was then suspended by the TCCB, triggering some lively back-page articles fulminating against the 'dodderers' and 'cretins' responsible for the ban. Lest anyone miss the point, Snow entitled his 1976 autobiography *Cricket Rebel*. More pertinently, he was a consistently helpful and generous *de facto* coach to Imran, who, as Boycott notes, now became 'not only a very fast bowler but a very clever one'. Some 15 years later, much would be made of the reverse swing phenomenon, that cricketing sleight of hand and aerodynamical oddity whereby bowlers such as Wasim Akram and Waqar Younis appeared to make the ball mysteriously veer off its true path. Imran was already practising this technique with some success in 1977. The Surrey and England batsman Graham Roope told me of an end-of-season game played 'in front of three men and a dog at The Oval' when Imran had appeared and suddenly 'made the old ball boom around at right angles'. There had been some 'disbelieving stares' and 'subsequent muttering' in the Surrey dressing-room, though Roope was at pains to stress that this was down to the shock of the new on the players' part, 'like African tribesmen seeing Concorde flying over for the first time'. Javed Miandad adds that 'the combination of pace, guile and reverse swing made Imran absolutely lethal. He started predicting his wickets ... He would often tell us he'd spotted a weakness in the batsman and how he was going to get him next ball. And sure enough he would.'

Sussex finished the 1977 season with home fixtures against Middlesex and Kent, who went on to be the joint county champions. Imran's contribution was a modest one wicket in each match, the latter of which was curtailed by rain. In his first five weeks of cricket in new colours he took 25 wickets at an average of 22.04, better figures than those recorded by the likes of Joel Garner, John Shepherd, Vanburn Holder and Clive Rice, all of whom were appearing on the county circuit. For its part, the Sussex yearbook describes the side's eighth-place finish as 'satisfactory', which perhaps carries the echo of one of those hospital bulletins describing the condition of a terminal patient as 'comfortable'. In fact, it was a significant under-achievement for a side which included players of the calibre of Javed, Greig, Mendis, Parker, Barclay, Snow and Imran himself, though even that eclipsed Worcestershire's 'sorry showing' at 13th.

Meanwhile, World Series Cricket was formally launched on 16 November 1977. It was not the immediate commercial success Kerry Packer had hoped: there were 1,690 paying spectators scattered around the Football Park, Adelaide, to see the inaugural Australia v. World XI fixture, which the visitors won, on 10 December. The first so-called Supertest between the Australians and the West Indians fared little better, attracting some 6,000 first-day fans in a Melbourne stadium seating 37,000. It's said that before certain WSC matches Packer could be seen disconsolately counting the cars in the parking lot. Nonetheless, the 'circus' was an idea whose time had come: night games were introduced; pads and balls changed colour; Dennis Amiss walked out to bat wearing a motorcycle helmet, a fashion that caught on. Packer and his managers made much play of the gladiatorial aspect of fast bowling, whose 'super-sizzling' and 'sexy' proponents – namely Imran, Lillee, Procter, Holding and Roberts – became WSC's most feted superstars. The organisers weren't shy about marketing their men, either, kitting them out in T-shirts emblazoned with the slogan 'Big Boys Play at Night', among various other lewd endorsements. For the first time in the game's history, cricketers were routinely staying in luxury hotels and being driven around in limousines. Thanks to Packer's ownership of his own television station and virtually unlimited advertising budget, the whole enterprise came to unite Australia as little else could. Along the dark miles of desert highway, the reassuring points of light were huge billboards featuring smouldering close-ups of the more photogenic WSC recruits. As Imran says, 'a major feature of Packer cricket was the personalisation and packaging of players ... In the absence of patriotic passions the game was promoted by emphasising its entertainment value and by glamourising certain individuals' – none more so than himself.*

Perhaps predictably, the Pakistani authorities reacted to the Packer affair with all the decorum and restraint of a *Fawlty Towers* fire drill. When Imran arrived at Karachi airport for an aborted attempt at a reconciliation with the BCCP, 'the customs officers eyed my luggage as if I was carrying gold bars ... I heard remarks like "I'd play for my country for nothing".' For their parts Abdul Kardar and Mohammad Hussain competed to heap abuse on 'the mercenaries' and more particularly on Imran, whose effigy was burnt outside the main gate of the Gaddafi Stadium in Lahore. Following that there were widespread street demonstrations against the 'traitors' and 'double-crossers', some of whose family members also received death threats. By contrast, the influential cricket commentator and sometime administrator Omar Kureishi felt able to issue an invitation on what he called 'the highest possible authority' for three of Pakistan's WSC players to fly back from Australia for the 1977–78 home series against England – which they did, only to have the door slammed in their faces.

---

* Imran also benefited as a bowler by being able to study the best in the world at close quarters. Dennis Lillee and Mike Procter were both 'significant' in helping convert the previously somewhat random run-up of anything between 10 and 15 stuttering paces into the well-oiled long jumper's gallop it became. It's mildly curious that Imran became a more fluent bowler in part by studying Procter, who, as the latter cheerfully admits, 'flung it down off the wrong foot'.

Farce first stalked the proceedings when Imran, Mushtaq Mohammad and Zaheer Abbas returned to Pakistan to play in the third and final Test of the series, at Karachi. Or so they thought. Both the previous Tests had been ill-attended draws, after the second of which the army chief of staff (and state president in waiting) General Zia-ul-Haq reportedly advised the board to 'pick the best team available' or to 'personally face the consequences'. Despite this high-level intervention no BCCP officers were on hand at Karachi airport to welcome the three returning WSC players – nor officials of any kind. The anti-Packer contingent, however, was there in force. Imran was eventually able to make his way through the protesters and on to a perhaps over-full minibus, which reportedly deposited him at the home of a friend near the National Stadium. He arrived at the trim, white-walled ground the next morning, to be met by a small but vocal crowd of demonstrators but, again, no formal reception committee. Imran had apparently had some trouble in gaining access to the pavilion and had to knock repeatedly, while curious onlookers gathered round him, before making his way in through the groundstaff entrance. There were supposedly similar difficulties when it came to his being admitted to the home dressing-room. At length Imran was able to change into his whites and report to Mohammad Hussain and his fellow selectors, who greeted him 'with a mixture of hostility, surprise and amusement that [I] thought [I] was going to play'. Even that reaction was positively effusive compared to the response of the new Pakistani captain, Wasim Bari, who looked Imran up and down and asked him, 'Who the hell invited you here?'

For their part, the England team were similarly indignant that the three 'Packerstanis', as the media dubbed them, might now be parachuted back into the national Test side. In the build-up to the match the tourists had issued a press release saying that they were 'unanimously opposed in principle to players contracted to World Series Cricket being considered for selection for International Cricket Conference Test matches'. The statement was read by Mike Brearley, the captain. It was his final act before flying home – Brearley's left arm had been broken in a zonal match against Sind, and he handed the responsibility of leading England to Geoff Boycott, a man of many sterling qualities but not, perhaps, particularly well versed in the diplomatic niceties. With characteristic bluntness, the Yorkshireman had already aired his own views on Packer's English and Pakistani recruits, whom he branded as 'disloyal traitors'. In short order, the authorities at Lord's sent a telegram warning their counterparts in Karachi of a 'potential boycott' (the pun, we can safely assume, was unintentional) of the forthcoming Test. Thirty-six hours before play was scheduled to begin on the morning of 18 January, Pakistan named a squad of 24 players. As he read the 'interminable' team sheet, Zaheer remembers 'only hop[ing] that sports editors had space to print the full list'. All two dozen candidates appeared at Pakistan's pre-Test net session, where, Imran reports, 'For the first time in my life I wanted a cricket field to open up and swallow me. All the officials and some of the players made [me] feel distinctly unwanted.'

Imran and his two colleagues were then called in front of the Pakistan selectors and told that they could play in the Test if they publicly denounced Kerry Packer. Imran declined the offer, but took the opportunity to ask the panel on whose authority Omar Kureishi had issued his invitation for the three men to return. Kureishi had 'no standing' in the matter, he was told. At that Imran, Mushtaq and Zaheer caught the next flight back to Australia, leaving the official Test team to eke out another draw with England; the visitors eventually took ten hours to score 266, during the latter stages of which the crowd pelted the outfield with oranges. General Zia was on hand somewhat incongruously to present commemorative medals to both sets of players at the finish. By flying to Karachi and back Imran had missed out on the chance to play in a WSC Supertest, for which his match fee would have been Aus $5,000. It remains a matter of debate whether or not the England tourists actually threatened to pull out had the Packer trio been reinstated, but, if so, the home board seem to have needed little further persuasion in the matter. As play got under way at Karachi, Mohammad Hussain and his colleagues issued a statement announcing that 'the BCCP has decided to depend on the talent that is available today and will be available in the future. [We] have therefore elected to restrict our choice to those players who will be available at all times to serve cricket, owing loyalty to the established authority and not to the highest bidder.'*

* In 2008, Mike Brearley recalled, 'While I was in hospital in London, there was the mother of all [rows] in Pakistan. I was getting phone calls and press visits asking for my comments, and I was also in touch with the MCC. I was less heated than the rest of the team about the issue, not least because I knew that I and others were in the side largely because of the absence of our own WSC players, and felt that there were personal reasons involved as well as principled ones. After all, we had played our Packer men in the previous series against Australia. Whether or not it was the result of the England team's threats that Pakistan didn't play Imran in that Test, I don't know.'

Exactly a week later, Imran appeared for a WSC World XI against the West Indians in a day-night game played in front of a full house at Melbourne. Packer himself flew back from a meeting in New York to watch the match. I was told by Asif Iqbal, 'Uncle Kerry bustled in to the dressing-room with a huge grin – he'd just counted the receipts – and announced, "I'm looking forward to this one, boys. What a pity the West Indies will walk it." I seem to remember him offering odds of 100–1 against us and several of the guys, myself included, taking him up on his generosity.' The West Indies scored 238 in their 40 overs, which the World XI passed with five wickets and an over to spare. In an epic of sustained hitting, Asif made 113 and Imran added 65 not out. The picture of a beaming 'Uncle Kerry' (who paid up in 'crisp bills', Asif recalls) with his arms around the two players ran on the morning's front pages, and did as much as anything else to put WSC on the map. Two days later, Packer called a press conference in the bar of his favourite golf club for which he appeared dressed in Bermuda shorts and a tight-fitting red shirt adorned by an 'I love Imran' badge. He accused the 'MCC establishment' at Lord's of hiring a public relations agency and of always wanting to get their names in the papers. 'Honestly, I'm past all that,' he said as the motor-drives whirred. 'All I care about is the cricket.'

Although enough major changes took place in Imran's career around 1977–78 to make his head spin, his success on the field was a constant. He emerged from the Packer affair an infinitely better player than when he went into it. As a fast bowler, he now commanded all the variations. Although Imran clearly remained partial to the short stuff – as Ashley Mallett, the Australian tail-ender who ducked into one of his bouncers and spent a week in hospital, could testify – he was always more than a mere 'enforcer', whose sole job was to put the wind up the batsman. No less a judge than the former England captain Len Hutton told me that by May 1978 the 'smooth Asian lad' was already as good as any bowler he had ever seen. Although Lindwall and Miller had been 'a handful', and Frank Tyson probably had the edge over even them in terms of pace, none of them possessed Imran's all-round ability with the ball allied to his 'fanatical self-discipline'. Hutton made his remarks as he and I watched the 'Asian lad' jog repeatedly around the outfield during a rain delay in an otherwise forgettable early-season match at Hove. For whatever reason, none of his new county colleagues joined him.

FOUR

'War Without the Nukes'

Considering the time and effort that went into his move there, Imran had mixed initial impressions of Sussex. The feeling seems to have been mutual. Several former county players echo the all-rounder Neil Lenham, who broke into the side some years later and who told me that Imran had been 'a good team man in his way', but one who, whether pounding round the ground on his solitary jogs or disappearing promptly at the close of play, 'essentially did his own thing'. A second team-mate 'always saw Imran as slightly intimidating, for some reason. In those days he was strictly a "Yep" or "Nope" kind of guy, and that kept you off balance.' To another colleague he seemed 'basically aloof, very sure of himself, and very careful to keep people from getting too close to him'. The Sussex and England batsman Paul Parker adds that there was 'a definite mystique' to the 'narrow-eyed, unshaven Immy' who – again – had 'more than a hint of Clint Eastwood'.

For his part, Imran, though enjoying the spirit at Sussex as a whole, had doubts about the newly appointed county captain Arnold Long, 37, whom he describes as an 'extremely affable man [who] was completely unsuitable for the job. Long was too inflexible and hated taking risks of any type ... His basic philosophy of the game was to make sure the team didn't lose, hence missing out on a lot of opportunities where with a little risk we might have won.' To compound Imran's frustration, his friend and mentor John Snow had been sacked by the county, and his eventual replacement, the hyper-aggressive South African bowler Garth le Roux, had only limited first-class opportunities in 1978. In their absence, Imran was obliged to share the new ball with the former Surrey and England warhorse Geoff Arnold, who at 34 was clearly nearing the end of an illustrious career. On the batting front, Javed Miandad was away playing for Pakistan for much of the season, Tony

Greig, suffering from epilepsy and a variety of other problems, emigrated to Australia, the versatile Keppler Wessels was doing military service and the Sri Lankan-born opener Gehan Mendis perhaps underperformed with an average of only 29. For all these reasons, Sussex finished a below-par ninth in the county championship, one place down from their 1977 position.

Rather more serious than mere playing disappointments was the 'institutionalised racism' Imran apparently encountered at 'varying levels of British society', if not, it should be stressed, at his new county. As mentioned, there were some harsh words from the crowd when he returned to Worcester for his first few matches there after leaving the club. In other cases, it may be harder to say where normal boorish behaviour ended and out-and-out racism began. One of the Sussex team told me of an occasion when, during a crowded rail journey to London, Imran got up and offered his seat to a black woman who would otherwise have had to stand. 'It was a typically chivalrous gesture, but one Immy apparently saw in a racial light. To him the reason no one else gave up their seat was "colour prejudice", while to me it was just a normal scene in a rush-hour train.' Always thin-skinned, and perhaps over-alert to the least sign of what he called 'colonial condescension', Imran tended to interpret many of the everyday knocks of British life as motivated by racial bigotry. In 1978, he writes in his autobiography, 'I attended a meeting of the Cricketers Association to hear sixty per cent of those present vote that English cricket would be better off without overseas players. I was amazed at their attitude, and haven't been to another meeting since.' Imran chose to ignore the Association's argument that a strong case could be made for limiting the number of foreign-born players purely on cricketing grounds. Comparable quotas existed in other walks of professional life and indeed in other countries, including his own. Similarly, Imran was reportedly 'unimpressed', or worse, by the part played by the TCCB and their distinguished secretary Donald Carr in the recent Karachi Test fiasco. If so, it may be relevant that this was the same Donald Carr who 22 years earlier had been captain of MCC in their ill-fated match at Peshawar, still a source of keen debate in Pakistan. Imran certainly encountered his share of heavy-handed treatment over the years, but it's arguable that he was over-sensitive to what he considered racial abuse.

Sussex began their season with four consecutive and eminently forgettable draws in which Imran did more with the bat than the ball.

Their fifth match was against Gloucestershire at Hove. Gloucester batted first and made 129; Sussex replied with 424–7, with Imran, profitably exploring the aeriel route over extra cover, scoring 167 at a run a minute. Thirty-one years later, one of the fielding side still remembered the subtle efforts of the bowlers not to catch their captain's eye and become the next victim. The 22-year-old Paul Parker, a fluent stroke-maker in his own right, was batting at the other end for the early part of Imran's innings. Sussex added 83 runs in the hour before tea: seven extras, nine to Parker, and 67 to Imran.

Gloucestershire came out to bat a second time. Zaheer immediately hit Imran for a four. As Paul Parker recalls, 'The Sussex lads were geeing Imran up. We all told him he never bounced Zaheer or any of the other Pakistani players. As motivation goes, it was crude but effective. The next over, Immy ostentatiously added a couple of yards to his run and came in like a freight train. The bare-headed Zaheer just managed to get a touch of his glove on the ball a split-second before it crashed into his forehead and ballooned up for a catch to gully. Ten of the Sussex players immediately appealed. The eleventh, Imran, rushed up to enquire about the batsman's health. "Zaheer, my friend, are you all right?" we heard. "Speak to me. Zaheer ... Zaheer ..."' Zaheer gave Imran a 'baleful look', but otherwise showed no after-effects of being hit on the skull by a 145 kph (90 mph) bouncer. He was given not out by the umpire, and went on to score 213. Sussex were left needing 87 to win in 20 overs, on a worn pitch. They finished on 84 for eight, which was about as good an advertisement for county cricket (and for the use of the crash helmet) as you can get.

It would be fair to say that Imran was an enigma to most of his team-mates, and perhaps consciously set out to be. He was inclined to oracular judgements and, as Parker recalls, tended to be 'friendly but cryptic' if asked for his advice by a younger player. One of his junior Sussex colleagues remembers 'getting up the nerve to ask Imran some technical point about in-swing bowling, to which the standard coach's reply would have been all about the correct grip on the ball and the exact angle of the left elbow at the point of delivery. Imran's four-word response was: "Be like a tiger."'

Ironically, Imran himself was curiously diffident when it came to his batting, which improved beyond all recognition in 1978. Immediately after the Gloucestershire match he scored 105 not out against Somerset, followed by 49 against Andy Roberts's Hampshire, 113 not out against Nottinghamshire, 65 against Surrey, 53 against Middlesex, and more in the same general vein. Most if not all these innings displayed not only technical skill, but coolness of judgement, a proper degree of aggression and the requisite 'bottle' against fast bowling; he was someone who could take it as well as give it. At the end of the season Imran had 1,339 first-class runs at an average of 42, which was to rub shoulders with the likes of Botham, Gooch and Gower. Not surprisingly, he was awarded his county cap. Yet, as Paul Parker recalls, 'Immy was strangely modest about his batting prowess. I remember David Steele, of all unprepossessing people, bowling for Derbyshire against us at Eastbourne. After studying Steele's innocuous little left-arm floaters for the best part of an hour, Imran approached the batsman at the other end, Paul Phillipson, and said a bit apologetically, "You know, I think perhaps I can hit this bloke." Phillipson's reply was "Get on with it."'

While Imran was settling in with Sussex, the Pakistani Test team minus its Packer players was touring England. The visitors were crushed in the three-match series, which saw the beginning of the Botham legend, and did little better against the counties. At times Imran found himself playing only a few miles away from where his sometime colleagues were going down to their latest defeat. The ensuing sense of 'debasement, discredit and disarray', to quote Wasim Raja's assessment of the tour, would have far-reaching ramifications for Pakistan's cricket administrators. Having deposed Zulfikar Ali Bhutto in a military coup, General Zia assumed the state presidency in September 1978. On his third day in office he dismissed Mohammad Hussain and his co-selectors and formed a new board under Lieutenant-General Azhar Khan, a former military governor. Khan was given orders to bring back Pakistan's WSC players at any cost, even if this meant doing business with Kerry Packer, a man General Zia described as 'a prostitute'.

Imran's working relationship with Packer wasn't the only liaison that would sustain him and bring him a certain controversy in these years. For all his aloofness, the Pakistani cut a dashing figure. A reporter for the London *Evening News* caught up with him during one 'rock star-like progress' through the capital. 'Imran Khan is the sexiest man alive,' she panted, 'dark and Othello-like, perfectly proportioned; has burning brown eyes, deep black hair, a bedroom pout.'

Most women Imran encountered individually at the time found him similarly engaging, and vice versa. It would seem that monogamy wasn't as yet part of his game plan. Meanwhile, Imran would recall that from around October 1978, when he turned 26, 'my mother actively began looking for a bride for me' in Pakistan. Among Mrs Khan's most promising early candidates was her son's former Oxford contemporary Benazir Bhutto. I was told there had been 'about a year' of serious matchmaking efforts involving the couple. Bhutto had returned to Pakistan in late 1977, only to see her father first deposed and then imprisoned by General Zia. The young woman who remembered herself as 'a waif ... abjectly await[ing] developments in Islamabad' was commonly thought one of the more eligible catches elsewhere. 'All the mothers were getting in the act and asking Benazir to dinner,' I was told by a particularly well-placed source in Lahore, reflecting on Bhutto's frequent visits to the city. 'You know, she was a good, intelligent, good-looking girl – and just as opinionated as Imran was.' Despite the apparent compatability, there's no evidence that Pakistan's two rising (and eventually opposed) political stars ever seriously considered Mrs Khan's proposal.

As we've seen, however, Imran did enjoy a full and varied social life both in England and elsewhere. By the late 1970s or early 1980s he was clearly beginning to develop a rather more elevated public profile than that of the average county cricketer. And generally speaking it was less Imran's prowess with bat or ball that attracted the interest of the British press than the insinuation that he was a robustly sexually active young man whose affairs were not entirely confined to a safe, committed relationship with one woman. Thirty years later, Imran would recall of his regular visits to London at the time that 'you could go out on four different evenings and meet four different sets of people [from] different parts of the world. I loved that.' It would be churlish not to take him at his word. Imran clearly enjoyed a wide acquaintanceship at all levels of society, with both sexes, in London, Lahore and several ports of call in between, making friends he later described as 'like brothers and sisters'. But perhaps it would be fair to say that there was a special place in his heart for the distaff side of this extended family. I spoke to a now middle-aged Englishwoman who had known him quite well in 1981–2. Towards the end of their time together it had been brought to her attention that Imran's relationship with her might not have been an entirely exclusive one. With heroic self-restraint, she told me, 'Imran was a people person. It would have been strange if he withheld himself from half the people.'

During his first year or two in Sussex, Imran's renown was confined pretty much to a local stage. A number of factors contributed to turning him into a national and international celebrity, not least his starring role in his nation's Test successes against her arch enemy India. But if there was a single defining moment that marked the beginning of Imran's decade or more as a global sex symbol, it was the day he was introduced to a fellow Pakistani expatriate in England, a gregarious hairdresser-cum-personal stylist known as 'Mr Dar', or simply as 'Dar'. Anyone familiar with the 1975 comedy-drama *Shampoo*, with Warren Beatty in the role of a priapic crimper, has only to think of that same character, transported to south Asia, and with a better sense of humour, to get a feel of the man. Until he met Dar, Imran was alluring but not polished. Left to himself his dress code tended to be a brightly coloured mishmash, dominated as it was by a variety of boots, wide-open shirts, neatly creased jeans and gaudy cricket blazers, for an overall look that might not have been out of place on stage in an edition of the *Top of the Pops* of the day. As Dar told me, Imran 'hadn't really cared about his image' up until then, although he 'wasn't unaware of himself'. This broadly confirms the assessment of several of his early county colleagues. At Worcester, Imran had been known to casually walk into the unassuming town centre shop of a barber named Toby Veale and request a five-shilling cut – adding, perhaps unnecessarily, 'Nothing fancy.' His departure from the county seems to have been the occasion of a personal as well as a professional makeover. By the time Kerry Packer and his advertising executives got hold of him in late 1977 Imran was already teasing his hair into what became the trademark bushy black bouffant, a style which evolved into an art form, known as the 'lion look', under Dar's expert curatorship. This carefully assembled package of clothes, hair and accessories contributed significantly to the public image of the 'sexiest man alive', who was quite self-aware enough to play along with it. By the mid-1980s, Imran walking in to a men's boutique was a bit like Elton John walking into a florist's shop, or Oliver Reed walking into a pub: he was happy to be there, and they were glad to accommodate him. In later years Imran became a partner in Dar's international salon business, which perhaps in part owed its continuing success to his patronage.

Dar provides a small but somehow touching example of Imran's growing celebrity at about the time he joined Sussex. Although indifferent to cricket, the stylist accepted his friend and client's invitation to travel down to Hove to watch him in 'some mundane county match'. Also present in the party was a 'fabulous-looking woman' who hitherto had proved strangely resistant to their host's charms, Dar recalls.

> Throughout the day, whenever Imran set foot outside the pavilion he was immediately swarmed by young boys with autograph books and scraps of paper. Out of earshot of the woman, he told all these kids to meet him at a certain gate at exactly six that evening, when he would be glad to sign for them. At exactly 6.05, the woman and I also turned up at the gate in question. Imran was standing there in the sunshine looking like a Greek god, surrounded by this adoring crowd of about a hundred kids and quite a few of their equally awestruck parents. It was like the woman had drunk an aphrodisiac. She took one look at Imran holding court and promptly went from ignoring him to fawning on him for the rest of the night. Privately, he was amused and appalled that she was quite so brazen about it.

Since ultimately it made all the power and the fame and the sex possible, it's worth repeating that Imran 'work[ed] like a navvy', to again quote Sir Len Hutton, to perfect his seemingly natural bowling action. (This was the same Len Hutton who remarked of one particularly well-known English player of the day that he was a 'show pony', and of another that 'He always gives me the feeling that a chorus line of girls is about to appear and start dancing around behind him.' Not a man to be easily moved, in other words.) It's fair to say that Imran started with the advantages not only of regularly playing on one of the world's quickest wickets, but also of having the classic fast bowler's physique. In a fine display of traditional English homoeroticism, the London *Evening Globe*'s cricket correspondent devoted a quarter of his review of a Gillette Cup tie to waxing eloquent over Imran's musculature. 'Khan stripped to the waist would put Adonis to shame. At a time when too many first-class cricketers in this country could be mistaken for the man who comes to fix your sink, the more obvious templates here are the Incredible Hulk and Valentino.'

Even so, there was always rather more to Imran's professional success than a fetchingly broad chest and a narrow waist. Beneath the luxuriant hair there were also distinct signs of intelligence. Paul Parker said to me, 'Imran was the world's hardest working bowler and probably about the most creative one. He never stopped thinking about his game ... Instead of just charging in, he'd experiment with the way he approached the crease. He'd vary the angle, com[ing] in wide and somehow swinging the ball away – almost unheard-of.' Mike Procter would also have cause to refer ruefully to Imran's speed and versatility after facing him on a fruity pitch at Hove. Another player remembered thinking that the young Imran had taken a 'somewhat mincing, medium-pacer's run' and was amazed to see the same bowler a year or two later 'more or less push himself off from the pavilion steps'. Imran's Sussex colleague and future captain Johnny Barclay adds: 'I played against the great man at Oxford. Back then he had a decent, open-chested inswinger, but he wasn't really quick in the true sense of the word. By the time he joined us he was *lightning* fast, sideways on, and he had the lot. And then some. That last-second jump he gave off the left leg was probably the most thrilling sight in cricket.'

Ten years after being casually asked to turn his arm over in the Pakistan Under-19s trial at Lahore, Imran was the finished article.

Added to his prodigous talent and old-fashioned oomph, he was also a remarkably consistent professional who was often in action for 10 or 11 months of each year. Imran's devotion to the job was essentially no different when playing in front of a handful of spectators on a wet afternoon in Uxbridge from what it was in front of a packed house in Karachi or Lahore. He drove himself hard, and eased up only when nature took its toll. ('He is human,' as General Zia was to remind us a few years later.) The first half of the 1978 season had seen Imran in rare form with both bat and ball. But even before soccer was back on the sports pages in early August, *The Times* delivered a blunt and critical assessment; he looked 'exhausted and feeble', they said. An example of what the paper meant by that came in the rain-affected championship match against Worcestershire, to whom Imran arguably had something to prove. Playing in a steady drizzle at the normally fetching Saffrons ground in Eastbourne, both sides seemed a shade under-motivated, managing just 539 runs in four innings. Imran's contribution was to score 18 and 0, and take one wicket. Sussex did, however, win the Gillette Cup, beating Somerset in the final at Lord's. Imran struck no less a judge than E.W. Swanton as 'under par' and 'the most restless fellow, pacing around with a frown in the outfield. His mind appeared to be elsewhere.'

Swanton may well have been right. Imran, who was nursing a torn muscle, had just been named in the Pakistan squad to play in a home series of three Tests and three one-day internationals starting later that month. It would be almost impossible to exaggerate the sense of anticipation among the players and spectators alike. Long before the first ball was bowled, much of the country was excited to the point of hysteria, with crowds thronging the streets, marching bands playing patriotic airs, and radios blaring sensational stories of moral lapses by the opposition players. In Lahore, whole families moved their homes into the open, sleeping under the arches of the Gaddafi Stadium for nights on end, all on the mere rumour of tickets. In due course there was rioting among some of the unsuccessful applicants. Imran's and the team's names were plastered over the front pages, and the forthcoming 'clash of the century' was discussed like a major state event, which in fact it was. After 18 years marked by incessant diplomatic rows and two wars, Pakistan were to play India again.

The home press again deployed their boldest headlines for the occasion, and the accompanying stories tended to the partisan zeal and hyperbole that were to be a prominent feature of fixtures between the two countries over the years. To one Karachi publication the visiting Indians were 'unholy' and 'to be humiliated, rather [than] beaten'. The newspaper's depiction of the tourists' predominantly Hindu players as 'infidels' gives a further flavour of the coverage. 'Know your enemy for what he is,' thundered the *Pakistan Star*, an expatriate weekly widely available in Lahore and other cities, 'a godless, ruthless and sinister foe who should be destroyed on the field of play.' (Somewhat belying this image of his team as a pack of 'thugs and vandals … spiritual descendants of the Evil One', the affable Indian captain Bishan Bedi would subsequently donate his blood to a Pakistani children's hospital, one of several such goodwill gestures the press either buried on their inside pages or chose to ignore entirely.) In what perhaps amounted to an exercise in reverse psychology, the same Pakistani media generally praised the wily tourists' technical skills to the skies, insisting that their famous quartet of spinners would be both 'wicked' and 'the devil to beat' on turning wickets. The whole, increasingly shrill build-up to the series swung to its zenith with Pakistan state television billing their ball-to-ball transmission of the rubber as 'the event of a lifetime' and large electronic scoreboards in city squares counting down the hours, minutes and seconds to the first Test. A global audience of some 300 million viewers would eventually watch some or all of the proceedings. Meanwhile, for their part the Indian press and public proved to be every bit as spirited as their Pakistani counterparts. There were an estimated 2,000 patriotic billboards appearing in either official or handwritten form along the main Delhi–Bombay railway, or an average of roughly three for every mile of the line. Many of these forcefully decried the opposition captain Mushtaq Mohammad and the other returning 'Packerstanis'. The Indian poet Khadar Mohiuddin would later satirise the ensuing series of matches he referred to as 'war without the nukes' in the lines 'Never mind my love for my motherland/What's important is how much I hate the other land.'

Perhaps inevitably, the cricket itself, though improving dramatically from a slow start, only rarely lived up to its advance billing. The first Test at Faisalabad was a high-scoring draw played out on a lifeless track. Imran recalled that the whole thing had been an exercise in futility from the bowlers' point of view, and 'the best Sarfraz and I could do was send down a liberal amount of bouncers to at least stop Gavaskar and company driving off the front foot. Without that, it would have been a slaughter.' Contrary to popular expectation, both the Test and the series as a whole would be played in a generally cordial atmosphere, and, as Zaheer Abbas says, 'anyone with strong feelings or prejudices [kept] them to themselves. [Pakistan] put the highest premium on maintaining courtesy and decorum.' Courtesy, that was, towards the *opposition* team; colleagues weren't necessarily eligible for the same consideration, and following the match Mushtaq informed a television reporter that Imran had 'bowled much too short' and employed 'some odd tactics' throughout. Rather understandably, Imran would remark, 'I was disgruntled at this ill-informed criticism by my captain. With the burden of public anticipation on my shoulders, I didn't need the extra pressure.' For the record, it was the 13th consecutive Test between the two countries to end in a draw, which perhaps lends context to what followed.

By contrast to Faisalabad, the groundsman for the second Test at Lahore produced a pitch which, if necessarily on the arid side (there was a drought), showed off Pakistan's fast bowling, quick-footed batting and agile close-fielding to full advantage. India were inserted and hustled out for 199, Imran taking four for 54. He later told an interviewer that he had felt under 'crushing pressure' both from his captain and the capacity crowd (which included Benazir Bhutto) to make an early breakthrough. 'As [a] result I found it almost impossible to control my line or length or movement. With each wayward over the accusing looks from my team-mates intensified. Fortunately, a bad ball got a wicket, which made me relax and bowl better.' Imran added 42 further high-quality overs in the second innings, and Pakistan were left to chase 126 in 99 minutes. They got there with eight wickets to spare, and General Zia proclaimed the next day a public feast.

With around 10,000 more people inside than the official ground capacity, the third Test at Karachi got off to a satisfactory start, meandered somewhat, and then produced an even better finish than Lahore.

Pakistan eventually needed 164 to win in just under two hours. Promoted for the slog, Imran responded with a ferocious yet chanceless 31, which included a four and two straight sixes off Bedi, the second of them an immense and perfectly struck drive over the sightscreen, to see Pakistan to victory. It was 19 November 1978, which was to be a major watershed in the popularity, if not the long-term fortunes of Pakistani cricket. A series which had initially produced all the attritional and tedious traits of past encounters between the two countries ended in scenes of delirious rejoicing. Pakistan's 2–0 victory, which promptly shut down the nation for a second day, represented 'a fulfilment of aspiration [and] pride never before seen in our history', to quote General Zia.

A senior and long-standing team-mate of Imran's told me that what struck him most around now was an apparent paradox in the character of his 'esteemed friend'. 'He was a model professional in the way he devoted himself to cricket, but he also had something of an amateur's mindset in his attitude to it.' His colleague saw Imran as an 'innocent' in the best sense, a man not exactly naive but 'pure'; his main motivation was 'enjoyment, not ego', and therefore he was sceptical, at best, about 'becoming overnight the most famous man in Pakistan. It was a mania ... There were stories about grown men who literally stabbed each other in fights about whether he or Hanif was the greatest of all time.' Imran himself broadly confirms this thesis when he says that 'cricket fever engulfed [us] and a whole army of fans was swept along on a tide of passion for a sport they didn't really understand ... I was singled out for much of the attention and consequently the [media] started to run wild.' Although Kerry Packer had begun the process of personalising and glamorising Imran, it was only now that 'everything went overboard. I was being followed around by the press ... stalked ... The result was a succession of ill-informed trash that portrayed me as [the] kind of sportsman who goes out with dumb blondes, rather than someone who plays a mentally taxing sport to a high degree of professionalism.'

In the midst of the Pakistani national celebrations, Imran left for Australia and his second and final season with World Series Cricket. The 'circus' eventually folded with a drawn Supertest between the West Indies and Australia, a subsequent would-be climactic one-day bash being washed out. On 30 May 1979, Packer announced the terms of an agreement with the Australian board, which gave him the exclusive rights to broadcast home Test matches as well as certain other marketing privileges. The 21-year-old Mark Nicholas, future Hampshire captain and doyen of Channel 4's cricket coverage, was then playing club cricket in New South Wales and told me he watched every WSC match. 'Imran made an immense impression. It was the aura, the stature, the mane, the staggering looks and the unbridled talent. His dramatic action, the approach, the leap and the follow-through were all pure theatre. He wasn't swinging the ball so much by then but, God, he was good – and stylish in a way even other fast bowlers could only dream of.'

Fresh from his Packer triumphs, Imran went straight to the generally less charged atmosphere of a three-Test tour by Pakistan of New Zealand. He added five more wickets in the first innings at Napier, favouring the Kiwis with a generous quota of throat balls, but otherwise recalls the series, which Pakistan won 1–0, as 'rather boring [and] inconsequential'. As such, it may have been a welcome relief from his recent experiences on and off the cricket field. Of these, Wasim Raja recalled, 'There were times [after the India series] when Imran didn't want to step outside, because he knew he'd be mobbed by fans and reporters. It took a lot of guts. And once he did he put on this front of being friendly and patient with all the bores, who must have driven him nuts.' One night in Auckland, safely back in the team hotel following a sparsely attended stroll through the city's streets, Imran exclaimed, 'No one hassled me!'

If Pakistan's fanatically supported series with India had been distinguished by its 'courtesy and decorum', as Zaheer Abbas says, a noticeably different tone prevailed when they agreed to a hurriedly arranged, two-Test tour of Australia in March 1979. In its quest to drum up support for the series – and sell papers – the home press made much of the residual ill-feeling between the Packer and non-Packer contingents, who would be playing each other for the first time in Australia. The resulting atmosphere, Imran reports, 'was as ugly as I ever knew in my career'. Asif Iqbal perhaps didn't help matters by adding his own version of Tony Greig's ill-advised 'grovel' remarks, insisting that the Australian team were 'no better [than] schoolboy level'. This was generally thought to have been counter-productive both to Pakistan and to Asif himself, who would spend much of his time at the crease fending off short-pitched deliveries from the general vicinity of his throat.

In the first Test at Melbourne, Javed Miandad ran out Rodney Hogg when the latter inadvertently strayed out of his crease to inspect the pitch. Imran described the incident as 'quite funny in its way' and perhaps not untypical of Javed, whom he characterises as a 'gutsy guy, but with a major inferiority complex – *very* into statistics ... someone who combined great passion with that scrappy, street-cricket approach to the game'. Hogg's response was to initiate a briefly popular practice among disgruntled batsmen by smashing his stumps on his way back to the pavilion. The Australian bowler Alan Hurst then provided a rare example of cricket's so-called 'Mankad' dismissal by running out Sikander Bakht when Sikander backed up too enthusiastically in the course of the second Test at Perth. At that, Sikander's partner Asif demolished his own wicket in protest. Some time later, the home batsman Andrew Hilditch courteously picked up the ball and lobbed it to Sarfraz, the bowler, after an innacurate return throw from the field. Sarfraz appealed and Hilditch was given out for handling.

Meanwhile, Pakistan won the first Test – again thanks largely to Sarfraz, who took nine for 86, including a spell of seven wickets for one run, in the Australian second innings. He was another of those uniquely gifted and self-assertive characters who seem to be a speciality of Pakistan. In his autobiography, Imran would write warmly of the versatile 'Sarf' that 'he taught me more about swing bowling than anybody. He is a bit of a loner [but] I always felt he tried his best for the team.' Twenty-five years after he said this, Imran, while again paying fulsome tribute to his old colleague's technical prowess, added that Sarfraz had been 'a misfit' who was 'chiefly concerned with himself', by no means the strongest words aired on the subject. Australia went on to win the Perth Test, and thus tie the series. Imran was carrying a back strain and consequently not at his best. In the six months from September 1978 to March 1979 he'd gone directly from playing in the English Gillette Cup final to the Pakistani Test training camp and from there to three international series staged in three different countries, while somehow also appearing in the gruelling day-night regimen of World Series Cricket. But the physical slog was only part of Imran's 'steadily growing sense [of] unease' about certain aspects of the Test side, which had seemingly lost momentum only weeks after the historic victory over India. As usual, Wasim Raja remarked, Pakistan's star 'always appeared to be either rising or falling, never just staying still'; this wasn't a side to make a virtue out of consistency. There had again been running disagreements in Australia between Imran and his captain Mushtaq, who the former believes had become 'increasingly defensive and nervous as his own form deteriorated'. The national selectors appear to have broadly shared this assessment. Later that spring Mushtaq, suffering a finger sprain and something of an attendant decline of potency as a spin bowler, was replaced by Asif, who would find it every bit as hard as his predecessor to consistently blend 11 individually talented cricketers into a united team.

Perhaps it was fated that the one constant factor of the 1979 World Cup, held, like its predecessor, in England, was the atrocious weather. It was the wettest early summer for years, with disastrous consequences for all eight sides' preparations, although for those arriving direct from the likes of Pakistan the shock was 'physical – like being dropped in an ice-cold bath' in Wasim Raja's vivid phrase.

Imran is a natural enthusiast, but even he acknowledged that Pakistan's World Cup campaign seemed to lack something in team spirit or, more bluntly, that 'we folded under pressure'. Asif's side saw off Canada and Australia in the tournament's early stages, but self-destructed in the tie against England at Leeds. Chasing a modest 165 in 60 overs, Pakistan, with vociferous support from much of the crowd, began well enough. With Majid in apparently sparkling form, and Willis in a generous mood, a target of a run every other ball was always on. When the score was 27 for no wicket, the live BBC coverage of the match broke away to broadcast a race from Epsom. By the time the cricket transmission resumed 20 minutes later, Pakistan were 34 for six. Coming in at No 9, Imran played a self-denyingly stubborn knock of 21, but ran out of partners. Against all expectation, England won the match by 14 runs. A number of the Pakistani expatriate community gave voice to their frustration that night outside their team's hotel. In the days ahead, Imran would frequently find himself being asked why he hadn't simply hit the English bowlers out of the ground to win the tie, a line of enquiry to which he responded with unfailing courtesy.

Despite the loss Pakistan advanced to the semi-final, where they met the West Indies at The Oval. Once again, Imran records, 'we cracked under the strain'. Chasing 293, Pakistan were 176 for one with Majid and Zaheer in full cry. Viv Richards, of all people, then took three wickets with his innocuous off spin, precipitating another Leeds-like collapse. The West Indies won by 43 runs and went on to lift the cup. It's not difficult to imagine with what delight the Pakistani team, after more than ten hours' cricket, then settled in to their London hotel for another night of loud abuse shouted at their windows. Back home, the euphoria of the Indian series gave way to a critical press reaction bordering on a hate campaign against some of the senior players, Imran prominently included.

Back in Sussex, he sometimes displayed what were called 'royalist tendencies' in stark contrast to the easy informality of most of the rest of the club. Nicknames were mandatory in the Hove dressing-room, as they were elsewhere. The man who was cheerfully addressed as 'Immy' to his face, which was bad enough, was now called 'the Great Khan' behind his back. At least one county colleague thought him 'somewhat limited in humour', although the name had less to do with any pomposity *per se* than with Imran's princely looks and what they all saw as a tendency for him to 'simply vanish at the close of play [rather] than sitting around playing dominoes in the pub'. Imran himself was sufficiently unsure of his prospects at Sussex in 1979 to later write that 'it became quite clear that they were thinking of releasing me', something I was authoritatively told was 'balls'. The county then had four overseas signings on their books, Imran, Javed, Garth le Roux and Keppler Wessels, only two of whom, under the TCCB regulations, could play at any one time. At the end of the 1979 season Javed left Sussex for Glamorgan, and the mercurially talented Wessels would prove neither as consistent nor as fit as some on the cricket committee had hoped. Under the circumstances, it was a reasonably safe bet that the county would somehow find a place for the man who was arguably the world's fastest bowler. One team-mate went away from a match against Middlesex in which Imran had 'pulverised them with the ball and then whacked their own attack into the street' with the strange impression that the Great Khan was 'actually a bit insecure'. He also sensed the faint air of anxiety and suspiciousness that others had seen at Worcester. 'He was basically not a confident man. Never thought he'd be picked for the next game. To put it mildly, the [club] were happy to have him, but in Imran's mind there was always a plot going on to get rid of him.'

Nothing reflects better this schizophrenic turn of affairs than Imran's playing figures for the second half of the 1979 season. He made his first appearance for Sussex at home against Hampshire immediately following Pakistan's exit from the World Cup. Coming in at No. 5, Imran scored 154 not out and then took six for 37 to send the visitors home a day early. That was in the last week of June. Before July was out the Sussex committee were quietly debating whether, far from sacking Imran, they should appoint him county captain after Arnold Long privately signalled his intention to retire in 1980. Although the bauble went elsewhere, the very fact that it was discussed seems to refute Imran's suggestion that the club were anything less than delighted to have his services. He continued to give what the file calls 'uniform satisfaction with bat and ball'.

Against Surrey at Hove, Imran took five for 33 in 15 overs of what Graham Roope described as 'non-stop improvisation. He'd let you have three screaming deliveries all coming at you from different angles, and then a fourth one that went straight. It was the sucker punch. The ball that got the batsman out was the one that did nothing at all.' Imran followed this up with figures of four for 64 and five for 50 against Middlesex. This gave him 600 career first-class wickets, not that he was counting them – there may never have been a less statistically minded bowler. Imran seems to have enjoyed playing Middlesex. Some 30 years later, Paul Parker dwelt fondly on the memory of the delivery which accounted for their batsman Graham Barlow in a fixture at Lord's. According to Parker, Barlow had been playing a typically gritty innings, shoving out his pad and disdainfully ignoring anything a fraction outside the stumps. 'Out of nowhere, Imran suddenly produced this booming reverse swing. No one saw it coming, least of all the batsman, who again shouldered arms. At the last split second the ball shot back and hit the top of his off stump. As Barlow reluctantly took his leave Imran strolled up, beaming, and said to us, "*That* was a clever trick".'

I spoke to several of Imran's colleagues at Sussex, most of whom broadly agreed with Neil Lenham's assessment that he'd been 'a good team man in his way'. The 21-year-old fast bowler Tony Pigott was just coming into the side in 1979. 'Lester', as he was inevitably known, remarked that the impassioned little pep talks favoured by certain other players weren't Imran's style. 'He wasn't the sort of guy to sit down next to you in the dressing-room and offer any encouragement,' Pigott said. 'As a fellow bowler, you could literally wait all day for a word of advice. But then again, just watching him in action was an education.' There appears to have been a general consensus that Imran didn't necessarily react well to criticism. On occasion he took abrupt offence where none was intended. Following one tactical post-mortem after a Sussex defeat, Imran left the room 'in a royal huff', evidently, 'even though no one had said a word against him'. He apparently saw something in the overall discussion as an attempt to point the finger of blame at him for the loss, or possibly he just disagreed with the whole tone of the thing. Another colleague who was present adds that Imran had made his departure with 'a glacial stare [rather] than any locker banging', and that this had made the protest all the more effective. 'I genuinely sympathised with him. After you've bowled out the Aussies in front of 80,000 people at Melbourne, it can't be easy listening to a bollocking in the Hove dressing-room from Arnold Long.'

Imran told me that his main reservation about county cricket as a whole remained simply that 'it was too defensive. There wasn't enough passion. You had certain players whose top priority was to keep their head down and secure their contract for the next season. There were times when they were literally praying for rain so they could stay in the dressing-room playing cards.'

In theory, Imran found English domestic cricket on the bland side. In practice, he found it all too robust, at least when it came to the matter of sledging. A Sussex player told me of a racially charged epithet the Yorkshire close fielders had once chosen to make when Imran came out to bat at Leeds. The original remark, while not enlightened, had sparked a 'truly spectacular' response, which had seemed to impress even that hardbitten home audience. Imran recalled that right through into the 1980s there had been occasional 'mutterings' from certain quarters when he appeared on the field. As a whole, these still inclined to the familiar 'curry' or 'Paki' references, and weren't necessarily restricted to his fellow cricketers. Imran reacted to one such comment from the crowd while batting for Sussex at Worcester by promptly smashing the ball for six into the section of the ground from which the offending phrase had come. Depending on one's perspective, he could come across as fiercely proud or mildly paranoid; either way, a number of his Sussex team-mates describe him as a forbidding, occasionally aloof, character. 'I wouldn't say Imran was hail-fellow-well-met,' adds one long-time colleague. 'He basically had two close mates at Hove, Garth le Roux and Gehan Mendis. He was intensely loyal to both. Immy thought the Test selectors ignored Mendis after he qualified for England because of colour prejudice.'

Imran ended the English season in a three-day match against Somerset at Hove. He took one for 40 in the visitors' first innings and six for 53 in the second. The then 22-year-old Somerset batsman Nigel Popplewell told me ruefully that 'notwithstanding my father's influence in enabling Imran to move to Sussex in the first place, I didn't get much reflected sympathy ... He came tearing up the hill at Hove and bowled at 95 miles an hour in the evening gloom, which was my baptism in county cricket. The thing about Imran was, you could tell when he was really trying because he crouched in his run-up before exploding into his slightly swingy action. If you saw him crouching, you really knew you were in trouble.'

A number of opposing batsmen had that feeling about Imran in 1979. He finished the season with 73 first-class wickets at an average of just under 15; not coincidentally, Sussex rose to a creditable fourth in the table.

During his playing days, Imran was a man absorbed equally with substance and image. He was also a man who desperately wanted to be appreciated, even loved. All professional sportsmen pay attention to what the media say about them, but none more so than Imran did in mid-career. Pakistan's self-inflicted failure in the 1979 World Cup coincided with, or perhaps triggered, a growing tendency on the part of the press to explain every disappointment on the playing field in terms of the players' extracurricular activities. And that chiefly meant Imran's. As every journalist in Pakistan knew, the public was fascinated with the Great Khan's private life, 'with the scope of its dramatic deeds, the amazing range of its celebrity couplings and the considerable body of contradictions it indulges', to quote the expatriate *Star*. It might be going too far, but if so not going entirely in the wrong direction, to say that much of the Pakistani media was clinically obsessed with Imran's sex life. His every rumoured relationship was immediate front-page material. At least one Karachi daily paper maintained a 'nooky watch' on his behalf. By 1979 long-time broadcasters such as Omar Kureishi and a new generation of rabidly ambitious tabloid journalists had made the Test team the centre of the nation's civic life. As a result, 'when we succeded, we were gods; when we failed, the devil incarnate,' Imran wryly noted to an English friend. After the bland and often catatonically boring Pakistani cricket scene of the 1960s, the press had been swept off its collective feet by the charismatic all-rounder newly attired in what the *Star* called, a shade anachronistically, 'the latest London togs and a Beatle pompadour'. Most of Pakistan's matches now featured youthful, banner-waving audiences that punctuated play with lusty chants of 'Imran! Imran!' Twenty years later, a suitably impressed political reporter would instinctively turn to Imran in the middle of a 'hysterically enthusiastic' campaign rally in Lahore, and in all innocence ask him whether he had ever seen anything like it before. 'Yes,' he said quietly, 'I have.'

So that autumn, when Imran chose to make one of his relatively rare appearances in Pakistani domestic cricket, he did so 'watched by a pack roughly the size of the White House press corps', to quote an AP reporter named Tony Gill, who was qualified to make the comparison. He repaid their interest in spectacular fashion. Playing at Lahore for PIA in the Invitation Trophy against Pakistan Railways, Imran returned figures of five for 31 in the first innings and two for 33 in the second. Appearing for the same team against National Bank, he took six for 49 and six for 56, missed the Quaid-e-Azam knockout match with the House Building Finance Corporation, but returned to bag four for 36 and three for 63 against Habib Bank, off whose attack, with Abdul Qadir to the fore, he hit a spectacularly aggressive second-innings 77. As a direct result, PIA claimed both major domestic trophies; Imran was the league's most valuable player, his 26 wickets having come at just over 10 apiece.

Attendances at Invitation Trophy matches showed a marked increase whenever Imran was playing, with a crowd estimated at 3,500 queueing outside the gates of the Gaddafi Stadium long before the start of the first day's play in the Invitation final between PIA and the Habib. A sizeable number of those in line were young women. When the players themselves appeared at the ground at 9.30 in the morning there was a 'mob explosion', according to one Anglo-Pakistani female spectator, whereupon Imran 'turned around, faced the girls, and raised his arms in a quieting gesture like Moses parting the water. Everyone immediately fell silent.' Some 90 minutes later, a rising young journalist named Aslam Anwar would be moved to abandon his professional sang-froid when watching Imran run out on to the field to take the new ball. 'He acknowledged the packed crowd with a combination of dignity, grace and responsive enthusiasm ... when the rumble of applause began, it was as though each person there had been struck by the lightning of that smile, the grandeur of that presence ... At the lunch interval all one saw were young ladies strolling purposefully back and forth outside the pavilion door, and, in the perimeter, nine-year-old boys enthusiastically practising their run-up technique.'

The Invitation Trophy also took on extra significance as players sought to attract the attention of the Pakistani national selectors, who later announced a squad of 28 to attend a training camp prior to an eagerly anticipated tour of India. Mushtaq Mohammad had been under the impression that he would return to captain the Test side, despite his not having appeared in the World Cup. The board disabused him of this notion by commenting in a press release that a man 'not fit for one-day cricket can hardly be considered for Test matches'. Despite this public rebuke, Mushtaq then let it be known that he would be 'happy to tour simply as a regular player', only to be snubbed a second time. Instead, the board kept faith with Asif Iqbal. Asif, who told me he was 'thrilled' to get the job, refused to go on tour with Sarfraz Nawaz in his side ('I wasn't prepared to spend 90 per cent of my time looking after one player; the guy was talented, but completely unmanageable'), putting even more pressure on Imran to succeed on the moribund Indian wickets.

According to Javed Miandad, Mushtaq's ousting was the result of 'a plot played out by a handful of players who each fancied himself as the next captain of Pakistan'. One former national selector recalled that his committee had sat down 'in a panic' at the prospect of appointing Asif, an undeniably fine player, but until recently 'a prominent member of Mr Packer's gang [who] was widely believed to have retired from Tests in 1977'. What followed was a tumultuous several hours in which at least one of General Zia's hand-picked board members argued for Imran's appointment as a 'leader of national unity'. The subsequent debate appears to have been a lively one, with 'fists thumped on tables' and the somewhat incongruous sight of a uniformed military figure with 'tears literally rolling down his cheeks'. At some point, a junior selector had taken a position opposed to that of the majority and a colleague remarked, 'I don't have to sit here and listen to some Lahori bullshit!'

Taking a leaf from the Pakistanis' book of a year earlier, Sunil Gavaskar, the Indian captain, indulged in some pre-Test kidology by publicly insisting that the tourists would 'easily' win the series, largely because 'Imran and their other bowlers are in a different class to our guys', and the visitors as a whole were so much better trained. This blizzard of logic, while true as far as it went, was perhaps to oversimplify the underlying state of affairs. As Imran recalls, the Pakistani cause was hindered by a series of 'bizarre' selectorial fiats, of which Sarfraz's omission was only the most glaring. The panel 'also thought our regular first XI was sufficient [and] gave little thought to the right reserves ... [They] assumed the wickets in India would turn, so they brought two slow left-armers, a leg-spinner and just three seamers. We were picked on reputation and the selectors ignored our lack of depth. That became a criminal neglect when I ran into injury problems.' Meanwhile, in a notable reversal of their earlier practice, most Pakistani media predictions now left little room for failure. 'WHITEWASH!' was the uncompromising forecast emblazoned in a banner headline across one Lahore daily. Three months later, Imran was to conclude that Asif had been ill served by the pre-tour publicity, which listed his team as the greatest ever to leave Pakistan. 'We had a lot to live up to ... The relentless publicity was too much. The team eventually gave up ... some of the players went to pieces.'

The scenes that greeted the Pakistani tourists on their arrival at Delhi airport moved even Imran, who by now was used to a certain amount of mass adulation. As well as the formal reception committee, possibly as many as 800 local cricket fans were jam-packed on to the terminal balconies, screaming and tearing at their clothes. In time an officially delegated young girl came forward and gravely presented each of the visitors with a garland – the first of many – before backing away again into the crowd, as if in the presence of royalty. An *ad hoc* ticker-tape parade ensued to the Pakistanis' city-centre hotel where a 'WELCOME' banner adorned with likenesses of Imran and the other players was splayed across the main street. After a second effusive greeting by representatives of the Indian board, the tourists were shown upstairs to their rooms, the floors of which were strewn with a regularly replenished supply of rose petals throughout their stay.

Now there was just the matter of the cricket.

The first Test, at Bangalore, was a draw, although one that did little for the tourists' morale. Zaheer, in particular, looked out of sorts, and the Indians could hardly recognise him as the destroyer who had taken their attack apart just 12 months earlier. Pakistan were perhaps fortunate to escape with another draw in the second Test at Delhi. No fewer than six of their men were down with a virus, and to compound their problems Imran then pulled a rib muscle and could bowl only 8.3 overs in the match. It proved to be the worst injury he had yet suffered as a professional cricketer. Back in the hotel, Asif remembers it suddenly dawning on him that this might not be Pakistan's series after all. 'That Delhi pitch was a seamer's paradise, as shown by the fact that Sikander Bakht took 11 wickets in the match. India were left chasing something like 390 in the last day and a half. We held on for a draw, but if Imran had been fit I would have backed us to win easily. Sometimes these lost opportunities take a lot of getting back, particularly when you're playing in front of 50,000 screaming fans in a blazing hot stadium in India.'

I asked Asif whether, given the nature of Imran's injury, he'd considered placing a call to Sarfraz, their main wicket-taker against India in the previous series, who was kicking his heels back in Lahore. 'No,' he said. 'Never, never, never,' he added by way of emphasis. 'It was made clear to me that our government expected there to be no incidents of any kind while we were in India. These were two countries who had been at war, remember, and our even going there was a huge event. Under the circumstances Sarfraz was literally the last man I would have sent for.' 'The guy was a time bomb,' another senior player confirms. Several other well-placed sources broadly concur about the talented but awkward Sarfraz, who was thought a handful even by the standards of Pakistani representative cricket, whose ranks also included a man who played a perpetual phantom golf game while fielding in the deep, a batsman who considered his loss of form to be the result of black magic, and a third individual who later tirelessly insisted he was a Mogul emperor and had the documentation to prove it. The articulate and always opinionated Sarfraz was eminently sane by comparison, but even so 'perhaps lacking in political skills', in Asif's measured phrase.

Imran promptly broke down again in the third Test at Bombay, and got through the next 15 overs only in excruciating pain. India won by 131 runs. At an ill-tempered press conference the tour management accused the ground authorities of doctoring the pitch after the match had started. One down in India generally takes some winning back, particularly when you have only three fit bowlers at your disposal. By now Asif was on tranquillisers and beginning to have renewed thoughts of retirement. Imran sat out the fourth Test, which was a draw. Adapting the trend seen in Australia, Sikander kicked down the stumps on having an appeal disallowed, one of several protests taking place in either verbal or material form against alleged bias on the part of the umpires; following the match Asif talked of calling off the rest of the tour, which the home team said they would not have been too sorry about. Once again the wicket would have suited Imran down to the ground, as seen by the fact that Kapil Dev took six for 63 for the Indians and, bias notwithstanding, Sikander five for 56 for the tourists. In those marginally more relaxed touring days there was often an interval of as much as two or three weeks between Tests. Imran needed the break, as it was to be nearly a month before he felt fully himself again. He celebrated his recovery by bowling flat out in the nets, whereupon he promptly strained his back. Omitting to mention this latest setback to his captain, he played in the fifth Test at Madras, which India won by

10 wickets. It says something for Imran's competitive spirit that even in acute discomfort he took five for 114 in India's first innings, which included his 100th Test wicket. The raucous celebrations which had broken out in Pakistan at a comparable stage the preceding winter now had their counterpart in India. The tourists at least salvaged some self-respect, and Imran had nine victims, in the drawn sixth Test at Calcutta.*

Nineteen wickets in the series may not sound a lot, but judging from his form at Calcutta a fully fit Imran would have doubled that total. Pakistan's real problem was their batting. Only Wasim Raja and Javed Miandad did themselves justice; Asif and Majid managed just 267 and 223 Test runs respectively, while Zaheer's average showed a not insignificant decline from 194.33 in 1978–79 to 19.62 in 1979–80. Back home, the Pakistani press executed a broadly similar U-turn in their treatment of the players. Once again, Imran was singled out; according to one front-page report, his back injury was the result of 'lecherous activities with Indian actresses', one of only 'many debaucheries by Asif's merry men', who in fact had been subject to a strict 10.30 p.m. curfew throughout the tour. By itself it was a trivial slur, scarcely a tabloid pinprick amid the much wider celebrity Imran had begun to enjoy. But it was the beginning of what he describes as 'a campaign of malicious [and] ill-informed gossip' that would continue right through his cricket career and beyond.

In contrast to the scenes at Delhi airport, the Pakistanis' late-night return to Lahore just 11 weeks later resembled an expressionist film set, all deserted grey corridors relieved only by the appearance of unsmiling customs officials with sniffer dogs. After what Imran describes as some 'rough treatment', the players walked out into the windswept car park, where a small but emphatic crowd had gathered to shout abuse at them. In the ensuing post-mortem, both the chairman of the board and Asif resigned. The latter was replaced by the 22-year-old Javed Miandad, whose appointment occasioned some surprise, not least to Javed himself. 'I came to believe, however, I was deserving of the

---

* In November 1998, Imran told a commission looking into allegations of impropriety in Pakistani cricket of a curious (though perhaps entirely innocent) event prior to the Bombay Test, 'when our captain Asif Iqbal told his Indian rival that he [Gavaskar] had won the toss without looking at the coin'. As a result, India elected to bat first, thus depriving Imran of another day's rest for his pulled muscle. As noted, Pakistan lost the Test.

honour,' he notes. 'Although there was some vocal dissent, I don't feel this reflected the general mood in Pakistan. I believe the majority of the public were behind me, and welcomed the board's daring move.'

Javed got off to a winning start in a three-Test home series against Australia, thanks in large part to some extremely slow pitches. Pakistan won the first Test at Karachi and drew the remainder. Imran managed to take a total of six wickets in the series, which was three more than Dennis Lillee. Lillee publicly vowed never to return to Pakistan.

Meanwhile, the new president of the board, Air Marshal Nur Khan (no relation), called Imran in to assure him that he had a very bright future in the team and that he would do whatever he could to advance his career. Short, that was, of making him captain. A long-time colleague adds that Imran 'appeared to have accepted the decision' and 'seemed philosophical when he told me about it. He sort of sighed deeply once or twice. He wasn't combative in any way.' Ten years after the event, Imran was to say that 'appointing Javed was a major error, which led to immediate problems. He was too young to handle the team.' The long-serving Zaheer, for his part, admitted he was 'crushed' not to have got the job. Javed responded by dropping Zaheer for the third Test against Australia.

It's a curious fact that Imran could be widely recognised as, on his day, the most hostile fast bowler anywhere in Test cricket, while assessments of him at the County Ground, Hove, were more reserved. He was never in serious danger of being released by Sussex, as he feared he might be. That would have been to display self-destructive skills beyond even the reach of most English cricket administrators. The club did, however, offer Imran only a one-year contract for 1980, thus paying him a full £4,850 (roughly £25,000 at today's prices) for some six months of his 'sole, unstinting and exclusive' services, as well as providing the usual subsistence-level food and travel allowances. At the same time the county lost Javed Miandad but gained Garth le Roux, whom Imran had originally recommended to the club after playing with him in World Series Cricket. The burly Cape Towner, though at this stage perhaps notable more for his speed than his control, was soon among the wickets. Ironically, Imran's generosity was initially to backfire on him when the Sussex captain, Arnold Long, somewhat eccentrically announced that it was 'too risky' to go into a match with both his overseas fast bowlers, who would therefore have to rotate. In the event, early-season injuries to several key players forced Long to rethink his policy, and the Imran–le Roux axis duly provided Sussex with one of the most dangerous new-ball attacks in their history. The county's batting also improved beyond recognition, owing not least to a free-scoring 20-year-old newcomer named Colin Wells. Wells was to hit numerous sixes in the general direction of the English Channel, and to pass 1,000 runs in his first full season. His team-mates did not nickname him 'Bomber' for nothing.

As already noted, on a personal level one or two of the county players had their doubts about Imran, whom broadly speaking they saw as that seeming contradiction in terms, an 'introverted snob', to quote one admittedly jaundiced ex-colleague. Other, rather closer friends deny he was any such thing, but allow that he was perhaps at the couth end of the Sussex dressing-room. Certainly, for whatever reason, Imran was to find the Eton-educated Johnny Barclay a more congenial club captain than his predecessor Long had been. The appreciation seems to have been mutual. Barclay says: 'Imran always tried his hardest for me. My only reservation about him was that he had a rather flexible approach to timekeeping. He wasn't one to exactly make a fetish of punctuality. You'd sometimes call a meeting promptly for 10, and Imran would tend to saunter in at around quarter to 11. But he was always there in the middle when you really needed him, and I found him a delight to captain.'

Barclay confirms the general impression of Imran the county cricketer as 'someone [who] was a model professional on the field, but otherwise largely invisible. If play finished at 6.30 in the evening, he would have vanished by 20 to seven.' On many of the nights in question Imran would take the first available train to London, where he found 'a much-needed escape [from] some of the frustrations and tensions of full-time cricket'. As a general rule, such relief tended to come in the company of various sleek young women. The Middlesex bowler Mike Selvey had first met the young Imran in 1971, and occasionally saw him socially in London. 'He had some stunning escorts at times,' Selvey confirms. While Imran's expeditions took in a wide variety of activities, and not just the one people most associated him with, the basic routine involved spending prolonged amounts of time with some of the more raffish elements of the British aristocracy, although he good-naturedly denied this when teased by his Sussex team-mates. Sometimes there would be a little dressing-room banter behind his back about all the upper-class totty. 'Imran claimed a lot of friends in comparatively low stations of life,' one colleague recalls. 'I don't doubt he was extremely gracious to the cleaner and the guy on the gate. But

I regarded them as his imaginary playmates. In my experience he was more drawn to the toffs, and clearly they were to him.'

Thanks to the vagaries of Arnold Long and the weather, Imran had to wait until the end of May to make his home debut for Sussex that season. He announced his return by taking six for 80 and scoring a fiery 82 against Kent, who included Asif Iqbal in their ranks. One of the visitors' spinners recalled that Imran had shown an exaggerated respect to his first over, but that he had soon come to realise this was only a temporary respite as the batsman played himself in. 'He then tonked most of my second over into the road.' A fortnight later Imran was back at Lord's, playing in a Benson and Hedges quarter-final tie against Middlesex. According to the report in *Wisden*, 'the match had an extraordinary start and an even more unusual finish'. Imran was involved both times. Opening the Sussex attack at 10.45 on an overcast morning, he swung the ball so extravagantly that he took three wickets and bowled 11 wides in his first nine overs. At the other end, Geoff Arnold uncharacteristically proved nearly as wayward. The total number of extras conceded by Sussex, 38, was higher than their eventual margin of defeat.

Seven hours later, Imran found himself batting with the Sussex No. 8 Tony Pigott, who was being bounced on average twice an over by Middlesex's Wayne Daniel. (Daniel had broken Keppler Wessels's hand with an earlier riser.) In Imran's account, 'I protested to [the umpire] Jack van Geloven about Daniel's bowling and asked for a ruling ... Mike Brearley spotted that the umpire was confused and came running up to me, rather than the umpire. We had a fairly rude exchange of words and Mike Gatting had to drag Brearley away.' Here some slight discrepancy exists with Brearley's own account of events. He told me, 'It was a bit rich for complaints about bouncers to be coming from Imran, who wasn't averse to bowling them himself. I wanted to get my point across to the umpire, I seem to recall, whom Imran was blatantly trying to influence. So I said something like, "Imran is pissed off because he couldn't get it up." Which I admit to be provocative. Imran marched towards me almost as if he was going to hit me with his bat. I stood firm. At this moment my arms were gripped from behind by my young colleague, who had come trotting in from mid-on, and who thus managed to deflect my ire from Imran to him. From the [press box] it may have looked like I was about to have a physical fight, which wasn't the case.' Both sides at least agree about the timely intervention of that master of diplomacy, Mike Gatting. In his report van Geloven stated that he had 'never heard such ripe language, either on or off the cricket field, as Imran's' – high praise coming from a man who had played for Yorkshire in the 1950s. As a result the TCCB asked each county to enquire and to take action. On 15 July the board's Disciplinary Committee stated that the matter was closed, as they were satisfied with the 'firm reprimand' Sussex delivered to Imran, and with Middlesex's perhaps lesser 'expression of regret' that Brearley had become involved. It remains a rare instance of two of cricket's otherwise most dignified figures 'showing all the finesse of a pair of Irish drunks', to quote, if not endorse, van Geloven's private account.

Despite or perhaps because of missing several early matches, and seeing others lost to rain, Imran was consistently able to operate at full steam that season, and often to pitch the ball fearsomely short. He came down on Hampshire, in early July, like a wolf on the fold. Imran hit the visitors' attack for a run-a-minute 114, including a six and 16 fours, then ran in to bowl with 45 minutes left on the first evening. Hampshire were soon 8 for one, which brought the young Mark Nicholas to the crease. He was to tell me that the memory of what followed was still quite vivid.

> Christ, it was horrific. Imran bowled up the hill, Garth le Roux came down it. I had a little school thigh pad and was wearing a helmet for the first time. I was so far out of my depth it was a joke. The umpire, Barry Meyer, muttered to me to get down to Garth's end, which was marginally safer, he felt. I didn't manage it for long. Next over, I was back facing Imran. The first ball whistled past my visor at startling pace. The next ball thundered into my gloves and the third caught the thinnest edge of the bat as I tried to avoid it. I often tell people that I shouted 'Catch it!' I turned and watched what seemed to be a slow-motion image of the dark red ball hurtling to the wicketkeeper's right side miles back. That put an end to my misery.

By this stage in the season, Arnold Long seems to have actively reconsidered his policy of playing Imran only in every other match. Sussex went straight from demolishing Hampshire to an away fixture with Glamorgan. Imran took four for 25 and four for 8 in the two Glamorgan innings, between which he hit their attack for 124 in slightly over 90 minutes. As a result, everyone went home a day early. For all that, Imran remained oddly diffident about his batting, or at least showed an exaggerated respect to certain bowlers, as again seen by Paul Parker. 'I remember him being deeply apprehensive in the dressing-room at the prospect of facing Pat Pocock, and another occasion when he and Bomber Wells were batting at Hove against Lancashire. "Flat" Jack Simmons was bowling at something less than warp speed, and Imran seemed positively mesmerised. He looked as though he'd never held a bat in his hands before in his life. He could sometimes do that against the spinners. Eventually Bomber hit Simmons for a four, and Imran promptly called a mid-pitch conference. "That was a fantastic shot," he said, with genuine awe in his voice. "How did you do it?" Bomber muttered something about using his feet, and Imran nodded as though this was a revolutionary new breakthrough. Next over he walked down the wicket and hit Simmons for six.'

Two months after their ill-tempered encounter at Lord's, Sussex and Middlesex met again at Hove in the semi-final of the Gillette Cup. Some residual warmth seems to have tainted Imran's performance. Mike Selvey remembers 'sitting upstairs in the Hove watching area as Imran bounced Wayne Daniel, who was our No. 10. From 80 yards away, I and the rest of the full house distinctly heard the Sussex keeper shout "You cunt!" before the ball had reached his gloves. Wayne, not a man to rile easily, was hopping mad and subsequently took six for 15.' Sussex lost the match.

There's something almost autistic about English cricket lovers, or at least the ones who faithfully attend county matches, wrapped up against the elements, as was the case throughout 1980, thermos in one hand and a pile of reference books in the other. I should know, as I spent much of that alleged summer huddled at various Sussex grounds obsessing over the players' statistics, most of which I knew better than my own family's birthdays. So before leaving the season, a final memory of Imran coming in to bowl against Nottinghamshire at the Saffrons, Eastbourne, on a typically dank morning in early August. On a pitch which offered a hint of swing but little perceptible bounce, even Nottingham's Clive Rice was to struggle to get the ball to rise knee-high. As the session progressed, one or two of his deliveries gave up the attempt and merely trickled through to the wicketkeeper, allowing for some good-natured satirical comment from the crowd about the wicket's resemblance to a 'rice pudding'. When Sussex came to bowl, the now 36-year-old Geoff Arnold, something of a past master of the conditions, went for roughly four runs an over. At the other end, meanwhile, Imran snapped into action with a full-service performance that was generous in its use of the late inswinger and hardly less restrained in the toe-crushing yorker and bouncer departments. He troubled all the Notts batsmen, the first four of whom were current Test players, scythed through the middle order, and wasn't afraid to slip in a seemingly innocuous slower one to account for the tail-enders, most of whom had edged in the direction of square leg by the time he came to release the ball. At the end of the session, Imran's figures were 13.3–5–11–5. Sussex took a first-innings lead of 156, and were ultimately denied only by a combination of Rice's second-innings century and the rain.

For the second successive season, Sussex were fourth in the county table; Imran took 54 first-class wickets at an average of 17.90, which was to bracket him with the distinguished quartet of Marshall, Procter, Hadlee and Lillee. He was again the leading all-rounder in English domestic cricket. But while there were few bowlers anywhere in the world to compare with Imran at his breeziest, he was always about rather more than raw power. There was also a functioning intellect. One of the Sussex players told me admiringly that Imran had been 'almost obsessive' in following the local weather forecast, and had often waited patiently for the Hove sea breeze to blow, 'at which point he would come steaming in at a hundred miles an hour, before just as suddenly slipping back a gear into a highly effective containment mode'. Such was his control, and his craftsmanship, that few batsmen played him with any sort of comfort even in the most lifeless conditions. In the last county match of the season against Gloucestershire in another mudbath at Hove, Imran bowled 25 first innings overs of brisk pace, with all the variations, and frequently made the ball pass disconcertingly close to the batsman's head. With any support from his fielders he would have returned better figures than his three for 71.

Imran's efforts for Sussex appealed not only to the cricket tragics who followed their team around to every match. They also attracted a much broader audience. It was noticed that, starting from the 1978 season, the percentage of female spectators at grounds where he happened to be playing rose beyond all previous recognition – one unscientific estimate is that there was an average of 700–800 young women at most such fixtures, and that 'they were there for only one reason'. Partly as a result, the Sussex chief executive, Roy Stevens, reported that the club's once 'crippling' overdraft would be paid off in the near future. In time various glossy magazines like *Vogue*, not previously known for their cricket coverage, sent correspondents to watch Imran in action. Such phrases as 'Bowls a maiden over ... Makes a nice catch ... Beautiful hair ... Thighs ... Sultry ... Imran is sex' duly went around like stops on the Circle Line. But the appeal was even more ecumenical than that. A then freshly elected MP named John Major remembers Imran as an 'inspirational figure'. To Margaret Thatcher and Ted Heath respectively, he was 'an adornment' and a 'role model', while one now middle-aged and eminently respectable female former Labour cabinet minister adds that there were 'few sportsmen capable of making an entrance with quite such a flourish. When I saw him, Imran ran on the field in a pair of tight white trousers, shirt unbuttoned, vigorously clapping his hands above his head. He seemed to be applauding the crowd, and of course we applauded him back.' As an exotic, Anglicised cricketer, perhaps Imran's only peer was Kumar Ranjitsinhji, later the Maharajah Jam Saheb of Nawanagar, who played with such distinction for Sussex and England at the turn of the 20th century. The swashbuckling 'Ranji' received the level of adulation then normally reserved for stars of the music hall. When he stepped out of a carriage or alighted from a train, reporters crowded round him, and there were impromptu press conferences at curbside and station – 'this was a man', *The Times* wrote, 'more famous in the great salons of London than any statesman'. Some 70 years later, much the same could be said of Imran.

Writing in his magisterial history of Test cricket in Pakistan, the journalist Omar Noman would say of the Khan phenomenon, 'His wider appeal was based on a lethal combination – sexuality and power ... The truth or the exaggerations didn't really matter; what was arresting was the marriage between sex, wealth and power. Some of the most glamorous women in the world seemed to be captivated by him.'

After the setback of losing to India, Pakistan soon continued their rapid ascent of Test cricket's unofficial league table. That was not, however, to preclude some lively internal debate. Imran, for one, was 'never totally convinced' by Javed's captaincy skills, and seems not to have been alone in his doubts. Wasim Raja referred to Javed as a 'precociously gifted batsman who was impatient with others who didn't come up to his expectations' – mild compared to the remarks of one former player who described his captain, in his no doubt jaundiced opinion, as a 'talented shit'.

As the Test team's most consistently successful player, Imran could and did command a respect among his colleagues that Javed himself could only feebly approximate. Wasim Raja likened the situation to one of those 'feudal regimes with a boy king [nominally] in charge while the first minister actually calls the shots'. By all accounts Imran's influence extended to everything from cricket technicalities down to certain of his team-mates' individual style choices. For example, he advised Abdul Qadir to affect a 'pointed French-style beard' on the grounds that it would help to unsettle the opposing batsmen, and had the advantage that 'it works with the women, too'. And, certainly, that bowler's ducal glare back down the wicket was a significant part of his armoury over the years. For the next 18 months or so, Imran increasingly came to be seen as a spokesman for senior players such as Majid and Zaheer in airing their views about Javed and the board. Below these men were various newcomers to the Test side, some of doubtful worth and others of real craft and enterprise. Taken as a whole, Pakistan would soon come to rival the West Indies as the pre-eminent team of the 1980s.

At the turn of the year, a side of young MCC players made a visit to the Middle East. In Dubai they came up against a combined Indo-Pakistan team including Imran. Notwithstanding his baptism of fire some five months earlier, Mark Nicholas recalls that 'I somehow got a few runs this time ... Imran was delightful, encouraging me to make the most of my talent and telling people I could play a bit. He was the most generous of opponents in that way. Not what you'd expect.' Imran's hostility might be professionally unnerving, but he had a sense of duty to promising young opposition players. A second tourist broadly concurs with Nicholas, adding that 'this seemingly aloof Pakistani' was only too ready to offer technical advice and coaching if approached by a suitably deferential junior. 'See Imran about it' became a by-word on the tour, he reports. 'In just about twenty minutes in the nets, he taught me more than the official management team, who were more concerned about what sort of blazer we wear at dinner.'

A small and touching example of Imran's celebrity status in Pakistan came later that winter when his father took him to inspect the harvest on the family farm in the rolling hills of Mian Channu, some 240 kilometres (150 miles) west of Lahore. This was not exactly a hotbed of pop culture, and most local inhabitants came by their knowledge of the outside world only from what they read in the weekly six-page newspaper. 'My father insisted that we ate at a crowded restaurant near the rest-house where we were spending the night,' Imran says. 'Next morning we were woken up by a panic-stricken *chowkidar* who insisted that unless I came out the front door would be broken down. When I did so, I found that there were thousands of people waiting outside. My father was genuinely bewildered.'

Some of the same general passion, as expressed by players and spectators alike, went into the always exuberant, frequently disputatious, albeit not invariably distinguished world of Pakistani domestic cricket. By common consent, the prevailing atmosphere was competitive bordering on the pugnacious. In particular, the sporting reputation of the Quaid-e-Azam trophy, the local equivalent of the county championship, was an unenviable one. As Zaheer Abbas remarks, many of the fixtures went ahead against a background of 'chair-fights, stone-throwing and ugly skirmishes with the police'. Relations between the players tended to be brittle, and displays of truculence were a way of life. The level of strife varied, but many of the encounters bore little relation to a game of cricket in the traditional sense of the phrase. Disparaging references to an opponent's immediate family remained a popular playing tactic. Sometimes satire gave way to more explicit observations on an individual's regional or ethnic origins. Many Pakistani umpires came to look on a degree of verbal or other abuse as an occupational hazard. I was told of one particularly heated exchange taking place in the 1980–81 season in which a player had ultimately seen fit to menace one of the match officials with his bat. After cooler heads intervened, there was a subsequent attempt to make amends during the tea interval. The umpire did not immediately accept the batsman's apology, and the two men ended up rolling around on the pavilion floor, discussing the matter. The incident could have just been 'one of those things', as the umpire himself later chalked it up, part of a 'regrettable failure of understanding, [a] mutual loss in perspective' engendered by the heat of the battle. This was to show commendable generosity on his part, although, with the best will in the world, it's hard to imagine quite the same level of animation being seen at, say, the Saffrons, Eastbourne. Wasim Raja offered still another explanation, years later, that may have been closest to the mark. The batsman in question, he opined, was, like all too many of his colleagues, 'a jackass'.

Imran made another of his comparatively rare appearances in the Quaid-e-Azam that winter, prior to the arrival of the West Indians for a four-Test tour. Appearing for PIA early in October in a three-day match against the House Building Finance Corporation, he took three for 31 and three for 20 in what was officially described as a 'decorous' contest. A fortnight later, PIA were involved in a perhaps more typically spirited affair against Muslim Commercial Bank (MCB) at the Bakhtiari Youth Centre, Karachi. PIA enjoyed a first-innings lead of 125. Imran bowled just four overs in MCB's second innings, during which the bounce of the ball is reported to have grown 'increasingly low and devious', though with the odd lifter that, by contrast, 'shot vertically towards the chin'. After one such delivery the opening batsman Anwar-ul-Haq retired hurt for the remainder of the proceedings. The next morning the MCB team declined to leave their dressing-room, although the umpires declared the wicket to be fit. PIA won by default. Needing to take their last two games they could manage only a draw against Habib Bank, and finished as league runners-up. Curiously, just three weeks later the same MCB team conceded another match, at Lahore, on the grounds that nine of their players were injured and unable to field.

Fresh from their successful tour of England, the West Indies reached Pakistan later in November. If the visitors' batting was solid, it was for its bowling – not always a thing of beauty, but rich in intent – that Clive Lloyd's side was most remembered. Once Michael Holding was injured, the attack consisted of four men, Marshall, Garner, Croft and Clarke, who between them claimed 54 out of the 65 wickets which fell in the Test matches. One can only wonder what they might have done on pitches which actually helped them. By contrast, Imran toiled in virtual isolation; as he says, 'For much of the series I was bowling with a spinner at the other end, which, apart from anything else, doesn't give you a lot of time to recuperate between overs. [I] was exhausted.'

The first Test, at Lahore, was a rain-affected draw. The ignominy of an early home defeat had loomed on the first afternoon when Pakistan collapsed to 95 for five, which brought Imran to the wicket. It could fairly be said that he rose to the challenge. Such was his temperament for the situation that he not only scored 123, his maiden Test century, but put it in a personal context by completing his international double of 1,000 runs and 100 wickets in the process. Every report of the match makes much of the fact that these landmarks occurred on Imran's birthday. One Pakistani journalist wrote, with perhaps a touch of hyperbole, that this was 'only befitting the nation's greatest sportsman, and perhaps her greatest citizen'. General Zia was to send a telegram noting the 'happy coincidence' of the date, something Imran himself seemed to endorse when he later wrote, 'I recorded my first Test century on the day I turned 28.' Under the circumstances it seems almost a churlish technicality to mention again that he was actually born on 5 October, and had thus celebrated his birthday some seven weeks earlier, in the less rarefied atmosphere of a pre-match practice session for PIA held at the Gymkhana Ground, Karachi.

West Indies won the second Test, at Faisalabad. A discreet veil can perhaps be drawn over the specifics: the spinners took all 20 wickets for Pakistan, and Imran's chief contribution was to drop Viv Richards at long off when he was on 5 – a costly error. Predictably, Pakistan's first defeat on home soil in 11 years was not well received by the local community. Several thousand fans stayed behind after lunch on the final day to express their misgivings about Javed's team. A number of those who had celebrated 'the fulfilment of our aspiration [and] pride' in the triumphant series against India now tore up posters of the players, burned them in effigy, and attempted to set fire to the team bus. This may be one of the occasions Imran had in mind when he later told the *Sunday Times* that he had come to trust his own judgement, not that of the crowd. 'Once, when I went out to bat, I was cheered all the way. I was out without scoring a run. They were shouting at me again, but this time they were telling me I was useless ... How can you let yourself be defined by views that change so quickly? If I took notice of what most people said, I'd never achieve anything.'

Javed's decision to bat first on a wet wicket in the Karachi Test was subsequently the subject of some lively dressing-room discussion; Pakistan were soon 14 for four, with Zaheer *hors de combat* after being struck on the helmet, producing an echo like that of a gong, by a Croft bouncer. In another keenly debated move, Pakistan had elected to go into the Test with only one fast bowler: Imran. He responded with four for 66 in the West Indies' only innings, sufficient to ensure a draw. The fourth and final Test, at Multan, had the same result. The match was delayed on the first morning by the late arrival of an umpire and on the second afternoon by Clarke's action in throwing a brick into the crowd. Play was suspended for 45 minutes by the ensuing riot. Imran took five for 62 in the West Indies' first innings. Unlike the opposition, he wasn't afraid to keep the ball up to the bat, even when Viv Richards was in full cry. Richards later paid fulsome tribute to 'the Great Khan's' arsenal of 'subtlety, accuracy and searing pace, [and to] his ability to regularly get reverse swing with the old ball'. He was the 'complete player', even if one Caribbean newspaper was to remark archly of Imran the fielder that he sometimes 'appear[ed] to be moving with his bootlaces tied together'.

Most if not every series in which Pakistan were involved seemed to result in a debate over the umpiring. This one was no exception. The West Indies had reportedly thought their opponents 'rather shrill' in their appealing, which *Wisden* later characterised as 'almost a case of affray ... The Pakistan way of approaching the umpires en masse, and the filthy language that was used, caused great concern.' A long-serving home official, Khalid Aziz, took the opportunity to tell the press that on several occasions he felt himself to have been 'pressurised' to bend the rules. Speaking on condition of anonymity, one of Aziz's Test match colleagues made broadly the same claim, adding that his health had suffered as a result. He was on 'pills' and could 'hardly sleep a wink for worry'; perhaps not surprisingly, there had been some 'shocking' decisions in the Tests. Rather than specifically defend their own officials, Imran and his colleagues instead pointed out that some of the umpires elsewhere in the world were just as bad. By 1981, the Pakistan board had taken up the cause of appointing two 'neutrals' for every Test, a campaign Imran vocally championed right through to his retirement.

For the time being, Javed Miandad remained Pakistan's captain and gave every indication he was in charge. His public persona proved a fair substitute for the Imperial authority of earlier years. Each match day he carried out a routine in which he was driven from his hotel suite to the ground, where a respectful crowd of spectators and journalists gathered to watch him put his men through their paces in the nets. Anyone incurring Javed's displeasure was subject to a stinging reprimand, as Zaheer, among several others, could attest. The captain's own form was steady if not spectacular, as shown by a Test average of 32 against the West Indies. For all that, there was growing pressure from the board both to reverse the recent downward trend in the team's fortunes, and to do so with 'the grace befitting our sporting culture'. Pakistan were to fall somewhat short of these ideals in their coming tour of Australia, which culminated in a players' revolt. 'Soon,' Imran recalls, 'there was much speculation about who was going to be the next captain. Matters became rather complicated when Javed and Zaheer both made it known that they would not play under each other.' At that, word came down from the highest level of government for the board to appoint a figure of 'national stature'.

FIVE

The Downhill Struggle

In 1981, just as Imran was being manoeuvred into Pakistan's most coveted job, not excluding that of the state presidency, he came close to being sacked by Sussex. The problem was nothing to do with his on-field performance. What seems to have concerned the club was their star player's relaxed approach to certain contractual details, or more specifically what his newly appointed county captain calls his 'flexible timekeeping'. At the risk of perpetuating a stereotype, a broader cultural factor may have been at work alongside any personal idiosyncracy. As often noted, there tends to be less emphasis in Pakistan than elsewhere in the world on a strict adherence to the conventions impinging on the individual's total freedom of movement, and a disdain for most forms of centralised authority. Anyway, Imran appeared two days late for the start of the new English season. Sussex fined him £400 and issued a very public 'firm reprimand'. He says that he came close to leaving the club as a result, whether by mutual consent or at his own insistence, and spent 48 hours alone in his flat brooding on the matter. One well-positioned source with a vivid command of simile says that it was all down to Imran's 'chronic disorganisation, and the club's heavy-handed reaction to it ... He was invariably 30 minutes late wherever he was supposed to be ... When he made appointments his hotel room became a bottleneck – it was like a Mexican brothel, so one gathers, with people queuing up outside his door for hours. I don't mean that it was in any way a knocking shop, just that there were constantly mobs hanging around.' Nor can a touch of vanity be completely discounted. In his first autobiography, Imran writes that 'Sussex said that the rules applied to all the players, but to me that seemed ridiculous ... The club felt that I was just the same as anybody else on the books, but cricket is not like that. We should never be categorised in the same way, because one player's value is different from another ... The club treated me like a schoolboy. It hurt my pride.'*

Imran's vocal displeasure may have been fuelled by the relative severity of the fine, which resulted in some hardship – £400 was a significant slice of his basic annual salary, which in 1981 rose to £5,450. (For purposes of comparison, the Survey of Hours and Earnings puts the average pay for a male 'unskilled or minimally skilled' manual labourer in the UK of the day at £5,800 p.a., rising to £6,340 in London and the South-East; as Kerry Packer remarked, most county pros were in the game 'strictly for sandwich money'.) On a point of principle, Imran declined a lucrative offer early that summer from Dr Ali Bacher, the former Springbok Test captain and future administrator, to play a season's cricket in South Africa. There was some initial confusion when Bacher referred to the sum involved as 'the sort of money Paul Newman makes'. The only Paul Newman with whom Imran was personally acquainted was the young Derbyshire all-rounder of that name, who would have been earning even less than he was. After the error had been discovered, it transpired that Bacher had had in mind a figure close to £20,000 for three months' cricket, which would have been 'irresistible' in other political circumstances.

Later that season, a mutual Indian friend introduced Imran to an entrepreneurial English designer and budding sports marketeer named Jonathan Mermagen. Imran told Mermagen that he was seeking to 'significantly enhance' his income by taking commercial or sponsorship work. By now the need to support an increasingly vibrant London social life placed additional strain on an already precariously balanced budget. But Mermagen was able to offer only limited immediate prospects. 'Most firms at the time wanted to do business with an Ian Botham or some other specifically English player,' he told me, 'and even then the sums on hand weren't astronomic – £10,000 for a Weetabix ad was considered good going.' Imran, who seems to have had a clear-headed understanding of market realities, then met an expatriate Pakistani businessman named Naeem-ul-Haque, who headed the London branch of the Oriental Credit Bank. He, too, was unable to offer much in the way of a personal financial lifeline. 'While I was happy to

* The county chairman who signed off on Imran's fine, Tony Crole-Rees, coincidentally had a vote of no-confidence passed against him later in the season, but refused to resign. It was symptomatic of a stormy year in the Sussex committee room.

be Imran's bank manager, it was all pretty basic stuff. The sad fact is that he was being paid peanuts.'

Within this particular limitation, Imran was to have a comparatively happy and successful fifth season at Sussex. The county had the best championship run in their history by playing purposeful, attacking cricket, with Johnny Barclay, in his first year as captain, positive and challenging in his attitude, and open to the occasional whimsical declaration in pursuit of victory. At 28, Imran was now at the senior end of the playing staff. In the group photographs taken each April, he'd edged ever nearer the centre chair, and at one point had been in contention for Barclay's job. He remained one of the less naturally effusive members of the team. Imran's usual practice both at Sussex and elsewhere was to offer advice, like a constitutional monarch, only when asked. 'He was a less warm guy than, say, le Roux,' one of the players adds. 'You wouldn't call him a barrel of laughs. But he could still gently take the piss out of everybody, including himself. [A colleague] once went nuts in the dressing-room after a match we lost and informed Imran that he was a fucking bouffant-haired ponce. Punch-ups have broken out for less. And Imran looked up and said, "Well put, sir. Spot on. Let me shake your hand."'

Imran's policy with women wasn't all that different from that with men whom he wanted to charm: he flattered them, listened to them, teased them and generally threw in some self-deprecating wit. Added to his looks, intellect and 'Oxford urbanity', as *Today* put it, it was a potent formula. His impressive train of girlfriends came to a temporary halt in 1981 when he met the 16-year-old Reynu Malla, a Nepali princess. Although apparently serious, the relationship ultimately foundered in the face of determined opposition by Reynu's mother. Where the likes of Marshall, Garner and Croft had failed, Mrs Malla had successfully 'intimidated' Imran, according to a close friend. 'He basically retreats into himself with anyone he doesn't know well. I often told him he was brilliant, unique – he wasn't pained by such suggestions – but also that he could perhaps make breaking the ice with people less obviously an effort.'

Umpires aside, the one issue inextricably linked to Pakistan cricket over the next decade was that of ball tampering. Imran was first to hear the mutterings about so-called 'anomalies' during the 1982 tour of England, when at least one newspaper took the opportunity to display a diagram of 'balls identical to those used in the Test', with arrows helpfully locating 'the seam' and 'shiny side'. Following another muckraking headline which managed to conflate a technically flawed analysis of seam bowling with the broader innuendo that 'the Pakis' were bad sports, a group of tabloid journalists and TV reporters with cameras in tow had taken up position behind the Lord's pavilion in order to await Imran's appearance at the close of play. He came out and went straight past them, causing one member of the posse to write accusingly of him 'wearing a blazer and flared slacks, calmly sauntering off towards his girlfriend, seemingly unconcerned about the claims against his team'. But the implied attack on his integrity had cut deeply, and Imran would find himself regularly challenged on the subject of ball abuse right through to 1996, when it became an issue in the libel case brought against him in the High Court.

Reverse swing, tampering's entirely legitimate and much envied distant cousin, also came to public view in 1981, when the TCCB introduced a new standardised ball for use in first-class cricket. The ball's thicker seam acted as a rudder for fast bowlers who, under the right conditions, now began to make certain deliveries apparently defy the laws of physics by sliding through the air in either direction, with no apparent change in the bowling grip. As a further (again legitimate) aid to the process, one side of the ball would generally be allowed to roughen with use and the other would be vigorously polished with sweat from the bowler's brow, or perhaps other agents. The theory and in some cases the practice was that the ball would then swerve towards the shiny side. A potent visual symbol of reverse swing was the hapless batsman who, having spectacularly misread the flight and declined to play a shot, was left surveying the total ruin of his wicket. As we've seen, Imran was among the first to master the art, and in particular the extravagantly curving 'banana ball' that was to bring him a rich harvest of wickets in 1981 and beyond. He told me that he'd first successfully applied the technique in the Melbourne Test of January 1977, when 'towards the middle of the match the pitch had gotten so hard it began to take lumps out of the ball, which then behaved like a boomerang'. Seeming to illustrate the point, Imran returned figures of none for 115 in the Australian first innings and five for 122 in the second. This was sometimes the only way to make the ball swing on the arid pitches in Pakistan, he added, 'where even club bowlers knew how to do it'. In later years, Imran became perhaps understandably tetchy when his critics continued to speak of reverse swing 'as if it were some kind of black magic', whereas 'really all you need are dry wickets and the right degree of skill'.

After paying his fine and settling his differences with his county committee, Imran had no further complaints about the 1981 season. By early August, while England were playing out their unforgettable series with Australia, the championship had come down to a race to the post between Sussex and Nottinghamshire. Once again, the festive Eastbourne ground, flag-strewn and filled to capacity, was the setting for a game of extraordinary fluctuations and drama when the home side took on Derbyshire. To quote *Wisden*'s account of the match, 'In a thrilling climax, Imran, who had earlier in the day taken four wickets in five balls, hit a swashbuckling unbeaten 107 to take Sussex to victory with five balls to spare. He hit three sixes and eleven fours, reaching his 50 in only 36 minutes, and his century in 88 minutes as Sussex chased a tough target of 234 in just under two-and-a-half hours.'

Wisden being a chronicle, this was certainly a fair and balanced statistical summary of the proceedings, but it hardly begins to do justice to what happened. The sides were effectively level on first innings. An untypical local heatwave appeared to sap the energy from the match, and both sets of batsmen were offered only cut-price bowling, which they treated with exaggerated respect. A draw seemed inevitable when, shortly after lunch on the third day, Derbyshire stood at 226 for five in their second innings. Seemingly desirous only to serve the batsman, Geoff Arnold and Colin Wells were wheeling away to David Steele, who by then had accumulated 59 in a shade over three hours. Johnny Barclay remembers that at this point 'Imran tapped me on the shoulder and said, "I can stand it no longer. Let me have a bowl." I said it was all right by me as otherwise we were all going to fall asleep, and at that Imran ran off and an over later ran back on again, having changed from his trainers into his boots.' There was a brief conference among the fielding side. As a result Imran took over from Arnold, and the immediate rise in pace was calculable in dozens of miles per hour. Derby lost their last five wickets for one run, with Imran returning figures of four for one. As Barclay adds, 'Perhaps still high on adrenalin, he then asked to be promoted in our batting order, and under the circumstances I was happy to oblige.' Imran went in at No. 4 and promptly erupted, smashing 45 off five overs before Derbyshire called for drinks, including a huge pull for six off Oldham which cleared the crowd and disappeared in the direction of the Town Clock, and then finished the job with two minutes to spare. I was there, and the general impression was as if a tornado had appeared out of a clear sky and touched down in the Sussex countryside, which in a way it had.

Imran's colleague Paul Parker adds one perhaps salient detail to what happened that sunny Friday afternoon. Whether or not it detracts from an extraordinary all-round performance is for others to say. Parker told me that, after running back on the field before his devastating final bowling spell, 'Imran said to me, "Watch this", whereupon he took a bottle-top from his pocket and roughed up one side of the ball a little bit.' If true, Imran's initiative might seem to contravene the spirit of Law 42.5, which states that 'No one shall rub the ball on the ground or use any artificial substance or take any other action to alter the condition of the ball.' It's worth mentioning here only because the match in question took place a fortnight or so before Sussex played Hampshire in a late-season championship fixture. Of the latter game, Imran would famously tell his biographer Ivo Tennant, 'I have [sometimes] scratched the side and lifted the seam. Only once did I use an object. When we were playing Hampshire, the ball was not deviating at all. I got the twelfth man to bring on a bottle top and it started to move around a lot.' One or both of the players' memories may be playing tricks on them, but it does seem as though they are talking about two separate incidents. Without condoning them, it's perhaps these isolated lapses which make Imran engaging; at almost all other times he was the embodiment of cricket's elaborate rules of gallantry and fair play, a man whom the umpire Dickie Bird calls 'the most honourable player' he ever saw.

The championship was effectively decided on the evening of 18 August, when Imran and Garth le Roux took the second new ball against Nottinghamshire at Trent Bridge. Needing 251 to win, the home side were 215–9, with their somewhat rotund last-wicket pair of Eddie Hemmings and Mike Bore – 'Tweedle-dum and Tweedle-dee' in one unkind but popular local chant – at the crease. Imran tore in to bowl and Hemmings, raising his bat, extended the pad. There appeared to be some mid-wicket exchange of pleasantries between batsman and bowler. Imran let fly again and Hemmings met him with a forward stroke of irreproachable correctness. A bouncer followed. Hemmings squatted underneath it. It became almost a *pas de deux,* with Imran consistently aggressive, straight and fast and the tubby tail-ender relentlessly defending. Nottinghamshire survived for the draw. The 16 points of which they deprived Sussex were 14 more than eventually separated the two teams in the table.

A week later Sussex beat Hampshire by eight wickets at Bournemouth. Imran took four for 50 in the first innings and then showed his all-round ability with a century in two hours. His batting average for the season was over 40. Garry Sobers was visiting England and thought Imran 'good enough to go in at three or four for any team in the world. In fact I asked him why a batsman as fast on his feet as he was felt it necessary to wear a helmet. He replied that cricket was his living, and he wanted to live long enough to enjoy it.' Imran contented himself with a cameo of 37 in the next fixture against Middlesex, while returning match figures of ten for 93.*

Nottinghamshire finally clinched the title by a whisker from Sussex, who were in the process of beating Yorkshire at Hove when confirmation came over the loudspeaker that they were officially runners-up. It was the county's best finish in the championship in 117 years, and would remain so for another two decades. A season which had begun with Imran sulking in his flat ended in an uninhibited display of irresponsibility, happiness and mass inebriation (though he himself stuck to milk). After seeing off Yorkshire, the entire Sussex squad stayed behind for a party, at the climax of which, led by their two overseas fast bowlers, they stripped off and streaked round the Hove ground. A resident of the adjoining block of flats named Beryl Kenworthy subsequently sent the county a note about the incident. Mrs Kenworthy, who was 83, told the club secretary that it was a sight that would 'long linger in the memory'.

Starting just five weeks later, Pakistan's tour of Australia was an altogether less congenial experience. The actual cricket was bad enough. To quote Imran, 'On paper a 2–1 defeat was adequate, [but] our solitary victory was on a slow, low Melbourne track reminiscent of conditions back home ... The sad truth [is] that the tour magnified our decline.' In the first Test Imran took four for 66 to help dismiss Australia on a good Perth wicket, but was then party to not so much a batting collapse as a full-scale implosion. As he says, 'Our first wicket fell as I was taking off one of my boots; our second went as the other one was pulled off and four wickets were down by the time I'd taken off my damp clothes. My batting boots were swiftly found and I walked out with the score 21 for five.' Not surprisingly, Pakistan lost that match, and went down in similar fashion in the Brisbane Test, where Greg Chappell hit a double

---

* Mark Nicholas recalls going out to bat for Hampshire that season in a Benson and Hedges tie at Hove. 'For some reason I came in without a helmet, sporting a wide-brimmed sunhat. Imran reacted with glee, relish and amazement. After the laughter had died down, he proceeded to bomb the hell out of me.'

century. The tourists' consolation win at Melbourne was a case of too little, too late. It says something for his colleagues' generally lacklustre performance that Imran, with 16 Test wickets at roughly 20 apiece and a batting average of 27, was named Pakistan's man of the series.

This being Australia, the cricket engendered strong emotions that more than once spilled over into what the tour manager's report called 'uncouth and unacceptable' conduct. Perth saw the infamous clash between Javed and Dennis Lillee. Although they varied when it came to the fine detail, both parties agreed on the basic facts of the saga. Javed, who was batting at the time to an accompanying chant of 'KILL, KILL, LILL-EE!', set off for a quick run and collided with the bowler, who then aimed a kick at him. This was the signal for each player to offer to knock the other's teeth out. Lillee's subsequent apology to the Pakistan dressing-room was not unanimously accepted. Meanwhile, Javed also found time to fall out with his vice-captain Zaheer, who at one point was close to leaving the tour. According to a first-hand source, the two men had 'gone mental' and 'hurled abuse around' in the course of a public difference of opinion in the Melbourne pavilion. Imran successfully kept the peace on that occasion, but later added that he didn't much care for Javed's captaincy as a whole. 'It was like a nightmare,' he notes. 'Throughout the tour, Javed was complaining that he hadn't been given the team he wanted, but then why did he accept it?' The always fickle Pakistani media now again decided that their cricketers were a national disgrace. After the tour was over, the board issued a statement blaming their team's failure in Australia on 'a sorry lack of cooperation' between the senior players and their captain. Ten of the players promptly issued their own statement, in which they declined to play any further Tests under Javed's leadership.*

Javed confesses that he felt 'something amiss' even before reading the players' views, several of the team having refused to speak to him (always a potentially ominous sign) during a training session held at the Gaddafi Stadium, Lahore, in February 1982. The following week, the Sri Lankans appeared for a brief tour of Pakistan. One of the visitors says that a senior Pakistani opponent had greeted him by asking, 'Are you here for the death-watch?' Later that same night Imran and his

* Amid the various ructions taking place in Australia, there were moments of light relief. The tourists' habit of shouting frequent encouragement to their young off-spinner Ijaz Faqih, as in 'Faqih, you've got him!' or 'Faqih, yes!' was always a popular talking point.

nine colleagues publicly confirmed that, while 'patriotic professional cricketers', they were not necessarily committed to the current regime, and would thus withdraw their labour. (Two of the signatories, Iqbal Qasim and Wasim Raja, later returned to the side after being pressurised by National Bank, their domestic employers, to reconsider their position.) The board backed their captain, with the result that Pakistan appeared for the first Test at Karachi with a somewhat unfamiliar look to their team. Four players made their international debut, and others like Haroon Rashid were recalled some time after their representative days had seemed to be over. In due course Ijaz Butt, the chairman of selectors, resigned as a protest against what he reportedly called the 'degradation' of his nation's cricket. Even with a second-string side, Pakistan won the first Test and drew the second, albeit helped by a number of hotly disputed umpiring decisions.

Not for the first time, Pakistan's cricket management seemed to be directionless, and no one immediately came forward to seize the wheel. As one Karachi news outlet complained, it had become 'quite impossible' to find anyone to explain exactly what was going on behind the scenes. In Javed's version, the air had begun to go out of the rebels' balloon as early as the end of the first Test, 'when I received word that Imran was very keen to return to the team and have a bowl at the Sri Lankans. However, the organisers of the revolt [put] immense pressure on him to stay put.' Another theory is that the board became alarmed by the prospect of their having to send a weakened team to England later that spring, particularly in the light of what had happened under similar circumstances in 1978. Imran himself recalls that 'there was a very real threat of crowd disturbances' should Pakistan have taken the field for the third Test at Lahore without their senior men. 'I think the tipping-point was reached then,' Wasim Raja told me, 'when people began throwing rocks at the committee room windows.' Shortly afterwards all parties were to announce a somewhat strained compromise: Javed would lead the side at Lahore, but resign the captaincy immediately following the match. As a result, the eight dissenters now found that they could play under him after all, if only for one last Test.

Javed won the toss at Lahore and decided to field. Imran had one of his more notable Tests, returning match figures of 14 for 116. Despite the loss of a day to rain, Pakistan won by an innings.

* * *

Imran's capacity to keep the different sides of his life 'oddly separate' from one another was something that struck at least one of his young team-mates at Hove. 'He'd turn up for pre-season training, and I'd say, "How was your winter?" He'd say, "Boring." I've just spent six months reading about brawls in Australia, and players' revolts and riots and God knows what, while I'm living at my Nan's house in Worthing. And to Imran it just wasn't worth mentioning. No one, nothing, impressed him that deeply.'

Quite apart from his more exotic off-season life, there was a widely held view among his Sussex colleagues, and one or two others on the county circuit, that Imran was 'different'; as one player told me, that there was a 'day-time Khan' and a 'night-time Khan'. The former was an unrelenting, resourceful, somewhat austere and utterly dedicated professional who could be relied on to give his all for the side. The latter was the gregarious, Oxford-educated smoothie who tended to go directly from the cricket ground to the latest scene. Somerset's Nigel Popplewell had occasion to see both Imrans at work. 'I'd go and stay with Sussex's Ian Greig, who I'd been chummy with at Cambridge, and Imran was often there. He was extremely courteous, and along with Greiggy and le Roux, always great company. Fun guys. But you could forget about getting any bowling concessions out of them simply because you bought them a beer the previous night. Ian Gould, when keeping for Sussex, had a ruse to fire up Imran and Garth. He would stand a couple of yards closer to the bowler who was bowling more quickly so that he took the ball above his head, or at least on the rise. He'd then shout to the other one who he thought wasn't bending his back enough, trying to get them to hit the gloves just as hard. The result was a blitzkrieg.' When Popplewell came in to bat in Somerset's first game of the new season, against Sussex at Taunton, he found five men around him with hands outstretched, as if expecting him to faint. His friend Imran promptly bowled him a bouncer and his university chum Greig held the catch.

Another Cambridge man, Alastair Hignell, was part of a Gloucestershire side that came up against Imran that month. In Procter's absence, the Gloucester attack looked 'grotesquely thin' when confronted by the world's leading all-rounder at full sail. Sometimes the only way to get him out was by boring him. 'Imran belted a four or two and was starting to look dangerous,' Hignell says. 'Anything could happen. After a hurried conference, we hatched a plan in the belief that he'd be so insulted by Phil Bainbridge's (very much) slower ball that he would want to hit it for six over square leg. The catch was that deep square was the longest boundary, and we reckoned that if we could get a fielder into that area without Imran noticing, he might just hole out. Accordingly at the changeover before each of his overs, Phil would mutter to me which delivery was going to be held back and, as he was running in for that ball, I would, as unobtrusively as possible, back-peddle to the boundary ...' The plan seems not to have worked, because in that particular innings, Imran was caught Stovold, bowled Shepherd, having hit 31 in a shade over 20 minutes. At the close of play he sauntered into the Gloucester dressing-room, thanked them for a fair fight, raised a glass of milk and then apparently slipped off alone for a quiet night in at his flat.

Some time later, Air Marshal Nur Khan, the urbane if, to his critics, somewhat feckless PIA president and chairman of the home authority, rang to offer Imran the captaincy of Pakistan. Despite pressure from General Zia, the board's decision hadn't been easily reached. 'Imran's name was suggested but many people were opposed to him,' the Air Marshal revealed. 'Some felt his performance would suffer while others thought he was too irresponsible. His playboy image didn't help.' In fact, until recently Imran's only backer of any importance had been the Pakistani team doctor, who was his cousin. A number of the senior players envied his widespread name recognition but thought his star quality would quickly fade in the heat of a Test campaign. For his part, Imran, too, had certain misgivings about the post. The general consensus in May 1982 was that the Pakistan side, though talented, were close to unmanageable; also, that the honour of captaincy tended to come with compensating personal drawbacks, as had apparently been the case in Ian Botham's unhappy term in charge of England in 1980–1.

Imran thought about it for two days, and then decided to accept the board's offer. He made it clear to them that he would expect complete freedom of action and a 'full voice' in selecting the team. Over 11 years, his progress through the ranks hadn't been easy. Alternately fawned on and knocked by the press, at the forefront of two players' revolts and tainted by World Series Cricket, he rose to the top through hard work, undisguised pride and an utter unwillingness to mince words. His principal conviction was that 'I knew I could do a better job than [Javed on] our dreadful tour of Australia', when the team had sometimes seemed to be competing against themselves more than the Aussies. Among the first to call Imran on his appointment was Zaheer Abbas, who 'didn't hide his disappointment' at again being passed over.

Zaheer was also not alone in having reservations about his new captain, whose only other first-class leadership experience had been at Oxford University. (Not necessarily impressive credentials, for a whole variety of reasons, to some of his more aggressively populist colleagues.) Only in retrospect does the appointment appear to have been a stroke of genius. At the time many people wondered what would happen to the already fissile Pakistan team now that the tough-talking, libidinous Pathan was in charge. Since around 1976, a consensus had formed about Imran that wasn't always that complimentary. He was, as one close friend allows, 'opinionated'. Compared with Javed and his other predecessors and successors, Imran was an anomaly in arguably the most insecure office in Test cricket: a fiercely proud but personally unaffected man who, when teased by a colleague that he would rather be right than captain, replied, 'I'd rather be anything than captain.' On top of that he was intelligent, gruff and kissed up to no one, including the home board. On the face of it, this would not necessarily seem to be the man to 'heal our national wounds', as General Zia put it a touch floridly.

As noted earlier, Pakistan had done well in the 1978–79 series by beating India twice in three Tests. It should have been the beginning of a process that created a united team of strong minds and a clear sense of self-worth – both as individuals and as a unit. Instead the side had gone on to be losers in four series and winners in two, with one drawn. It was hard work and they stuck to it well enough, but there was rarely that all-important sense of authority from the top. This was perhaps the great failing of Mushtaq Mohammad. A supremely affable man and an Anglophile, he had become an increasingly defensive captain who tended to treat Test matches as though they were all part of the county championship. As Imran says, 'Mushtaq would use the phraseology of English team captains about "pitching the ball up and let [ting] it do the work", even when this was courting disaster.' It was part of a larger mindset that had seen successive Pakistan touring sides be almost absurdly deferential, both on and off the field, to their British hosts. Under Imran, the first order of business was to slay the inner Mushtaq and 'impress on the world that we were as good as anyone'.

The defining characteristic of Javed's tenure had been not so much excessive modesty as it was the captain's apparent inability to get along with most of his team. Here, too, Imran was to signal a clear break with the past. Although not immune to playing favourites, he was to prove a unifying force who was at once open to suggestion – 'a good listener' according to Intikhab, the new team manager – and swift to put an end to the practice whereby there had often 'seem[ed] to be 10 or 11 Pakistan captains all muttering away' in the field. It would be fair to say that Imran came to enjoy the loyalty if not always the unbridled affection of his men in a way hitherto unknown in his country's 30 years of Test cricket. Essentially a federalist who saw the many diverse elements of Pakistan as a single entity, he was to rally the various troops under his command into a 'lean [and] cohesive fighting unit', in much the way that Frank Worrell had moulded the West Indians into a world-beating side in the early 1960s. The cricket-loving author Jeffrey Archer believes that the more obvious comparison is with England's Mike Brearley, albeit with one critical distinction not lost on Imran himself. 'When the chips are down, the players want someone to come out and actually score runs or take wickets,' he remarked. 'In a war, the last thing the troops need to see is their general lying dead at their feet.' Geoff Boycott adds that Imran was a 'thinking man who was very clear about what he was doing – I would have played for him in a flash', rich praise coming from one who has mixed views on most modern Test captains. Imran combined mutual respect with a certain detachment from his team. Wasim Raja said that one or two of the side had been 'healthily afraid' of him, and that Imran's otherwise 'highly polished' pep talks had often featured a 'bollocking' of any under-performing players. During his tenure few serious rivalries arose in the Pakistan dressing-room. Imran was also among the first to make extensive use of video and other modern coaching aids, was readily approachable at least up to nightfall, when he tended to vanish, and struck most of the foreign press as a breath of fresh air – to quote Peter Smith, long-serving correspondent of the *Daily Mail*, it was like 'talking to an Archbishop who dressed like Mick Jagger'.

Within 12 months Imran had emerged, partly through circumstances, partly through his own playing ability and his own character, partly through the patronage of General Zia and other parties desperate for success on the field, as the unquestioned tsar of Pakistan cricket, and the object of a rapidly growing personality cult. In time even Javed would come to recognise certain unique qualities in his immediate successor. 'When Imran became the captain, he led from the front and created an atmosphere in which there was no room for mediocrity. He made selection strictly performance-based. Everyone feared for their place in the side, and it motivated them to give of their best. Secure in his own abilities, Imran feared no one. This made everyone, the players as well as the cricket establishment, fear him even more.'

By nature, Imran was a 'disruptive element', Wasim Raja believed, to the men in blazers who administered Pakistan cricket. A source then close to the head of the national government refers to it as a case 'enjoyably like that of Dr Frankenstein and his monster'. It seems fair to say that Imran made little attempt to conceal his sense of superiority over the faceless bureaucrats, most of whom had never risen above club level, if even that, as players. There was also the fact that, unlike Javed, he was a university-educated product of the professional classes. Somehow this still seems to be more of an asset for the captain of a cricket team than might be the case in other sports. As Imran's friend the journalist Fareshteh Aslam says, 'He had the education and, perhaps more fundamentally, the self-confidence to take on the board when he had to.' As a result there was to be a 'steady drumbeat of official criticism' of Imran's tactics, even as these helped transform Pakistan's cricketing fortunes. 'The man we appointed,' in the austere words of one 1983 memo, 'remain[s] totally unwilling to bend or compromise with [his] employers.' It was the same with the players, to whom Imran gave some individual leeway, 'although ultimately all the leashes [were] held in his hand'. Wasim Raja was to characterise the team's reaction to their captain as one of respect and trepidation, rather than warmth, 'which was probably no bad thing'.

It's a truism that a captain is only as good as his resources, but, unlike Javed, Imran went out of his way to ensure that he at least got the team he wanted. The most obvious case in point was the gifted but enigmatic leg-spinner Abdul Qadir, who at that stage had played 11 Tests without ever threatening to impose himself on the side. Although his claims to a place on the England tour were impressive on purely cricketing grounds there was a general perception that the 26-year-old Qadir was, to quote one colleague, a contrarian of 'uneven mood' – in short, trouble. Imran not only insisted that his fellow Lahorite be on the plane to England. He allegedly phoned Qadir and personally invited him to tour; reportedly Qadir said nothing, but 20 minutes later rang back, accepting, explaining that he had lost his composure, 'Because, captain, no one has ever asked me to do anything for my country. You are the first one.' Imran similarly assured his mercurial predecessor that he had a full part to play in the side. In the event Javed had an indifferent series, managing just 178 runs in three completed Tests, but that was arguably more due to technical deficiencies than any man-

management issues. Imran described Javed to me as 'a great player in his day, who really became just a nudger from around 1982 [in] part because he didn't believe in weight-training, or even training, too hard'. A third member of the awkward squad, Sarfraz Nawaz, also went on the tour and gave no cause for complaint.*

On the downside, even Javed was to question Imran's treatment of his cousin and senior batsman Majid Khan, whom he 'ignored for the first two Tests ... It caused a good deal of tension, which affected team morale. It got to the point where Majid wouldn't join the team for practice sessions. While the rest of us worked away in the nets, Majid could be seen in some corner of the ground, sitting around in street clothes, showing no indication that he was part of our outfit.' A quarter of a century later, Imran conceded that his 'tough decision' to omit Majid from the first Test had been badly handled. 'I got the tour manager to give him the news' – which, not surprisingly, Majid received 'without enthusiasm'.

While most of the Pakistanis performed well enough in England in 1982, Imran himself was the weapon of destruction. He took 21 Test wickets – more than twice as many as his opposite number and fellow pace bowler Bob Willis – and enjoyed a batting average of 53. These were figures that effectively settled the debate about whether or not he would rise to the challenge of being both the team's captain and its star turn.

The Pakistanis arrived in June as firm underdogs to an England side that had memorably won the Ashes the year before. Defeat in both one-day internationals when the frailty of their batting on damp, green pitches was exposed, typically dour resistance in the Tests by Chris Tavaré, who took nearly seven hours over his 82 at Lord's, and a series of disputed umpiring decisions provided a stern examination of the tourists' character. Gradually, however, as England faltered and Imran's stature as a leader grew, they showed distinct signs of becoming a team.

Twenty-eight years earlier, the English captain Len Hutton had taken the decision to drop his long-serving bowler and friend Alec Bedser, who was 36, minutes before the side went into the field against

---

* Abdul Qadir formed a particular affection for his captain and mentor, and named his first son after him. Years later, as the proprietor of a Lahore Marriage Hall, Qadir began to worry about Imran, who remained a bachelor into his early forties. 'He should get betrothed as soon as quick,' Qadir said, 'otherwise there is a question mark.'

Australia at Sydney. The first Bedser knew of it was when the tour manager pinned the team sheet to the dressing-room door. Hutton told me that 'in the flurry of events' – a late arrival at the ground, dealing with the press, changing, tossing up – he'd simply 'failed to have [the] quiet word with Alec' that protocol demanded. 'These things happen in cricket,' Hutton added phlegmatically. Indeed, something very similar took place between Imran and Majid shortly before the first Test got under way at Edgbaston on 29 July 1982. The new 'Pakistani strongman', as the *Daily Mail* called him, had slept poorly and was understandably edgy at leading out a team which had mutinied against its previous captain and which contained no fewer than six former captains or vice-captains in its ranks. It's arguable that Majid, then 35, deserved to be dropped purely on form: his 11 previous first-class innings on tour had been 12 not out, 0, 8, 88, 16, 47, 8, 23, 5, 42 and 6, giving him a distinctly modest average of 25.50. Rival candidates such as the 22-year-old all-rounder Tahir Naqqash would seem to have been more in line with Pakistan's renowned youth policy. Whatever the rights or wrongs of the case, there were fireworks in the visitors' dressing-room. The 'bloody stab in the back' was carried out in a way Majid himself clearly found unacceptable. Thereafter a perceptible coolness descended between the two cousins for the next decade or so, with a gradual thaw later in the 1990s.

Quite apart from that, Imran's introduction to the captaincy was a baptism both of fire and water. The ground was a quagmire, with heavy rain sweeping from end to end only hours before the start, before drying out nicely just in time for Randall to score a century. A few isolated but vocal elements of the crowd then took it upon themselves to barrack the tourists, whose dressing-room, according to Wasim Raja, 'frequently appeared to be in volcanic eruption' as a result. 'We were reacting to racial abuse and to certain other language' which, in Raja's assessment, was 'ripe'. Adding to the already combustible atmosphere were the now somehow familiar-seeming umpiring controversies. In the Pakistan first innings Mudassar was lbw in unusual fashion when he turned his back on a ball from Botham and was given out in what Imran calls 'one of the poorer decisions' in Test cricket. Earlier in the season, England had hosted India in a three-Test series which the home side won 1–0. The Indians had asked that David Constant be struck off the list of match officials for the tour, a request the TCCB agreed to. It would be fair to say that Imran and his men were unenthused to learn that Constant would return just a month later to officiate against them.

England had made 272 in their first innings at Edgbaston, with Imran, although rumoured to be carrying a thigh strain, taking seven for 52. As it frequently would on the tour, the visitors' batting let them down. When they went to grab their chance, midway through the match, it evaporated as quickly as it had appeared; maybe it had never really existed. Earlier, it was thought that Imran had betrayed some tactical naivety by keeping his tired opening pair on against the English last-wicket duo of Willis and Taylor, who were able to survive and even engage in a relatively free-scoring partnership. Their stand of 79 was effectively the difference between the two sides. After an hour or so of this, even Imran was reduced to using the weapon of more mortal fast bowlers when frustrated – the bouncer. One can perhaps imagine his emotions on being slashed for four over the slips by Willis, a man whom he seems to have believed guilty on at least one occasion of using unduly provocative language to an opponent. Eventually set 313 to win, Pakistan on the fourth morning slumped to 98 for seven, with only Imran, who scored 65, delaying the inevitable. Mudassar was out for his second nought of the match, causing his captain to 'speak' to him, an experience the self-effacing batsman would 'not soon forget'. England won by 113 runs.

A fortnight later, the two teams met at Lord's. England were led by David Gower when Willis dropped out at the last minute with a sore neck – he could still barely move his head as a result of facing the Pakistan bouncer barrage at Edgbaston. In his absence, Robin Jackman and Ian Greig did much of the bowling for England. Despite this stiff challenge, the tourists scored 428, with Mohsin Khan making a double-century. England replied with 227; extras top-scored with 46, including 10 wides by Imran. One of the Englishmen recalls having to face this 'increasingly flamboyant' attack while simultaneously dealing with the problem of Javed making 'high-pitched bird noises from his position a few feet away at silly point', all part of the 'quite extensive' Pakistani psych-ops programme. There also seemed to be a generous amount of appealing, much of it conducted from the direction of long leg. Ian Greig was later to remark that one of England's batsmen had been 'clearly out', caught off Qadir. The batsman survived because, on that occasion, 'none of the Pakistanis said anything'.

While batting, Ian Botham was to have the first of what became a series of run-ins with Imran and the Pakistanis broadly related to law 42.5, dealing with tampering. '[I] could see that the quarter-seam was coming up and had been picked at. I took the ball to the umpires and asked them to have a look at it, and they were clearly worried by the state it was in. At the end of the over I had a word with Imran about it and he said, rather ambiguously, that the English bowlers might get it to swing a bit more if they "looked after it a bit better".' While there's of course no reason to doubt Botham's version of events, it's also true that Dickie Bird, one of the umpires in question, denies ever having had a problem with the Pakistanis in general or Imran in particular, whom he calls 'a gentleman'.

After Tavaré and the rain frustrated Pakistan on the fourth day, the tourists were left to make 77 runs to win. At a critical stage Imran had thrown the ball to Mudassar and suggested that he perhaps make amends for his pair at Edgbaston. Mudassar, an occasional seamer, took six wickets. Pakistan got home, in a steady drizzle, with less than five overs to spare. It was only the second time they had beaten England (the last one was in 1954), and the first time they had done so at Lord's. The result marked perhaps Imran's greatest personal triumph in the captaincy, and unleashed another round of both official and wildly spontaneous celebrations in Pakistan.

Obeying the unwritten rule which seems to demand that every Pakistani success be followed by a setback, they met with what Imran calls 'crushing disappointment' in the final Test at Headingley. Things began poorly for the tourists when both Sarfraz and Tahir pulled out with injuries shortly before the start. As a result Imran was forced to enrol the portly part-timer Ehtesham-ud-Din from the Bolton Association side, Daisy Hill. The 32-year-old seamer promptly pulled a muscle, took one wicket in the match and scored no runs. He did not play Test cricket again.

Imran having won the toss and chosen to bat, the tourists perhaps failed to make the most of a pitch that started untypically firm and flat. Their 275 was summarised by their captain, who top scored, as '50 below par' for the conditions. It was still too much for England once Imran had swapped bat for ball and taken five for 49 in 25 zesty overs. There was to be a 'regrettable lapse of decorum', to quote the late Sir Gubby Allen, in Pakistan's second innings, when Sikander Bakht was given out, allegedly caught by Mike Gatting at short leg. Neither Sikander nor his partner Imran seemed actively to relish the decision. And not just because the umpire was David Constant. As the television replays appeared to show, Sikander's bat had never remotely been in danger of making contact with the ball. Vic Marks, the bowler in question, told me that 'it was probably not a great call [and] one which seemed to colour Pakistan's view about English officials for years to come – the feeling was mutual'. A few hours earlier, the same David Constant had turned down a sustained Pakistani appeal for a catch at the wicket against David Gower when he had made only seven. The batsman went on to score 74. Gower recalls 'a very thin edge and the highly vocal displeasure of virtually the entire opposition. Imran didn't necessarily stand out in that department at the time but most of the words directed at me were in, I guess, Urdu, with the odd Anglo-Saxon epithet thrown in.' He adds that 'given the relations between the two teams in that era – strained at best – not walking was not hard to do. In fact, it was compulsory.' The subsequent feeling in the visitors' dressing-room was that between them these two decisions had cost them the match. England were left 219 to win, which always looked reachable, although at one stage they slipped to 189 for six, with Imran in full flow, coming around the wicket because the footholds on the other side had broken up. In another quite versatile performance he was to claim eight victims in the match, as well as to enjoy a batting average of 113. Pakistan lost the Test by three wickets.

In the series, incident-prone, certainly, but over time elevated into some mythic triumph of English fair play over Pakistani whingeing, there was roughly a cigarette paper between the teams. Or perhaps a disputed caught-behind decision. Although Pakistan narrowly failed to press home their advantage, the tour was widely seen – at least by them – both as a moral victory and a watershed in the country's cricket history. They would not lose to England in another series, home or away, for 19 years.

Chosen as the man of the series (and not exactly seething with excitement when Tom Graveney presented him the award), Imran generally lived up to his reputation and his own exacting standards. At nearly 30 he remained one of the world's fastest bowlers – '*the* briskest', in *Wisden*'s account – as well as strengthening his claim to a place among the world's top all-rounders. One of the delights of the tour, in this context, was watching Imran take on Ian Botham: two robustly self-confident players at their peak. Some 15 years later, Botham was to say that Imran had 'bowled beautifully' in the 1982 series, but had perhaps made something of a meal of his issues with David Constant. 'If Constant made a mistake, it was a genuine error, the kind that all umpires make because they are human,' Botham added.

Writing immediately after the England series, Imran would pay a reciprocal tribute to his 'friend' and 'opposite number'. 'I admire Ian for getting to the top while still remaining true to his individualistic instincts ... He's a dynamic cricketer ... He attacks in his bowling as well, giving the batsman a chance by pitching it up and trying to experiment.' Alas, instead of improving over time, Botham's bowling languished. 'Although he's supposed to have a bad back,' Imran was forced to conclude, 'I don't believe his action has suffered because of that. His main problem is that he's overweight.' Several years later, Imran summarised Botham to me as an 'extremely competitive player [who] was already in decline in his late twenties', at least in part because 'he lacked the training discipline' of certain other all-rounders. When I contacted Botham he told me, rather clearly, that he had nothing to say about Imran.

Although he did well with the bat and ball, the outstanding recollection of Pakistan's new captain would probably come not on the field of play but in the hour or so immediately following the end of the Headingley Test. After managing a somewhat wan smile on the pavilion balcony, Imran promptly went on from there to share some views about the English umpires. 'Constant cost us the match,' he told a press conference. 'Everybody knew that Gower was caught behind in the first innings ... Then came the decision against Sikander. I was at the other end and couldn't believe it.'

From roughly this point on, relations between David Constant and the Pakistanis began to deteriorate rapidly. Imran soon let it be known that his side had 'no confidence' in the umpire. Constant was reportedly keen to give his side of the story, but was prevented from doing so by his employers the TCCB. The mutual ill-will turned in fair part on personalities, as do most cricket controversies – few turn on cheating. Imran told me that it was Constant's 'high-handed manner' the Pakistanis had most objected to. Perhaps inevitably, this could, and did, lead to 'occasional grief' with a team always alert to the slightest hint that they were being condescended to. 'Everyone makes mistakes,' Imran conceded, 'but I felt that David's personal likes and dislikes were too near the surface. The man was uncouth on the field. In my hearing he once shouted out, "Oi! Get on with the game," after refusing an appeal.' Constant himself declined to comment, but one of the players recalled a 'small but vivid' incident in the second Test at Lord's when Abdul Qadir had enquired for lbw against Ian Botham, who had played all round the leg-spinner's straight ball. Qadir had been in 'a frenzy' and 'continue[d] to jump up and down and scream "Howzat?"' long after Constant's verdict of not out. The bowler eventually went into 'a war-dance of fury'. At length Constant had strolled across to consult his colleague Dickie Bird, and then 'quite clearly' announced that he would suspend the proceedings should such behaviour continue. 'Hold on, Conny,' Bird had muttered, whereupon he conferred briefly with Imran. Imran in turn spoke to Qadir, who then 'immediately turned around [and] bowled without further incident for the rest of the day'.

Debate about the Pakistanis and, more specifically, their 'dishy' and 'gym-honed' crumpet of a captain was everywhere in Britain. Newspapers, television shows and private conversations were awash with speculation about his social life. Not since Keith Miller 30 years before had a touring sportsman had so electrifying an effect on female spectators wherever he played. Unlike Miller, however, Imran was to be regularly splashed over the tabloids, part of a process he describes as 'journalists writing me up as some sort of playboy figure breezing through the staid world of cricket'.

It's perhaps possible to discount some of Imran's protests at his subsequent public image. Anyone who chooses to appear in the *Daily Mirror*'s centre-page spread 'stretched across his hotel bed wearing only a petulant expression and a pair of tiny, black satin shorts', to quote the paper's feature writer Noreen Taylor, is at least complicit in his own downfall. The news coverage as a whole deteriorated from then on, with pages of 'analysis' in broadsheets and tabloids alike, accompanied by endless gossip and supposedly intimate profiles, enlivened by various young women brought forward to attest to Imran's astonishing virility. Although he went along with it, much of what was written at the time struck even the *Mirror*'s (and later the *Sun*'s) cricket correspondent Chris Lander as toe-curlingly inept. 'It was prurience,' he noted, 'masquerading as news.'

Interesting scenes followed, often at the back doors of various English pavilions, where Imran demonstrated to foreign throngs some of his home appeal. He was frequently mobbed at the close of play, not least at Lord's, where Lander once saw him step outside into a waiting crowd of 'literally scores of journalists, news crews and a veritable chorus line of hopeful young women [while] a row of assembled schoolchildren waved Pakistani flags'. Imran easily entered into the hyperbole of tabloid fame; he was well aware that many of his interviewers knew little or nothing about cricket, but was too polite ever to say so. More than a quarter of a century later, one of his colleagues was to recall his impressions of that tour as 'a vast Imran love-in all the way ... tossed flowers, cheers ... constant flashbulbs'.

Though he would later become famous as a champion of the indigent and socially disenfranchised, at this point Imran still tended to prefer dating well-connected English girls with names such as Susie Murray-Philipson, Lady Liza Campbell and one Lulu Blacker, an intimate of the future Duchess of York. Another young woman from an immaculately smart family in Worcestershire went out with him several times in July and August 1982. 'Imran looked like a god, and was rather treated like one,' she reflects. 'People would approach him in the middle of a restaurant with that half cheesy, half apologetic grin that meant they wanted an autograph, if not something more. I seem to remember there was also a procession of bimbos slipping him notes, some of which I saw, with quite complicated messages like "My parents are in the country – ring before 10.30".' In between dealing with the interruptions, Imran was 'very solicitous' to his companion, asking what she planned to do with her life and what she thought of various issues. 'It was heady,' she recalls.

Another testament to Imran's trans-cultural charm was a recent boarding-school graduate who then found herself cooking directors' lunches in the City of London while waiting to be discovered by Hollywood. Now in her mid-forties, she speaks warmly of their few, 'strictly platonic' dates together. 'Imran gave new meaning to the phrase "playing the field",' she admits, 'but oddly enough you always felt you were the only girl in the world when you were with him. Very few men 30 years ago actually listened to women. Imran treated you seriously and was never one of those guys you sometimes met who told you your face was your experience and your hands were your soul – anything to get those knickers off. Your big rival, of course, was cricket, [where] sometimes his enthusiasm ran away with him: this was a man who thought it OK to plonk you down on a damp rug for eight hours to watch him take part in what, for me, was a meaningless encounter between two sets of men dressed like loony-bin orderlies.'

The setting of many of Imran's social encounters from around mid-1982 was Tramp, the private nightclub in London's Jermyn Street founded by a former Brighton bookie named Johnny Gold. Jonathan Mermagen put his friend up for membership when the Pakistan team was passing through London that summer. 'Johnny G was delighted and immediately started doing bowling actions, which I took as a yes,'

Mermagen says. 'After the likes of the Lahore Gymkhana, Tramp was a natural habitat for Imran, who virtually lived there for a time. He tended to be a fixture on the nights when he had a game anywhere within about 80 miles of London.' In its prospectus, the club offered its clientele the alluring promise of all-hours drinking and dancing. Oddly enough, Imran himself avoided both these activities. 'He tended to anchor himself at a table in the main dining-room where he could watch the action,' says Mermagen. 'As you know he never touched alcohol in general, let alone champagne. At some stage, though, he must have at least tried the stuff. I once asked him if the reason he didn't drink it was a religious thing. "No, I just don't like the taste," he said.'

Tramp was and remains a high-visibility haunt that attracts celebrities such as Andrew Lloyd Webber, Joan Collins, Jerry Hall, Elton John and the late George Best, the last of whom virtually became its in-house mascot. As a result there tended to be a lively tabloid interest in the club, with paparazzi routinely in attendance at the door. So even as he remained an 'intensely private' man, one who didn't bare his soul to others, Imran sometimes found himself in the limelight as a result of his social life. Another woman who met him in Tramp in 1982 assures us he was 'the most charming and courteous host' (although, as later became apparent, 'a snorer') who remained 'incredibly modest' given his achievements and connections: 'I only realised how famous he was when General Zia started leaving him messages.' Similarly, one of the Pakistan team reports to being impressed by the number of hats his captain wore while on tour. 'Next to Nelson Mandela, he was the most interesting man I ever met,' his colleague raves. 'He was surrounded by a fascinating aura, a magnetic field, and whoever he turned to, great or small, was energised [as a] result.'

One hot evening in August 1982, Imran made his way through a crowd of admirers and out of the Grace Gates at Lord's. After eventually hailing a taxi, he was off to a playing-fields fundraiser in central London. He was the star of the event, signing scores of autographs and telling one of the organisers that he also wanted to line up behind various environmental causes, which he later did by generously supporting the World Development Movement and Friends of the Earth.

At eight that same evening, Imran was at a gala to raise money to buy sports equipment for disadvantaged schoolchildren. Again, there were long queues for autographs. At ten he was at dinner in the West End with two male friends, one of whom remembers the 'innocent glee

Imran took in hearing all the gossip about people's love affairs'. Around midnight he was listening attentively to a spectacularly pert young woman seated next to him at a low-lit corner table in Tramp. A famously androgynous-looking British rock star and his entourage were sprawled around. Imran was very probably the only person on the premises to be drinking milk. Less than six hours later, one of the embedded Pakistani journalists would glance out of his hotel window to see his team's captain, clad in a green tracksuit, setting off for his early morning run, 'plough[ing] off into a steady grey drizzle with only a passing milkman or two for company'.

It was vintage Imran.

'When I reached the age of 30 I felt that the time had come for me to settle down,' Imran writes in his book *All Round View*. 'Just as I was becoming reconciled to the idea of an arranged marriage, I became involved with an English girl.' Although he fails to identify the woman in question, she was a 22-year-old artist named Emma Sergeant. They met at a small London dinner party given while the Pakistanis were touring England. Not long into the meal Imran had turned to Sergeant and said that he wanted to get to know her better, an understandable desire. At least two authors have since paid tribute to her 'dreamy, pre-Raphaelite beauty accentuat[ed] by lashings of golden brown hair', as well as to her 'arresting figure'. Smart, well read and socially ambitious, Sergeant, the daughter of a prominent City journalist, would cheerfully admit that she knew nothing about cricket. Johnny Barclay, Imran's Sussex captain, recalls, 'Emma was a bit aloof, which I think he probably liked. She certainly didn't fawn over him. I remember him once scoring a magnificent century at Eastbourne, and then coming through an adoring crowd at the close of play to find Emma sitting with her back to the field, putting the finishing touches to a painting of the pavilion clock. She possibly hadn't even been aware he was batting.'

In the 'fiercely independent [but] loyal' Sergeant, Imran had met the woman who would come to eclipse the charms of a contrived marriage in Pakistan. The result was a true and time-tested relationship. For domestic consumption, however, Sergeant would remain merely Imran's 'acquaintance'. In the elaborate protocol of Muslim life as it was familiar to the Khans, single men and women were generally allowed to meet only under closely controlled conditions, and sexual relations outside marriage remained a criminal offence, albeit one that required four witnesses to prove. The President's 'Zina Ordinance' of 1979 had gone some way to further formalising the rules on the subject. By the autumn of 1982, Imran had acquired a devotional status in his home country. In particular, for his team to have beaten England at Lord's struck some as a feat of almost folkloric proportions, one which 'in more mortal terms, stands beside the glorious march on Palestine [of AD 637]', in the words of one of those military-sporting analogies frequently heard on state radio. A degree of discretion was thought appropriate when dealing with the motivating force behind this coup. Even in England, the papers usually referred to Sergeant, if they did so at all, as 'one of Imran's companions' or, at the tabloid end of the spectrum, as a 'good' or 'close' friend. This concession to Pakistani sensibilities, often at the whim of individual editors, was only partly successful in conveying the impression that their nation's cricket captain led a blamelessly celibate life while in England. 'If I was written about in the gossip columns in London my parents sent me letters immediately,' Imran notes ruefully. 'I hated being portrayed as a playboy. I wasn't one – cricket was always my obsession.'

In the 12 months to September 1982 Imran had played seven Tests against three countries, quite apart from his prominent role in the 'gruelling' act of regicide that led to Javed's departure and his own appointment as Pakistan's captain. The timing of a three-Test visit that autumn by the Australians was unfortunate. Both Imran and his opposite number Kim Hughes were to remark that they and their men needed a rest, something not readily available in the gladiatorial atmosphere of the six-week series. Hughes threatened to end the tour almost before it had begun if any of his players was hurt by the repeated stone-throwing at the National Stadium in Karachi, which led to two walk-offs during the first Test. Trouble had seemed to be brewing as early as the pre-match knock-up, when the crowd had set fire to a boundary marquee. A month later, the third and final one-day international, also at Karachi, was abandoned after less than an hour's play, by which time at least three of the Australians had been struck by missiles. Hughes led his team off and declined all requests to return, at which point a full-scale riot erupted inside and outside the stadium.

In between these events, Pakistan comprehensively won all three Tests and both the completed one-day matches. It was their first ever whitewash of an opponent. Imran and his protégé Abdul Qadir were the main destroyers, with 13 and 22 Test wickets respectively. Compounding the public-order problems were the now regulation umpiring controversies. The Australians formally asked that the officials for the first Test not stand again in the series. Despite apparently 'solemnly agree[ing]' to the request, and issuing a statement to that effect, when the time came the Pakistan board reappointed the two incumbents. In the third Test, at Lahore, Imran took four for 45 and four for 35, as well as contributing runs from the middle order. Pakistan won by nine wickets. The Australian captain was to remark that if this was Imran when he was tired, he would hate to meet him when he was fit and rested.

Just 22 days after the Australians' abrupt departure, the Indian side under Sunil Gavaskar arrived for a 10-week, six-Test tour. For Imran there was a personal point to prove. Three years earlier, in India, the general consensus was that his younger rival Kapil Dev had decisively won the battle of the all-rounders. For a variety of reasons, the two men weren't personally close. 'The press had been very harsh on me and how I had clearly been eclipsed by Dev, sometimes forgetting that I had been injured,' Imran remarked. Although not a man in thrall to statistics, it would be fair to assume that he had a healthy awareness of his rightful place in Test cricket's pecking order. No one, it might be said, makes a living out of professional sport for 20 years without a certain inner competitiveness. In the event, Kapil Dev took a respectable 24 wickets in the series. Imran took 40.

For days beforehand, the home press had wondered if there would be any play at all in the first Test at Lahore. It was a reasonable question; for much of the preceding week the pitch was under water. As it was, the match was sparsely attended. There were just 955 paying customers on hand for the first session, the men and the women segregated in their own stands – disappointing in a stadium then seating some 38,000. Before the match the BCCP had sold the sponsorship rights to the series to the Paasban Finance Corporation, and between them had then raised the price of a five-day enclosure ticket from 400 to 1,500 rupees, or some £100, exclusive of handling fees. For real skinflints there were a few 'restricted view' bargains at 1,200 rupees. A couple earning 75,000 rupees a year after the now-mandatory *zakat* (income tax) would have to spend a fortnight's salary to watch the match without the aid of binoculars. Admission prices gradually fell, but the series was pathetically badly attended given the two teams involved. At Lahore, Zaheer scored a double-century in the soggy draw. Imran took three for 68 in the only Indian innings. Earlier, one of the junior Pakistan players had watched his captain practise alone in the nets during one of the lengthy rain delays on the first day. 'Imran bowled three successive balls which hit off, middle, leg. Then he reversed the order. Next he called for a volunteer to come in, and promptly uprooted his centre stick. The ball shot off the greasy turf and dipped in about a yard. It was literally unplayable. I speak with some authority because I was the batter.'

Imran's Aitchison contemporary Yusuf Salahudin met up with his old schoolfriend on the eve of the second Test at Karachi. Salahudin told me that they had stayed out perhaps later than was wise before a match of that importance, particularly as Imran was reportedly suffering from a mild case of flu. The team doctor had apparently advised plenty of rest. 'I was quite worried, because we'd rather overdone it,' Salahudin added with a chuckle.

A few hours later Imran captained Pakistan to the biggest victory over their arch rival in their Test history. He took 11 wickets in the match, which saw him pass 200 in Tests. It was a rout. The Indians got off to a less than ideal start after being sent in on a green pitch by losing Gavaskar, run out from a direct hit by Imran, who then accounted for Vengsarkar with a rare away-swinger. One of the Indians remarked that the very sight of the opposition captain 'eventually got to us, [and] when he came in to bat the next day I saw one or two of the guys quietly take a step back in the field. Actually, several steps back.' Imran scored a run-a-ball 33, part of a Pakistani total of 452, which gave them a tidy first-innings lead of 283.

What happened in the last session on 25 December 1982 is part of Pakistan history. Bowling with a familiar sea breeze at his back, Imran took five wickets in the space of 25 balls for seven runs. Asif Iqbal was in the pavilion and confirms that this was 'high speed bowling with all the trimmings. I'll always remember the ball he bowled to Viswanath, which swung in a yard to flatten the off stump as the batsman shouldered arms. The crowd was beside itself with glee. Vishy looked stunned.' Imran's second-innings eight for 60 was Pakistan's best individual analysis against India, and among the best returns in Test history. In the past, great fast bowlers had tended to be either the sort who had pace or those who had control, a Trueman or a Statham respectively. At Karachi, Imran combined both these ideals, while again exploiting the dark art of reverse swing. India's agony ended early on the fourth morning, when they lost by an innings. By the time the tourists arrived at Faisalabad for the third Test, spectators were holding up banners likening Imran to the F-16, the American-built jet fighter, 40 of which were then being delivered to the Pakistan air force. Unfortunately, the aircraft in question were to prove distressingly difficult to maintain to full operational level, another analogy to the national cricket captain over the next two years.

As usual where these particular teams were involved, the matches went ahead in a spirited atmosphere, with constant, loud, ball-by-ball vocalisations from the fielding side, as well as a generous amount of straightforward sledging. Javed Miandad remained the master, though by no means the sole proponent of what a former England Test captain euphemistically calls the 'gentle art of social interplay' between the players. As a rule, Javed's muttered remarks to the batsman on strike tended to be blunt and not necessarily distinguished by their Wildean wit, although, as noted, he also periodically varied the routine with some quite accomplished bird and animal impersonations. One Indian player said to me that before the series Gavaskar 'had told us just to ignore any abuse that came our way. The captain's advice proved to be easier [given] than taken. You have to imagine facing Imran Khan hurling reverse swinging thunderbolts at you while also dealing with a noise like an angry bee buzzing around your ear to get an idea of the challenge.' A well-directed radio microphone picked up a classic reciprocal bit of repartee on the first day of the Karachi Test when one of the Indian fielders greeted an incoming Pakistan batsman with the time-honoured enquiry, 'How's your sister?' For the most part, Imran himself remained above the unseemly taunting of opponents, though he seems not to have actively discouraged the practice among others. It's reasonable to say that the Pakistan players would have listened to him had he done so. By his eighth Test in charge Imran was proving himself to be a hands-on captain whose attention to detail was rightly legendary. His team-mates did not nickname him 'the General' (of particular resonance in a military dictatorship) for nothing.

Other than maintaining his own form and dealing with the team, Imran had two particular priorities as captain. He spent a large amount of time, every day, studying the press, briefing the press, warning his side about the press, berating the press – and then declaring himself indifferent to the press. In Wasim Raja's view, 'Imran saw the media as irresponsible because of the way they treated him. Every match he didn't take five for 50 or score a ton it was supposedly because he'd been out on the town the night before with an actress. They couldn't just accept that sometimes he had a bad day.' Imran's second preoccupation was with the home board of control. Here his tenure was to mark a clear break from the 'consensus captaincy' of his immediate predecessors. He would later characterise his experience of dealing with the BCCP over the years as 'a nightmare'. Although the parties seem to have co-existed well enough when it came to selecting the side (if only because Imran generally saw to it he got exactly the names he wanted) it would be made increasingly clear that it was the team captain, not the administrators, who ran affairs on the field. When the board secretary once invited himself into the home dressing-room for a 'chat', Imran promptly had him evicted. That particular sanctum was a 'working area' and not for 'gossip', he noted.

The third Test, at Faisalabad, was another personal triumph for Pakistan's supremo. On an unhelpful pitch, he had match figures of 11 for 180 in 56 overs against an Indian batting line-up strong enough to include Kapil Dev at No. 8. In reply to the tourists' 373, Pakistan were 367 for five midway through the third day, when Gavaskar would remember entertaining the hope that his team's first-innings deficit might be less than fifty. That was until Imran appeared. Over the next session and a half he scored 117, which included nine fours and five sixes. Most of the bowling was done by Madan Lal and Amarnath, a moderate pairing by Test standards, it has to be said, so that Imran at least had an opportunity to play himself in. Even so, he seemed to rise to the occasion. At 5.40 that evening, Kapil Dev came back into the attack. Imran deposited the third ball he faced from him back over the bowler's head and into a pastry stall. A short time later, he reached his second Test century. There was pandemonium. The game stopped. In due course Kapil Dev strolled up to shake him by the hand, followed by most of the rest of the Indian side. Salim Malik and Imran continued for a while, their partnership producing 207 until Imran succumbed, possibly exhausted. He became only the second player to have scored a century and taken 10 wickets in the same Test match, the other being Ian Botham, also against India, three years earlier.

Pakistan won the Test by 10 wickets, giving them a 2–0 lead in the series. A 'quite pleased' Imran collected his second man of the match award in succession. All that remained now was the traditional umpiring wrangle, which came when the manager of the Indian team, the Maharaja of Baroda, pronounced himself dissatisfied with the 'bungling' home officials. There was some passing talk of the Maharaja and a number of his men leaving the tour prematurely. The crisis blew over with the release of a statement by Sunil Gavaskar expressing his personal confidence in Pakistani fair play, which was sufficient, at least, to bring an end to the latest round of anti-Indian rioting.

January 1983, Hyderabad, was one of those peculiarly Pakistani occasions when a national triumph was soured by factional in-fighting. The bare facts are that after winning the toss Pakistan scored 581 for three declared in two days. Javed Miandad devotes a full chapter of his autobiography to an almost real-time account of his innings of 280 not out, and more specifically to whether or not Imran reneged on a promise to let him, Javed, chase the then record 365. Arif Abbasi, the treasurer of the home board, was one of those who believed that the captain went back on his word. 'On the third morning, Miandad got nearly twice the agreed number of runs,' Abbasi claimed, 'but then Imran declared.'

Checking the truth behind some of Pakistan's Test match history, particularly when it took place more than 25 years ago, is a time-consuming business. Javed Miandad declined, or ignored, my request to interview him. Another interested party did speak quite passionately, and on the record, only to apparently have a change of heart, signalled by a one-sentence letter informing me that our 'arrangement' was cancelled. Reflecting on the incident, Imran agrees that 'I told Javed something like "If you get near the target I'll give you a bit longer"', but denies having made a specific time commitment. Somewhere in the subsequent spat would seem to be the age-old question of whether cricket is a team sport or an opportunity for individual players to see their names etched up on the pavilion honours board. At the time Pakistan declared, Javed was scoring at roughly 30 runs an hour, and was still 85 short of equalling Sobers. It could be added that there were no fewer than 14 intervening Test scores of 280 or more. None of which particularly troubled Javed, who cheerfully notes in his autobiography, 'records are certainly important [for] me, and only a fool would say that they're not'. For his part, Imran remained that strange creature, a world-class sportsman bored by statistics. It's true he was generally aware of when he had a better all-round match than a Botham or a Kapil Dev, but he never worried about his personal averages. Once or twice, he misquotes these, to his disadvantage, in his own books.

Imran told me that the wicket at Hyderabad had been 'stone dead', and that at 581 for three it was high time to have a go at the opposition. 'If you have your enemy down then you never let him up,' he added, in a perhaps revealing overview of his wider management style. In the event, India scored just 189, roughly 400 less than the Pakistanis. Imran took six for 35. The home team won by an innings, with two sessions to spare. Imran received some noticeably tart press coverage for his alleged 'stab in the back', 'act of betrayal' and 'insult' towards his immediate predecessor. There was flak, too, from a well-known state political commentator who described his nation's Test captain as 'duplicitous'. No one could possibly be that and survive in Pakistani public life, the theory went. Javed himself eventually 'forgave' Imran, whom he describes as 'the most successful all-rounder of his day' and 'the best leader', although, in Wasim Raja's assessment, relations between the two 'never quite recover[ed] their old lustre'.

A few years later, one of Imran's female English press admirers was to write that what happened to him in 1983 was a tragedy of literally biblical proportions: here was 'a great and charismatic man [who] at his hour of triumph sacrificed himself for his people'. That might be pushing it, but the basic facts are stark enough. Imran told me that he had felt so physically fit during his first year or so in charge of the Pakistan team that 'I often found myself wondering, "How do people get old? How do people slow down?"' The answer was to come on the second morning of the second Test at Karachi (the one in which he nipped in for eight for 60), when Imran got out of bed and felt a throbbing pain in his left leg. The discomfort would come and go throughout the remainder of the series. Initially ignored, then misdiagnosed, the problem was eventually revealed as a 'gaping' crack in his shinbone. After the Indian series he was unable to bowl properly in a Test match for three years. Back in London, Imran would have a 'tough time' of his convalescence, according to Jonathan Mermagen. 'I remember he tended to limp off by himself in the afternoons. He was depressed ... I don't think any of us, Imran included, knew what would happen.'

Under the circumstances, certain other cricketers might have opted to sit out the last two Tests of the India series, given that Pakistan had already taken an unbeatable lead. Imran played in both matches, both of them drawn. One was curtailed by rain and the other, at Karachi, by riots. Despite visibly limping in his run-up, Imran took five wickets in the final Test, to finish with 40 in the rubber at an average of 13.95. When the time came to name Pakistan's man of the series there weren't many contenders, and the verdict was quickly reached. During the closing ceremony, Imran was lustily booed by some of the Karachi crowd. To put this in context, the city's leading local English-language paper had just published a stinging (and unsigned) front-page article rebuking the country's 'Lahorite captain' and his alleged cronyism, particularly as applied to Abdul Qadir.

Not everyone in Pakistan, then, was delighted with their team's comprehensive defeat of India. At least one highly respected radio commentator called for Javed's reappointment, an appeal the player himself didn't actively go out of his way to prevent. There were continued public protests at the board's decision to hand over the Tests to commercial organisations. Meanwhile, another group with a perhaps narrower focus attempted unsuccessfully to have the series banned from television, claiming that attendances at mosques had fallen away sharply between December 1982 and February 1983. A spokesman for the group, which petitioned the president, noted that the media's main purpose should be 'to implement and propagate Islam and not give mileage to a game more British than Asian'. As we've seen, certain regional news outlets also got tetchy, making it a point of honour to show their independence by carping. Imran earned himself some of the critical yappings and shin-bitings that invariably seem to greet even a successful Pakistan captain.

Then again, most public reaction was everything he could have hoped for. The celebration of Imran started like the feting of other Pakistani folk heroes of the day – generals, macho film stars, squash champions and so on. But it acquired a quality of its own and far outstripped the others. Omar Kureishi, the Asian equivalent of John Arlott, remarked that Imran's status as a combined sports star and sex god was especially noteworthy in a country that was 'frequently seen as a dour, sad and corrupt place. Things got particularly bad during Zia's early period when Pakistan went through one of its puritanical phases', relieved only by 'a sort of collective frenzy for our national cricket captain'. Omar's nephew, the British-born writer Hanif Kureishi, had a taste of this phenomenon in the mid-1980s when, on his first visit to Karachi, he came across an '18-year-old kid strung out on heroin, danc[ing] around and pointing to his quite prominent erection, which he referred to as his "Imran Khan"'.

Clearly, something unusual was going on. Even in that relatively recent past, Test cricketers tended to be the poor relations of the international sports scene. As a whole, they were badly paid, travelled around the world in economy class on flights or steerage on boats and existed on match-day meals of cheese sandwiches and tea rather than the latest upscale steroids. Imran may not have been the first player to enjoy his own cult following, but he was more or less single-handedly responsible for sexualising what had hitherto been an austere, male-orientated activity patronised at the most devoted level by the obsessed or the disturbed. And he did so on the basis of rather more than just a fetching haircut. Imran took 88 Test match wickets in 1982. It seems reasonable to say that the figure would have been higher had he made himself available for all three home Tests against Sri Lanka, given that he took 14 wickets in the one game he did play. Two months after they lost the series to Pakistan, the Indians under the captaincy of Kapil Dev began a tour of the West Indies. They were again comprehensively beaten. The journalist Dicky Rutnagur covered the series and believes that India 'were still both shellshocked and intrigued as to how Imran destroyed them'. He effectively ended whole careers. Within 12 months, four of the Indian top order including the veteran Gundappa Viswanath would be permanently dropped, or have retired. Along with England's Ian Greig and certain other players, so the *Jang* believed, they 'never quite recovered from their going-over at the hands of the "Orient Express"'.

Even Richard Hadlee paid Imran the compliment of comparing their bowling philosophies, in 'see[ing] every ball as like a bullet. There are six balls in an over, and six bullets in a chamber. Each one is a chance to hit.' Considering this tribute came from an arch rival, one can begin to appreciate the sheer depth of Imran's popularity at home in Pakistan. There was something akin to a civic nervous breakdown when it was announced that he might not be fully fit for the 1983 World Cup in England. New X-rays taken that spring showed that the bone in Imran's shin was not only cracked but close to shattering completely. A specialist named Peter Speeryn advised him against bowling for at least three months, but left open the possibility that he could play in another capacity. In time General Zia involved himself personally in Imran's treatment, insisting that the state would provide him with whatever facilities he needed or, failing that, fly him to England for surgery. The president's initiative was widely reported in Pakistani newspapers, at least one of which speculated that Khan would 'retire from the fray and accept a government position'. Imran appears to have had no particular political interest at this stage in his career, although both Jeffrey Archer and Johnny Barclay recall that he admired Margaret Thatcher for her sense of resolve, if not always for her specific policies. Imran eventually accepted a request from the BCCP that he play in the World Cup solely as a batsman.

In the factionalised society of Pakistan, even this compromise excited strong emotions. 'I had become the target of a planned campaign by certain journalists,' Imran recalls. 'A leading Karachi daily, the *Star*, carried a headline that I had sold out to the bookies' by allegedly faking his injury. Imran chose not to sue on that occasion, Pakistan's libel laws generally being less than congenial to the plaintiff. Many of the home press, in fact, seemed to be gripped by an advanced form of schizophrenia when it came to reporting on the nation's most famous citizen. On the one hand, there were constant editorials rightly remarking that Imran had smashed the inferiority complex affecting Pakistani cricket. On the other hand, these same proponents of national unity felt able to engage in an almost psychotic discussion of whether or not 'the great pilot' was in reality a Lahore partisan who viewed the rest of Pakistan with barely concealed contempt. In January 1983, it reached the point where Imran's attempts to discourage a pitch invasion at the National Stadium were seen by the *Star* as 'blatant discrimination [against] Karachi crowds'.

Pakistan had little trouble in disposing of Sri Lanka in their first World Cup group match, before losing to Richard Hadlee's New Zealanders. Things really started to unravel against England at Lord's, where the 34-year-old Sarfraz and his seam bowling partner Rashid Khan took just one wicket between them on a green pitch. All Imran could do was to watch impotently from mid-on as his side was thrashed with some 10 overs to spare. Three days later Pakistan played Sri Lanka for a second time. Midway through a rain-affected morning they were 43 for five, with the ball swinging around 'square' according to *The Times*. Imran won the day by scoring 102 not out. Pakistan then lost again to England but beat New Zealand thanks to an unbroken stand of 147 in 75 minutes between Imran and Zaheer, during which they took 47 off Hadlee's last five overs, enough for them to qualify for the semi-final.

The match produced two heroes, one on either side. Pakistan's opener Mohsin Khan held one end for 57 of the alloted 60 overs on what Imran calls a 'damp and uneven Oval wicket' (but which *Wisden* curiously describes as a 'good, firm pitch') to account for nearly half his team's 184. For the West Indies, Richards batted with a nuggety determination, first withstanding an onslaught from Rashid while he played himself in, and in the latter stages taking the battle to the enemy for an accomplished, unbeaten 80. Once again Imran could only watch passively, resisting any temptation he might have had to bowl, as his team crashed out by eight wickets.

In the glory-and-shame culture of Pakistan, this was another national humiliation, all the more so as India then somehow beat the

West Indies in the final. One Lahore-based journalist reached Imran by phone in London a day or two later. Although ostensibly an interview, their conversation had some of the trappings of a therapy session. 'I appreciate how you handled the business of the injury,' Imran said, referring to an earlier article in the man's paper.

'Think nothing of it,' the journalist assured him.

'No, I really mean it,' Imran protested. 'It means a lot. I'm very grateful.'

Fearing that Imran was about to turn maudlin, the scribe asked him if he would be available for that winter's tour of Australia, and Imran replied merely that he hoped to be. There was a 'very obvious tone of frustration and fatigue' in his voice. Back in Karachi, the *Star* was busy attacking Imran's captaincy and tactics, while remaining noticeably silent on the fact that he had topped the Pakistan batting averages. One prominent state television commentator then blasted 'King Khan's' team selection, and in particular his decision to play Abdul Qadir in the one-day side at a time when these rarely included a leg-spinner, or indeed a spinner of any sort. This would seem to have been another case of selective criticism. Qadir had figures of four for 21 against New Zealand and five for 44 against Sri Lanka, and could have turned the semi had Richards not been dropped off him when still in single figures. He topped the Pakistan bowling table.

In a frustrating, difficult time, Imran was as exasperated by certain aspects of county cricket as he was by his injury. Meaningless late-season fixtures played in front of a few hundred spectators would cause his eyes to glaze over. He needed the stimulus of the big occasion. After 12 years' experience of the personalities involved, Imran had further refined his views on what he called the 'old pro' syndrome. For these individuals, of whom every club had its share, 'cricket [was] a job, and they have played for so long that they're basically bored by it ... Because of his understanding of the game, the old pro spots talent very quickly, but is then envious, rather like the old man Salieri is of Mozart in *Amadeus*. They always told me not to experiment with my bowling action lest I lose whatever I had. A draw is a good result for them.' (Somewhere in the above, as well as a canny overview of the county circuit, would seem to be a healthy self-appreciation on Imran's part.) One such Sussex player was known to report to the ground in the morning dressed in a dark business suit and carrying what looked suspiciously like a briefcase. Imran, for whom cricket, while competitive, was 'fun – the world's greatest game', would never be mistaken for a bank manager. Nor, as noted, was he exactly 'one of the lads', eschewing, for instance, the spirited farting competitions that remained such a popular item among at least one element of the home dressing-room. Rather, he remained a 'princely cunt', in the view of one of his possibly less admiring and jaundiced county colleagues. By the time his team-mates made for the nearest pub at the close of play, Imran was typically on the fast train to London for a night at Tramp or dinner at some equally chic restaurant. This detachment, or limited involvement, became an increasing part of his life at Sussex, for whom he would play on a more sparing basis from the 1983 season onwards.

Curiously enough, while Imran was unimpressed by the 'old pro' in general, he had a soft spot for the *ne plus ultra* of the species, Geoff Boycott. The Yorkshire and England stalwart, then aged 42, was a 'self-absorbed' player, to whom making runs sometimes seemed nearly as difficult as making friends, but one possessed of 'almost incredible' powers of concentration. Imran would add that swashbuckling stroke-play was all very well, but Boycott 'was the one I admired over time ... I only wish Pakistan had had a few like him.' Twenty-five years later, Boycott in turn went out of his way to make his views on Imran known. 'He had a gift from the gods,' he said. 'There weren't many who could do what he did. It's fucking hard work, fast bowling.'

As if to prove the point, Imran limped through his next half-dozen county appearances following the World Cup. He continued to play for Sussex solely as a batsman, and, Boycott apart, it would be hard to imagine a stronger-minded one on the English scene. The club promoted him to No. 4 in the order, from where he enjoyed a season's average of 57. Imran eventually resumed bowling in early August, off a shortened run and at an appreciably less fearsome pace than when at full cry. He operated in some discomfort, and his pogoing leap had an unfortunate impact on his damaged leg. Even so, he took six wickets for six runs, including a hat-trick, in a losing cause against Warwickshire at Edgbaston, a match in which he also top-scored in both Sussex innings. There appears to have been some lively interplay between Imran and the home team's bowlers. The following week, the TCCB 'severely reprimanded Khan for continuing verbal abuse directed at the opposition after he had been hit on the chest by a short-pitched ball, and warned him as to his future conduct'. The language employed throughout was 'raw', according to the report. Sussex were handicapped by a variety of other problems during the season, including a bizarre injury to Ian Greig when he fell from the window of his flat, trying to gain entrance there after apparently misplacing his key. As a result, they finished a disappointing 11th in the table. Imran topped both the county's batting and bowling averages.

After six years at Hove, Imran and his English employers had come to know what to expect of one another. One of the club committee members would recall his star turn's 'amiable haughtiness ... [Imran] condescended to us. He seemed to think, and made us feel it, that one or two of the players possibly weren't quite his social or professional peers.' The county captain, Johnny Barclay, felt that Imran sometimes chafed under the various rules and regulations, and 'wasn't necessarily well suited to the treadmill of six- or seven-day a week cricket'. Another interested party was the Hove groundsman, who was occasionally required to double up as the club's switchboard operator. Some years later, this luckless man was to tell the *Sunday Times* that among his most onerous duties had been 'fielding endless phone calls from girls begging for Imran's number'.

This was funny, and it had the added value of being factual. Since arriving in Sussex in 1977, Imran had taken a series of comfortable but sparsely furnished rooms close to the county ground. He once remarked that he had 'basically only ever kept a bed' at Hove. Now even this small concession to standard club protocol was discontinued. From mid-1983 Imran's home became a fashionable split-level flat in London's Draycott Avenue, just off the King's Road. Taken as a whole, this was not your average county cricketer's lair. An indoor forest of gaudy statuettes and figurines, ethnic Pakistani rugs, brightly coloured cushions and exotic plants could have doubled as the clubhouse of an oriental cult or the set of a rather heavy-handed Grateful Dead biopic. There were several prominently displayed works by Emma Sergeant on the walls. Among them was a large painting of a burqha-clad Afghan refugee, which hung alongside a series of Mogul miniatures and an arresting portrait of a man holding a teacup in one hand and a woman's breasts in the other. The living-room took up the whole top floor of the flat. Downstairs was Imran's bedroom, with a gold-pleated canopy over the bed and two paintings of tigers at its foot. According to one visitor, the ambient smell was of incense. Among subsequent furnishings was a sofa covered in grey-fawn velvet and a vivid oil painting of Imran himself reading a book, the whole bathed by special 'moody' lighting. The overall impression was of a sixties art gallery crossed with a Sultan's harem. Imran seems to have taken a justifiable pride in his new accommodation, which remained his primary residence even after a fire destroyed most of his bedroom a decade or so after he bought the flat.

In his practical and optimistic way, Imran saw Draycott Avenue as both a convalescent home and a place to party. As his banker and friend Naeem-ul-Haque says, 'For someone who was thought aloof, he loved a good "do". He and Emma would hold court at his place or hers, usually with about 12 or 15 people sitting around on the floor. Lots of gossip. On Sundays we returned the favour, and they came to dinner at our house in Wimbledon.' Jonathan Mermagen adds that Imran was in the habit of returning with various man-of-the-match champagne awards, several of which were on ice in the Draycott Avenue bathtub at any given time. Imran's guests would enjoy the fruits of his labours, while their host stuck to milk – 'There were a lot of pissed English girls as a result.' Mermagen confirms that 'women in general tended to like Imran', whom he now told, 'You're a growing brand, mate.' Although in every other way the model professional, Imran sometimes struggled to balance his full social life with his playing schedule. One of the Sussex team remembers being amused at the way 'the great Khan would tear out of the ground and fling himself on to the first train, still wearing his tracksuit, at the close of play, then return again with minutes to spare in the morning'. British Rail being what it was in the 1980s, Imran's brinkmanship occasionally went awry. A colleague told me a story to illustrate this, although it's only fair to add that two or three other Sussex players I mentioned it to couldn't remember it. The story goes that Imran once arrived at Victoria station only to see that a particular train was delayed due to the familiar 'essential engineering work' on the line. As a result, he reached Hove a few minutes late for a group photograph with one of the club's commercial patrons. Feeling snubbed, a Sussex marketing executive later took the opportunity to lecture the entire squad on the importance of the brave new world of corporate sponsorship. Imran had 'bridled a bit', recalled a participant. 'It took five minutes to get through that situation ... [The official] was not pleased.'

There's absolutely nothing to suggest that Imran's affair with Emma Sergeant was anything other than a respectful, mutually fulfilling relationship. But it's conceivable it may not have been an entirely exclusive one. Imran's Sussex team-mate Tony Pigott remembers that there was always a 'large female crowd' waiting outside the Hove pavilion door on match days. Of course there's not a shred of evidence that they were specifically there for any one player, though Pigott detected 'a heightened sense of alert' whenever Imran appeared. Another colleague remembers leaving Hove at seven o'clock one evening 'sometime in the early eighties' (and thus possibly before Imran met Emma Sergeant) to drive to Cardiff, where Sussex were playing Glamorgan the following day. 'Just as I was starting off, Imran appeared and mildly enquired if I minded detouring to London on the way to Wales. He had a certain quite well-known actress with him. I said that was fine, so we drove to London, where the young lady in question alighted. Imran and I then continued on to Glamorgan, where we arrived at around two the next morning.'

Imran's friend Fareshteh Aslam was struck at how 'open and direct' he was with women, though, to her knowledge, his socialising never affected his cricket. 'Whatever the distractions, he was supremely dedicated.' Nor, by all accounts, would anyone promised a romantic night out by Imran have had much cause for complaint under the terms of the Trade Descriptions Act. Romance was somewhere he was very much at home. One knowledgeable source assured me that 'he wasn't one to make love by shouting "Phwoar" and taking a long running leap to join his mate on a bed which then collapses. You tended to get rather more in the way of candles and conversation than that.' Another party adds: 'You can forget about what you hear about all his womanising. He wasn't macho at all ... he *courted* me. Imran was a very, very sweet guy. You'd laugh all night with him, sleep in a canopied bed and in the morning you'd sit in a flower-filled conservatory, where he served you breakfast. What's not to love about a man like that?'

In mid-September 1983, Imran accepted an invitation from Shell, the festival's sponsors, to turn out for an International XI in a series of three one-day matches against the West Indies in Jamaica. In retrospect, he might have been better advised to spend the time with his feet up at home in London, particularly with Pakistan's five-Test tour of Australia starting just a month later. When Imran returned to England, X-rays showed that the fracture in his left leg had opened up again. There was a serious risk of his being left crippled should he take the decision to bowl at any time in the forseeable future.

In Imran's absence, Zaheer had captained Pakistan on a short tour of India. Having once declined to play one another for 18 years, the two sides had now met in four out of the last five seasons. On this occasion Sarfraz was absent for disciplinary reasons, and Abdul Qadir was omitted owing to a financial dispute. All three Tests were drawn. Imran then informed the BCCP that he was available to play in Australia as a batsman, an offer they accepted. They further asked him to captain the side. Imran pointed out that in that case he expected to be allowed to choose his team. This tested the board's patience too much; over Imran's reported objection they announced that the young opener Shoaib Mohammad, Hanif's son, would be included in the squad. The subsequent dispute led to the mass resignation of the Pakistan selection committee. Meanwhile, Imran was already enthusing about a whippy 17-year-old fast bowler and lower-order batsman named Wasim Akram. He would make his international debut 12 months later, taking 10 wickets in his second Test. Like Abdul Qadir before him, Wasim became something of an Imran protégé; it wasn't lost on certain sections of the Karachi press that all three men came from Lahore. For its part, the *Star* was lobbying for Imran to go to Australia as a batsman under Zaheer's captaincy. Another Karachi-based daily assured its readers that the 'pernicious Khan' was paying the price for once having kicked a local boy who ran on the field during a Test when he was batting. The boy had thereupon put a curse on Imran's leg, which would remain *hors de combat* until its owner sought out the boy and apologised. This was quite rich stuff even by the standards of the Pakistani tabloids. I asked Imran if he remembered the incident. 'Yes,' he said. 'Unfortunately, I kicked the boy with my right leg and it was the left one that had the fracture.'

On 17 October, an already largely unfancied Pakistani tour party arrived for four months in Australia. On his first full day there Imran consulted a specialist, who told him not to even pick up a bat until after Christmas. A second opinion confirmed the diagnosis. At that Zaheer assumed the responsibilities of captaincy, and promptly issued a statement bemoaning the fact that the team was not the one he would have chosen. With Imran immobilised, the tourists' fast bowling would be largely in the hands of relative newcomers like Azeem Hafeez and Rashid Khan, men who had acquitted themselves well for the likes of Allied Bank, but who were now faced by batsmen of the calibre of Greg Chappell and Allan Border. Midway through the tour, the Pakistanis called up the now 35-year-old Sarfraz Nawaz, who after a three-day search was eventually located in Bombay. The great contrarian undoubtedly enlivened the dressing-room, but like his colleagues was unable to do much about the Australian batsmen. Even the highly touted Abdul Qadir finished the series with a Test match bowling average of 61. In something of an understatement, Qadir later remarked that he had been 'outmanoeuvred'. His failure in Australia was seized on by the Karachi press as evidence that he was only in the team as Imran's pet, or an 'apple-polisher' who never missed a chance to play up to his captain – an obvious and vile calumny, not that there was any telling his critics that.

On doctor's orders, Imran sat out the first Test at Perth, which Australia won by an innings. There were to be heated words in the visitors' post-match inquest. Zaheer, perhaps reasonably enough, asked whether, under all the circumstances, Imran might not prefer to fly home to London rather than to sit glaring at the team from the players' balcony. Imran said that he wouldn't. A two-day thunderstorm saved Pakistan in the second Test at Brisbane, which Imran also missed. From their bunker in Lahore, the BCCP then issued an invitation for Zaheer to assume the 'full and unfettered' captaincy of the side for the balance of the tour, though Imran would remain on hand as a potential player. To some surprise, Zaheer declined the board's offer. He would captain the team on a Test by Test basis, but nothing permanent. The belated arrival in Australia of the BCCP chairman added yet another layer of perplexity and rivalry to the tour hierarchy. Disgruntled players knew that they could lobby either the chairman or the formally designated captain, Imran, to reverse decisions by the caretaker, Zaheer. Wasim Raja, who was on his 10th overseas tour, later called the whole administrative set-up a 'rolling disaster'.*

It seemed to be more of the same in the third Test at Adelaide, until Javed remembered why he was there and started hitting Lillee back over his head on his way to a century, one of three in Pakistan's first (and only) innings of 624. It wasn't enough. The tourists' attack, a farrago of the up-and-coming and the over-the-hill, failed to capitalise, and Australia were able to bat out time for a draw. Imran then had another X-ray, which showed no significant improvement after his two months of enforced inactivity. However, it was felt that his mere presence on the field was worth 'a gift of 40 or 50 runs' in Wasim Raja's unscientific, but reasonable estimate. There was a full meeting of the Pakistan committee on 15 December, the eve of a four-day match

* To add to the already Byzantine arrangements, the former Test captain Intikhab Alam remained the Pakistanis' official manager. Fortunately, the easy-going 'Inti' harboured no professional or personal ambitions, a rarity on that tour.

against Tasmania at Hobart. In his best peacekeeping mode, Intikhab reportedly asked if everyone would be happy if 'the Skip' now made his tour debut, but with no promises about his possible return to the Test side. Various batting options were discussed. Zaheer hemmed and hawed. Finally it was left at this: Imran would go in at No. 3 against Tasmania. When Intikhab so informed Wasim Raja, the latter 'actually sighed with relief'. As he later said, he felt this was 'the end of all our worries in Australia'.

Not quite.

Imran scored 13 and 19 in the match against Tasmania, which Pakistan narrowly won. As a result there seem to have been two schools of thought on what to do about team selection for the fourth Test, which started at Melbourne on Boxing Day. There were those who saw a non-playing captain staring at them from the pavilion as necessarily being something of a spectre at the feast, and thus not exactly a boon to team morale. On the other hand, Imran could hardly ask another batsman to make way for him after the Pakistanis' huge total in the previous Test. The tour committee eventually came up with a compromise solution. Imran would captain the side at Melbourne, where he would appear as one of no fewer than seven specialist batsmen. The committee elected to drop the 36-year-old off-spinner Mohammad Nazir, sometimes known as Nazir Junior, who had achieved a return of one for 217 in the first three Tests. 'I felt his absence wouldn't make much difference,' Imran notes, accurately if perhaps a touch clinically. In the event, the veteran bowler never played for his country again.

Pakistan batted first at Melbourne and made 470, thanks largely to a century by the opener Mohsin. Imran scored 83, which took him all but four hours. Lillee once told me, 'We thought he could make 50 every time he went to the wicket.' Imran had done so often enough when Pakistan were in trouble to lend force to that argument. He had ample time to reflect on his injury during the Australian reply of 555, in the course of which even Zaheer was forced to bowl 22 fruitless overs. Imran had previously taken the opportunity to warn his predecessor as captain that he 'might have to turn his arm over'. Abdul Qadir took five for 166, over four sessions, in the latter stages of which he reeled about like a dazed flyweight boxer. In their second innings the tourists collapsed to 81 for five, which again brought Imran to the crease. He scored 72 not out and effectively saved the match. The pain in his leg returned about midway through the day, causing him to eschew the quick single and hobble somewhat between the wickets. Although he didn't yet know it, his stress fracture had opened up to something approaching twice its original size. As in the first innings Imran was again unchivalrously encircled, with some of the sledging not so much making note of his infirmity as seeming to actively revel in it. The word 'hopalong' was used. In all he batted for some seven hours in the course of the match, compensating for his imposed limitations with a dour, Boycott-like concentration.

Australia won the last Test at Sydney by 10 wickets, and took the series 2–0. Imran paid a gracious tribute to the better side, making particular reference to Chappell, Lillee and Marsh, all of whom retired from representative cricket. Zaheer then flew back to England, saying that he needed to prepare for his benefit year with Gloucestershire. A semi-regular column continued to appear under his name in the Karachi-based *Dawn*, recording Imran's many alleged defects as a captain. Zaheer again reminded the board how positively he would respond to any approach they might care to make to him in the matter. Meanwhile, Imran stayed on in Australia to lead the team in 10 one-day internationals, nine of which they lost. The whole protracted saga finally ended in early February, when Imran and his men flew back to a muted reception in Pakistan. Perhaps predictably, the home board was toppled in a coup and replaced by a rival group headed by General Safdar Butt, a keen mountaineer with no known prior interest in cricket. Their first act was to appoint Zaheer as captain. The board then falsely informed the press that Imran had 'diverted' money from some of the junior players in Australia, a smear several of the Karachi papers saw fit to report in regular banner headlines over the coming weeks.

In March 1984, Zaheer's Pakistan beat England 1–0 in a three-Test series. England had warmed up for the event with a brief tour of New Zealand, where they, and Ian Botham in particular, were accused of converting their dressing-room into an alleged 'opium den', to quote one local paper. Peter Smith of the *Daily Mail* would remark that he 'still didn't know what Both thought of the "investigative" press at this point' ('the scums of the earth', he later discovered), but confirmed that it was an obviously 'edgy' relationship. In the event Botham flew home early from Pakistan for knee surgery. While convalescing in London he gave a radio interview in which he spoke of the respective charms of various Test-playing countries. Pakistan, he concluded, 'is the kind of place to send your mother-in-law for a month, all expenses paid'. The TCCB swung into action and set up a full-scale disciplinary hearing, which fined Botham £1,000. Like millions of other people in Pakistan, the staff at the Lahore Hilton soon got to hear of the interview and showed their displeasure by briefly going on strike against the English cricketers still in residence there. Sarfraz Nawaz conspicuously failed to lower the emotional voltage of the whole affair when he referred to Botham as a 'drug-crazed opium pusher'. It's fair to say, then, that some mutual coolness existed between the Pakistanis on one side and England's most famous sportsman on the other, a situation that lends context to the drama of what happened 12 years later.

On General Zia's authority, Imran flew to London in April 1984 for experimental surgery on his leg. The initial procedure involved the doctors exposing his shin and clamping on a small metallic device which passed therapeutic electrical currents down the bone. The basic clinical facts somehow don't quite convey the stakes involved. Although the operation itself was a success, Imran was told that he would be in plaster for six months, and that even then his days as a professional sportsman would almost certainly be over. Back home, several of the more regionally fanatical Karachi papers tacitly celebrated the news. Having first built up the 'great Khan', they were ready to chop him down again. On some days, when a particularly venomous article appeared, even his parents were forced to endure the catcalls of the small mob milling around outside their home in Lahore. 'This was the most difficult period of my life,' Imran remarks. Like so many Pakistan captains before him, it seemed his career would end in pain, recriminations and failure.

top left Imran in July 1971, on his first, largely undistinguished tour of England.

top right Jahangir Khan, one of nine of Imran's relatives to play first-class cricket; he once managed to kill a sparrow when bowling against the MCC at Lord's.

left Pakistan captain Intikhab Alam introducing his young all-rounder to the Queen at Lord's. The other players are smiling because Intikhab has forgotten his teammate's name.

Cambridge batsman Alastair Hignell taking evasive action when facing Imran in the 1975 University match. Hignell, who was also the England rugby union full-back, recalls it as a 'terrifying barrage'.

top left Imran's superbly controlled bowling action, culminating in a last-second leap an full-stretch whip of the body.

top right Imran's transfer from Worcestersh to Sussex in July 1977 and his subsequent move to London brought about a personal, as well as a professional makeover.

left The 'feisty little bugger' and doggedly accomplished batsman Javed Miandad.

Imran bowling for the first time as Pakistan's Test captain, against England in 1982. He was the man of the series. In private, the tourists had certain misgivings about the English umpiring.

Imran batting in 1982. Essentially orthodox, if liking to smash it around on occasion, he finished his career with 3,807 Test runs at an average just under 40.

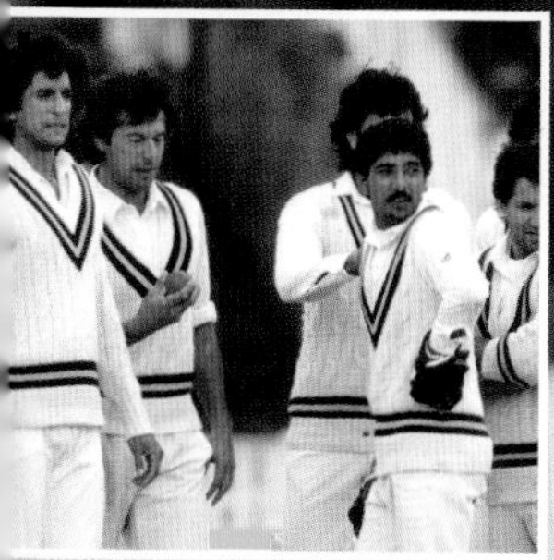

top left Wasim Akram (left), Imran and teammates on tour of England, 1987. After some bruising encounters, Pakistan won the Test series 1–0.

left After apparently retiring from international cricket, Imran was back to lead his country in 1989's Nehru Cup. Pakistan beat the West Indies in the final, played in front of 103,000 animated fans in Calcutta.

kistan's euphoria on becoming world champions in 1992 proved short-lived. After a orly-received victory speech (inset) and a misunderstanding with some of the team about nuses, Imran announced his retirement not long afterwards.

Tyrian Khan White (left), whom a court ruled to be Imran's daughter, seen wit her mother Sita White and one of her stepfathers, acto and former 'Marlboro Man Alan Marshall.

Imran's London home, whe one visitor impression was of 'a Sixties art gallery crossed wi a Sultan's harem'.

As famous in the tabloids f his social life as his sportin prowess, Imran's celebrity friends included Susannah Constantine and Jerry Hall among others.

The Princess of Wales visited Lahore in 1996. In the weeks that followed, Imran's
olitical rivals lost few opportunities to play up his reputation as a lothario.

David Frost's television show.

Dar, seen here adjusting his client's hair into the trademark 'lion look'.

left Nothing came to obsess Imran quite as much as the building of the Shaukat Khanum hospital, named after his mother and something of even greater long-term national consequence to him than winning the World Cup.

'Don't bring back a foreign wife,' Imran's mother had told him when he left for England in 1971. Twenty-four years later he married the heiress Jemima Goldsmith.

The military-backed President Musharraf, whom Imran described as a 'conman and a coward', among other unappreciative remarks.

Ian Botham and Allan Lamb's 1996 libel action against Imran led the front pages ar even managed to disrupt England's Test match preparations. Imran won the trial.

spite a number of personal distractions in 2004, the Tehreek-e-Insaf party chairman kept a dogged attack on the Musharraf and Bush administrations.

:007, Imran's anti-government stance landed him in a cell at Dera Ghazi Khan prison. k in London, Jemima Goldsmith told the media that her ex-husband might be executed as rrorist.

With sons Qasim (left) and Sulaiman, enjoying a day at the cricket.

Still campaigning in 2009. Imran told the press, 'I know, God willing, I am going to succeed And that's not very far away.'

SIX

Captain and Crew

Imran was 31, an age by which even a fit fast bowler has normally begun to review his career options. He had played 51 Tests, leading his country in 14 of them. While initially successful, his captaincy had conspicuously failed to unite Pakistan's cricket establishment behind him. One English friend called in at Draycott Avenue shortly after the patient's release from the Cromwell Hospital. Imran's condition was worse than he had been led to believe. 'He was in the truest sense of the word a pathetic figure.' An unshaven Imran 'sat with his leg propped up on a chair, an orthopedic walking-stick by his side'. Equally worrying was his mental state, which seemed to border on full-scale depression, though there were as many opinions about this as there were of Imran's performance as a captain. To Naeem-ul-Haque he was 'down, obviously, in a funk, often wondering aloud if he had a future in cricket', but still managed to exercise daily and thus 'keep himself remarkably fit, if not cheerful, under the circumstances'. Another visitor to Chelsea thought his host 'distraught' and 'completely cut off from the world'. Not so, says Jonathan Mermagen, who remembers Imran hobbling home in the afternoons, but remaining the life and soul of the party in the evenings. One of his Pakistani colleagues, who hadn't seen him since Australia, nevertheless now pronounced him 'in good health and spirits'. Writing in his autobiography three years later, Imran himself admitted, 'I was extremely depressed and bitter ... For six weeks I hardly left my flat in London. I stopped following cricket in the newspapers or watching it on television. I did nothing but read and wallow in self-pity.'

Over time, one or two respected commentators would find greater significance in Imran's injury than was apparent in other cases. To Ian Wooldridge of the *Mail*, it was a morality story. A man 'who[m] the gods seemed to have touched' was mortal like the rest us, after all. A few of Imran's enemies went further, and positively gloated at recent developments. One aggrieved Pakistani Test player remarked, 'The situation [in Australia] was impossible. Imran was up on his high horse. I wasn't the only one in the team happy enough to accept a new captain.'

By now, Emma Sergeant was enjoying some success of her own in the art world, and was instrumental in snapping Imran out of it by introducing him to a life outside cricket. One night she decided it was time he became acquainted with opera, and took him to see *Carmen*. As she recalled, 'Imran saw the shattering end when Carmen was murdered, put his finger up in the way an umpire does and said, "That's out! That's back to the pavilion."'

Although Sergeant kept her own flat in Kensington, friends remember her as more or less a fixture at Draycott Avenue. She enjoyed her role as hostess, and generally left an impression on visitors. Johnny Barclay recalls that she was 'bohemian, talented, and probably the one person who could tease Imran and get away with it'. A more cynical colleague found call to criticise Sergeant's wardrobe and figure, which in his opinion made her look 'like a brightly coloured tapeworm'. There was also, perhaps more damningly, a 'touch of [the singer] Stevie Nicks' to her 'floaty-scarf-and-bangle' ensemble. To Naeem-ul-Haque, by contrast, she was 'beautiful and charming with it'. At the conclusion of one dinner party, Sergeant made a gift of her family piano to the Haques' six-year-old daughter. Acknowledging that she was visually over the top, with 'various ribbons, baubles and bits of bone hanging off her frock' and a tendency to 'possibly overdo the makeup', another visitor, a well-known radio personality, judged that Sergeant was 'self-consciously arty', adding rather grudgingly, 'Imran was obviously taken by that whole Chelsea scene fill[ed] by authors who never seemed to write a word and film-makers begging for money.' Geoff Boycott also happened to meet Imran one day when the latter was hobbling around with the aid of a cane. In his inimitable way, the Yorkshireman looked his sometime opponent up and down and remarked, 'You may be in plaster, son, but don't tell me you're not still getting your leg over.'

In the summer of 1984, Imran briefly attached himself to a visiting tribal warlord from the Balochistan region of western Pakistan, named Sher Mohammad Marri. Marri and his personal guard of four *parari* (fighters) spent a month in London as part of a European fundraising tour. On arrival they were put up for several nights at a sympathetic diplomat's house in Hampstead. The neighbours' view of the group enjoying a traditional Balochi feast of a roast sheep served in a makeshift barbeque on the back lawn was the village's major talking-point, although the sight of Marri and his men calmly strolling up Hampstead Lane in their native regalia also made a strong impression. He was to cut something of a similar swathe on his more formal public appearances. According to one observer, Marri 'donned the mantle of warrior-scholar with great elan'. At public meetings, 'he railed against western decadence, read his rather florid poetry, and propounded Maoist political philosophies with more fervour than reflection'. Also known as Babu Shero or the 'Balochi Tiger', he favoured an armed struggle for independence from the government in Islamabad. Only then, he wrote (in translation), would come the 'happy day, all despots subdued, all tyrants slain ... What object could be more compelling than the universal ambition to see Freedom live and reign the monarch of the world? Supreme consummation! Hail, righteous cause! Glorious revolution, all hail!' A week or so into the visit, Naeem-ul-Haque took Imran and Marri to dinner at a suitably discreet restaurant in central London. He reports that it was an 'enjoyably spirited' occasion, and one which was apparently to have long-term consequences. 'Imran was totally fascinated by what he heard. Marri was this wonderfully colourful, ferocious character, and he obviously left an impression. To me, that was the moment Imran first began to think seriously about politics.'

Meanwhile, Johnny Barclay captained Sussex to a respectable sixth in the county championship, though they made an early departure from both knockout tournaments. In Imran's absence they found it hard to dismiss opponents once, let alone twice. Barclay himself led from the front. He said that he wanted to win more games, acknowledging that this could mean losing more – about which he was right. Twenty years later he added that, like Tony Greig before him, he'd 'tried to make the players feel appreciated, [and] to give each of them a certain leeway'. Barclay's relaxed style of leadership – amateurish in the best sense of the word – worked well when Sussex were reasonably successful, but, as he was the first to admit, 'we rather missed having the world's greatest all-rounder in our ranks'.

On 1 October, new X-rays showed that Imran's leg had healed completely. It was just under two years since he had limped out of bed that morning in Karachi. His London surgeon was cautiously optimistic that he could now play again. One long-time colleague met Imran at Draycott Avenue and went out with him on a celebratory run through

Hyde Park. 'He left me standing,' his companion reported. Although less than match fit and evidently still in pain, Imran handled it in typical fashion: 'He pushed himself even harder.' For the rest of the month he alternated between the indoor nets at Lord's and playing host to his parents. Shaukat Khan had developed colon cancer and flown to London for surgery. Along with his own injury and his exposure to the neo-communist musings of Mohammad Marri, this event was to mark a seminal change in Imran's life. For 15 years he'd essentially lived only for cricket and sex, generally in that order. As a result, he now became – philosophically, intellectually, politically – a radical in the truest sense. He developed a marked aversion, for instance, to the sort of society that left the vast majority of Pakistani cancer patients to die, and a privileged few either to seek treatment in one of the clinics reserved for the ruling elite or to fly to the West. Such things are never other than devastating. After one wrenching hospital visit, Imran reportedly put his head on a friend's shoulder and wept. Only he knew how lucky he was to have had Shaukat for a mother, only he could guess at how much he owed her.

On 9 October 1984, just as Imran was going through his paces in Hyde Park, the Indians arrived for their now annual winter Test series against Pakistan. Even by recent standards, it was a disaster. In the words of the Pakistani commentator Omar Noman, 'Meaningless hundreds and double hundreds proliferated ... There was unpleasant acrimony over umpiring, with the generally mild Sunil Gavaskar issuing a strongly worded statement that the adjudicating in the Lahore Test was "pre-planned and malicious and it was a miracle that we escaped with a draw".' Zaheer, the home captain, suffered a stiff neck during his first innings of the series, and this proved to be a painful experience for his team. Both completed Tests were ill-attended draws. Indira Gandhi's assassination on 31 October led to the abrupt abandonment of the tour, which one critic likened to a 'case of euthanasia'. Zaheer's generally defensive captaincy came in for widespread abuse, particularly when compared to that of his predecessor. Even some of the Karachi press appeared to have revised their opinion of Imran. One four-page weekly paper, which only a year earlier had given over most of its space to publishing an article under the headline 'Khan an embarrassment in Australia', was now eagerly calling for his return and proclaiming him 'a strategic genius'. Almost as if he were running for political office, the press again covered his every move. If he was spotted, walking in or out of Lord's or jogging up Brompton Road in his Pakistani tracksuit, it was in the paper the next morning. Meanwhile, the requests for him to play cricket were coming in from all over the world. One in particular caught Imran's attention.

It came from New South Wales, a side which had finished a disappointing fourth (out of six) in the previous Australian season's Sheffield Shield. A contact from the Packer days made the arrangements, which reportedly called for a modest salary on top of 'distinctly generous' accommodation and travel allowances. Imran flew in to Sydney on 2 November, the same day as Gavaskar's Indians were making their own rapid departure from Pakistan. Although apparently just one representative from the club was at the airport to greet him, there were several dozen ordinary fans on hand to enliven the occasion. One of them, a then 24-year-old zoology student named Jan Harris, remembers waiting with the sort of lively, clock-watching anticipation that sometimes precedes a rock concert: 'At exactly 4 p.m., an hour late, the glass door slid open and there, dressed in black trousers and an unbuttoned white linen shirt, hand outstretched in greeting, was Imran.' The next day he was in action playing Grade cricket for Sydney University, thus resuming his career within a mile or two of where it had left off nine months earlier.

Imran chose to make his full State debut the hard way, appearing for New South Wales against the touring West Indies. Batting at No. 6, he scored 30 and 9, but perhaps more to the point bowled a total of 19 overs in only mild discomfort. In answer to their enquiries, Imran assured everyone, including the team doctor, that he was 'fine'. The New South Wales captain with the name of a 1950s action hero, Dirk Wellham, prudently used his shock weapon in controlled bursts of three or four overs at a time. Wellham later reported himself 'well pleased' with the results. Imran, by contrast, remembers staying up all night during a match against Tasmania in order to analyse what was going wrong with his bowling action, which he estimated to be at 'around 70 per cent' of its pre-injury effectiveness. Deciding that his newly shortened run was the problem, he slipped himself in the Tasmanian second innings, taking four for 44 as a result. In the Sheffield Shield final between New South Wales and Queensland at Sydney, a tactical duel broke out between Imran on one side and Allan Border on the other. At the time the latter had scored 45 in an innings of calculated savagery, and looked set for many more. As he came in to bowl his first ball of a new spell, Imran abruptly halted in mid-run, ostentatiously studied the field and then loudly requested his captain, Wellham, to 'just move that man there' – John Dyson – 'a foot to his left'. Everyone waited while Dyson fractionally altered his position at third slip. Seemingly as an afterthought, Imran then called down the pitch for the man in question to take an additional half-step backwards. Meanwhile, Border continued to lean on his bat, watching the manoeuvres going on in front of and behind him with a show of disinterest. After two or three further minute adjustments, the field was eventually set to Imran's satisfaction. The next ball he bowled slanted across the left-handed Border, took the edge of his bat and flew directly to Dyson, who held the catch. New South Wales went on to win the final by one wicket.

In between his playing commitments, Imran regularly flew home to Pakistan, where his mother's condition had worsened. It did not help that she had been misdiagnosed as having only a 'mild stomach bug' when initially seeking treatment in Lahore. Sadly, Mrs Khan's case wasn't untypical of a country where cancer was widely regarded as the 'great dread'. Treatment was often late, usually faulty and almost always primitive; thanks to government fiat, painkillers such as morphine, even used medicinally, remained illegal. 'It was the most traumatic and painful period of my life,' Imran repeated in several interviews. 'My mother was sick for six or seven months and suffered terribly at the end.' In the next bed in the hospice where she was eventually taken lay an old man, also suffering from cancer. He was visited each night by his brother. Imran made enquiries and learnt that the brother, himself in his seventies, was working as a labourer to be able to pay the medical bills. The system itself was 'sick', Imran concluded.

Shaukat Khan eventually succumbed to her disease on 10 February 1985, aged 63. Imran seems not to have dwelt on his loss with any of his cricket colleagues in Pakistan or Australia, apparently preferring a process of internal grieving. Over the coming weeks he continued to show what a close friend calls the 'most flagrantly unfashionable sense of self-restraint'. Back in Sydney, one team-mate claims that Imran didn't even mention the matter to anyone until a radio reporter happened to enquire about his parents in the course of an interview. 'I've just lost one of them,' Imran said quietly. The team-mate reports that he 'nearly fell off [his] chair' at this revelation. Imran would remark that for the next two years he blotted out the memory of his mother's illness, at which stage he decided to build Pakistan's first public cancer hospital in her honour. In time this was to provide him with a somewhat different focus in life from the standard retired cricketer's lot of doing commentary or running a pub.

Despite the obvious distractions, Imran enjoyed his one and only season for New South Wales. He was to compare the working environment ('like me, passionate about cricket') favourably with that of the English county championship. The state won not only the Sheffield Shield but also the 50-over McDonald's Cup, a notable double for a team the Sydney *Herald* had greeted in a banner headline as 'LOSERS' just a year earlier. From a cricketing point of view, he achieved everything that he and his employers could have hoped for. Off the field, the reviews were perhaps more mixed. Richie Benaud felt that Imran did all that was expected of him, and was 'always happy to pass on to his team-mates the valuable information of the correct positioning of the seam and the shiny side of the ball' to effect the mysteries of reverse swing. One of the team-mates in question, the 19-year-old Steve Waugh, remembers rooming with Imran on a six-day trip to play Queensland in Brisbane. 'I wondered if I had been chosen as a promising all-rounder or a potential secretary,' Waugh recalls. 'Imran really was a legend, to the point that I was so busy answering enquiries about his availability that I didn't have time to get nervous about the match.' (In the event it rained almost continually.) With some restraint, Waugh adds merely, 'I wasn't a priority for Imran.' He was perhaps more attentive to his senior colleagues, with one or two of whom he would occasionally sit down to exchange technical chat. But what he chiefly seems to have enjoyed off duty was going out and being seen in public. At the end of the season, Imran threw a star-studded party which moved from a downtown Sydney restaurant back to his penthouse flat in the city's exclusive Connaught apartment complex. Steve Waugh watched as 'for the first time in my life, I saw people using marijuana'.

Meanwhile, Zaheer captained Pakistan in a brief home series against New Zealand, another international relations debacle. Several of the Kiwis were later to remark that, so bad was the umpiring, they had effectively had to bowl the opposition out twice every innings. The visitors had to be persuaded not to leave the field after one particular decision went against them in the Karachi Test. A month later, the same teams met in yet another series, this time in New Zealand. The BCCP reappointed Javed as captain. In the course of a zonal match with Wellington, words were exchanged between Zaheer and Abdul Qadir when the latter made no attempt to stop the ball as it trickled past him to the boundary. The details of what followed are unclear, but it seems fairly certain that Zaheer remonstrated with his younger colleague, and that the two fell into a noisy quarrel. Qadir was then sent home from the tour. When Imran finally rejoined Pakistan in late February for a limited-overs competition in Australia, he found team morale 'pathetic ... There was no commitment or spirit left. Everyone was playing for himself because no one had any confidence in the selection process, and players were only interested in retaining their own places.'

On 22 March 1985, Imran appeared under Javed's captaincy in the Pakistan team taking part in the four-nation Rothmans Cup in Sharjah. The press release touted this as a 'unique' and 'thrilling ... duel in the desert, featuring some of the world's most finely honed athletes'. (This might have come as a surprise to the 'willing but flat-footed' 45-year-old Norman Gifford, who was captaining the England side.) To the former Test captain and latter-day sports writer Tony Lewis, by contrast, the tournament was all about teams composed of club cricketers with one or two superstars thrown in, 'playing each other for a lot of money on a rough wicket. The whole event was run by what a well-placed Bahrain journalist described to me as the "spiv" element in Gulf sport.'

On his first appearance at Sharjah, Imran took a seemingly match-winning six for 14 against India. Back in Pakistan the hurriedly produced Karachi AP headline read, 'The Lion of Lahore is back: Official'. Unfortunately, so were certain other characteristic aspects of Pakistani cricket. Set 126 to win, Javed's team could manage just 87. Overnight, the once upbeat domestic news stories had to be hastily rewritten. To the AP, Pakistan's 'abject collapse' was a 'blot [and] a disgrace on a once proud escutcheon'. For the next two days, crowds in Karachi and Lahore took to the streets to voice their dissatisfaction, and burn posters of the senior players.

As early as the first morning of Imran's first home match back for Sussex, which happened to be against the Australians, colleagues noticed that he had 'something about him'. For one thing he'd altered his bowling action, which now featured less by way of a whirling right arm as he went into his climactic leap. More significant, perhaps, Imran came back a more determined player than ever. 'That was the first thing I marked,' a senior colleague recalls. 'Then, he'd usually wanted to win. Now, he always wanted to win.' One of the earliest conversations he remembers that summer was one in which Imran factually remarked,

'At 32 you've got more cricket behind you than in front of you. It's no use even playing unless you put body and soul into it every time.' He was as good as his word. Not many bowlers hope for glitzy figures when operating uphill into a stiff breeze, but in 21 overs of sustained hostility that day at Hove Imran took three Australian wickets, and would have had three more had the Sussex slips done their job. One had to admire the dignity and cool self-possession he showed when the various catches went down. Although in the heat of the Test match arena Imran had exposed his inmost feelings to the public gaze with an emphasis and frequency rare even for a Pakistani cricketer, now he just turned around and walked smartly back to his mark. The only visible hint of emotion was when he then adopted his pre-run crouch, always a sign that he meant business. One or two of the opposition looked distinctly put out to be bounced quite as often as they duly were, and, once again proving the cyclical nature of cricket, Imran wasn't spared by the Australian quicks when it came to his turn to bat. Despite the barrage, he top-scored with an unbeaten 44 in the Sussex second innings, allowing his side to hold on for a draw with their last pair at the crease.

The Somerset batsman Nigel Popplewell attests to Imran's 'well-developed sense of competitiveness' and 'total lack of sentiment' on the field, both characteristics which seemed to grow more pronounced the longer he went on. It's a side of him several of his county colleagues recall fondly from the mid-1980s. 'With Imran "good enough" wasn't good enough,' one team-mate writes. '"Show me a good loser," Imran told two or three of us, "and I'll show you a loser."' There was more in the same general motivational-talk vein. 'Imran said it was all a question of "being willing to pay the price". After a loss, he would say, "You've got to remember this feeling, because it's not something you want happening again. You've got to hate to lose, and that means that once you do, then you fight harder."'

Which brings us back to Popplewell, who at 28 was retiring from first-class cricket to go into the law. Nearly 25 years later, he would recall his swansong for Somerset, which came in a late-season Sunday league match against Sussex at Taunton. The visitors went into the game first equal in the points table. 'The highlight of my day came when the Sussex fielders did me the honour of clapping me all the way to the wicket.' From this gratifying start, 'things seemed to go downhill from the minute I took guard [and] looked up to see Imran crouching into his run in the mid-distance. Something about his body language suggested that I shouldn't expect any favours. Sure enough, the next few seconds confirmed that he wasn't interested in giving me a generous final run. None of your typical "one off the mark ..." Even though Imran was coming off a shorter run, he was still lightning and bowled me a couple of overs of absolute jaffers. Fortunately, I was so out of nick that I never got anywhere near them, and somehow managed to hang on for a few with Viv Richards to win the match.' Another participant confirmed that Imran had given all the Somerset batsmen 'the full treatment – inswingers, yorkers, bouncers, everything. He almost went berserk when Viv once stepped back and hooked him for four in the direction of the river.' But, the same source adds, 'Immy was also the first to saunter in and congratulate [Somerset] after the match, despite the fact that as a direct result, Essex, not Sussex, won the league that year.'

In an age when English county professionals were known to play as many as 120 days' cricket of various sorts every summer, it seems almost wilfully eccentric that the world's foremost all-rounder should appear in only a dozen county matches and a handful of one-dayers. Imran's captain Johnny Barclay is one of those who thought him a 'rhythm bowler' who 'need[ed] regular and prolonged competition to be at his best'. Another interested observer saw it slightly differently. 'Like a carefully preserved vintage hot rod, Imran was still firing on all cylinders. You just don't take a car like that out of the garage when you want to pop down to Tesco.' In his abbreviated season, Imran took 51 first-class wickets at 20 apiece, and enjoyed a batting average of 68. A highlight came in early July, when he scored an unbeaten century and fired out half the Warwickshire side at Hove; after being worked over by Bob Willis and the rest on their previous meeting, he had a score to settle with them. Sussex finished seventh in the championship table and were never in the running in the knockouts.

No wonder, then, that the county committee wrote to enquire if Imran would perhaps 'increase [his] playing commitment' to the club in 1986. Most of his team-mates seem to have felt the same way. By now it must have borne in on them that, while he was never likely to be the first one down to the pub at the close of play, Imran remained a forceful and on the whole benign presence in the dressing-room. To the 19-year-old Neil Lenham, 'Immy wasn't a barrel of laughs, and lacked the nonstop heartiness of certain other players. He was intelligent. He read books. That isn't to say he couldn't gently take the piss out of you.' Lenham remembers Imran appearing on the first day of the new season and 'gravely informing the follically challenged Garth le Roux, "Don't worry, my friend. Over the winter, I discovered a cure for baldness."' According to another Sussex player, 'Imran made a little humour go a long way'.

The Chelsea bachelor pad and the glamorous friends were trappings of a lifestyle that marked Imran out from the field. Even other contemporary Test players were able to slip back into private life more or less unnoticed. Not him. Naeem-ul-Haque joined his friend and several other cricketers to watch a day's tennis at Wimbledon that summer. 'Coming out, Imran was surrounded by a crowd of several young women and had to break into a run to get away from them. It was all but a riot. My abiding memory is of Imran disappearing through the gate while the Australian bowler Geoff Lawson muttered, "Christ, it's never like this when *I* go out in public".' For all the new-found sense of perspective his mother's death and his own injury seem to have brought, there was still a trace of a self-confident, occasionally cocky nature when he was around people he had no particular need to impress. In the mid-1980s, the *Sun* briefly engaged Imran to contribute a wide-ranging series of articles on the state of world cricket. His ghost-writer on the paper considered him an 'imperious bugger'.

The Test team that Imran rejoined in 1985 was a sorry sight.

Perhaps it would be fairer to say that the overall state of Pakistani cricket, and more particularly its administrative arm, left something to be desired. General Butt was to prove an only moderately capable president of the BCCP. Tacitly confirming that he cared little about cricket, and knew even less, he once asked Abdul Qadir why he bowled off such a short run when West Indians like Michael Holding and Joel Garner took such a long one. There seemed to be a perennial financial crisis at the top, and regular umpiring controversies on the field. The new board secretary, one Rafi Naseem, was a former soldier turned poultry farmer who was only partially successful in his alternative role as cricket administrator. Imran describes him as 'a small-minded, self-righteous man [who] loved to throw his weight around'. When Pakistan played Sri Lanka that winter, Naseem had a friend of his appointed to umpire in the Test at Sialkot. Entirely coincidentally, Pakistan won by eight wickets.

In time, the board further overextended itself by seeking to meddle in Imran's social life. Emma Sergeant made her second visit to Pakistan in late 1985, ostensibly to paint while her partner was playing cricket.

Much fur was to fly over a published story that on the night before a subsequent one-day international with the West Indies in Peshawar, Imran and his guest had stayed in the same hotel room. A number of the reports were to quote a 'senior board official' as their source for this, to some, shocking exposé. In the months ahead, there were to be various other articles about Imran's nocturnal activities, the most complete if not always balanced analysis of which was to be found in the Karachi *Star*. No doubt Naseem, not a man endowed with natural ambassadorial tact, and who was about to be forcibly banned from the Pakistan dressing-room, had an axe to grind. By most accounts, he and the other board members hadn't even been staying in the hotel in question. However, the secretary at least seemed to have known his man in general terms, and little about his specific allegation, including his reported claim to have heard about it from another player, fails to make sense, unless one is flatly determined to refuse to believe that Imran at any stage in his playing career spent the night with a woman.

Whatever the merits of Naseem's personal moral crusade, Emma Sergeant did apparently 'tend to flag a bit' when confronted by the sheer intensity of the emotions Imran stirred in the Pakistani public as a whole. These ran the gamut from near-religious adulation to the regular issuing of kidnap and death threats.* Another cricketer recalls seeing her standing by the door, while Imran worked a crowded reception room full of dignitaries and well-wishers, as if afraid to venture in. Even that small incident struck him as a sign that the couple were perhaps drifting apart. From Sergeant's perspective, Imran might not have been ideally suited to the artistic but ordered home life to which she aspired. She wanted a partner, not a legend. Then there was the whole matter of the press and its 'constant obsession' with them, even in the laxer moral climate of Britain. Shortly after her return to London, Sergeant was to conclude that their cultural differences were too great. 'The things that mattered to him didn't matter to me, and vice versa,' she remarked. After a suitable interval, Imran would be seen with the 27-year-old fashion guru Susannah Constantine, among others, whom he typically entertained at Tramp. As Emma Sergeant has good-naturedly observed, gossip columnists like Nigel Dempster

---

* One popular advertising billboard prominently displayed in Pakistani bus and train stations in the late 1980s showed a chiselled-looking profile of Imran with dozens of men, women and children lying prostrate at his feet. Although not sanctioned by him, it wasn't untypical of the personality cult at the time.

'didn't need to ring Imran, since he was usually sitting at the next table'.

In October 1985, the Sri Lankans arrived for a brief three-Test tour of Pakistan. While not in itself, perhaps, a sporting occasion of the first rank, the series was still marked by feverish domestic press interest and wildly enthusiastic crowds. On 15 October, the night before the first Test at Faisalabad, a mass meeting was held outside the Iqbal Stadium 'to give expression to popular gratitude to one player – the King of Swing, for his signal services to Pakistan Test cricket in conducting the mighty Stars to victory', in the muted report of the *Daily Asas*. At 33, some 21 months after last playing at that level, Imran was set to attempt the most difficult trick in sport – the comeback.

Although Sri Lanka were on something of a roll, having just won a home series against India, the official opposition hardly mattered. Not for the first time, the Pakistan team were to prove their own worst enemies. Captained by Javed, the target of a players' revolt three years earlier, the side also contained Shoaib Mohammad, whose selection had become a resignation issue for the home panel prior to the ill-fated Australian tour, as well as the now seemingly permanently disgruntled Zaheer (currently on the outs with his colleague Abdul Qadir), and Salim Malik, who after several well-publicised misunderstandings with Imran was to remark that 'with no superstars in the side, we are happier'. A fairly representative Pakistani fighting unit of the time, in other words. They did well to beat the Sri Lankans 2–0. Imran took nine wickets in the second Test, and 17 in the series at an average of 15.94. It comes as no surprise to report that there were to be a variety of umpiring controversies. The visitors went home deeply aggrieved, a feeling the Pakistanis came to know all too well when they, in turn, toured Sri Lanka just three months later. At one stage in the latter series Javed was given out in what he considered a 'pathetic' decision, and then promptly ran into the crowd to remonstrate with a spectator who had thrown a rock at him. Salim later appeared on the field of play with a copy of *Wisden* in order to draw the officials' attention to the current lbw law. After that General Zia had to get on the phone to both the team manager and the president of Sri Lanka to ensure that the tour continued.

For all that, Imran was back. In contrast to other recent series, the Sri Lanka Tests were well subscribed by home fans, more especially so by the young and female ones. A professional appreciation for the 'Lion of Lahore' often brought with it a more personal component. Judging from the various slogans on display at the Tests, a significant proportion of Pakistani women related to Imran in much the same way their opposite numbers in the West had done to the Beatles or their various doe-eyed successors. Banners held aloft at subcontinental cricket grounds were nothing new, but it's hard to imagine them having been quite as enticingly customised in the past as they were now. Predictably, not everyone was delighted by this renewed outbreak of the 'cult of Khan', as it was called in *Dawn*. Just as he had three years earlier, a religious leader, Dr Israr Ahmed, complained that mosque attendance suffered when cricket matches were shown on television. He went on to note that Imran's practice of rubbing the ball on his trouser leg 'had a sexually stimulating effect on the feminine populace'. Dr Ahmed's reproach was one of several reactions to the man who had become the most polarising public figure in Pakistan. By around 1986, a wide gap had opened up between what could be called the cricket establishment and the mass of ordinary fans who actually paid to watch the game. To many of the professional administrators and others, Imran had simply become too important for their own good. It was an axiom among the press, generally reflecting a Lahore–Karachi split, to be either 'pro-Khan' or 'anti-Khan'. Only the public, it seemed, could hold in its head simultaneously the ideas that Imran had grappled with the unique challenges of Pakistan cricket; that he was occasionally wilful; and that, on the whole, he deserved all the credit he got.

Shortly after the home Test procession against Sri Lanka, Javed again opted to resign the captaincy in Imran's favour. Here some small discrepancy exists between the two men's versions of events. Writing in his autobiography *All Round View*, Imran notes matter-of-factly, 'Javed had faced severe criticism for his handling of the team in the three one-day defeats to India early in 1985: he chose to go and I was appointed in his place.' Javed's own account seems to imply a notably less consensual process. 'I had the chance of continuing as captain, but decided against it,' he says. 'I did so because Imran didn't give me his full cooperation in that [Sri Lanka] series, and it was a great disappointment for me … As captain, I would tell Imran to bowl a certain way, but he refused … He didn't observe cricket discipline … After that experience, I decided never to captain Pakistan if Imran was also playing. What would be the point if I couldn't rely on my leading bowler to fall in with my plans?' Neither of these versions, it's fair to add, entirely squares with what Imran told me in 2008, which was that the whole thing was down to the BCCP, 'who basically treated the captain like their employee, and generally hired him for only two years ... There was no such thing as job security.' As before, Javed resigned after a winning Sri Lankan series and, as he puts it without any pretence of enthusiasm, 'fell in line' behind his successor; a somewhat strained transition.

As captain, Imran nonetheless did a creditable job of leading a team who frequently seemed to be fighting among themselves as much as they were against the opposition. Sarfraz and now Zaheer had both retired, but in players like Abdul Qadir and Qasim Omar, as well as the twice-deposed Javed, Pakistan were blessed with men as individually opinionated as they were talented. Although Imran made no intimate friends, he had 'good working relations with nearly all the side', with the significant exception of Salim. (Shoaib Mohammad would be rested pending a recall to tour India in 1987.) Imran's primary challenge remained dealing with the home board. Rafi Naseem was perhaps the most obvious but by no means only example of the amateur-hour approach that seemed to typify the BCCP in its various duties: this was the man whom Imran *twice* evicted from the Pakistan dressing-room, as he wandered about fecklessly trying to cheer up the players, the second time nearly leading to a fist-fight. The metallic voice of General Butt called the shots on matters of 'pressing strategic urgency' (his team's pay among them), while a constantly replenished pool of retired lieutenant generals, many unburdened by any knowledge of cricket, issued fussily annotated lists of the players and officials selected for each match. Another BCCP functionary chose a moment when Imran was sitting padded up waiting to go in to bat in a one-day international to walk up with his son and ask his team's captain to 'be a good fellow and collect everyone's autographs' for the boy. Imran signed his own name, but declined the larger request. The official reported him to the disciplinary panel. At the end of the series, Rafi Naseem appeared once again and handed Imran a piece of paper which stated that he was no longer captain.

In time, the BCCP convened an inquiry committee, reportedly to look into the 'breakdown of leadership and discipline in Pakistan international cricket', while, it should be noted, acknowledging its star player's contribution with the bat and ball. Its conclusions, in no particular order – they were interchangeable – were: 'arrogant individualism of Imran Khan Niazi ... un-cooperative ... discourtesy ... never known the necessity of following orders ... inflexible ... brazen ... reputation ... rumours ... activities at night.'

Despite calling on an impressive number of witnesses and eventually producing a thick draft report, the inquiry committee failed to find a viable alternative to Imran. Javed was apparently sounded out about a possible third term in office but refused it. The 30-year-old Mudassar similarly declined the job. Most if not all the Karachi newspapers kept up a relentless drumbeat against Imran (as a captain, that was, not a player), summarised by one daily's headline, 'OUT!' For all that, no one could actually come up with any specific allegations against the national captain, apart from his impossibly tasteless lapse of having an attractive English girlfriend. Perhaps that was enough. In Pakistan, cricketers are more than just cricketers. Pakistanis look to their sports heroes not simply for excitement and entertainment, but for a way of life. The clerics provide an unfailingly rigorous definition of good and evil. But it's in the rare men like Imran that Pakistanis find their role models, people who are meant not just to play better but also to be better than ordinary mortals.

In the end Imran survived not only the BCCP inquiry, but most of the board officials. General Butt and several of his senior colleagues stood down in February 1988. Imran's *bête noire* Rafi Naseem lasted only until 1986. On retiring he became an occasional journalist. Seventeen years later, Naseem himself fell foul of the BCCP's successor, the PCB. In May 2003, the board council issued a writ against their former secretary claiming damages of Rs50 million (roughly £36 million) for 'tarnish[ing] the reputation of the officials and officers by writing articles against them'. Naseem claimed free speech. Among other things, he was alleged to have called the chairman of the PCB a 'petty dictator'.

Whatever the rights and wrongs of this case, whose outcome, if any, would remain sealed, and which elicited no further public comment, Imran perhaps had the last word in the matter. In July 1999, the PCB announced sweeping administrative reforms in which, among other steps, a council of professional officers, chosen by ballot, effectively replaced the old patronage system. Imran had campaigned for the abolition of the closed shop and the introduction of 'free and fair' elections more than a dozen years earlier.

Under Imran, Pakistan beat India but lost to the West Indies in the three-nation Rothmans Cup (not to be confused with the bi-nation Wills Series, or indeed the four-nation John Player Gold Leaf Trophy, both of which followed over the coming weeks) in Sharjah. Javed had broken his thumb shortly beforehand and had to be persuaded to make the flight. 'The medical advice for me was not to play, but the captain would have none of it. He made a huge fuss about how I was indispensable to our batting. I, too, was conscious of my batting responsibilities and relented,' Javed shyly admits. He scored 53 runs in the tournament.

Pakistan lost the subsequent home one-day series with the West Indies 3–2. It was a moral victory of sorts, given that the visitors had just completed a 'blackwash' of England in one Test series, and were about to do so in another. Imran went straight from the awards ceremony to an appearance in front of the BCCP inquiry committee. Although the board had to be satisfied with passing a rule that allowed their officials access to the home dressing-room whenever they wanted, they were 'a nasty lot of political manoeuvrers', according to the former captain Javed Burki. In early January 1986, the writer and broadcaster Omar Kureishi raised an all-star team to undertake a brief tour of Bangladesh. Kureishi's son Javed recalls that 'Imran immediately agreed to go, which caused the president of Bangladesh to remark, "Oh my God, we'll have to lock our women up."' Pakistan were due to make a two-month, three-Test tour of Sri Lanka starting in February. Despite feverish press speculation, the board did not decide to dump Imran; nor did they immediately decide to keep him. Instead they delayed their selection of the captain and players until just four days before the team's departure. While awaiting developments, Imran happened to meet his old bowling partner Sarfraz Nawaz, who was by now both the husband of a Bollywood actress and an elected member of the Punjab provincial assembly. According to Sarfraz, 'Immy was cheesed off with all the aggravation' and at least tentatively considering an offer to play in Australia. It was almost as if the home board enjoyed the thrill of keeping both their team and the public in a state of suspense. On 12 February, Imran was formally reappointed as captain, and went to see the relevant BCCP committee in Lahore. When he returned from the meeting, one of the board officials, speaking on background, remarked to a journalist that 'there was some lack of warmth'.

If so, the atmosphere turned positively glacial when the Pakistanis arrived in Sri Lanka, which happened to be undergoing a civil war. On the first morning of the first Test, the umpire Allan Felsinger turned down a spirited lbw appeal by loudly advising the tourists to 'shut up'. He added that this was 'not Pakistan'. The umpires later walked off the field, taking the players with them, after the hard-hitting Sri Lankan batsman Arjuna Ranatunga had been called a cheat by the Pakistani slips while on his way to a brief but action-packed score of 18. When Ranatunga then appeared in the visitors' dressing-room to discuss the matter, he asked Imran to apologise on behalf of his team. Imran said that he would if the Sri Lankans also agreed to do so for their 'provocative' behaviour. Outside, the crowd grew restless. When the match eventually resumed, the tourists' first four batsmen were then given out lbw with just 52 on the board. The on-field exchange of pleasantries continued, with numerous references both to the players' parentage and to their female relatives. Pakistan's eventual victory was made possible by their spin bowlers, who hit the stumps eight times in the Test, a feat beyond even the umpires' ability to quibble.

In the second Test, Ranatunga was back in action, having mellowed somewhat in the intervening fortnight; this time he scored a match-winning 77 in a shade over five hours. With the third Test drawn, the series ended one-all. Imran took 15 wickets. 'The hostility was unrelenting,' he remarked. 'Even the waiters in the hotel and the people in the streets were rude to us ... The souring of a series due to an uncertain political situation wasn't new to me, but on this tour it was as bad as it could possibly have been.'

Politics aside, Imran's return as Pakistan captain was among the more successful second acts in the history of a nation whose secular idols, whether military or sporting, rarely seemed to retire gracefully. It also came at exactly the right time, given the nature of the forward-fixtures list. After the Sri Lankan trip Pakistan would host the all-conquering West Indies, then in short order tour India and England before taking part in the fourth World Cup, which was to be held in the subcontinent. In between times, Imran had commitments to play in a seemingly endless series of tobacco-sponsored one-day carnivals as well as a contract to fulfil at Sussex. A relentlessly full schedule for anyone, let alone a fast bowler approaching his mid-thirties. By the spring of 1986, Imran had achieved his immediate goal of seeing off the home board and its inquiry committee, and had re-established himself as a public personality. His picture was on patriotic posters. Everyone in Pakistan had heard about him as the comeback kid – 'almost a case of reincarnation', in General Zia's only half-facetious view. People had read about his injury and seen pictures of him hobbling in and out of hospitals in London. Now they saw him back in Pakistan colours, and he looked just fine. He was aggressively resilient and unburdened by self-doubt; the image held for the rest of his cricket career – and beyond, into politics.

Imran's immediate priority was a five-nation limited overs cup, played in Sharjah in April 1986 as part of the Cricketers' Benefit Fund series. Pakistan won off the last ball of the final against India. An estimated television audience of a billion people were watching as Chetan Sharma ran in to bowl to Javed Miandad, with Pakistan still three runs adrift. Javed carted the ensuing full-toss over the midwicket boundary. The subsequent reaction back in Pakistan was, perhaps understandably, a trifle warm: a public holiday was declared, presidential telegrams were dispatched and, according to Omar Noman, 'thirty-six songs were released on the theme of Javed's six'. The batsman reports that on his triumphant return to the dressing-room, 'the whole team was there. Everyone had tears in their eyes, including Imran. Two of the youngsters, Mohsin Kamal and Zulqarnain, were openly bawling. The atmosphere was enough to make anyone speechless, and I was.' The winning team drove away in a convoy of honking cars with an *ad hoc* honour guard of several hundred motor-scooters intermingled with jogging pedestrians. It was another notable high on the emotional roller-coaster that Pakistani cricket had become.

For all that, Imran still hadn't quite got back to fulfilling his principal function of bowling lightning fast for extended periods, which is why he readily accepted a tenth annual contract offered by Sussex. As his county captain had remarked, he was a 'rhythm bowler' who needed prolonged exposure to the three- and five-day versions of the game to perform effectively. Imran now embarked on what could be termed his Late Period at Hove, which may have brought his most personally fulfilling season at the club. Although lacking a yard of pace the sheer variety of his arsenal, which now included every known kind of cutter and swinger, made him a true attacking bowler, astute at adapting to conditions and capable, also, of containment. His colleague Tony Pigott remembers an early-season championship match against Middlesex at Lord's.

> Imran came in off a short run, and still fairly hurled it down. He had two of their guys out lbw off successive balls. After the second one we went into a team huddle, in the midst of which Immy looks up with a mischievous grin and enquires, 'What shall I bowl next, guys?' 'Exactly the same again,' we promptly tell him. The clear implication was that he could have just as easily sent down one of about half-a-dozen different balls, each of them as lethal as the next one. Meanwhile, over my shoulder, I can see the new

> Middlesex batsman coming in. He happened to be playing his first or maybe second ever match at that level, and let's just say he didn't look happy. The word 'apprehensive' would just about cover it. At that Imran strolls back, turns, takes a largely perfunctory run, and bowls the guy a devastatingly fast inswinging yorker. It's totally unplayable. My memory seems to be of the middle stump cartwheeling out of the ground and nearly hitting our keeper on the way back. As we go into another huddle, Immy trots up and says, 'Thanks, guys. I was thinking of giving him a bouncer, but that seemed to work.'

Imran took eight for 34 in the Middlesex second innings; Sussex won the match by seven wickets.

As we've seen, Imran generally rose to the occasion when playing at Lord's. He seems to have enjoyed Edgbaston almost as much, it being the ground where he'd gone to hone his craft in the indoor school some 15 years earlier. Sussex appeared there to play Warwickshire in their last county match of the 1986 season. One of the fringe benefits of Imran's shin injury was the opportunity his enforced lay-off from bowling had given him to make himself a better batsman. His innings on an overcast September morning at Birmingham was a case in point. He opened his account at a clip, driving Small straight for four with a full pendulum swing, and in the same over lashing him first bounce into the Thwaite scoreboard. Next he pulled the evergreen Gifford for six and, seemingly within moments of arrival, passed his 50 amid generous home applause. In all Imran scored 135 not out. Memory had to grope back a long way to recall an innings as simultaneously violent and classically correct as this was. Imran's batting average that year was 48.66, on top of which he took 37 wickets in his nine first-class matches. Despite his all-round contribution, Sussex finished a dismal 14th in the table. Johnny Barclay retired, aged 32, and the captaincy passed to the wicketkeeper Ian Gould, who resigned after only one full season in charge, noting that the county needed two or three international-level seamers, a couple of top-quality batsmen and a class spin bowler if their position was to improve.

Sussex did, however, go all the way in the NatWest Trophy, beating if not actually trouncing Clive Lloyd's Lancashire in the final at Lord's. It was another of the pomp and circumstance affairs, with a capacity crowd and a television camera perched precariously on a crane at the

Nursery end, that seemed to bring out the tiger in Imran. He certainly flung the ball at the wicket with impressive speed if, for once, no particular pretension to subtlety. Meanwhile, at the other end Dermot Reeve took four for 20 with his hitherto innocuous seam. The Lancashire batting was somewhat thin on paper, and never quite recovered from Lloyd being out for a third-ball nought. They managed 242 from their sixty overs. Imran came in to bat when Sussex, largely thanks to Paul Parker, had reached a solid but heavy-going 156 for two. The authority and power he immediately brought to the scene shook the match awake. He began so aggressively, carrying Allott high through the covers, that umpire Bird, standing at the bowler's end, 'thought it was all too good to last'. It did; Imran scored 50 not out, seeing Sussex home by seven wickets, with two overs in hand. Bird added that this was batting 'of the top rank ... Imran saw the ball early, had a nice sense of timing and was very straight. That match may have been the best I ever saw him play.'

It almost goes without saying that Imran remained a popular and diligent county professional, the sort who tended to go out jogging rather than sit around with his feet up during a rain delay. One admiring colleague recalls that he 'put in longer hours and trained more intensely than anyone else', even if 'unlike the rest of us, he chose when or when not to actually play'. Intensity was clearly a theme for Imran, who also worked quite hard at his social life. A chronological rundown of some of the women he was popularly linked with after Emma Sergeant would include the actresses Stephanie Beacham and Goldie Hawn (a client of his stylist Dar), the Thane of Cawdor's daughter Lady Liza Campbell, the *Vogue* 'it girl' Caroline Kellett, the Duchess of York's friend Lulu Blacker, Susannah Constantine and a quite well-known journalist. The list isn't exhaustive.

The intensity occasionally showed itself in other ways, too. For a professional sportsman who describes himself with some understatement as 'competitive', Imran had learnt to control his temper to a rare degree, indeed to use his anger as a spur, transforming it into an internal challenge to do better next time. He had a way of turning negative emotions into positive assets. Even so, like most cricketers he occasionally gave vent to his feelings on the field of play. Derek Pringle, the former Essex and England all-rounder, told me 'Imran was aggressive but fairly straightforward. He did sledge, if nothing witty. I remember he once found himself bowling to a young opener for Essex called Mike McEvoy, who had the gall to face him without wearing a helmet. Immy told McEvoy he was going to "knock his fucking teeth out".'

As the year wound down, politics heated up. Imran was fighting the board once again over team selection for the home series against the West Indies. The captain is reliably said to have shared his views with the panel about both Qasim Omar, who played in the series, and Shoaib Mohammad, who didn't. The BCCP also ultimately agreed to Imran's repeated request to appoint neutral umpires, and took the brave and somewhat quixotic decision to hire two officials from India, who were thought unlikely to be accused of any pro-Pakistan favouritism. In the event the only altercation came between umpire Reporter and the West Indies bowler Malcolm Marshall, who was unhappy about being no-balled in the Karachi Test. After a lively debate on the subject, the board also chose to play the Tests on pitches that were characterised by their uneven bounce, as reflected by the failure of any batsman, Viv Richards included, to score a hundred.

The playing conditions would become an issue as early as the first morning of the first Test at Faisalabad, when, on a minimally prepared pitch, Pakistan found themselves at 37 for five, with the ball skidding around erratically at what Javed Miandad describes as 'variable' height. All things considered, among them Salim Malik's abrupt departure with a broken arm, the odds would have been against the home team reaching three figures. At that point Imran produced a captain's innings which, on that malevolent trampoline, was as physically courageous as it was technically sound. His 61 off 75 balls began a spirited counter-attack which saw Pakistan to the comparative respectability of 159. According to Javed, Imran was less than enthralled by Malcolm Marshall's policy of bouncing him on average twice an over. 'When the captain returned to the dressing-room he was fuming, and he told our guys to have a go at Marshall when he came out to bat.' No one who played in the game or watched it, or who saw it on cable, or who listened to it on the radio, many of them in Pakistan's most remote outposts, could have been left unimpressed by the subsequent assault. Between them, Imran and Wasim Akram bowled 46 of the most hostile overs imaginable, taking one for 32 and six for 91 respectively. Marshall spent most of his brief time at the wicket ducking under a succession of bouncers, and departed for only five.

To beat a side like that, Pakistan still needed to bat with rather more grit in their second innings. They did. The fightback was epitomised by a chanceless 66 by Wasim, and by Salim, who came out with his arm in plaster to face three overs from Marshall and Walsh. The tourists were left needing 240 to win in four sessions. A beamer from Marshall had split the index finger of Imran's right hand, which made it painful for him to grip the ball. Despite the handicap, he disposed of both West Indian openers and took four for 30 in all; Qadir did the rest and Pakistan won by 186 runs.

The West Indies managed to score just 218 in the second Test at Lahore, with Imran taking five for 59. It was still enough for them to win the match by an innings, with two days to spare. Pakistan were bowled out for 131 and 77. Imran was soon back arguing with the board about his team's batting line-up. To others, the captain himself was the issue. No deep psychological exercise was needed to predict that the Karachi press would again weigh in by calling for a change at the top, with Javed Miandad's name being floated by the *Star*. Javed's masterly batting at Lahore was a sparkling counterpoint to the domination of the West Indies fast bowlers. In the end Imran survived to take eight wickets, including a spell of five for 10 in six overs, in the third and final Test, which was drawn. It was another finish of such protracted drama that there were subsequently riots – of relief, presumably – in the streets outside the National Stadium. On the last day Imran was at the wicket with his side at 125 for seven, chasing 230, when bad light brought proceedings to an early conclusion. It was perhaps fortunate for Pakistan's sporting reputation that it was the Indian umpires who took the brave, if justifiable, decision to call off play with nine overs still to be bowled.

A tense and somewhat schizophrenic series ended 1–1. Imran reports that he was 'particularly proud of our performance [in] holding the strongest side in the world'. In other countries that might have been enough. In Pakistan, the three-way in-fighting between the board, the press and the team captain seemed almost automatic. The controversy took another twist following the West Indies series when the Kenyan-born batsman Qasim Omar went into print accusing his team-mates of discrimination, among a host of other offences. Omar was subsequently banned for seven years after making hotly denied charges of drug abuse against Imran. Equally unproven claims that 'senior colleagues' had both engaged in match-fixing and accepted prostitutes as bribes resurfaced some 15 years later. 'The other Pakistan players couldn't cope with my popularity,' Omar informed the BBC.

Spurious allegations from inside the team were the least of it. Just weeks after the West Indies series, Imran was in Australia to take part in the four-nation Benson and Hedges Challenge, a 50-over tournament designed as a sideshow to the America's Cup. Pakistan lost to England in the final. As he came off the field in Perth, Imran was told that the BCCP had announced the squad for the coming full-scale tour of India in his absence. He was not pleased. 'I was sorry at how Imran and the board went at each other,' a well-placed source remarked. 'It was a total communication breakdown [and] not just about team selection. There was a basic personality clash. Imran thought the board were inept, and they thought he was a control freak compared to previous captains. And in a sense, they were both right.'

SEVEN

The Contrast Principle

Pakistan's five-Test tour of India in early 1987 was the fourth series between the arch national rivals in as many years. On this occasion, there seems not to have been any falling off in public interest in the result. When the Pakistanis arrived in Faridabad on 23 January, there were more than a thousand students milling about, shouting derisively, carrying unwelcoming signs, and raising a regular cry of 'Death to Islam'. As Imran led his team into the Mayur Stadium, those in the rear of the crowd began throwing oranges, coins and the odd small rock. Not for the last time, the police were called on to ensure the visitors' safe passage. The tour in general became a rallying-point for critics of Pakistan's disputed claim to Kashmir, and for an assortment of other long-term grievances. According to *Wisden*, 'The touring team were subjected to a harrowing time by the crowds in Ahmedabad and Bangalore, where any convenient missile was thrown at the Pakistani players. However, the captain's sporting approach to the niggling problems which occur on a tour of India helped keep matters from getting out of proportion.' Another journalist would watch in admiration as, some 10 weeks later, Imran, having disposed of the few specific cricket points, then fielded questions of a broader cultural nature in the tour's final press conference at Jamshedpur. 'He was a model of good sense and statesmanship. Everything was fine. India was a wonderful country … Although [the interview] itself was eminently civilised, that was not true of the streets outside. Spit, fruit and pebbles again rained down on the building.' It would of course be quite wrong to say that the entire tour took place in a hostile working environment, or that the relations between the two teams were generally anything less than cordial. But even so, the combination of diplomatic, tactical and playing responsibilities was enough to reduce Imran's weight by almost a stone.

The travel writer Mark Shand accompanied Imran in India and thought him a born leader, who kept himself somewhat apart from his men. 'I always felt he was a proper sort of captain, a bit aloof with very strict ideals. He was a jot higher than the others in the dressing-room.' A general consensus was that Imran could be stubborn to the point of obduracy when it came to his preference for some players over others. An obvious case in point was that of his protégé Abdul Qadir. The Lahore spinner had appeared in 41 Tests, turning in some undeniably deft performances without ever quite threatening to become a consistent match-winner, and simultaneously running up a disciplinary record of some note. Conversely, Saeed's brother Younis Ahmed, the 39-year-old batsman who had last represented his country in 1969, now returned to play twice in India. After his second appearance he complained of a sore neck and was ordered back to the team hotel to rest. Instead, Younis went to a disco. Imran ensured that he never played for Pakistan again. Javed Miandad recalls another occasion on the same tour when even his captain's single-mindedness apparently gave way in the face of a sustained debate. 'Before the Bangalore Test Imran had determined to play Qadir rather than Iqbal Qasim. I knew that Qasim would be far more effective on that track, and urged Imran to change his mind. It became a testy exchange and I finally ended up invoking God and country before Imran relented.' Qasim took nine wickets in that match, which Pakistan won.*

For the most part, the first four Tests of the series had reflected the largely sullen atmosphere in the stands. Anyone familiar with the facts of England's tour of India under Keith Fletcher five years earlier, once described as the cricketing equivalent of a coma, has only to think of that grim series, but played on even worse pitches, to get a feel for the occasion. The basic pattern was for the Indians to run up huge first-innings totals which would put pressure on Pakistan batsmen forced to cope with slow, turning wickets and umpiring that was not of the very highest calibre. Just 21 wickets fell in the course of the first, drawn Test at Madras. Imran scored a deliberately paced century, his third and highest in Tests to date. Wasim Akram came in to join his captain when the latter's score was in the upper twenties. An hour and a half later

* Imran has a somewhat different recollection of the selection process at Bangalore. He told me, 'The only discussion was whether to pick an extra spinner or a seam bowler. I went against Qadir because the Indians had already played him so well on the tour.'

Wasim was out for 62, by which time Imran had moved on to the mid-forties. His eventual 135 not out included five sixes and 14 fours and took six-and-a-quarter hours in all, which suggests he thrashed the bad balls and otherwise put up a brick wall of Boycott-like solidity. Three days later, the teams regrouped in Calcutta, to produce the same result. Sunil Gavaskar declined to play because of his past treatment at the ground, bringing to a close his run of 106 consecutive Tests. If the home crowds were thought hostile to India's greatest batting hero, they were unlikely to be well disposed to the Pakistanis. The visitors duly came under a continual shower of asterisked abuse. Imran was not at his best, taking none for 93 in India's one completed innings.

Gavaskar returned for the third Test at Jaipur, marching out under a huge electric sign proclaiming '10,000 RUNS – AND MANY MORE TO COME'. He was out, off Imran, first ball. The Pakistanis' reaction to the dismissal was not notable for its restraint, with at least one reported reference to the outgoing batsman's immediate family. From this point on, the playing atmosphere began to deteriorate rapidly. There were a number of incidents of gamesmanship, with both sides apparently competing to be the more flamboyant in their appeals. When the Pakistanis arrived for play on the third day, which followed the rest day, they found that rain had seeped under the covers. There was a 'football-sized' damp patch to one side of the pitch on a convenient length for the Indians' left-arm spinner Maninder Singh. Elsewhere the wicket appeared to have been sprinkled with sawdust, which the Pakistanis claimed had been used to dry the turf, in contravention of the Laws. The ground authorities countered that the 'foreign matter' must have been blown there by the wind. It was possibly this sort of thing that *Wisden* had in mind when it referred to the 'niggling problems' that can occur on a tour of India. In the almanack's account, 'the umpires then dragged their feet over a resumption as Imran threatened to refuse to bat, and eventually defused the situation by abandoning play for the day', thus condemning the match to another draw. Perhaps unsurprisingly, crowd trouble ensued in the fourth Test at Ahmedabad, where the Pakistani outfielders were pelted with rocks. Six of them subsequently took the field wearing crash helmets. Imran had earlier scored a three-and-a-half-hour 72. Quite apart from his bowling, he was now about as solid a batsman to be coming in at No. 7 or 8 as anyone in recent Test history. His first-class average in India was a shade under 60. After the Ahmedabad Test – another draw – Kapil Dev issued a statement blaming his opposite number for 'negative cricket'. An indifferent Imran replied that Kapil was just deflecting criticism of the Indian team's failure to force a result. In his private rebuttals, he laid it on a bit thicker, labelling some of the playing conditions 'subnormal', and remarking that even good home umpires were no substitute for neutral ones. A Pakistani cricket figure familiar with both players provided a blunt and critical assessment of the Imran–Kapil relationship when he told me that the latter, though a fine all-round performer, didn't care for the 'constant gibes about how good-looking Immy was compared to himself'.

The final Test, at Bangalore, coincided with the Hindu ritual of Holi, or spring festival. To enliven the proceedings several of the Indian players took the field in beads and brightly coloured face paint. The cricket was also appreciably more vibrant. After nets the previous evening, Imran had reportedly taken Iqbal Qasim aside and told the Karachi spinner that his services wouldn't be required in the match. 'I thought it was the end of my Test career,' Qasim remarked, 'and asked the captain if he would at least turn up at my benefit games. He said he would.' After a muscular debate with Javed, Imran reversed himself, apparently, just 20 minutes before play began. Qasim took five for 48 and four for 73 in the match, which Pakistan won by 16 runs to record their first series win in India. It was one of the great unifying moments in the nation's 40-year history. An estimated quarter of a million fans were jam-packed on to the streets of central Lahore, screaming and tearing at their hair, to welcome their cricketers home. It was a scene of Beatlemaniacal proportions. As far as it could be judged, the crowd's consensus favourites were Imran, Javed and the 'destroyer of nations', Iqbal Qasim. Whether the reported chanting of 'Death to India' was apocryphal or not, it summed up the sentiments of many of those present.

Two days after the Bangalore Test, Imran informed Qasim that he would not be included in the tour of England that summer. Or, at least, not in a playing capacity. Instead, the captain offered to find him an administrative role as what was officially called 'assistant manager', and which was reliably described elsewhere as a 'net wallah and bellboy'. In the event he never played a Test under Imran again. 'I felt disappointed,' Qasim remarked with some understatement. 'I was never sure why Imran did not have much confidence in me. I admired him greatly ... Abdul Qadir is a good friend and a great spinner and I was always very happy for him and the faith Imran had in him.'

In the round-robin Sharjah Cup which followed the India tour, Pakistan again beat their eastern neighbours in the match billed as the final. Thanks to the tournament's inscrutable rules, it was actually the unfancied English who won the trophy by virtue of their superior run-rate. On the flight back to London, Imran sipped milk and savoured his recent triumphs. After Bangalore, even the *Star* had taken to billing him on its back page as 'Super-Khan'. Elsewhere, he was variously 'the lion', 'the king' or 'the miracle worker'. At 34, and about to enjoy his benefit year, Imran was clearly nearing the end of his international career. Under his captaincy, Pakistan had seen off both India and Australia and tied a series against the West Indies. After he landed at Heathrow, Imran told waiting reporters that he had just two small sporting ambitions left. 'I want to beat England and win the World Cup,' he said.

'Cornhill Insurance welcomes Pakistan, for the summer both sets of players and their supporters have long been looking forward to,' trumpeted the sponsors of the 1987 Test series in an ill-timed press release just as the two national boards went to war with one another. At least initially the main bone or contention was the professionally well-regarded if occasionally brusque David Constant. It seems not to have escaped the visitors' attention that although the TCCB had agreed to a request by the Indians to have Constant barred from their 1982 tour of England, the authorities had refused a similar appeal from the Pakistanis later that same summer. Pakistan's current tour manager Haseeb Ahsan wasn't alone in seeing a double standard at play. Ahsan went on to publicly criticise Constant, who stood twice in the 1987 series, and at one point described him as 'a disgraceful person'.

Before the cricket began, there was a five-hour meeting between Imran, his tour manager and a representative of the BCCP on one side and Alan Smith, the new chief executive of the TCCB, and two assistants on the other. It went badly. Citing the 1982 precedent, Imran asked that Constant be appointed for only one Test, if that, and appears to have expressed broadly similar doubts about Constant's colleague Ken Palmer. Smith flatly refused to accept any restrictions on the TCCB's freedom of action to choose whichever umpires they wanted. One side or the other (reports vary) then leaked the Pakistanis' request, and the TCCB's response to it, to the press. Smith promptly issued a statement from the English first-class umpires in support of their colleagues on the Test match panel. Haseeb Ahsan went on the counter-attack, insisting that he and his team were the victims of rank prejudice. 'It was absolutely hysterical,' he would later remark. 'The English press were adamant ... They instigated nationalist fervour to prove that the real cheats were Pakistan.' ('I did sense a certain jingoism that built up over the summer,' Imran confirms today.) A number of the tabloids, notably the *Sun*, in something of a fit of cricket patriotism since England's successful winter tour of Australia, began hounding the Pakistan captain to apologise for 'having called our officials' integrity into question'. All this time David Constant was actually standing in the Test match at Lord's. It also quickly became clear that Imran was unlikely to bond with the England captain Mike Gatting, a model pro of the old school who seems not to have actively gone out of his way to assuage the tourists' concerns about gamesmanship. As the series progressed, relations between England and Pakistan deteriorated both on and off the field. In the one-day international at Birmingham, in late May, there were 'ugly scenes beyond the boundary,' noted *Wisden*, 'provoked by racial pride, racial prejudice and alcohol'. By the time of the Test match at the same venue two months later, there was a daily contingent of 820 police and stewards to keep order at the ground where total attendance was just 37,000 over five days, a ratio of one minder for every nine paying customers.

On the broader level, the Pakistanis' objection to David Constant opened a new chapter in the 'neutral umpires' saga which Imran had taken up as a personal crusade. In a rare display of unity, the BCCP and their national captain had jointly tried to elicit Alan Smith's support for the initiative by pointing out that this was a case where 'the so-called colonials' had taken the lead over the 'ex-mother country'. The phrasing of the Pakistanis' claim was not untypical of the mood whenever administrative matters were discussed that summer. But Smith and his team still weren't convinced. The journalist Chris Lander later described Imran as 'building up a good head of steam' about the perceived arrogance of the home authority. He went on to say that the tourists' manager was 'pop-eyed with anger' in his account of the clash of wills between the two boards. At home in Pakistan, even Karachi's leading weekly had temporarily called off its campaign against Imran and gotten on board with the 'neutrality' issue. 'We can readily acknowledge that there were problems with our umpires, but our lords and masters won't deign to follow suit,' it wrote.

Seeming to add to a generally stormy tour (literally so, as it poured throughout) was the Pakistanis' staggered and occasionally fractious arrival in England. 'We were treated with disdain by the TCCB, the press and even the Customs from the moment we landed,' Imran recalls. 'At Heathrow the team was made to stand aside, while other passengers looked on as sniffer-dogs went through our luggage.' In the ensuing news conference, Imran fielded a half-hour's worth of questions about his personal life and then calmly announced, 'We believe we will beat England well.' After the sniggering had died down, a young female reporter from the *Mirror* leapt up to ask the Pakistani captain whether he was 'seeing anyone special' in England. 'Look,' Imran replied, 'I'm here to talk about cricket and I don't think most people care about what I do outside of that. All they're interested in is this series.' The reporter gave it a second, and then asked her follow-up question: 'Are you still living with Emma Sergeant, Immy?' That concluded the interview.

Meanwhile, Javed Miandad, the vice-captain, was still at home in Karachi, where the tax department had taken an interest in the Mercedes awarded him after his match-winning six against India in Sharjah. While negotiating with the authorities, Javed was also awaiting the birth of a son. Abdul Qadir would similarly miss the first eight weeks of the tour because his young wife was under medical care for a variety of issues in Lahore. In the end Iqbal Qasim agreed to accompany the party as Haseeb Ahsan's deputy, apparently with the promise that he would play if circumstances allowed. Despite Qadir's prolonged absence, Qasim bowled just 18 overs in the 15-week tour, none of them in the Tests.

Imran declined to appear in Pakistan's first three warm-up matches, which were respectively abandoned, drawn and lost. When he did return, against Essex, he ran in at half speed and bowled Graham Gooch with his first ball of the tour. That was the prelude to several miserable weeks for Gooch, who later announced that he was giving up the county captaincy to concentrate on his batting. Although Imran rarely if ever slipped himself on the tour, no one doubted his powers of motivation or self-discipline. Peter Smith of the *Mail* called him 'fifty per cent more rabid' than any other Test cricketer. Sport was his life, and he concentrated single-mindedly on the struggle. Even on a rare day off, Imran was known to choose to go for a run by himself around Hyde Park, after which he typically put in a full afternoon in the nets at Lord's. On match days he jogged into the ground ahead of the other players, inspected the wicket, checked the weather forecast and for the next 90 minutes installed himself in a corner of the dressing-room where he would brief individual players about what was expected of them. Javed Kureishi sometimes watched Imran 'prowling around the room, practising his shots with an almost trance-like concentration before walking out to bat', which may help to explain why the BCCP official's intrusion of a year or two before had been so poorly received. After eight or nine hours' cricket, he then met with his tour manager, dealt with any tactical or disciplinary issues arising from the day's play, briefed the press and stepped outside to sign autographs before retiring to Tramp or a similar nightspot. Although 'geriatric' for a fast bowler, in *Today*'s uncharitable view, Imran suffered his only significant injury on tour when he strained a stomach muscle while lifting weights two days before the full internationals began. Despite being advised to rest for at least a week, he was the first player on the ground for the first Test at Old Trafford.

On the match itself, a draw, it's best to be brief. Just over half the playing time was lost to the weather. Even so the English batsmen were able to indulge their new-found habit of walking down the pitch to punch gloves with one another after a routine forward defensive, or even after playing and missing. Botham's innings of 48 in 130 minutes was punctuated by an orgy of hugging throughout. Another feature of the match was the Pakistanis' over rate, which was relaxed at the best of times. With Imran off the field for an X-ray of his thumb, the tourists sent down just 62 balls in an hour after tea on the second day. When Micky Stewart, the England manager, commented that this seemed to him to be a bit on the slow side, Imran reacted by saying, 'We always get slagged off and called cheats. I object to that.'

Lord's, the next venue, was under water on the first morning and under water again on the last evening. Between the floods, there was only seven hours' worth of cricket. Pakistan never got to bat. Conditions were only marginally better for the Headingley Test. Even by 1987 standards it was a bruising encounter, with what *The Times* referred to as 'indecorous' behaviour on both sides. Chris Broad was unlucky to be given out, caught behind off Imran, in England's second innings, a decision that left the batsman visibly unimpressed. Some time later, the Pakistan wicketkeeper Salim Yousuf enthusiastically claimed a catch off what appeared to be the second if not third bounce from Botham's outside edge. The umpire was not happy. Nor was Botham, who shortly after the match conceded that, in the heat of the moment, 'I may have accused the keeper of sharp practice.'

This was a notable paraphrase. What Botham actually told Yousuf was, 'You cheating little bastard. If you ever try that again I'll knock your head off.'

At that the umpire, Ken Palmer, advised Yousuf to conclude his appeal and go back to his position. Botham writes, 'At the end of the over, Imran came across and I asked him what he was going to do about it. He told me that if I hadn't sworn at Yousuf he would have been forced to make an apology.' *Wisden* has a slightly different version, praising the timely intervention of both umpire Palmer and Imran, the latter of whom 'reacted smartly, dressing down Yousuf in no uncertain manner'.

The other significant development in England's second innings also concerned Imran, who was now 'fairly satisfied' with his fitness and confirmed the point by taking seven for 40 off 19 overs. On the way he became the eighth bowler to capture 300 Test wickets. Among the crowd was the former England captain Ted Dexter, who still recalls 'watch[ing] Imran take the old ball and suddenly produce this prodigious swing. It was the "reverse" phenomenon all over again.' Dexter, a keen student of the physics of cricket, was later intrigued to come across 'an article by an American academic' – Imran's old grammar school friend Rabi Mehta – 'involved with the space programme, [who] authored a paper on the dynamics and effects of the airflow over a ball. In time I managed to arrange a meeting with him at Lord's, where some super high speed photography and demonstrations took place, although some like [former England bowler and chairman of selectors] Alec Bedser remained unconvinced.' It was all a bit confusing. A year later, however, Mehta published a further, much quoted paper on the science of reverse swing, which essentially confirmed the Pakistanis' long-held belief that there was nothing particularly mysterious about the whole process; it just needed 'the right kind of ball', and 'the expertise to use it'.

Thanks to Imran's bowling, Pakistan won the Leeds Test by an innings. There were still nearly two days' play in hand. Some of the large Pakistani contingent in the crowd, armed with impromptu instruments, saluted the occasion with native music and dancing on the outfield. Imran was man of the match. 'He led the team well,' Javed allows. 'He was a good listener ... I liked to share my insights, and the captain was always receptive.'

After that there was little to do but play out another draw at Edgbaston, where England finished at 109 for seven, chasing 124; Imran took a further eight wickets. The tourists had a single county match, against Hampshire, before the fifth Test. Although nominally the captain of the visiting side, Imran took little active part in the proceedings. He did, however, find time for a public tongue-lashing of the Hampshire captain Mark Nicholas, who told me about the incident.

> Imran didn't appear on the second day of the game, 'resting up' in his hotel after batting quite well on the first. On the third morning he swanned in suggesting that Pakistan use the day for batting practice before the Test as a result was unlikely. I said I thought he should make some quick runs and declare to set us a target and thus entertain the crowd. He said he wasn't there to entertain the crowd, and I said I wasn't there to help his team warm up before a Test against England. This became a full-on row beneath the press box in front of the members. Eventually Imran stormed off, calling me an arrogant public school boy. I shouted back that it took one to know one.

The match was drawn. 'Javed led the side while Imran was back at the hotel,' Nicholas adds, 'and kept telling me he couldn't do a thing without his captain's agreement ... It was all pretty childish,' he admits.

The final Test, at The Oval, saw Pakistan score 708. Javed was in his element and made 260, apparently once again in failed pursuit of Sobers's Test record. Just before the match, Imran had announced that this was to be his last appearance for Pakistan. He scored 118. In one 30-minute spurt on the second afternoon he and Javed put on 44, which consisted of 43 to Imran and a leg-bye. Following on, 476 runs behind, England escaped by virtue of 150 and 51 by Gatting and Botham respectively. Before the match Imran had chaired a long and reportedly heated meeting of the tourists' selection panel, most of whom felt that Abdul Qadir was out of form and should be dropped. I was told that Javed, among others, had again made a 'sustained' case for Iqbal Qasim, just as had happened five months earlier in Bangalore. This time Imran persevered and Qadir played at The Oval; he took his best Test figures of seven for 96, including a spell of four wickets in 35 balls, in England's first innings.

After beating India and now England on their home grounds, Pakistan were on a roll. If Imran was indeed going out, he was doing so at the top. Not only had he fulfilled most of his ambitions as a captain, he'd maintained his own form both as batsman and bowler. Reflecting on the 1987 series, Ian Botham was to write, 'I still regard Immy as my greatest rival in the world all-round stakes.' It was a generous tribute, if one the facts only partly support. In the five Tests that summer,

Botham had a batting average of 33 and took seven wickets at a fraction under 62 apiece. Imran had a batting average of 48 and took 21 wickets at some 22 each. 'The bounding, big-hearted Both [was] still good value,' *Today* correctly observed, but there was only one all-rounder's name up in gold leaf on Test cricket's 1987 honours board.

In county cricket, unlike most sports, financial rewards tend to be a result of longevity rather than exceptional talent or popularity. After an extended period of service, even the journeyman player can look forward to a benefit season with the prospect of earning a six-figure sum, tax free. Despite having exasperated at least half the county membership at one time or another during his 22 years there, Geoff Boycott would net £147,954 from Yorkshire in 1984. Graham Gooch did even better at Essex the following year. Imran's turn came in 1987, exactly a decade after his controversial move to Sussex from Worcestershire. When all the figures were added up he made an eminently respectable £100,000, roughly ten times his basic annual salary from the club. 'I am both flattered and honoured,' he wrote in his fundraising brochure, 'and deeply thankful for all the friendship and support shown me by players and members alike. It's been more like a home from home than just a cricket club.' For all that, Imran's notion of what constituted a dignified benefit differed significantly from that of many other players. 'It was just legalised begging,' he later remarked. 'I thought when I saw a sheet being carried about for supporters' money during Mike Procter's testimonial year that a great cricketer was being degraded. I vowed that I would do things differently.'

'Basically, Imran wanted a benefit, but he didn't want to walk around shaking a collecting tin,' says Jonathan Mermagen. Mermagen sat on the organising committee, and came up with a number of 'perhaps more select' celebrity events involving the likes of Bill Wyman and Adam Faith, as well as a gathering of 2,000 fans at the Hammersmith Palais. There was also a star-studded match at the county seat of cricket's Anglophile patron Paul Getty. Getty 'went ballistic', a witness reports, 'when Imran, who had been out at a club the night before, was 20 minutes late in appearing for the toss'. Tony Pigott also attended some of the functions, among them a glittering black-tie dinner in Brighton. 'Imran was perfectly friendly, but it was pretty clear his heart wasn't in it. You certainly wouldn't call him the life and soul of the party. He sat there at the top table, listened to the tributes, and then stood up and made a speech in which he said something like, "I don't actually need this. I don't really want your money", and about five hundred faces around the room fell flat.' Another player says bluntly, 'The timing of the whole benefit was an exquisite cock-up on someone's part.' Thanks to Imran's international commitments, his one appearance of the year at Hove was when Sussex hosted the Pakistanis before the first Test. Eschewing sentiment, he took five for 61 against his sometime county colleagues. Imran declined to join Sussex for the last month of the season, but did appear for the Rest of the World against the MCC in the club's bicentenary match at Lord's. For once, the sun shone. Imran enjoyed a run-a-minute partnership of 180 with Sunil Gavaskar in the Rest's first innings. Some half an hour into the stand, pace gave way to the gentle off spin of John Emburey, who had played in four of the summer's Tests against Pakistan without taking a wicket. His first ball, dropped short, was deposited by Imran into the president's box above the Tavern concourse. Hadlee returned to the attack soon afterwards, and went for three off-side fours in an over. Gavaskar scored 188, Imran 82, and the match was drawn.

In the watering holes of Kensington and Mayfair, the reaction to Imran was, if possible, even more effusive than in Pakistan. A self-styled 'old deb' and future journalist named Alix Gibb was on hand for a late-summer London charity fundraiser where a number of women, in ball gowns, escorted by a liveried butler, moved from room to room and 'finally entered the inner sanctum, at the far end of which Imran was standing, with his hand in his pocket, leaning casually against a mantelpiece ... Our party slowly advanced, some of the [women] bowing their heads as if in the presence of royalty ... Imran stood quite motionless, apparently oblivious or indifferent to the homage paid him.' Another guest at the same event remembers Imran 'surrounded by a sizeable mob of female admirers bent on touching the hem of his coat, if not considerably more'. Certainly his fan base had long since ceased to be confined to the sports world. 'It was the same sort of frenzy – slightly more localised – that Barack Obama enjoyed 20 years later,' Gibb now reflects. 'It was a great thumping love-fest. Imran appeared to be genuinely thoughtful and in earnest about his desire to make the world a better place. Between that and the big brown eyes, what could a girl do?'

It's a tribute to all parties' discretion that Imran and his various companions only rarely ended up in the gossip columns. One notable exception to the rule was an Anglo-Pakistani named Homaa Khan (no relation), a GP who then worked at St Bartholomew's hospital in

London. 'Yes, Imran is charming,' she informed *Today*. 'But if you tell me that women envy me, I can only say, what is all the fuss about? There are many more attractive men about, I would have thought.' Perhaps not surprisingly, the relationship ended soon afterwards.

When Imran announced his retirement from international cricket there seems to have been a certain amount of doubt, at least in some people's minds, about whether or not he meant 'with immediate effect'. Initially, several of the Pakistan papers had taken him at his word and published full-scale Test career obituaries of the 'miracle worker' and 'great helmsman', almost as if eulogising a fallen populist statesman. Even in the hitherto tetchy Karachi media, virtues were discovered that had somehow previously failed to surface. It was obvious now that the editors of the *Star* took to this 'magnificent beast' and 'national icon' in a way which few had ever suspected. On the other hand, anyone who had listened carefully to Imran's announcement would have heard him say, quite clearly, that it was only the five-day version of the game he was bowing out of. The recently retired Wasim Raja would remember being in a meeting with two senior members of the Pakistan government discussing his possible appointment to an advisory board; as the three of them talked, one of the ministers volunteered his opinion on the burning issue of the day. 'I just can't believe that Imran's work is finished,' he declared.

Nor could he. By early October, as he turned 35, Imran was back training with Pakistan in the run-up to their first tie in the Reliance World Cup, as its sponsors insisted it be known, in Hyderabad. The home side began their campaign in a possibly excessive mood of self-confidence. One much-circulated press cartoon suggested that the whole event would be a coronation for the Pakistanis. 'It almost seemed natural and inevitable that Imran should finish his career on a winning note. Mentally, we had won the World Cup before it had started,' Wasim Akram recalls.

Pakistan duly edged Sri Lanka in their opening match, before pulling off nail-biting wins against England and the West Indies to eventually earn a semi-final tie against the unfancied Australians. At that stage it would be fair to characterise the mood both in the team and the country as a whole as one of supreme optimism. As Wasim Akram says, 'the match itself seemed like a formality. The Australians hadn't even made any provision for televising the final on [the basis] their team wouldn't be in it.' Imran remarks that he had stayed up late in his

Lahore home the night before the match trying to envisage any possible scenario in which Pakistan could conceivably lose. 'I honestly couldn't think of one,' he adds.

Of course, everything went wrong. The in-form opening batsman Mudassar pulled out at the last minute with a neck injury and was replaced by Mansoor Akhtar, who scored 9. Less than half-way through the Australian innings Pakistan's wicketkeeper Salim Yousuf took a ball to the mouth and Javed Miandad had to step in and don the gauntlets. He tried hard, but it was a major break for the visitors. The total number of leg-byes conceded in the Australian innings, 19, was one more than their final margin of victory. 'The force just wasn't with us that day,' Imran would reflect. Another significant factor was the bowling of the left-arm medium-pacer Saleem Jaffer, which only rarely lived up to the inherent promise of his surname. Jaffer went for a vital 18 runs off his last over. When Pakistan came to bat, the old warhorses Imran and Javed put on 112 for the fourth wicket before Imran was caught behind on 58. 'There's some controversy whether umpire Dickie Bird made an error on that particular decision,' Javed remarks. 'I don't think he did.' Imran demurs. 'I missed the ball by six inches but was given out.'

Some people left the Gaddafi Stadium with tears in their eyes, and others vented their disappointment by rioting on the streets of Lahore. A 'disheartened' Imran confirmed his final retirement. 'I wanted to leave at the top, partly because I was aware that the cricket establishment was gunning for me. I didn't want to put myself at the mercy of the selectors,' he adds. The Lahore Crisis Clinic received over 400 calls on the day he officially announced his decision, roughly twice the usual number. Three months later there would be demonstrations outside Imran's home calling on him to return to the game and captain the national team in the West Indies. Two fans, one in Multan, the other in rural Kashmir, went further than this and killed themselves in apparent grief at the outcome of the World Cup, which Australia went on to win. In the national furore that followed the tournament, the ever colourful Sarfraz Nawaz accused the Pakistan players of having taken money to throw the semi-final. Imran heatedly denied the charges. Undeterred, Sarfraz then named Javed Miandad as one of those who had allegedly been bought off. Javed sued, but eventually dropped the case after it had degenerated into an administrative stalemate.

* * *

Over the winter of 1987–88, a succession of government ministers and ordinary fans continued to urge Imran to come out of retirement, even if the board officials were generally conspicuous by their silence. Meanwhile, Javed once again assumed the captaincy of Pakistan. For Imran this was a period of 're-evaluating my priorities [after] 17 years of non-stop sport'. He had now played in 70 Tests and four World Cups. One of the early milestones of his chosen exile came when he found himself sharing a Greek holiday villa with the American-born journalist Charles Glass, who made headlines in 1987 when he was taken hostage for 62 days in Lebanon by Hezbollah, the Shi'ite Muslim group, before escaping. Glass got the impression that, even then, Imran resented Islamabad's apparent servility to the Reagan administration, and the demands of Washington's 'corrosive' foreign policy. 'He [saw] a class of people in Pakistan merely responding to Western interests [rather] than to their own kind.' At a dinner in London, Imran would exchange views on American imperialism with the playwright Harold Pinter and a similarly imposing line-up of other literary and academic guests. These were perhaps deeper waters than those steered by the average retired cricketer. At about the same time, Imran began to take up a variety of environmental causes, in which he was something of a celebrity pioneer. By the late 1980s he was giving his time and money to the World Development Movement and Friends of the Earth, and later publicly cut up his credit cards in protest against either the banks' policy on Third World debt or on the rainforest, depending on which version you read. In time Imran became a spokesman for Save the Children, and as such regularly outshone even his fellow travelling ambassadors such as Peter Ustinov. Ustinov good-naturedly remarked that following 'the cricket player' around anywhere in India or Pakistan was 'roughly akin to be[ing] the uncarved side of Mount Rushmore. The word "ignored" would be the key one.'

For all that, nothing motivated Imran quite as much as his 'now burning ambition' to build a cancer hospital in memory of his mother. It stamped for ever and changed the lives of those most directly involved – not only Imran and his immediate family, but a host of administrators, doctors, patients and those who donated their money. Back in London, Jeffrey Archer threw one of his shepherd's pie-and-champagne Christmas parties, at which sports and film stars mingled with members of Margaret Thatcher's cabinet. 'Imran talked about politics,' Archer recalls, 'but at that time he was much more interested in [fundraising] for his hospital. It was clear that he was absolutely dedicated to achieving this before [anything] else.' He was described elsewhere as being 'just slightly obsessed' by the project.

England's winter tour of Pakistan was ill-conceived and poorly timed, coming only a week after the two teams' mutual disappointments in the World Cup, and promptly lived down to its billing. After what had happened in the previous English summer, it perhaps didn't take a genius to predict that certain administrative issues might arise. In the event, the acrimony began before the first ball of the first Test. England's refusal to entertain Pakistan's objections to umpires Constant and Palmer some four months earlier now came back to haunt them. According to *Wisden*, 'The [Englishmen's] protest about the appointment of the controversial Shakeel Khan in Lahore was ignored. The tourists claimed afterwards that no fewer than nine incorrect decisions had been given in favour of Pakistan's bowlers, while during the match their disgust and disillusion had boiled over in an extraordinary incident involving Chris Broad. Given out, caught at the wicket, by Shakeel, Broad refused to accept the decision, and almost a minute elapsed before he was at last persuaded by his partner, Graham Gooch, to depart the crease.'

Not a good start. After a relative lull in the zonal match played at the Montgomery Biscuit Factory at Sahiwal, England moved on to the second Test at Faisalabad, which proved to be one of the more acrimonious games in cricket history. The third day's play was lost while England's captain Mike Gatting tortuously composed an apology acceptable to the umpire Shakoor Rana, with whom he had publicly exchanged finger-prodding insults the previous evening. Compounding the problem was the elusiveness of both the BCCP president and secretary, respectively Sadfar Butt and Ijaz Butt, who were variously reported to be 'unavailable', 'resting' or 'out to dinner' throughout the impasse. (Imran himself was incommunicado most of the winter, shooting partridge in the Pakistani highlands.) The two Butts were eventually located, and the whole bilious tour at least continued as scheduled. A member of President Zia's cabinet was later to remark only half-jokingly that it would perhaps be just as well for diplomatic relations if the Pakistani and English sides refrained from appealing altogether in future Tests against one another.

Despite Imran's consistent calls for neutral umpires, and his own occasional misgivings about Shakoor Rana, it would be wrong to state that he condoned the tourists' less than ambassadorial conduct at either

Lahore or, more particularly, Faisalabad. But it's at least arguable that, had he been playing, he would have defused the situation earlier than his recurrent stand-in Javed Miandad did. 'When Javed was captain there was always some controversy,' Imran recalled.

What seems beyond dispute is that the events of November and December 1987 only increased the calls for Imran's comeback. Despite being an unlisted number, his phone at Zaman Park was 'going crazy ... People were calling literally begging him to return, threatening suicide if he didn't,' I was told. Distraught fans had similarly jammed the wires of the BCCP offices in Lahore. One widely quoted report stated that Lieutenant-General Butt and his board received some 80,000 letters and cards signed by a quarter of a million people. The office of the state president in Islamabad received additional thousands of letters addressing the issue of the national captaincy. They ran 150 to one in Imran's favour. The president himself had expressed regret that his 'esteemed friend [should] go gentle into the night'.

Still, only Imran's opinion counted. He told me that he had been 'earnest' about his retirement, but added that he'd always relished the personal challenge of playing the West Indies, where Pakistan were to tour in the spring of 1988. Imran was also shrewd enough to know that his returning to captain Pakistan would give him the sort of international profile that could serve to help turn his dream of a cancer hospital into a reality. Javed himself endorses this theory, adding, 'Our guys subsequently donated all kinds of prize money – from team awards as well as cash from man of the match awards – to the cause. On one occasion one of the players was awarded an automobile, which was also handed over to help with the hospital.' All of which is true, including the bit about the team's financial generosity, although it's perhaps worth mentioning that it was Imran himself who furnished the car, which he won in Australia in February 1990.

What linked the ordinary citizens demonstrating outside Imran's house with the highest reaches of the Pakistan government was their fanatical support of the national sport and their obvious concern for its future. In mid-January 1988, the state president hosted a dinner to celebrate the cricket team's achievements during the past year. It was a glittering occasion, which was broadcast live on Pakistani television. After presenting each of the players and officials with a gold medal, General Zia turned to fix Imran with his shark-like grin – the terror of political opponents over the past decade – and said, 'It is good to know when to go out gracefully. But a sportsman should also be like a soldier who is always ready to serve the country.' The president than sat down and the camera panned on to Imran. Given the circumstances, he might be thought to have been under a fair amount of pressure when forming his reply, which was heard by an estimated audience of 30 million people. 'I am always ready to serve the nation and the game,' he said. It was almost as if, in another culture, Lazarus had risen from the dead, such was the immediate and nationwide effusion – although, as in the biblical tale, there were also those, among them certain members of the home board, who resented the comeback being effectively imposed on them by a higher authority.

In short order, Imran had plugged himself back in like a neon sign. He spent the next six weeks training eight hours a day, giving interviews, meeting with the board and helping put in place the groundwork for a Pakistani Cricketers Association designed to protect the players from just the sort of 'crazy' itinerary they faced in the West Indies. The tour itself was a mixed success. Pakistan lost the one-day international series 5–0. 'Imran was treated lightly,' according to one report. But they recovered sufficiently to win the first Test, at Georgetown, thus handing the West Indies their first defeat on home soil in 10 years. Bowling with an improving back strain and a worsening toe infection, Imran took seven for 80 and four for 41 in the match. 'Two things really kept me going,' he remarked. 'The team depended on me so much, and my pride was hurt by [certain] fans saying I shouldn't have come to the West Indies because I was past it.' As Imran's detractors should have known, such gibes only served to spur him on. When Pakistan's manager suggested that the team might be more enthusiastic if they spent more time on the beach, Imran responded by doubling the regimen from one to two practice sessions a day. On duty he was a 'joyless, single-minded leader', a player recalled approvingly; one who 'expected you to live up to his own high standards'.

Now carrying a leg injury, Imran took another nine wickets in the Trinidad Test, bowling medium-paced inswingers. But for some overly patriotic umpiring, he might have improved his tally to 12 or 13. Other than that, the gripping moments came on the final day when Qadir, the No. 11, survived the last five balls from Richards to preserve Pakistan's lead in the series – a role-reversal case of a batsman bowling to a bowler. The West Indies narrowly won the last Test at Bridgetown, in the course of which a frustrated Qadir threw a punch at a heckler in the crowd, an assault for which he later received a court summons, before the charges were eventually dismissed. At one stage on the final morning, Richards came down the wicket to block Imran with an extravagant gesture, at which point the bowler stood in mid-pitch and announced, 'You really love yourself, don't you?' 'Yeah,' said Richards, 'I learnt it from watching you.' A combative series finished 1–1. At a time when the best most touring teams to the West Indies could hope for was to lose with dignity, it was a rare achievement – and a personal triumph for Pakistan's now middle-aged captain, who took 23 wickets at 18 apiece in the three Tests.

A large and appreciative crowd was on hand at the airport to welcome home Pakistan's cricketers in late April. In a departure from previous practice, a party from the BCCP was reportedly waiting with a local government delegation to greet Imran personally. He duly descended first from the team plane – impassive, grave and distantly preoccupied in the midst of all the delirious excitement around him. He exchanged salutes and handshakes of congratulation with the officials and, as rapidly as he could move, which wasn't very fast, passed through mobs of cheering well-wishers and on to a brightly decorated bus. A chorus of screaming bystanders, hooters, klaxons and an intermittent blast of distant rifle fire accompanied the players throughout their short journey to the formal civic reception, outside which onlookers in the tens of thousands had gathered with their green-and-white flags and banners. 'Imran's [return] had been anticipated as keenly as an Eleventh Commandment or a book tour by J.D. Salinger,' one British newspaper stringer wrote. 'He did not disappoint.' The possibly inapt comparison apart, it seems fair to say that Imran's comeback had capped off a collective triumph. As he said, 'By drawing the series in the Caribbean and beating both England and India on their home grounds, Pakistan were now considered the best team in the world together with the West Indies.' But his reputation cut rather deeper than that of merely a successful cricket captain. Essentially, Imran provided a sort of sports-assisted therapy for a nation still struggling to fully accommodate itself to General Zia's move from a secular form of government to a religious one. Nor was his fame restricted to a domestic audience. According to the Associated Press, when dignitaries from other Commonwealth countries visited Pakistan for the first time, they typically 'asked to see the Khyber Pass and Imran Khan', though, as the correspondent was quick to add, 'not invariably in that order'.

It's worth dwelling on Imran's stature once more, if only to show the contrast between the scale of the stage he occupied internationally, and the one he operated on back in Sussex. After playing in front of a full house in the gladiatorial atmosphere of Bombay or Bridgetown, it was always going to be difficult to rise to the occasion on a wet afternoon in Horsham. In the event, the county offered Imran a contract which bound him to one-day games but to only a handful of championship matches of his own choosing. 'It soon became something of an embarrassment to the club,' reports *Wisden*. One of his senior Sussex colleagues put it to me more strongly: 'By then, it was pretty clear we were just a pit stop on the grand prix of Imran's career. He handpicked [his] appearances, which was probably better than his not playing at all – he was still a great all-rounder – but wasn't an absolutely genius move in terms of team morale.' Compounding the problem, Sussex were in a state of some disarray, having changed their captain, coach and club secretary and lost Garth le Roux, Dermot Reeve and no fewer than five other first-team players over the previous 15 months. As Imran remarks, 'The side I came back to in 1988 wasn't a shadow of the one I left two seasons earlier.' In retrospect it might have been better for all parties had he made a clean break from the club immediately after their winning the 1986 NatWest Trophy, thus ensuring he left English first-class cricket while still at the top.

Among others on the county circuit, attitudes were mixed. Although an 'imperious bugger', as his ghostwriter remarked, Imran could also be the charmer, gliding smoothly across the social classes. 'Educated at Aitchison and Oxford, equally at home in Islamabad's presidential palace as at Tramp, he can mix it with all sorts,' according to the *Sunday Times*. If you were a player, an official or even an ordinary fan at another English county, the chances were that Imran would be friendly, considerate and interested in you individually. To a long-serving ground supervisor at Lord's named Gus Farley, who'd 'seen it all', he was 'alert, sharp ... he looked good, very vigorous, very strong', but, more importantly, he was a 'diamond' who 'remembered people's names and signed their autographs'. A self-styled 'security consultant and VIP courier' who sometimes took Imran to and from the airport told me:

> Most people, after arriving off a long-haul flight, come in the terminal like zombies. They can barely make it to the door ... Now, here's a guy, you had to move when he moved. And he *moved fast!* He'd trot by with a couple of bags, and you had to catch up. I knew when I met Imran I had to be on my toes, because otherwise he'd

be out the door and probably jogging half-way down the M4 before you'd missed him.

Imran returned to Sussex in time for a Sunday league game against Gloucestershire in early May. It was raining. Opening the Sussex batting he scored 6, and then took no wickets in the abridged Gloucester innings. After that he was in action against Middlesex at Lord's, where David Constant was one of the umpires. Imran made 71, but was again wicketless. 'The sting had gone,' one of the opposing Middlesex batsmen assured me. 'I couldn't believe how much he'd lost from only a year earlier. He still had the model action, but he was about as fiery and hostile as my granny.' Imran was back at Lord's for a county match at the end of May. He took five for 50 off 22 overs in the one Middlesex innings, 'bowling', said the *Cricketer* magazine, 'with a speed and skill that tested all the batsmen, and physically damaged at least one of them'.

Still, Imran's all-round prowess was unpredictable, and his *chutzpah* now sometimes fell a bit flat. On 19 June, Sussex narrowly won a Sunday league game against Leicestershire at Grace Road. Imran under-performed. Three days later Sussex hosted Derbyshire in the NatWest Trophy first round at Hove. Tony Pigott remembers Imran drawing him aside on the way into the ground 'and announcing with great conviction, "Forget about [Leicester]. I'll get a hundred here today."' In the event, he was to fall somewhat short of his boast. Imran came in to bat at 11.07 and departed again at 11.09, not having troubled the scorers. The destroyer was his old rival Michael Holding, whose return of eight for 21 was then the best in any English limited-overs competition. It was a poignant moment, according to Pigott, 'because you sensed Imran couldn't just turn it on at will any more'.

He did a bit better the following Sunday, scoring 50 and taking three wickets against Warwickshire. On figures he was just about holding his own in the county side, although that may not have been his main value to Sussex. Exact totals are hard to establish, but a well-placed source at Hove believes that 'there were still at least two or three hundred extra bums in seats whenever Imran was playing, most of them female' – statistically significant for a ground only holding some four thousand. On 24 July he was in the side for a one-day tie against Northants, who included the 39-year-old Dennis Lillee in their ranks. Imran took one for 24 and Lillee managed one for 18. Two days later, the same teams finished a miserably wet championship match at

Northampton. Although no one knew it at the time, it was to be Imran's last professional appearance in England, coincidentally against the same opponents as his first one had been 17 years earlier.

As county cricket grew less riveting, dealing with the media became a positive chore. It sometimes seemed that Imran was more concerned about and angry with the press than with his on-the-field opponents. In England, the continuing obsession was with what *Today* called the 'swarthy Khan's' love life. Quite apart from taking the opportunity to run a whole series of pictures of young women in short skirts, the press generally spun their headlines to depict an England that was fine with multiculturalism – 'many of his best friends are fledgelings from our oldest established families [and] fully respect his beliefs', an anonymous insider assured one Sunday paper. At the same time, some of the more sneering coverage was designed to imply that Imran, a mere cricketer with no great financial prospects, was supposedly getting above himself in 'openly seeing toff author Susannah Constantine, the on-off flame of Viscount Linley'. Many of Susannah's well-heeled friends were 'amused', it seemed. Clearly there was only so much goodwill to go round, and now that the likes of *Today* were becoming so laid-back about race it was apparently still all right to raise 'the inevitable questions [about] circumstances and compatibility', which might just conceivably have been taken as the code for 'class'. In Pakistan, of course, Imran had long since grown used to being treated as everything from a secular saint to a national pariah. No wonder that when his friend Fareshteh Aslam announced she was thinking of becoming a cricket writer, he told her, 'You have no idea just what a filthy business it is', and, having said that, 'supported and encouraged me by giving me access to the Pakistani team'.

In the summer of 1988, Imran became the latest celebrity to invade his own privacy by publishing what the accompanying handout called his 'full and shockingly frank' memoir *All Round View*. It sold some 23,000 copies in its hardback edition, which is around 20,000 more than many cricket autobiographies. Imran's views on the English establishment in general and more specifically the Test and County Cricket Board probably weren't improved when the latter formally reprimanded him and banned his book from sale at certain outlets on the grounds of its 'unacceptable' criticism of David Constant, among others.

On 31 July, Sussex were due to play a 40-overs Sunday league match against Glamorgan at Eastbourne. Some small discrepancy exists as to why exactly Imran arrived at the ground as late as he did. Jonathan Mermagen told me that it had been down to a combination of 'making a punctual start from Badminton, but then running out of petrol on the way'. Tony Pigott, who was playing at Eastbourne, believes his sometime team-mate 'had been at a party in Gloucester the night before and, not untypically, misjudged the time'. Imran himself recalled that 'it was the middle of a bank holiday weekend' (which wasn't the case) 'and the road was busy'. Whatever the cause, the result was that the Sussex players went out on to the field without their star all-rounder. Just as the first ball was about to be bowled, Tony Pigott looked up to see 'a red-faced Immy chugging across the ground carrying his cricket bag' to confer with his captain Paul Parker – who told him that he wouldn't be playing. Although Imran's 'unreserved' apology was accepted, the following morning the club announced that he would not appear again until the last match of the season. In the event he missed that one, too, owing to injury. It was the end. In his 11 years at Sussex, Imran had scored 7,329 first-class runs and taken 409 wickets, as well as putting several thousand paying customers in their seats.

'It was a sad way to go,' says *Wisden*, a view broadly endorsed in the press as a whole. But was it? Imran himself saw the break as the 'natural and inevitable' outcome of a growing disenchantment with English county cricket that had set in as far back as 1981, when Sussex had finished as runners-up in the championship. A theme throughout his time at both Worcester and Hove had been his low boredom threshhold and aversion to merely going through the motions in certain late-season matches. He'd found the playing atmosphere altogether more congenial in Australia, where the domestic competition was geared more towards producing results than long-term job security. 'When I finally finished in England, I asked myself why I hadn't done so years before,' Imran recalls. 'Cricket was my passion, and the idea of it being a routine job just didn't appeal to me.' Paul Parker also discounts the 'Eastbourne saga', which he sees as only the last milestone of a 'very long road both for Imran and the club ... By then it seemed to me that although the committee wanted him around for the gate money and the sponsors, it was a step backwards to actually play him in the team. What happened was a natural winding down of a great career.'

* * *

Had he wished, Imran could have gone into the political bully-pit in 1988, nearly a decade before he actually did so. In discussing various sinecures late that spring, President Zia had given a colleague to understand that 'the country's number one hero' was of old Pathan stock, the son of a hard-working father and a late patriotic mother, that he was a fresh face in Pakistani party politics and, not incidentally, 'was known himself to be an honest and honourable man'. Strong credentials under any circumstances, but ideal for what the president had in mind when he decided to form a committee of 'intellectuals, scholars, *ulema*, journalists and distinguished others' to act as a national brains trust, answerable to himself. Imran in turn described the president as 'not exactly a friend because he was the Head of State', but plainly someone for whom he felt a mutual respect. It's unclear whether there was ever a formal job offer, and if so whether Zia saw his national cricket captain as a 'real executive [or] just as window dressing', as a Pakistani team rival put it. According to one biographer, in the weeks following his *de facto* retirement from Sussex, Imran went to the trouble of consulting a clairvoyant, who told him that he would be assassinated if he went into politics. Later that month, on 17 August 1988, a military plane carrying Zia, as well as most of his senior generals and civilian advisers, and the American ambassador to Pakistan, crashed shortly after take-off from the airfield at Bahawalpur, south of Islamabad. There were no survivors.

In somewhat strained circumstances, Australia's sixth tour of Pakistan got under way a fortnight later. Imran declined to participate. In explaining his decision he told the press that it was absurd to play cricket in September's summer-monsoon conditions simply because it suited the two boards; and, besides, he didn't think that the Australians were good enough to win a series in Pakistan. He was right: Javed's side took the three-Test series 1–0. There were umpiring rows and crowd disturbances throughout. In Imran's absence Iqbal Qasim returned for Pakistan and was his team's leading wicket-taker. After that, he would never represent his country again.

In private, a number of the Australians expressed the view that Imran had been a touch *de haut en bas* (I sanitise somewhat) in refusing to come out and play against them. The Pakistani public, meanwhile, were as confused and divided as were its cricketers. A widely quoted opinion poll of 12 October showed that 53 per cent wanted Imran to return as captain, while 44 per cent were opposed. At least one elderly

Lahore man in the former camp was prepared to illustrate his views by going on hunger strike. In Karachi, only 13 per cent favoured replacing Javed. Given the contradictions of their national selectors, it was small wonder the public were nonplussed.

In due course the domestic media again dusted off their career obituaries. As many of them were at pains to point out, competitive nerve tends to be a wasting asset. At 36, Imran was thought unlikely ever to return to his peak form, and what's more he apparently wasn't going to give himself the chance. In Pakistani sport, however, things are rarely as straightforward as they first seem. 'The board asked me to continue after the Australian series,' Javed insists, 'but Imran wanted the job back. Things could have turned ugly. I had stepped aside before to accommodate Imran and I did so again.'

A measure of the Imran manner and outlook was the way he conducted his irregular but lively meetings with the BCCP, generally speaking one of the more memorable events in the bureaucrats' diaries. 'You might as well have been negotiating with a cyclone,' one of the now retired board members recalls. In a break from the precedent set by other captains, Imran was 'prodigiously intelligent, opinionated and determined. He once announced that he would argue the merits of a particular player all day if necessary to ensure his selection, and proceeded to do so.' The official, who was himself 'not punctual', he cheerfully admits, also notes of Imran, 'The calls on his time were always quite obvious, and we were never sure if we would speak uninterrupted. When he excused himself for just a minute, he would sometimes be back half an hour or an hour later.' The other board members could each tell their own stories of Imran's exceptional diligence, the long hours he kept and the fact that he took the job '*very*, very seriously. He spent virtually every waking moment working at being captain, and wouldn't settle for anything less than the team he wanted.'

Having sat out the Australian series, Imran now consented to lead Pakistan on their tour of New Zealand. This was conspicuously hard luck on Javed, who, whatever else one thinks of him, never gave less than his all to his country. It's not clear to what extent Imran based his decision on popular demands for his return, or whether he simply relished the challenge. On balance, the latter seems more in character. Imran hadn't played Test cricket against his fellow all-rounder Richard Hadlee since early 1979, when he, Imran, clearly hadn't been firing on all cylinders. So there was a point to prove, which was probably motivation enough. From the start of his career, even when playing for county seconds or Under-19 sides, Imran had made a habit of doing it his way, against the wishes and even the orders of those above him, while displaying an equally healthy competitive streak when it came to the official opposition. The twin goals were independence and superiority, at whatever level he was operating. By now his life priorities may have changed, but his need to dominate was as strong as ever. In January 1989, a young Pakistani team-mate ventured, in a rare moment of conversational reflection as they were walking out to the Auckland nets together, to say to Imran, 'Skipper, this will probably make you smile, but I have a curious feeling that you are heading for a very great triumph here.' Imran simply gazed off into the distance and replied in a deadpan voice: 'Yes, I do, too.'

On taking over from Javed, Imran had had a number of spirited sessions with the Pakistani national selectors. His confidence in his own judgement of his subordinates seems to have grown along with his disillusion with and contempt for the compromise option. Imran now took up the cause of a 16-year-old Lahore-based seam bowler named Aaqib Javed. Unsurprisingly, the BCCP mandarins had never heard of Aaqib, whose few first-class appearances to date had brought him six wickets at some 40 runs apiece. Despite these modest credentials, Imran insisted that the lad be included in the squad for the triangular Benson and Hedges 'world cup' in Australia, where the hosts disposed of Pakistan in the early stages. Aaqib took 10 wickets in the series, which was three more than Imran himself. The young seamer then went on the tour of New Zealand, and would eventually play 22 Tests and 163 one-day internationals in the course of the next 10 years. On his retirement, Aaqib would say of Imran, 'Once he was convinced about something, he would never retreat. Never.'

In a subsequent meeting, Imran further insisted on picking Shoaib Mohammad, the Karachi opener whose selection he'd vocally objected to five years earlier. Shoaib's return was not met with great enthusiasm on the part of the selection panel. There was a brief but vigorous debate, which Imran reportedly brought to an end by announcing, 'If he doesn't go on the tour, nor do I.' A witness to the scene remarks, perhaps superfluously, that Pakistan's captain was 'not a man to trifle with'. Shoaib duly went to New Zealand and responded with a batting average of 137.50.

In brief, the first Test at Dunedin was abandoned owing to a lake having formed on the outfield, and the second and third Tests were drawn. *Wisden,* departing from its proprietary brand of critical sang-froid, would deplore the 'filthy language' employed during the series. 'It seemed that the tourists, sensitive to the claims that umpiring in Pakistan was questionable, set out to show that New Zealand umpires were also incompetent. That was the word used by the captain, Imran Khan.' Other than that, the brief and ill-tempered rubber was notable only for a few individual knocks. Javed hit a nine-hour 271 at Auckland, again falling short of Sobers's record. Imran became the third player after Botham and Kapil Dev to score 3,000 runs and take 300 wickets. In the two completed Tests his batting average was 140 and his bowling average was 28; Hadlee's figures were 27 and 34 respectively.

Not, then, a glisteningly brilliant series. The personal coups no doubt gave Imran some pleasure and served to reassure him that he was still up to the job, but it's very likely that nothing at this time brought him greater satisfaction than the news that the government of Punjab was to donate 8 hectares (20 acres) of wasteland on the southwestern outskirts of Lahore on which to build his cancer hospital.

Little did he know it, but finding the land for the site was to be the least of his challenges. The eventual construction costs would soar impressively, while Imran faced a barrage of criticism, much of it coming from the Karachi area, to the effect that the project was more about a giant ego trip on his part than about helping the sick and dispossessed of Pakistan. 'There was negativity through envy,' said Imran's cousin, Dr Nausherwan Burki, who became the hospital's first chief of staff. The scope for bribery and outright fraud was also apparent from an early stage. One alleged surgeon who sent in his CV for consideration was later revealed to be a 'serial lunatic' who had received his sole medical training by watching imported American television sitcoms. Other would-be staff were similarly sent packing, guilty, apparently, of some form or another of financial scheming that Imran and his board of governors found unacceptable. By mid-1989 fundraising was well under way, with an initial target of some $8 million. Twelve months later it became clear that the $8 million would barely cover start-up costs, and that Imran would be committed to keeping the enterprise afloat for years to come, if not for the rest of his life.

Meanwhile, Pakistan's cricketers of the day were never quite certain if and when their officially designated captain would join them on the field of play. Sometimes only Imran himself knew much in advance whether he would deign to appear in a particular series. To call him the Frank Sinatra of the international sports world would be to confer a somewhat flattering sense of consistency on a player who seemed to rest, or retire, and then come back on roughly an annual basis. Of course, it's also fair to say that he had rather more in the way of extracurricular activities than the average Test cricketer. A friend remembers Imran going up into the Pakistan highlands around October 1989 for a long weekend to get away from it all. In the event, on all three nights he stayed up until nearly dawn writing his hospital development material. Back in Lahore, he spent most of the next month at the same task.

Imran, then, worked typically hard to see through a project taking place in a country where large-scale capital works tended to attract the attention of interest groups, politicians seeking rewards for providing the necessary building permits and contractors earning grossly inflated sums to work outside their strictly prescribed hours. He read every available regulation on Pakistan's national healthcare system, an impressive feat in itself. He also visited dozens of clinics and doctors' surgeries around the country. The existing situation was 'a disaster', Imran concluded. Years later he would recall going to one state-run hospice in Lahore where 'three or four small children suffering from cancer had to share a filthy bed'. There were no funds for modern equipment or even the most basic sanitary requirements, although, curiously enough, the government was able to maintain its own lavishly furnished hotel-cum-infirmary for members of the ruling party and senior military officers. By contrast, Imran vowed to provide treatment for anyone who needed it. Under his proposals, all patients would receive hospital service and follow-up care irrespective of their ability to pay. Although the basic start-up costs were met by private donations, Imran's plan inevitably brought him into contact with a number of national and provincial officials of the administration now headed by president Ghulam Ishaq Khan and his prime minister Benazir Bhutto. By all accounts, the ensuing meetings followed much the same pattern as Imran's sessions with the national cricket selectors. If the bureaucrats balked at his requests, he just asked for more. There was nothing unusual about a Pakistani citizen being rebuffed by his appointed representatives. What was novel was a citizen who, when repeatedly rebuffed, refused to back down.

An example of how Imran 'lorded it over the game of cricket in Pakistan', to quote the then president, came in his approach to the competitively dubious but well-subscribed one-day internationals staged in the desert fastness of Sharjah. Immediately after having hosted Australia, the Pakistanis flew in to take part in a triangular tournament against India and the West Indies. Despite a number of high-level requests, Imran declined to join the party, citing his lack of match fitness, along with his apparently waning enthusiasm for instant cricket. A fortnight later, Pakistan were in action in the 45-overs Wills Asia Trophy, where they narrowly lost to the Indians. Still no Imran. Yet in March 1989 he was back in harness for what would appear on the face of it to be the even less alluring two-leg Sharjah Cup series against Sri Lanka. Pakistan won the showdown 2–0. As usual, Javed Miandad was the man who had led his country when Imran wasn't available, and who stood aside again when he was. 'It was a strange arrangement,' in Javed's measured description. 'I became used to the charade. Imran was always able to call on me when he was captain; but when I was captain, I didn't have the same luxury.'

Imran had exercised supreme autocratic power on behalf of the Pakistan team, and over the team, for nearly seven years, but it was power he never particularly enjoyed. As we've seen, there were recurrent clashes with the home board and its various sub-committees and panels. Try as he might, he only rarely had the luxury of a close working relationship with his national co-selectors. Imran hardly ever managed to get his way without a fight, and his apparently high-handed methods and attitude to what he saw as 'meddlers' and 'incompetents' only added to official unease about his leadership. Among the players, there were those who worshipped Imran and those who feared or even loathed him. By and large, they weren't lukewarm. Over the years he'd had well-publicised disagreements with Majid, Zaheer and Javed, to name only the three most obvious. In 1989 he finally managed to fall out with his old bowling partner Sarfraz Nawaz (by no means a unique achievement on Imran's part), Sarfraz slamming the phone down on him following a heated exchange. It was much the same story in Pakistan at large: he was either fanatically popular or the target of nearly psychotic abuse. And he was still single, which was considered eccentric in a society that put the premium on settling down from an early age to marry and raise a family. As even the *Star*, which had directly contributed to the phenomenon, was to remark, the Pakistani public 'appear[ed] to have the ultimate love–hate relationship with Imran'. For much of the past 15 years, he seemed to have figuratively been either in the village stocks or at the head of a triumphal procession such as no Roman emperor could have dreamt of.

So it may have been with a degree of relief that Imran sat out the 1989 English summer, giving him his first extended break from cricket of his own choosing in two decades. He was apparently approached to play for Yorkshire, of all unlikely clubs, and there were protracted talks about him turning out on a limited basis for Middlesex. Nothing came of them. The popular assumption, at least in *The Times*, was that it was 'madness' for the world's leading all-rounder to voluntarily miss out on the action. But the madness was not without method. From March to October that year he was based in London, and seems to have had no trouble in filling his time. There was more work to be done on the hospital appeal, with Imran tapping both commercial organisations and a number of his celebrity friends for support. Mick Jagger gave a reported £20,000. Other activities included hunting and shooting, visiting Tramp and continuing to serve as a spokesman for Save the Children and UNICEF. He was also beginning to speak more and more often, in somewhat Delphic terms, about the iniquities of life both in Pakistan and the West. To at least one Lahore newspaper, it would later seem that Imran's politicisation had been the logical result of 'coming into close and prolonged contact with the physically beset' in the course of his hospital research. The hint of things to come was enough to lead the current premier, Benazir Bhutto, to remark that her Oxford contemporary would make a 'valued' public servant.

Meanwhile, he was still squiring a formidable number of attractive young things, quite apart from Susannah Constantine, around town. Whenever the cameras caught him with the latter, there seemed to be a boyishly happy leer on Imran's face. Whether or not the couple were ever engaged, as some speculated, he invited her to go with him on a Test tour of Australia that winter, where, in all innocence, she once suggested that Imran might care to lead his opponents out on to the field of play as a gesture towards her favourite charity. (He declined the offer.) Back in England, Constantine took Imran to shooting parties at various country houses, where he once distinguished himself by appearing in a 'hideous sweater with pheasants on it. It went into the bin,' said the future co-host of *What Not To Wear*. Within a year or so, the couple had drifted apart. If anything, Imran seems to have then only stepped up his love life, while shunning anything remotely resembling a commitment. 'And why not?' an intimate friend remarks; 'he was a bachelor, so why grudge it to him? And no one was ever hurt.'

The women? One or two of them may have had longer-term designs on Imran, but everyone understood soon enough that there was nothing doing. One overnight acquaintance recalled having been 'distinctly unmoved' when he allegedly shouted out the wrong name ('his own name', in some scurrilous versions) during sex. But on the whole an atmosphere of good humour and urbanity prevailed. 'I wasn't a saint,' Imran conceded, reflecting on this phase of his life. 'But nor was I a typical playboy. I didn't drink, smoke or dance, and I never went out of my way to have a great social life. I kept to a few places I knew. If you were flying off for a wild weekend in Paris or somewhere, I wasn't interested.'

In the midst of these other activities, Imran had begun studying the Koran. His renewed interest in the subject came in the wake of the publication of Salman Rushdie's novel *The Satanic Verses* and the subsequent offering of a large sum of money by Ayatollah Ruhollah Khomeini, the 86-year-old Supreme Leader of Iran, to suborn the murder of the author and his associates. Rushdie's Japanese, Italian and Norwegian translators would all duly be killed or attacked, while Aziz Nesin, his Turkish translator, was the intended target in a July 1993 massacre when a mob of protestors set fire to a provincial hotel where he was staying. On that occasion 37 people died. Imran was to remark of *The Satanic Verses* that it led him to a fresh respect for his religion, and that 'people like me, who were living in the West, bore the brunt of anti-Islam prejudice which followed the Muslim reaction to the book'.

Back at Tramp in the summer of 1989, sitting with the club's owner and a small group of friends, Imran had given one of them the tip that he wouldn't play international cricket again. He had spoken of the 'humiliation' of dealing with the BCCP bureaucrats. Most of the media weren't much better. However, two compelling factors now combined to help change Imran's mind. His cousin and patron Javed Burki had been made chairman of the Pakistani selectors, while his hospital board of governors were similarly keen for him to return to high-level competition as a platform from which to publicise the cause. The result was that Imran agreed to lead Pakistan in the six-nation MRF World Series, also known as the Nehru Cup, staged over three weeks that autumn in India. Even the Karachi press went into raptures at the news. Over and above the genuine enthusiasm for his return, there was a simple reason for the sudden outpouring of goodwill. Without knowing it, Imran was employing what social psychologists call the contrast principle. Another example of this phenomenon would be the plumber who, after gravely examining your leaky bathroom pipe, and muttering about the 'cowboys' let loose on it last time around, informs you you have a serious problem but that, given time and effort, he can solve it. By and large even the most battle-hardened consumer will be pathetically relieved at the end result, which is sold to him much like a miracle, and all too glad to pay the bill. Which is to say that certain members of the Pakistani media had apparently come to realise how much they still needed Imran only when he had begun to make himself unavailable. They had good reason to be grateful for his latest comeback. Imran led Pakistan to victory over the West Indies in the Nehru Cup Final, played in front of 100,000 spectators in Calcutta. He was both man of the match and man of the series, leading some to wonder what he might have done had he been fully match fit.

On 10 November 1989, Pakistan played India in front of a sold-out house at the Gaddafi Stadium, Lahore, on behalf of the Shaukat Khanum Memorial Hospital fund. The event raised an immediate 2,902,600 rupees (roughly £250,000), with some twice as much again coming in matching pledges over the next two weeks. The Indians then began another full-scale Test series against Pakistan, their 10th. A civil war having erupted in Kashmir, the contest attracted its fair share of public attention on both sides, and seems to have been another challenge that Imran felt unable to miss.

In the event, India's third non-military tour of their neighbour in six years proved sadly anti-climactic. All four Tests were drawn. Imran got his way in insisting on neutral umpires, but failed in his bid to adjust the actual hours of play. 'The first sessions were generally something of a lottery, if they happened at all, because more often than not we found ourselves having to bat and bowl in a heavy morning mist,' he told me. Several early runs were scored by the expedient of pushing the ball past the bowler and snatching a quick single while the fielders tried to find it. There was a generous amount of external participation as a whole, with the fourth Test at Sialkot repeatedly delayed both by rain and by the crowd pelting the players with rocks.

At 37, Imran now seemed to be coming into his own as a batsman. If the situation required, he could deal in what *Wisden* called 'bloodless efficiency' and even a Boycott-like intransigence. One quite celebrated England all-rounder told me that bowling to him in the 1987 home series had been like 'bouncing a rubber ball off a wall'. Equally at home going in anywhere between Nos 3 and 9, Imran could also announce himself, as he once did to Kapil Dev, with a languid pull for four off the first delivery he received, and liked nothing more than a good hell-for-leather run chase. In short, he had it all, as anyone who had seen him hit Wayne Daniel over the Lord's outfield, some temporary seats and a pile of builders' supplies and into the back of the 'Q' Stand bar could attest. Imran's batting average over the first five years of his Test career was 19.42; in the five years after he took on the captaincy it hovered around 44, while from 1987 until he retired, the figure rose to 67.60, which was to mingle with the likes of Gavaskar, Richards and Border. Accountancy isn't everything, but the numbers are perhaps worth mentioning if only because they tended to get prominently splashed over the Pakistani media. In the first innings of the first Test, at Karachi, Imran scored 109 not out in a three-hour, slow-fast march which included 17 fours and a six. He would end the series with an average of 87.33; and this wasn't one of those statistics flattered by a run of not outs and did-not-bats – when he swaggered out to the middle to face Kapil and the other Indian bowlers, 'he actually *looked* like he'd score about 87', one of them recalled.

Meanwhile, some of the zip may have gone from Imran's bowling, but at 23 his hand-picked successor Wasim Akram was making a fair go of replacing the irreplaceable. Wasim took 18 wickets in the series, more than any other bowler on either side. And yet another prospect was coming up behind, fast. A few weeks before the series began, Imran had turned on his television and seen an impressively brisk 17-year-old turn his arm over in an otherwise forgettable fixture between United Bank and a similar institution. The teenager in question, Waqar Younis, had already caught the eye of the Pakistani Under-19 selectors. But Imran, recognising true firepower when he saw it, insisted that Waqar be fast-tracked through the ranks and straight into the senior team, where he responded by taking four for 80 in the first innings of his debut against India. A further 369 Test wickets would follow before Waqar was finished. A sign of Imran's confidence in his two protégés, and possibly also of self-confidence, is that he now generally preferred to let Wasim and Waqar take the new ball. If and when the batsmen had seen off the opening pair, Imran himself would stride up, all business, and consent to bowl half-a-dozen overs off a smooth, deceptively short run which still let him hit the crease with a high-jumper's elevation, the whole performance followed as often as not by an ear-splitting appeal. It remained a thrilling thing.

A mark of Imran's stature came when *India Cricket* magazine decided on its list of its five international players of the year for 1989–90. As a rule, it seems fair to say that this particular publication had tended to favour its native sons: since the annual tradition began in 1946–47, some 65 per cent of those honoured had been Indian born, although there was generally some provision for a particularly distinguished visiting Englishman or Australian. A total of four Pakistanis had been included in the previous 43 years. So it was a gracious gesture now for the magazine to move to recognise Imran, who had 'contributed so much not only to his country, but to world cricket'. Back home, the main Karachi weekly joined the chorus. 'The national captain cannot, should not – must not – retire,' it insisted.

The hortatory blast had little, if any effect. As Imran made abundantly clear to friends, he was now just playing for his hospital. The fact that he had no remaining professional ambitions and that 'I genuinely don't care about breaking records' came up repeatedly, although he was known to add in passing that, after four failed prior attempts, winning the World Cup might be nice. After more muscular pressure from the two Burkis, one the chairman of selectors and the other the hospital's chief of staff, Imran did agree to tour Australia in December 1989. At least one major Karachi-based manufacturer had gone on record with the somewhat vaguely worded promise to make a 'substantial donation' to the Shaukat Khanum, 'if only our boys will turn on the style against Allan Border's side'. Imran remarked to a colleague that he would take this as a firm commitment, whether they meant it that way or not.

The Pakistanis made their traditional staggered arrival down under, with one of the selected players reportedly missing his scheduled flight, a second phoning in injured, and a third who reported to the airport both fit and on time but was subsequently found to be missing his passport and other documentation. Abdul Qadir then returned home with a finger problem after bowling a total of only 50 overs on the tour. Perhaps unsurprisingly, Australia won the first Test at Melbourne by 92 runs. Imran struggled to find his rhythm, although Wasim took 11 wickets in the match. Terry Alderman was awarded five lbw verdicts, at least two of them debatable, in the Pakistan second innings. Imran chose not to dwell on Alderman's good fortune when invited to do so at the post-match press conference. He later conceded that he had been 'not happy' with the home officials. 'Had Pakistani umpires given the decisions that were given against me and Yousuf, there would have been an outcry. After the way that the Australians had behaved in Pakistan, it took a lot to remain silent.' According to the local *Herald*, this was the 'new and improved', 'ultra-dignified Khan', who was 'clearly embarking on a global lap of honour before slipping into retirement'.

This was perhaps to downplay Imran's combative instinct. In the drawn Test at Adelaide he scored a second-innings 136, part of a match-saving partnership with Wasim that included some notably robust interplay with Australia's Merv Hughes. The two Pakistanis batted with a beautifully effective mixture of resolve and panache. Imran was at the crease for 485 minutes, hitting ten fours in what was to be his sixth and final Test century. He added a cameo of 82 not out in the deflating anti-climax of a rainy draw at Sydney, giving him a Test batting average of 70 (as compared to a bowling average of 42) for the tour. Richie Benaud reflected general opinion when he described Imran as being at the peak of his form with the bat, and a 'worthy ambassador' to boot.

By previous Pakistani standards the touring party was generally a happy one, and they kept any doubts they had about the umpires to themselves, or at least until they were home again. The loyalty of those around Imran was total, and bordered on hero-worship among several of the younger players – some of his own team were 'quite intimidated' when he strode up to bowl, one of them recalled, especially if there happened to be any unseemly 'verbal' going on with the opposition. It was as if, in the twilight of his long career, John Gielgud had suddenly materialised on the set of a Vin Diesel film. The 19-year-old spinner Mushtaq Ahmed would remember once dutifully picking up his captain's cricket bag for him, only to hear a crisp voice say, 'Please don't do that. I have two arms and two legs, and I carry my own luggage.' Some time later in the tour the same bowler was hit for 76 off 10 overs in a one-day international at Brisbane. In the break between innings, Mushtaq, already feeling miserable about his performance, was told to report to the captain's room. Anticipating a rollicking, the actual review caught him by surprise. 'You bowled absolutely brilliantly,' Imran said, in a voice that could be heard throughout the Pakistan dressing area. It was one of those 'little touches of class' that 'kept all of us going', Mushtaq would remember.

In short, it seemed that with the Imran era drawing to a close, and the Wasim–Waqar one just beginning, there was a promising atmosphere in which some fresh spirit of accord and common purpose could, and certainly should, take hold among the Pakistan side in the run-up to the World Cup. The one-time comedy team of cricket were finally in danger of being taken seriously. In the meantime, Imran won the Australian player of the year award, along with a sports car which he donated to the hospital fund. Other than his bowling, about his one significant failure on the tour was the launch of his short-lived *Cricket Life* magazine, which arguably never fully recovered from Imran's introductory speech made to a room full of contributors, backers, press and other potentially interested parties. 'It's amazing how so many of you know nothing about cricket,' he told them.

It was a rare misfire. At the end-of-tour World Series international in Sydney, confetti showered down and a band played the Australian and Pakistani national anthems. Imran stepped to a microphone to say thank you. Right around the stadium, said the *Sun*, there were people 'waving, cheering, shouting out to him'.

EIGHT

Dropping the Pilot

For all the recent talk of retirement, Imran had actually ceased to be a mere professional cricketer as long ago as November 1978. The job title seems wholly inadequate to describe what he became over the course of the next decade. If one were to pinpoint the exact moment when he'd gone from smouldering young pin-up to the embodiment of Pakistani national pride and aspiration, it would be that evening at Karachi when he smashed India's Bishan Bedi for a four and two sixes to win the first series staged between the two rival states in 18 years. 'Overnight, I became a star,' Imran allowed. 'I was hailed as the match winner, which was a little unfair on some of my colleagues, [but] we were all amazed by the adulation ... Within a few days, most sports shops in Pakistan had sold out of cricket equipment, and posters of the players sprang up in bookstalls, airports and railway stations.' Imran modestly failed to mention that it was actually the beginning of a major personality cult. Back in Lahore that night there was an impromptu street party whose ranks stretched for almost a mile. Many of the revellers carried banners and signs, some bearing only Imran's name, and others with a phrase or a statistic characterising some aspect of his life or career. Police estimated their number at 50,000.

So when Imran once again came to contemplate retiring early in 1990, there was a marked degree of public interest in the outcome. The state president may no longer have personally involved himself in the matter, but nearly everyone else in Pakistan seemed to have an opinion. Imran's pragmatic decision to become a batsman who could bowl a bit meant, at least in theory, that he could carry on at the top level into his early forties. Or that was the widespread hope. Javed had had a wretched tour of Australia, and it would seem to have been no time for Pakistan to lose both their senior players. That spring, when someone started a rumour that Imran would be unavailable for the six-nation Austral-Asia Cup in Sharjah, one Lahore paper published a special 'Nation mourns' edition, its front page rimmed with a black border.

In the end he did play at Sharjah, and with significant results. The two-week, two-group, 50-over tournament got under way on 25 April and, for all the incessant hype, had its share of longueurs in the early stages – 'sheer mismatches, one-sided games, ties that didn't matter much or that were simply short of action or drama or interest' according to one report. Even Pakistan's keenly anticipated opening Group B clash against India seemed to fall into a sort of coma. For hours on end this so-called 'duel in the desert' involved a good deal of nudging and nurdling, eked out against dourly tight bowling and defensive fields. Pakistan prevailed on that occasion, and similarly disposed of Sri Lanka in a group match two days later. Imran had bowled a total of three overs in the tournament thus far. The Pakistanis' next fixture, against New Zealand, lasted only two-and-a-half hours, having never quite recovered from the Kiwis being bowled out for 74. Waqar took five for 20. That meant Imran's side would face the World Cup holders Australia in the final. After the recent tour it had become fashionable among some of the Australian press to murmur wisely that it would perhaps be inadvisable to take the Pakistanis too lightly. In particular, the *Sun-Herald* made the point repeatedly in the build-up to the competition final. 'Never underestimate the sub-continentals,' it said on 2 May. In the *Age*, the anonymous sports-editorial writer advised: 'The golden rule is, do not underestimate Imran's men.' 'Do not,' opined the *Courier-Mail*, 'underestimate the bookies' underdogs.' By all accounts, Imran, to the extent that he thought about it at all, appears to have been mildly amused by the overall tone of the coverage. In his view it was rather more important not to overestimate the Australians.

The final did at least live up to the advance billing. There were blue skies and a capacity crowd, among which was what appeared to be a cheerleading cabaret dance troupe, with conga drum ensembles, and a contingent of gaudily shell-suited stewards who darted about like a shoal of carnivorous fish. Anyone acquainted with the Scarborough festival has only to think of that end-of-season bash played in tropical heat to get some of the feel of the occasion. One of the Australians later recalled, 'The squealing and screaming for Imran coming from one particular stand was reminiscent of what Elvis would have copped.' Pakistan won the toss, batted and scored 266; Salim Malik made 87, Wasim 49 not out, Imran 2. With Steve Waugh, Border, Taylor and

Jones in their ranks, the odds at that stage would seem to have been marginally in Australia's favour.

As it happens, bookmaking was very much on the Pakistanis' minds at Sharjah. Some eight years later, Imran told an anti-bribery commission in Lahore that several of his team-mates had been offered 'considerable sums' to throw the final. When he had heard this, he said, 'I was worried. It was quite unusual ... after careful thinking, I finally decided to wager all the money we had made in the other matches on our team.' The idea was apparently to provide the Pakistanis with an added incentive to try even harder to win. One of the players adds that, as a further insurance, the captain had had each of his men swear on a copy of the Koran that none of them stood to profit by Pakistan losing. Imran's twin secular-spiritual initiative seems to have worked: Australia were bowled out for 230, with Wasim taking a hat-trick to close the innings. As well as their betting profits, Pakistan pocketed a cheque for US$40,000, Imran's share of which went to his hospital fund.

To some, including the venerable commentator E.W. Swanton, Sharjah might appear to be 'just some out-of-season Middle Eastern flummery'. To others, primarily based either in Karachi or Lahore, Pakistan's stunning triumph over the world champions marked the climax of Imran's career. If, as was again widely rumoured, he was now about to announce his retirement, he would be going on a high. Pakistan, Australia and the West Indies were clearly in a super-league of their own at both the long and short versions of the game. Of the three, the Pakistanis arguably had the most mercurially gifted pool of players at their disposal. Wasim, Waqar and Aaqib were the tip of the spear, and each in large part owed his place in the team to Imran's personal patronage. He consistently sought out and encouraged new talent, usually, if not invariably to the team's long-term gain – a distinct leadership skill that went beyond anything any of his predecessors had dared to try. In the case of Waqar, he'd backed his judgement against the persistent and vocal opposition of most of his co-selectors. Rather than wait for young players to gain experience, as the board had argued, Imran acted, and by acting he'd given them experience.

For this reason, Imran had earned and deserved what was billed in *Dawn* as his 'farewell bash' or, more lyrically, his 'last hurrah in Sharjah'.

Somewhat whimsically, under the circumstances, New Zealand chose to send what was effectively a reserve team to play Pakistan early that autumn. Richard Hadlee had reportedly retired, and four other regular first-team members made themselves unavailable. The tour was not without incident. Imran broke off from his fundraising activities long enough to decline the BCCP's invitation to captain Pakistan against what he curtly dismissed as a 'B side'. He subsequently appealed to the board to cancel the series altogether. In Imran's absence the captaincy again passed to Javed Miandad, in the latest round of what *The Times* described as 'the cricket equivalent of a game of musical chairs'. Javed, too, was unimpressed by the calibre of the opposition. 'They're sending a second XI against one of the best sides of the world and this is ridiculous,' he remarked. On the whole, Imran and Javed's scepticism was justified by the results. The home team won all three Tests, which were played in half-full, eerily calm stadiums.

No series involving Pakistan could be entirely placid, even so, and on their return home the tourists' manager, Ian Taylor, accused the opposition bowlers of having doctored the ball 'by lift[ing] the seam or damaging the surface [to] obtain extra swing'. Mr Taylor went on to admit that Chris Pringle, the New Zealand bowler, had experimented with such tactics during the Faisalabad Test, from which he – Pringle, not Taylor – had been chaired off by his team-mates, having taken seven for 52. The non-playing Imran and the other Pakistanis hotly denied the charges. The whole ball-tampering saga would tick on for another 18 months, at which point it duly exploded.

Two years earlier, Javed had led Pakistan to victory against Australia and, despite being told he would be captain 'for an indefinite period', had promptly stood down to accommodate Imran. Something very similar now happened again. In a dignified statement, Javed announced that he was 'resigning for the greater interest of the game and the country, [and] will extend support to my good friend and successor'. Once Imran had decided the interests of his hospital would be best served by his prolonging his time as a national leader, his stand-in's days were abruptly numbered. It's possible there may have been a degree of professional motivation behind his latest comeback. Imran had played a total of two days' competitive cricket in the previous six months, but told me he was taken by the challenge of beating the West Indies, who were due to tour Pakistan in November 1990 for what amounted to the unofficial Test championship of the world. There seems to have been the usual amount of administrative upheaval beforehand. The BCCP began by announcing that Imran was now 'apparently domiciled' in England, and thus debarred from participating in a series of matches taking place thousands of miles away. It was 'all over', one of the board members informed the press. The same unnamed but erudite source went on to compare the situation to that of his hero Cincinnatus, the Roman general 'who retired gracefully at the height of his powers'. There appear to have been further discussions on the subject, because on 3 November, just six days before the first one-day international against the West Indies, Imran flew in from London. The next morning, he was formally named as Pakistan's captain.

In Lahore, fireworks, banners and kites were promptly produced to celebrate this supreme moment. But Imran himself, after pausing to describe Javed's gesture as 'great', was said to have 'quietly retired to the nets'. Two days later, in Karachi, he met up with the rest of the Pakistan team, and any minor impatience or irritation on their part reportedly dissolved in 'fraternal scenes' as they greeted the man they had followed for months if not years, but few had thought they would play under again. By all accounts, there seems to have been a similarly positive response among the general public. After 20 years the affair between Imran and Pakistan's cricket-watching masses was clearly less of a summer romance and more of a marriage, with a full quota of spats, shared disappointments and, towards the end, a mellowing sense of mutual appreciation, even on the part of some of his long-term critics. Anyway, by late that week the ground authorities had disposed of around 95 per cent of all available seats for the three West Indies Tests, a marked improvement on the recent New Zealand series.

As a rule, when raw talent overcomes solid professionalism, sport itself is the winner. Such was the gist of the contest between Imran's volatile yet gifted players and Desmond Haynes's West Indians, who over the previous year or two, with Richards and several others on the way out and Lara not yet fully on the way in, had generally been less about class than commitment. This time around, the BCCP solved their perennial selection crisis by the expedient of simply giving Imran the team he wanted. The Lahore contingent was substantial: Akram Raza, Salim Malik, Zahid Fazal, Abdul Qadir, Wasim Akram and the captain himself. Pakistan swept the one-day internationals 3–0. Imran was man of the match in the final game at Multan, where he top-scored and took a tidy if not devastating one for 26 off eight overs.

As several of them would later remark, a somewhat enigmatic relationship had emerged of late between Imran and his men, for all the warmth of their reunion. While not exactly a skipper of the 1930s school with his own changing room and a personal valet to go with it, it was fairly clear by this stage that he was in the officer class. A certain amount of deference from the ranks was thought in order. When Imran took Richardson's wicket at Multan, the Pakistani fielders had instinctively set off in an animated posse to offer the obligatory high-fives, as per the modern custom. At the same time, the capacity crowd had given full voice to its own pleasure at the dismissal. About the only exception to the general effusion was Imran himself, who merely stood there, hands on hips, with a dignified half-smile. Then, when the first three or four of his colleagues were about a yard away from their target, a curious thing happened. To a man, they applied the brakes. Something in his demeanour apparently discouraged closer proximity. In one account, 'the dust kicked up behind [the Pakistanis] as each in turn came to an abrupt, skidding halt', rather like Merrie Melody cartoon characters approaching a cliff edge. With exquisite decorum, Moin, the wicketkeeper, then extended a gloved hand and briefly allowed it to rest on Imran's left shoulder. Apart from this modest, scarcely perceptible gesture, there was no further direct physical contact between the wicket-taking bowler and his team-mates. Just as quickly as it had formed, the congratulatory committee drifted away again. 'Imran had millions of fans and thousands of acquaintances,' I was reliably told, 'but except for Qadir and maybe Wasim none in the team could be called warm friends.'

On the other hand, the man voted the 'most influential Asian sportsman of all time' in an online poll published that December didn't attain the position simply through being an 'imperious bugger', to again quote his British ghost. He was, by 1990, a benevolent dictator. He could gently correct the senior players if the situation demanded, as well as indulge the junior ones. The young Mushtaq Ahmed would remember bowling to his captain in the nets before the first Test against the West Indies at Karachi. Imran, who was experimenting with a new guard, repeatedly fluffed his usually reliable pull shot. Finally, Mushtaq spoke up. 'You are not doing this well,' he said. After a prolonged silence, Imran took a few steps towards the bowler, removed his sunhat and enquired politely, 'What should I do?' Mushtaq, with a career batting average to date of 6, remarked that Imran might have better luck with the stroke if he kept his head still. There was another short pause. According to a first-hand observer, Imran 'reacted to this fairly elementary advice as if he was now hearing it for the first time. He seemed to ponder a bit, before warmly congratulating Mushy on his insight, and go[ing] back to the wicket to play the next few balls with exaggerated care, like Geoffrey Boycott on the first morning of a Test. The message that went out loud and clear to the head of selectors down to the most junior player present was that Imran would take direction from anyone, provided it was in the right spirit.'

Pakistan won the Test at Karachi, where Imran scored a five-hour 73 not out. As even his critics allowed, it showed maturity to deny the attacking principles on which his game had been founded for 20 years by refusing to be tempted by the short ball, of which there was an ample supply. To all intents and purposes, Imran was now playing exclusively as a batsman. At Faisalabad, a seamer's Test where the highest team score was 195, he not only didn't take a wicket, he didn't put himself on to bowl. The West Indies won there, setting up the decider at Lahore. Imran chose to open the attack again on his home turf, removing both Greenidge and Haynes in his first five overs. There was to be a less distinguished moment in the West Indies second innings when Wasim Akram took four wickets in five balls, but was denied a hat-trick when Malcolm Marshall dollied up a catch to mid on, where Imran dropped it. 'I don't think the skipper was concentrating fully,' Wasim remarked diplomatically. Pakistan were left notionally chasing 346, a tall order against the likes of Marshall, Ambrose and Walsh on an under-prepared pitch. Imran came in with the score at 110 for four, with some five hours to play. Like his batting partners Anwar and Wasim, he kept his nerve under heavy fire, and a particularly generous quota of what was described as 'various beamers, toe-crushers [and] chin balls'. At stumps Imran was undefeated on 58. The series was drawn. If the tourists had had marginally the better of the last two Tests, Imran enjoyed the satisfaction of not losing a rubber to the only other side in serious contention for the title of the world's strongest cricket team.

Nine days later, Pakistan were back in the United Arab Emirates to contest the 45-over Sharjah Trophy with Sri Lanka. In a curious arrangement, this so-called 'world knockout bout' was staged over two legs, with each team duly winning once. It was the sort of commitment-phobic cup final only cricket can produce. There was one at least mild note of interest when, in the course of the second tie, Imran exchanged words with the Indian-based umpire P.D. Reporter. There seems to have been some difference of opinion over the regulations governing the calling of wides in one-day competition. This eventually became a muted replay of the Gatting–Shakoor Rana incident, with the two men locked in a toe-to-toe, finger-wagging debate before Reporter set off for the pavilion in protest. Calmer heads persuaded him to return, and play, such as it was, continued.

Imran restricted himself to one day's competitive cricket over the next 12 months. He missed little of note, since Pakistan's international schedule consisted of only a few spurious limited-over and/or exhibition games, but his absence was still enough to revive the old gibes in certain quarters of the Karachi press about his being 'more elusive than Godot' (among less elevated descriptions) when it came to appearing in the likes of the domestic Quaid-e-Azam trophy. Nevertheless, Imran's unflagging energy, his willingness to spend nearly half his time in planes, his skills as a man-manager and negotiator, his knowledge of the world, his high-octane friends, and his personal flair all combined to make him more than just another over-the-hill, 'resting' sportsman. For most of 1991 he devoted himself to three specific areas where he tried to be as bold and innovative as he was on the cricket field, if with mixed success.

First and foremost was his hospital. More than two years after he publicly committed himself to it, the project was in some disarray. There were positive developments, certainly, including the government's initial grant of land and the symbolic laying of the building's foundation stone by the prime minister, Nawaz Sharif, in April 1991. A firm plan now existed to convert the architect's drawing into a sprawling, five-storey complex which could eventually cope with up to 6,000 admissions and 120,000 out-patients annually, the indigent among whom – some 70 per cent – would be treated without charge, and who would have access to state-of-the art diagnostics and operating theatres, presided over by 40 full-time surgeons and a number of visiting specialists housed in guest chalets on the grounds. Although still relatively modest compared with the better-endowed of the West's cancer facilities, for instance New York's Memorial Sloan-Kettering with its 9,000 employees, this was a radical departure from Pakistan's notoriously archaic public healthcare system. The fundraising drive continued apace: Imran threw himself into a round of charity dinners, auctions and floodlit, celebrity cricket matches typically involving the likes of Roger Waters and Sting. A sympathetic New York businessman subscribed $60,000. In a whirlwind, 36-hour tour of Bahrain Imran raised a further $175,000. A number of smaller individual contributions came in from ordinary Pakistanis, including a desperately frail old man who bicycled to the building site in order to donate five rupees, and a group of Lahore schoolchildren who made a gift of their milk money.

Hospital trustees were in place in Britain, the USA and Australia, and the whole project looked to be on track to open its doors in the early part of 1994.

On the debit side, there were unsourced but persistent rumours that certain of the hospital's administrators were so-called '10 percenters' – those who, for 10 per cent commission, used their supposed influence to secure contracts for various favoured suppliers.* As mentioned, the trustees were also regularly being inundated by charlatans or outright con artists passing themselves off as benefactors. 'Crooks were coming out of the woodwork and saying, "I had a relation die from cancer and I'll help you",' Imran's cousin Dr Burki recalled. One or two churlish commentators remarked that it was debatable whether a single, 115-bed facility would be of any significant help for the estimated 275,000 Pakistanis diagnosed with cancer each year, and that the funds might have been better spent on a network of regional clinics. Imran took additional flak for his alleged ego trip in naming the hospital after his mother, a 'crass indulgence' that particularly irked the perhaps not unbiased Karachi *Herald*. There was more in a similar vein. A sportsman of formidable gifts, powerful intellect and great passions was, perhaps, only now coming to grasp what it was like to deal with the more opinionated of the nation's political commentators. In a generally negative review of the scheme as a whole, the *Herald* complained that neither Imran nor his 'well paid' staff 'appear[ed] to be the slightest bit interested in any meaningful attempt [to] help stamp out cancer in the first place'. It was left to Dr Burki to reply that public information campaigning of that sort was traditionally best left to the government. 'Our job is treatment,' he noted.

Of course, the hospital project was only the most visible sign that Imran's priorities had altered somewhat in his thirties. 'The mind must be open, unperturbed, empty of physical things,' he'd reportedly noted of late, in something of a progression on his previous policy. Most of us, in his view, would pass through life without seriously challenging our own handed-down truths, or questioning the bigger picture. Imran's friend and sometime banker Naeem-ul-Haque believes 'he underwent a really profound change towards the end of his cricket career, in fact almost a rebirth. When Imran was fundraising for the hospital he came

---

* These unsubstantiated allegations of bribery and corruption at the Shaukat Khanum hospital were never levelled at Imran himself, and could only have been politically motivated had they been so.

up against the true scale of the really massive public corruption in Pakistan for the first time. I remember him saying that the problem was too big for a few well-meaning social reformers to tackle. It would take an unusually dedicated national politician to clean it up.' Pending that, Imran continued to work on behalf of a variety of children's and environmental causes. Of his religious convictions, a matter he knew to be of some interest domestically, he said that, while it had been impractical for him to pray towards Mecca five times daily when playing cricket, of late he'd found enlightenment both in the Koran and in Muslim scholars like Charles le Gai Eaton and Ali Shariati. Among other things, they had taught him that God's will was paramount. 'My own inability to control my future has made me realise there is another power,' he remarked. Speaking of his hospital fund, Imran added, 'In Islam, the hoarding of wealth is the biggest sin. The moment you identify your needs, you can give the rest of your capital away ... This is a transitory place and we redeem ourselves in the way we deal with other human beings.' At times, when speaking of the corrupting influence of money or his preference for trekking around the world with his possessions in a single, small suitcase, he sounded more like a holy man than an intensely competitive professional athlete.

Along with the hospital and the other worthy causes, Imran was also able to maintain his social life. By the early 1990s he had become a semi-regular guest at the London-based Kitkat Club, a combined debating society and dinner group organised by Ghislaine Maxwell, the daughter of the posthumously disgraced financier Robert Maxwell. Imran's soft spot for pretty women appears to have survived his deepening adherence to the Islamic faith. In the summer of 1987, when Pakistan were touring England, he had met and befriended a flaxen-haired, 26-year-old socialite named Sita White, an eventual heiress of the multi-millionaire Lord White of Hull, co-founder of the Hanson Group and one of the most prolific corporate raiders of even the Thatcher era. The relationship had apparently cooled around early 1989, by which time Susannah Constantine was on the scene. But the couple had met again for what White called a 'last night of love' in Hollywood on 2 October 1991, when Imran had found himself on a west coast fundraising tour prior to taking part in a one-day competition in Sharjah.

'Ms White got pregnant,' her ubiquitous California attorney Gloria Allred later informed a judge, 'and Imran told her he hoped it was a boy. When it was learnt it would be a girl, he expressed disappointment and said the child would not be able to play cricket' – a vile calumny, obviously, as he would have known that the women's game goes from strength to strength – 'where he has some renown.' According to Ms Allred, Imran had urged his 'distraught' lover to have an abortion, but she refused. He would later vigorously contest this part of the story. In any event, Tyrian Jade White was born on 15 June 1992, at Cedars-Sinai Medical Center in Los Angeles. Five years later, California Superior Court Commisioner Anthony Jones ruled that Imran was the child's legal father. He added that it was a default judgment, since 'neither Mr Khan nor his attorneys have deigned to appear here'. 'We did not request child support today,' added a tremulous Ms Allred, whose thirst for justice seemed to be matched by an equally well developed flair for the dramatic. 'But we hope that one day he will open up his heart to his beautiful young daughter and give her the love, respect and nurturing every little girl deserves.'

A few years later, Imran would apparently decide to take an at least limited role in Tyrian's upbringing, though his own availability would turn out to be at the mercy of more global events.

A year after participating in the 'world knockout bout' against Sri Lanka, Imran was back in Sharjah to play in a three-nation, 50-over, $60,000 tournament sponsored by the usual tobacco giant. Pakistan promptly lost two of their four opening matches but, thanks to the event's Kafkaesque rules, survived to beat India in the final. There were to be shades of their Sharjah performance four months later in Australia.

Between accepting donations and lifting awards, Imran was becoming a proficient speechmaker. As a rule he went over every line, worked 'painstakingly' on getting the right tone and aimed, above all, for simplicity. His various press conferences showed a similar disdain for convoluted structure and high-blown phrases, if not for occasional displays of irascibility and defensiveness. When asked to comment on the new one-bouncer-per-over rule, Imran called it 'without doubt one of the most brainless pieces of legislation ever passed by the International Cricket Council.'

From Sharjah, Imran flew back to Lahore to lead Pakistan in a home series against Sri Lanka, the last stop on a grand farewell journey en route to the 1992 World Cup in Australia. The visit wasn't without administrative controversy. The BCCP appointed home-born officials, Shakoor Rana included, in all three Tests, thus ensuring that the Sri

Lankans left thoroughly incensed at what they perceived to be biased umpiring. Meanwhile, the ICC-installed referee was none other than Donald Carr, an administrator of unimpeachable probity, but, to some, forever tainted as the man who had allegedly debagged Idrees Beg 36 years earlier. So the Pakistanis, in turn, had cause to feel aggrieved. Imran then managed to fall out with Javed Miandad when he made the provocative suggestion that the latter change his position in the batting order. According to Javed, 'In the first Test he sent me in at No. 5. I wasn't happy about this. I had been a career No. 4 batsman and made clear to the captain I had no intention of batting at any other spot. But Imran, never an easy man to dissuade, insisted I be tried at No. 3 or No. 5 or No. 6.' These negotiations were still taking place right through the Pakistanis' World Cup training camp, and indeed during the tournament itself.

Imran's men, even so, achieved their stated aim of a series win against Sri Lanka, a side which, if not exactly among the titans of world cricket, had acquitted themselves with credit on recent tours of both England and Australia. The generally sparse crowds were rewarded by some watchable batting and one or two genuinely inspired bursts of captaincy. Any romantic souls who believed that the game was still about swashbuckling 'amateurs' who put the needs of the team ahead of their own individual interests would have found plenty to applaud in the first Test, at Sialkot. Sri Lanka batted first and scored an about par 270. Light rain then fell at the start of the Pakistan reply, which became a three-day marathon of prolonged umpires' inspections and sardonic catcalls from the crowd. By the fourth afternoon the score stood at 423 for five, with the captain on 93 not out. Concluding that a lead of 153 was good enough and that his bowlers needed match practice, Imran declared the innings closed just short of what would have been his seventh Test century. It was a self-denying gesture of the sort that one somehow can't imagine coming quite as readily from, say, Javed, had he been in the same position. In the event the Sri Lankans held out, but even the Karachi *Herald* allowed that Imran's leadership showed 'class and imagination' and had been the 'best part [of] an otherwise soggy draw'.

Pakistan eventually took the series 1–0. Imran allowed himself just nine overs in the three matches, without taking a wicket. If his bowling was now 'little more than a joke', as one report insisted, at least it was still a practical joke, as figures of three for 15 off eight overs in the one-day international at Hyderabad illustrated. Meanwhile, his batting average was 57.50. Imran played his 88th and, as it turned out, last Test from 2 to 7 January 1992 at the Iqbal Stadium, Faisalabad. Having made his international debut more than 20 years earlier, when cricket was still known fondly as the 'gentleman's game', he'd survived to see a time of lost certainties and frenetic, floodlit slogs played between teams clad in fluorescent tracksuits. The arc of his career spanned more change in the sport than had been seen in any previous period of its history. Born only five years after Pakistan came into being and vividly aware of the country's colonial heritage, he'd eventually led the national team not only to victory over England, but to become arguably the best, and certainly the most bellicose, side in the world, despite the internecine rows. The responsibilities he bore were like those of no other Pakistan captain before him, and he more than met the test. Imran even went out on a high, with a win at Faisalabad, even if his own last innings wasn't his most distinguished: lbw, b. Wijegunawardene, 0.

The Pakistanis' build-up to the fifth World Cup, jointly hosted by Australia and New Zealand, had a degree of self-satisfied masochism to it that was quite pronounced even by their standards. As per tradition, there were a number of heated meetings of the BCCP's selection committee. One, which the team captain didn't attend, was held in a split-level room at the Gaddafi Stadium which was reportedly so crowded that 'some voting members had to squeeze on to a narrow upper gallery', from which they intervened in the debate below 'like gargoyles hissing down'. In a subsequent session, Imran was to argue persuasively for the inclusion of the cherubic and dapper Mushtaq Ahmed in the squad of 14, despite his not having appeared in the Sri Lanka series, and being only partially secure in the United Bank side. Mushtaq's services were to be much in demand over the coming weeks. Pakistan's most successful strike bowler of the previous two years, Waqar Younis, had to fly home before the first match of the competition because of a stress fracture, and both his stand-in Ata-ur-Rehman (later banned by the ICC for his alleged involvement in a match-fixing ring) and the opener Saeed Anwar fell unfit. In their absence, the selectors chose a 21-year-old Multan batsman named Inzamam-ul-Haq, a self-proclaimed 'visual cricketer' who came to combine some of the flowing style of Majid with the imposing bulk of Colin Milburn, and one or two other finds of less consequence. For its part, the press was broadly divided between those who thought the Pakistanis would win easily and others who believed them to be the worst group of professional sportsmen ever to leave home shores. If so, they weren't the worst prepared: Imran was able to persuade the board to send the whole party to Australia a month before the start, so as to 'bond and acclimitise', he told me. Even then, something of the Pakistanis' uniquely chaotic travel arrangements and fragile communications skills remained. Javed Miandad had strained his back during a practice match at the team's training camp and wasn't initially named in the touring party. The *Star* was not alone in believing that the 'talented and spunky' batsman had finally reached the end of his long career, and the Karachi AP wrote a speculative obituary to that effect. Such observers underestimated Javed's obstinacy and resilience, as the BCCP's Arif Abassi recalls.

> Indeed Miandad was left out of the squad, and the players left for Australia without him. But he worked on his game, and the selectors were convinced that he was fit enough to go. In due course they announced him as vice-captain without the knowledge of either Imran or Salim Malik, who thought he was the number two. When Javed was put on the plane to Sydney, Imran did not know about his departure.

Reflecting on this, and the calibre of the Pakistan squad as a whole, one Karachi news organisation was to remark, 'Imran's men are the most complete fumblers and blunderers this nation has shipped overseas in a long time.' But perhaps more representative were the millions of civilian cricket fans who remembered their team's frustrations and despairing near-misses in four previous tournaments, and who believed that 'the wheel [would] now finally turn', to quote the state president. There was a certain burden of popular expectation. The Pakistanis' campaign would take place over the course of five weeks, and involve up to 10 matches, in an event which for the first time brought together all the trappings of a modern limited-overs cricket competition – coloured clothing, floodlights, white balls, black sightscreens, and a bizarre 'rain rule' which famously reduced the semi-final between England and South Africa to a lottery. Imran was later to inform his hosts that their World Cup was the worst organised of the five in which he had played. His own tournament got off to a bad start when he tore his right shoulder in practice and missed Pakistan's initial qualifying tie against the West Indies at Melbourne. In his absence, Javed led the side in what the AP called the 'psychologically vital' first fixture. West Indies won the match by 10 wickets.

A league phase had been introduced to the tournament's opening rounds to sort the wheat from the chaff, and Pakistan's early experience down under suggested that the system was working. The side which had swept all before them in Sharjah, winning five international competitions in four seasons, now struggled to dispose even of Zimbabwe. Although restored as captain, Imran neither batted nor bowled in that match. There seemed to be an inordinate amount of mediocre, low-stakes sport in the round-robin stages of the cup as a whole, which nonetheless generated thousands of hours of television and the equivalent in newsprint. As well as reporting on the actual play, media organisations such as the Fairfax Group were letting their women's page editors loose on the cricket for the first time. Imran looked 'tip-top ... his hair perfect. When I found my voice, I asked him how the heck he stayed so young,' one wrote. But even then the grilling wasn't quite over. 'My admiration and wonder at his laid-back way of looking at things, and his obvious rude health ... reached a new high.'

Unknown to his interviewer, Imran was actually spending most of his off-duty hours strapped to a machine which sent electrical currents through his injured shoulder, while simultaneously swallowing painkillers and undergoing a daily course of cortisone injections to the torn cartilage. 'I knew the agony he was in, but he never showed it,' his team manager recalled. There appears to have been some question of whether he might even drop out of the team but remain in Australia as a non-playing captain, much as he had eight years earlier. But the reporter was at least right when she remarked on Imran's essential optimism. The veteran Pakistani commentator Omar Kureishi would recall a 'dark night in Hobart, when [our] side was in some disarray, and on the verge of being eliminated. With just three weeks to go to the final, the captain was still hurt and there were question marks about several other players' form and fitness.' Despite these concerns, Imran still 'exuded a certain quiet confidence' as he briefed Kureishi on the team's prospects. 'We will bring the trophy home,' he told him.

Imran's prediction showed commendable self-assurance given his side's disastrous start to the campaign. 'It's hard now to understand how far down they were,' Kureishi later observed. Pakistan 'made just about the worst start of any team in the tournament's history,' winning just one of their five opening ties. Rock bottom probably came on 1 March, in a match against England at Adelaide from which Imran either dropped or rested himself. The Pakistanis were skittled out for 74, the lowest total by a Test-playing nation in any of the five World Cups to date. England were cruising at 24 for one in reply when steady rain began to fall and the match was declared void, with one point to each side. Later that night the Pakistan team straggled into their manager's hotel room for what they assumed would be 'the mother of all bollockings', to quote a party who was present. Not for the first time in his captaincy, Imran defied convention. 'Be as a cornered tiger, come out and fight,' he announced to the assembled group. It was the same oblique advice he had once given a colleague in the Hove dressing-room. 'Just bowl flat out; I don't care about any wides or no balls,' he added, in reply to a question from Wasim, and that completed the tactical talk. 'The skipper was unshakeable'; he spoke in his 'usual determined, skilful and spiritual way', and 'convinced almost everyone present in the room they could actually win', according to the players' quoted remarks. Imran was also realistic enough to know that the Pakistanis' fate rested to a large extent on injuries, accident and luck – although since he believed the future of his hospital was also at stake, he may have felt a degree of divine providence was involved. The 'overriding point' was to 'be ready [to] seize the ring'.

Imran's fighting spirit also surfaced rather more literally with regard to Qamar Ahmed, the London-based journalist in whose flat he had been a frequent guest some 15 years earlier. 'We were boarding the plane in Adelaide after Pakistan were saved by the bell against England,' Ahmed recalls. 'A certain Indian journalist had told Imran that I was talking rubbish about him in the press box. It absolutely wasn't true. But obviously it left an impression. On the flight Imran wouldn't talk to me, and when I asked why he became rude. Things deteriorated from there ... We nearly came to punching each other [until] Miandad intervened and got hold of Imran and some Pakistan journalists dragged me to my seat. We didn't talk to each other after that for another 10 years.'

Imran returned to the team for their matches against India and South Africa, both of which they lost. By now the home media was close to unanimous in writing the side off. 'THE CENTRE CANNOT HOLD' was the headline in, curiously, both the Lahore and Karachi main morning press on 9 March, the day after the defeat by South Africa. Events, even Omar Kureishi believed, were 'chipping away at Imran's sanguine belief that destiny can be commanded with sheer courage and perseverance'. Ladbrokes now offered Pakistan at 40–1 to take the cup. Still, not even the most gnarled journalist was making any firm predictions in what *The Times* called the 'most open global competition of all'. England had the batting talent to win, if not quite the gumption or the hunger; having followed their one-day form of late, one somehow couldn't see their campaign ending with a tumult of national merrymaking in Trafalgar Square. The holders and early favourites Australia found that for once they didn't enjoy the playing resources to match their ample self-belief. The West Indies had omitted Richards and Greenidge from their squad, and spent most of the qualifying rounds coming to terms with the fact. Half-way through the tournament, the experts thought the most likely outcome was an India–New Zealand final, although South Africa, back in international competition after some 20 years' isolation, remained the 'sentimental favourites'.

The convoluted process by which Pakistan eventually beat the odds included three wins inside seven days against Australia, Sri Lanka and New Zealand. Then, in order for them to make the semi-finals, the results of two other matches in which they weren't participating would also have to go their way. Improbably, both did. In their last qualifying match, England managed to lose to Zimbabwe, who were coming off a trot of 18 successive one-day international defeats. Graham Gooch's side were bowled out for 125, with a Harare chicken farmer named Eddo Brandes taking four for 21. In an almost equally unlikely result, Australia rallied to beat the West Indies in a day-night fixture at Melbourne. When all the figures were totted up, Pakistan, to general surprise, were found to have qualified for a semi-final tie against New Zealand. Everything had fallen in place to allow a side which had been widely thought down and out to advance to the knockout phase. 'It was enough to make us feel we were being specially guided toward a great destiny,' Javed remarks.

As noted, Imran was not at his personal best, having bowled just 44 medium-pace overs for six wickets in the contest to date. His shoulder had only partly responded to treatment, and he remained on a heavy regimen of cortisone shots which apparently also affected his batting, where he currently had an average of 16. There appears to have again been some debate within the Pakistan camp as to whether that was sufficient representation of his role as the 'world's greatest all-rounder'. In his 2003 memoir *Cutting Edge*, Javed writes, 'As the World Cup was coming to an end, our team had become sharply divided off the field, Imran versus the rest.' Some four years after his book's publication, Javed went on to recall that the cup had nearly slipped through Pakistan's fingers just prior to the semi-final because of a players' revolt against their 'domineering' captain. 'The mutiny took place before that [New Zealand] match. But to me the country was more important and I convinced the players to carry on,' Javed adds. The opener Ramiz Raja later termed this account of events 'absolute tripe'. He told the India *Telegraph*, 'Actually, Miandad is perfectly qualified to talk about revolts. He saw three against him, the first when he was captain and twice when he was Pakistan coach.'

Imran gave a stirring, nothing-to-lose speech before the semi-final against New Zealand at Auckland, but then rather spoilt the effect by an indifferent bowling performance of none for 59 off 10 overs. The New Zealanders' score of 262 was punctuated by a technically sound, if somewhat languid innings of 91 from their captain Martin Crowe. The 35,000 home spectators gave Crowe a rapturous standing ovation on his dismissal, and received a sheepish wave of the bat in acknowledgement. With 15 overs to go, the Pakistan reply stood at 140 for four, by which time the crowd were so confident of victory that they were chanting 'Easy, easy' as Inzamam-ul-Haq took guard. When Inzamam departed again, having clouted 60 in 45 minutes, the target had been reduced to 36 from five overs. Javed and Moin Khan duly finished the job. Pakistan won by four wickets, with six balls to spare. As Vic Marks recalled in the *Cricketer*, 'As the final shot reached the boundary, the jubilant Pakistan team rushed on to the field and submerged the batsmen. Among them was the usually subdued Imran [who] was beaming like a Cheshire cat rather than a Pathan tiger.' In the second semi-final, England defeated South Africa after the tournament's rain regulations had made a farce of the run chase.

The build-up to the Melbourne final was, much like the match itself, a clash of styles: the efficient but dour automatons versus the mercurial, potentially implosive flair players. England spent much of the 48 hours before the game diligently bending, stretching, pumping iron and jogging around the outfield of their training park. Perhaps not coincidentally, they reached their climactic fixture carrying seven injured players. Imran, by contrast, restricted his team to one collective net session and a series of individual briefings that appear to have been as much about personal motivation as they were about tactics. 'We discussed Graeme Hick,' Mushtaq Ahmed told the journalist Lawrence

Booth. 'He was the in-form batsman. Imran said to me in the meeting, "Mushy, if Hick comes to the crease, you make sure you bowl to him." I said, "Hang on, the guy who has been the cleanest hitter of the ball – and he can hit a long way – and I'm bowling to him!" But the way Imran said it, I could see the passion in his eyes. He was telling me I was the guy who's responsible to get him out. That makes my imagination go.' It was the sort of counter-intuitive input that one tends not to hear in the average English dressing-room.

When the day came, of impressive humidity, 87,182 spectators were jammed into the Melbourne arena, which resounded to the klaxon, whistle and bugle of fanatical Pakistan support. If anyone in Australia was magnanimously hoping for the Poms to win, they were keeping it to themselves. According to Ian Botham, 'It was not good-humoured banter [but] barely disguised hate. The English fans in the stadium suffered some terrible abuse. I should think that about 80,000 of the crowd were chanting for Pakistan.' To at least some of those in attendance, the cup final was symbolically over before it had started. With roughly some 12 playable hours of daylight remaining, the two captains appeared for the toss: Gooch amiably lumbering up, sporting a droopy moustache and a slight but perceptible pot belly, Imran wearing a tight-fitting, ribbed T-shirt emblazoned with a tiger. One England player watching from the balcony told me that it had looked to him like a case of an 'Edwardian music-hall performer shar[ing] a stage with a guy from Aerosmith', and it had 'not been a promising start, from a purely body language point of view'.

Pakistan batted first, and were in some bother at 24 for two. Imran had promoted himself up the order and had made just nine from 16 overs when he skied the ball to midwicket, where Gooch dropped it. It set the tone for the match. In the World Cup semi-final at Lahore five years earlier, Imran and Javed had rebuilt the Pakistan innings with 112 in 26 overs, only to lose to Australia. Something of the same patient bricklaying approach went on here, though to better effect. Imran restricted himself to a series of broad-bat defensive lunges and occasional trotted singles. Under the tournament rules, a new ball was in use at each end. As a result 'we had to keep playing ourselves in,' Imran told me, 'not to mention being conscious that we had a young and inexperienced team whom we needed to protect'. About half-way through the innings, he ended the period of anonymous accumulation with one of those surges of acceleration beloved of Jeremy Clarkson on *Top Gear*. Imran seemed to signal his intention when, in the 28th over, he calmly lifted Richard Illingworth for six. Another straight biff and two pounded fours followed in short order. The two old lags, with exactly 200 Tests and half-a-dozen leadership rows between them, were to smash and grab 76 runs in the next nine overs. In all their third-wicket partnership was worth 139, with Imran going on to a 110-ball 72. Inzamam and Wasim then ran riot, enabling Pakistan to reach 249 – not an impossible target, but apparently enough for a tired England team who would have to bat under lights. 'The mood in the dressing-room was a bit subdued,' Derek Pringle told me. 'We felt we'd had them on toast at one stage and then let them escape.'

Sure enough, England made a nightmare start, losing Botham for a duck in the third over. The outgoing batsman's mood was not improved by one of the Pakistan fielders, Aamir Sohail, enquiring, 'Why don't you send out your mother-in-law now? She couldn't do any worse.' Stewart, having exchanged some similarly pungent words with his opponents, soon followed him to the pavilion. Meanwhile, Imran pulled the strings as tautly as usual, not least when making his bowling changes. With his score on 17, Hick played round a Mushtaq googly and was plumb lbw, the vocally pleased Mushy having won that particular duel on his captain's behalf. Imran then summoned another protégé, Wasim Akram, for a second spell. At 141 for five, Chris Lewis, the latest England player on whom the 'next Botham' mantle had thudded, came to the crease, showing immediate signs of pugnaciousness by playing extravagant air-shots on his way out. He lasted one ball. Botham would call Lewis's dismissal by Wasim 'one of the most extraordinary deliveries I have ever seen. It started wide of off stump, suddenly swung in like a banana and smashed into the timbers.' Hardly had the crowd savoured the moment, stretched and resettled than Aaqib had beaten Fairbrother, and it was effectively all over.

The last rites were at least studded with a few flailed cameo performances. England's procession of all-rounders finally gave the Union Jack-waving contingent something to cheer, with Reeve and Pringle to the fore. DeFreitas thrashed around gamely, though defiance at that juncture had a slightly forlorn ring to it. Wasim bowled magnificently throughout to finish with three for 49. But for sheer sentimentality, nothing would perhaps rival the moment when Imran came back to take the final wicket with what proved to be his last ball in competitive cricket. No working scriptwriter would dare contrive such a climax. It was 25 March 1992. Pakistan won by 22 runs. There were four balls left for play.

'I recall most of the England team feeling a gross sense of injustice at the result,' says Derek Pringle. Pakistan had certainly taken their time to come to the boil in the tournament, and were supremely lucky to have been saved by the rain at Adelaide. But midway through the competition they had discovered a defiant streak of self-belief, as well as a resilient team spirit that contrasted with the in-fighting, bickering and bureaucratic officiousness of previous campaigns. It's hard to believe that this was entirely unrelated to Imran's motivational pep talks, or an even more august source, as some thought. A number of the players would later attribute their success in the final to *Inshallah*, which roughly translates as the hand of God. Whether or not divine intervention played a role, Pakistan were clearly the better team on the day. Both their batsmen and bowlers displayed a patience and versatility beyond that of their highly touted opponents. Imran's own innings certainly wasn't the only reason for yet another crushing England demise. But as captains' knocks go it was one of the best of modern times, a measure of his determination to overcome a problem and of his cricketing intelligence. Richie Benaud, who knows something about man management, recalled that Imran had not only batted with real nous, but 'led his team with skill, courage and common sense'. Of course, things might have been different had the Pakistan captain been out for 9 instead of 72. Gooch's dropping of his opposite number somehow summed up a generally lacklustre England team performance which, one fancies, rather remains the default position 17 years later.

Reflecting on Pakistan's triumph in the following days and weeks, Imran spoke with becoming modesty, frequently making reference to the part played by the Almighty. 'I was thankful to Allah that I was able to leave cricket with dignity. It is a blessing that has been denied to greater men than myself,' he observed. Unfortunately, his immediate post-final remarks were considerably less polished. Climbing on to a rostrum and holding aloft the Waterford crystal trophy, a sweating, somewhat manic-sounding Imran seemed to forget himself. For once his oratorical skills failed him. 'I would just like to say that I want to give my commiserations to the England team. But I want them to know that by winning this World Cup, personally it means that one of my greatest obsessions in life, which is to build a cancer hospital … I'm sure that this event will go a long way towards completion of this obsession … It is my dream … I feel very proud that finally I have managed to succeed …'

It was language that, to many, seemed oddly self-centred and out of place to celebrate what had, after all, been a team win. One journalist would remark that the Pakistan captain 'sound[ed] as if he had just taken part in a single-wicket competition'. Of equal concern to some in the audience, there seemed to be an implicit threat to dedicate the cup, and the financial rewards accruing, to Imran's hospital. The 'great Khan', it was said, had let both his country and himself down, his choice of words 'pompous and megalomaniacal'. Imran himself later joined this consensus, admitting that he'd been 'high on emotion' when called on to step up to the podium and speak live to some 600 million television viewers around the world.

That was hindsight. At the time, most neutral observers declared themselves unimpressed by Imran's 'rant', which ignored the normal protocol of thanking the event's organisers, hosts, sponsors and paying customers. 'I remember thinking his victory harangue was somewhat immoderate and rather more self-absorbed than is usual in team games,' Ted Dexter allowed. 'Now I know that [Imran] was just warming up for life as a politician.'

But if non-partisan reaction to Imran's *de facto* hospital fundraiser was tepid, the response of some of his Pakistani team-mates bordered on volcanic. Qamar Ahmed remarks that 'the captain's whole performance was in poor taste and very naive', an opinion broadly shared by the winning players. The future national captain Ramiz Raja and Imran's old friend Salim Malik were among several colleagues reportedly left uneasy by the thought, however misguided, that certain cup-winning bonuses and gifts might be directed to the Shaukat Khanum facility rather than themselves. In Javed Miandad's opinion, 'Imran would perhaps have been better off staying quiet that evening. He made a real hash of it.' In the coming days, Javed added that he and 'the guys' would be setting out on a nationwide fundraising tour to capitalise on their success in the World Cup. 'He made it clear,' according to one published report, 'that these appearances have nothing to do with Imran's ambitions for a cancer hospital – they will be purely for the players'. Even at their moment of supreme national triumph the Pakistanis were now to demonstrate what even General Zia had called their 'uniquely delicate wiring', and to exercise self-destructive skills of a high order. When he took over the team 10 years earlier, Imran had shown a steely willingness to carry things through, a resolve that had included the immediate sacking of his cousin and mentor Majid. As noted, he could be equally single-minded when it came to various non-playing parties. In particular, his relations with the home board had only rarely reached that ideal of 'mutual tranquillity and common goodwill' of which the chairman had spoken in 1982. But Imran had been 'taking it', to use one of his phrases, too long, and a series of misconceptions that arose out of his victory speech and subsequent events brought an inglorious end to his captaincy.

Normally a day of rest, Friday 27 March, when the news and analysis from Melbourne was first broadcast in full, was a busy day in Pakistan. The press went into overdrive, and there were street carnivals and improvised tickertape parades, though without the players themselves, in Karachi and the other major cities. This was the apogee of the national cricketing revival that, by general consensus, had begun in 1971. Alone of the current squad, Imran had been there at the start. The chain of events that had led to Pakistan winning the World Cup was to a large extent of his making. Recent studies that measure managerial skills seem to be describing Imran when they stress 'multidimensional thinking' and such other desirable attributes as 'getting groups to collaborate well', 'using forms of influence to build alliances' and 'boxing smart'. It's true that there had been various local ructions along the way. As the preceding pages have, perhaps, shown, Imran and his near contemporary Javed Miandad hadn't always been as close as they might have hoped. One particularly well-placed source characterises their relationship as that between 'two scorpions in a bottle'. But generally public reaction in the wake of the World Cup was everything Imran could have wanted. As well as the donations in cash and kind that came in for his hospital, he was presented with the nation's most prestigous civil award, the Hilal-i-Imtiaz, or 'crescent of merit'. (He later returned this in protest when the Pakistan government gave the same award to Richard Boucher, the US Assistant Secretary of State, whom Imran considered a warmonger.) To the British journalist Kate Muir, who travelled with him in 1992, it was as if he was 'Gazza, the Beatles and President Kennedy rolled into one in a country famished for idols'. Had he chosen to put himself forward then instead of waiting as he did, it's a fair bet that Imran might have met with electoral success, if not actually been appointed state president for life.

There were those who held back from the general effusion. Nawaz Sharif, the one-time first-class cricketer and current prime minister, was not an unmitigated admirer of his nation's World Cup-winning captain. Five years later, Sharif could still reportedly 'vividly remember' the scene when, in his role as Punjab chief minister, he had gone to Lahore airport to welcome back the team after they had beaten India. The future premier had been 'nearly skittled over' by the crowds who had stampeded through the official reception committee in their rush to greet Imran and his men. Now Sharif sent orders that the cup-winning players' return flight should leave late and take the most circuitous route possible, not landing until after dark. The delay made little difference. In the improvised stands the army had erected alongside the Allama Iqbal terminal, a crowd of three to four thousand people broke into cheers and whistling applause as the plane finally came into view. Several dozen others scrambled into the branches of trees for a better look. 'Nothing compares to the feeling of an entire nation pouring out its love and respect to you,' Javed notes. Nawaz Sharif himself was not among those present at the airport. The general feeling among the press was that he had no wish to be upstaged a second time.

By then it was nearly a week since Imran had lifted the trophy on that sultry Wednesday night in Melbourne. The next morning, 16 of the 17 Pakistan players had flown on to a state-funded shopping trip in Singapore, while an 'exhausted' Imran, still on a course of daily, but diminishing painkillers and steroid shots for his shoulder, stayed behind in Australia. When everyone was reunited the following Monday morning, the air of collective euphoria soon dissolved. 'We were in the Singapore transit lounge, on the way back to Lahore,' Imran says. 'A friend of mine arrived and handed over a cheque for £5,000. It was money raised by the Asian community in the area, and it was clearly and unequivocally meant for the hospital. Unfortunately, two or three of the players were infected by greed, and put it about that all the bonuses and appearance fees raised from then on would go to the cause and not to themselves. It absolutely wasn't true.' Within a fortnight of the players' return to Pakistan, a full-scale slanging match had broken out in the press. Imran continued to insist that the team, or at least some of its prominent members, were labouring under a mass delusion. 'Where there was a dinner specifically arranged for the guys, of course they were the rightful beneficiaries. It never even occurred to me to interfere.' Eventually, there were two parallel laps of honour being undertaken by the Pakistan squad, one a commercial endeavour by the players and the other a charity fundraising tour by their captain. Imran later told Mushtaq Ahmed, 'I treated you like my son, and what you did was not great. I was hurt.'

Nor was he feeling the love he'd enjoyed when the BCCP had first appointed him. The board and even the government itself were up in arms; according to a well-placed student of Sharif's premiership, the cabinet's view was that the spectacle of 'one group of players apparently engaged in a highly public monetary feud with another' was not necessarily conducive to 'Pakistani national dignity'. In time the issue turned into a face-off between those BCCP officials broadly in league with senior members of Sharif's ruling Muslim League (Nawaz Group) party, at least some of whose instincts were pro-Karachi, and by extension pro-Javed, and the 'most influential Asian sportsman of all time'. After a period of reflection in the mountains, Imran emerged to announce that he would not be available for Pakistan's tour of England in the summer of 1992. In explaining his decision, he cited his nagging shoulder injury, proof that he could no longer bounce back as he had in his twenties, as well as the 'misconceptions of a few senior players and others' surrounding his fundraising activities. According to one leading British political figure and cricket fan, 'One had to hark back to Churchill's exit immediately following the defeat of Nazi Germany for a comparable example of a national hero being so swiftly replaced at his moment of ultimate glory', although at least in that case there had been a democratic election.

The tour Imran missed was a fractious one, even by modern standards. Once again under Javed's captaincy, the Pakistanis took the series 2–1. There were frequent innuendoes of underhand practice, with the *Sun* cordially referring to the visitors as 'bloody cheats', among other remarks of an unappreciative nature. In his autobiography, Ian Botham recalls batting in a one-day international at Lord's when his attention was drawn to the state of the ball. 'On one side it was so badly chewed up that it looked about 300 overs old. The other side was perfectly normal.' Botham adds, 'Over the years I've seen Pakistan players fiddle with the ball illegally, and [that summer] they were at it again.' It should be added that Javed and his bowlers vigorously denied the allegations, insisting that it was all simply a case of legitimately 'work[ing] on the orb', to quote the press statement, to induce reverse swing. As one of the team later remarked, 'When we did it we were called con men. When the English bowlers did it against Australia in 2005, they were called heroes.'

At the end of the series, the BCCP announced that they were awarding their players a hardship bonus to compensate for their 'outrageous reception' in England. There was some talk of whether sporting relations between the two nations would survive. Following events from the press box, Imran wrote in the *Daily Telegraph*, 'No official Pakistan team will ever set foot in this country again.' Although a shade drastic, it expressed a view that many people, both English and Pakistani, held at the time.

Imran may not have had much of a gift for prediction, in common with most of us, but he generally made a good fist of analysing what exactly was going on out on the field. Stylistically, his journalism, for which the *Telegraph* paid him £1,000 a column, was more in the school of Ian Botham than Neville Cardus. He tended to pick a subject and then bludgeon it with a characteristic mix of persistence, intelligence and unshakeable faith in his own judgement. The paper gave Imran his head, and from the first he exhibited signs of a marked independence. Javed later complained that his predecessor 'wrote pieces where I thought he was trying to disclose our weaknesses and our strategy ... It wasn't as if he was revealing state secrets to the enemy, but it wasn't the sort of thing you expected from your immediate past captain.' Behind the scenes, Imran would in time let the board know that in his view Wasim Akram was the best man to be leading the team. He reports that his advice was 'not well received'.

Apart from his articles and a coffee-table book on the tribes of Pakistan, Imran was busy organising a series of fundraising galas for his hospital. As a whole these tended to be well-attended, financially robust affairs whose organisation wasn't always as pronounced as the enthusiasm that went into them. In mid-July, Imran hosted a floodlit pan-Asian cricket match at Crystal Palace. With a summer-festival atmosphere, despite the rain, and the euphoric chanting of the 17,000-strong crowd, the event billed as 'the greatest party of the year' initially nearly lived up to its hype. Unfortunately, the game got off to a late start and was bedevilled by a variety of further weather delays and other interruptions. The English seem to have patented the concept of the al fresco evening involving a mass audience and large amounts of drink which then duly goes wrong. The general exuberance of the occasion eventually spilled over into a series of pitch invasions and a running brawl between rival factions of Indian, Pakistani and non-aligned spectators. At one stage Imran himself had to get on the loudspeaker to make a forlorn appeal for calm. Most of the print media (whose own, hastily erected tent collapsed in the mud as the match approached its climax) were negative in their overnight reporting of the event, which nonetheless raised some £75,000 for the Shaukat Khanum centre.

When Imran subsequently came back to London from a fundraising tour of the United States and Saudi Arabia, he threw a party for the Pakistan team. Javed Miandad reports that 'he invited the entire squad with the exception of three people – Ramiz Raja, Salim Malik and myself'. Casting modesty aside, Javed adds that he was then enjoying a 'fabulous' tour of England, and that Imran's efforts were aimed at 'try[ing] to create an intrigue against my captaincy'. One of the senior players confirmed to me that there had been a 'certain affection' among the side for their departed captain, 'who only ever criticised you from love', and even some hope that he might make a comeback. It had happened before. 'There's an old proverb that applies very well in the situation we found ourselves in while we were trouncing England in 1992. "When drinking the water, don't forget those who dug the well."' The player listed a number of team-mates who had benefited from Imran's patronage. 'We don't forget our friends.'

Early the following January, Javed led Pakistan to victory on a short tour of New Zealand. When the team returned home the captain was invited to a meeting with the board, who informed him that he was being replaced by Wasim. Javed was caustic throughout the interview. He reputedly belittled Imran, recounting his various alleged screw-ups. 'Today you have destroyed Pakistan cricket,' he advised the assembled bureaucrats. Nonetheless, Javed agreed to tour the West Indies that spring under Wasim's captaincy. The series got off to a poor start from the Pakistani point of view when both the new captain and his deputy, Waqar Younis, found themselves in gaol on a variety of drugs charges, which were subsequently dropped. The West Indies won the series 2–0, the beginning of a decade-long slump by Pakistan.

Javed notionally retired not long afterwards, having played 124 Tests and enjoyed every success, bar unmitigated popularity, the game has to offer. He wrote a well-received if somewhat self-serving memoir in 2003. By then the Pakistanis had just played the West Indies again, and beaten them comprehensively. It seemed to some that the 'bad old days' were behind them; only Javed wouldn't let them go. Among other things, he claimed that the players had nicknamed Imran 'Meter', implying 'a little money counter that was always ticking', at the time of the 1992 World Cup. A cynical observer might conclude that Javed, a fine bat and a fanatically ambitious sportsman, had been driven almost to madness by his resentment of having had to act as a recurrent stand-in for his more famous contemporary over the years. Both men could at least agree about the various perfidies and idiocies of their home board. In March 2001, Javed stepped aside for the second time as Pakistan's team coach. He blamed the 'cadre of senior players', the media who had 'managed to somehow make me directly responsible if the team performed poorly', and the bureaucrats who had 'also fallen in with this mind-set'.

Imran formally announced his retirement in September 1992, just before his 40th birthday, which the world celebrated 51 days late. His career had often heard the distant drums before, notably in 1983–84, but this time around there would be no miraculous return. In his 88 Tests he took 362 wickets at an average of 22.81, scored 3,807 runs at 37.69, and held on to 28 catches. For many years, Gubby Allen, the MCC's *éminence grise* and one-time national chairman of selectors, used to say that the 'proper and consistent' way of assessing an England Test cricketer was by his record against Australia. Perhaps it still is. Starting in October 1978, when they resumed play after a break of 18 years and two wars, the same could be said of the Pakistanis with regard to India. Here Imran's record is even more striking. In 23 Tests against his country's South Asian rivals he took 94 wickets, including six innings in which he took five wickets or more, and scored 1,091 runs at an average of 51.95. What the figures don't show is the extent to which Pakistan's all-important sense of national pride and regional machismo came to be linked to Imran's captaincy. During his tenure, the team never lost a Test to India.

For almost a decade after his international debut, most people underestimated Imran, and it was only in the late 1970s or early 1980s, when Pakistan started beating the likes of England, that they came to recognise his virtues. It had taken that long for a cosmopolitan, bookish temperament and a lifelong commitment to the key Pathan code of self-assertion and revenge to be seen as traits of some importance to his nation's sporting fortunes. It would be fair to say that, over and above these qualities, Imran sometimes seemed to suffer from an advanced case of *noblesse oblige*. It's also true that he was something of a slow starter, and that his batting, at least, actively improved towards the end of his career. But for the stress fracture and one or two other, self-inflicted absences from the national team, he would have been a member of the 4,000 run and 400 wicket club chartered by Kapil Dev, who played 43 more Tests. And he did all this while leading a fairly full life off the field. Imran undertook a schedule that roughly tripled that of an Intikhab or Mushtaq, moving guests in and out of his hotel room with dispatch, signing autographs in shifts, meeting the press, posing outside nightclubs for photographers, making excursions to Beverly Hills, delivering speeches on healthcare and the plight of impoverished children, and flying on average 80,000 miles a year. And it was hard to ignore the playing style, which involved an essentially sound batting technique and a bowling action so upwardly propulsive it deserved its own runway. Although a recognisably 'modern' performer with his teased hair and medallion, Imran also appealed across the ages. Len Hutton, Richie Benaud and Godfrey Evans are only three of the immediate post-war greats to list him in their all-time World XI. Imran was a 'classical cricketer who'd listened to *Sergeant Pepper*', Evans once told me.

'Khan embodies the hypocrisy of Muslim elites who inveigh against the West by day and enjoy its pleasures by night,' the *Weekly Standard* wrote in a generally unadmiring May 2005 profile. The paper quoted Imran as having remarked, with some reticence, of his love life, 'Er, by answering that question I put myself in a difficult position because this will get quoted in Pakistan. I respect my own culture and a lot of young people look up to me. It's a big responsibility for me not to make these admissions in public. Everyone knows I'm a single man and a normal man. But there's no need to stick it down their throats.' To anyone mildly acquainted with the facts, Imran's reply was a *tour de force* of evasion and understatement. One former lover was less discreet and later informed *The Times* that he 'juggled his girlfriends extremely elegantly … and he likes mangoes'.

By contrast, the man whose image was perpetuated by his charity fundraising was almost saintly. At the age of nine or ten, one friend assured me, Imran had 'gone out in winter in a new overcoat and returned without it – he'd given it to a ragged urchin he had seen shivering in the cold.' There would be a number of broadly similar tales over the next 30 years. That the *Weekly Standard*'s spoilt-brat view of Imran is something of a simplification we have, I hope, established. But it would still be an inadequate picture of the man to claim he was totally without his humanising contradictions. 'In 1995, Khan denounced the West with its "fat women in miniskirts",' the *Standard* factually reported. 'Presumably the skinny ones in miniskirts he dated were OK, then?'

At around the time he retired from cricket, Imran met a tall, attractive, 26-year-old brunette named Kristiane Backer. She was the

German-born presenter of MTV Europe, and as such based in London. Over the years, Imran had shown himself to be an attentive companion who would listen with sympathy while women talked about themselves, their lives, their jobs and even sometimes their slightly dotty New Age philosophies. Ms Backer (whose own skirts tended to be of the token variety) would later write in praise of her adopted home town, 'It has always stood for respect (not just tolerance!) towards other cultures and religions. It has graciously welcomed its guests, black, white, yellow, green or pocadot [sic]. In fact, The Queen is proud of Great Britain's multi-cultural heritage. David Bowie once asked to have his photograph taken with me! ... I also adore Islamic art and architecture. They are always harmonious and pleasing to the eye ... My extensive travels throughout the Muslim world have given me the opportunity to dig deep into the intricate cultural fabric of Muslim societies and gain a knowledge of their religion and way of life. Rich in colours, spices and scents, my experiences in the Orient, the people and their values inspired and challenged me at the same time ... I also hosted many live music shows in Europe with acts like Take That, the Backstreet Boys and Lenny Kravitz.' Imran and Kristiane Backer, who went on to qualify as a homeopath, were to be together for some two years.

A longer-term priority was Imran's growing concern with social justice, which also began in earnest around 1992. The obsession was startling in its sweep and boldness. Imran doesn't seem to have proclaimed the fact: he just acted, building on a groundswell of progressive opinion within Pakistan. In its way, the transformation was almost as total as the one which had turned him in his late twenties from being a county trundler to a world-class bowler of Caribbean fire. Imran's new constituency would be the hitherto largely silent majority of ordinary citizens whose rulers had spent some $10 billion in outstanding loans from the US government on such projects as an opulent new prime ministerial secretariat in Islamabad and a fleet of several thousand American yellow taxis, which Nawaz Sharif's government saw fit to distribute throughout every small town and village, regardless of whether or not they had roads. With both Sharif and Benazir Bhutto coming to face corruption charges in Pakistan's courts, Imran must have sensed that the country would be receptive to an honest, socially conscious politician who already happened to be a national hero. In the meantime, he continued to concentrate on his hospital, to which he gave his full World Cup winner's bonus of some £85,000.

Imran's new calling would require a certain amount of sacrifice both from himself and those around him. As Kristiane Backer observed, 'His working life changed so completely. The circumstances of Imran's life altered incredibly when he [retired]. He had great plans for his country and, as Nelson Mandela said, regrettably, when your mission is the struggle there's little time left for family.'

NINE

'If They Say They Were Squeezing the Ball – Fine; They Were Squeezing the Ball'

Imran's eventual decision to enter the briar patch of Pakistani state politics wasn't unprecedented for a former Test player, and his old bowling partner Sarfraz had chosen the same career path some years earlier. But it still presented rather more of a challenge than he would have faced had he slipped into the more typical retired cricketer's world of providing occasional colour commentary on Sky Sports and opening provincial supermarkets. Crudely put, it meant asking people who were your social inferiors to vote for you. It meant entering an arena where the privileges of birth could be counter-productive. It meant being on familiar and friendly terms with every adult on the electoral roll, or at least as many as practicable, and kissing their babies. And, in Imran's case, it meant putting himself at the mercy of a small but fanatical band of enemies from his playing days who could be expected to oppose him out of personal malice rather than high-minded conviction.

On the upside, there was a large and potentially receptive audience waiting for him. Many Pakistanis saw in Imran a slightly more glossy reflection of themselves: he was fiercely patriotic and rightly concerned about his country mortgaging itself to the West; he was not a multimillionaire; and he wasn't part of any establishment. His elderly father and his four sisters were all still working productively. And he exhibited, or at least projected, some of the grit and defiance of the Pathan tribesmen he had written about in two books.*

---

* At least one of these required the services of a ghostwriter. Speaking 18 years after the event, the former literary agent Jeremy Lewis recalled Imran arriving in his office to deliver a manuscript. 'He handed me a leatherbound notebook or diary containing a few jottings and autobiographical snippets. It took me, at most, five minutes to read them; and that, it soon became apparent, was all we had to go on.' The work in question was called *Indus Journey: A Personal View of Pakistan*.

Imran warmed up for his new role by taking an unpaid position as 'special adviser' to the Pakistan Board of Control. This was not the sort of job ideally suited to the nervously inclined. Imran's tenure was punctuated by the familiar ongoing rows, mostly centred, it appears, around the question of Javed Miandad's suitability as captain. The decision to remove Javed in early 1993 split the BCCP into two factions. Infighting was not a skill that the bureaucrats had allowed to grow rusty following Imran's own resignation from the side. In making his ill-tempered departure, Javed accused his predecessor of being a 'conspirator and a manipulator' behind the scenes. Salim Malik came to echo the sentiments when he found himself omitted from Pakistan's subsequent tour of the West Indies, allegedly on Imran's advice.

As the board's representative, Imran also attended meetings of the International Cricket Council at Lord's, where he put the case for staging the World Cup on the subcontinent again. Although the other delegates eventually fell in with the idea, not least because the Pakistan, India and Sri Lanka contingent (quite legally) got the ICC Associate Members on board by promising them £100,000 each, Imran told me, 'I was appalled ... Most of the Englishmen still treated us as though we represented some junior colony.' He was to resign his position only a year later, amid some controversy.

Coming back to Lahore offered the first real reward of retirement. Imran still 'absolutely loved' the chaotic, over-full city with its Mogul tombs and town-centre cricket stadium jostling up against a growing number of shops that were almost Parisian in their luxury. While in Pakistan he spent most of his time living in a well-heeled suburban home with his father and close family. There were also frequent excursions to the area around Mianwali, some 320 kilometres (200 miles) to the west at the foot of the Salt Range mountains. It was here that the Niazis had first settled in the 13th century. Imran liked nothing more than to wander off into the hills with a few friends and shoot partridge, even in this remote spot often coming across groups of fanatical cricket supporters. A companion and occasional travel writer told me of a weekend trek up the banks of the Indus when a crowd of elderly tribesmen, 'look[ing] sad, shabby and world-worn as they sat around their campfire, serenaded by jackals', had 'sprung to life' on seeing Imran and then begun to pepper him with intensely technical questions about his various Test performances. 'You could tell he was more in his element here in this tribal outpost than he was in some meeting or another with the suits at Lord's.'

While Imran decompressed from his 21 years in the limelight, he was arranging for construction of the cancer hospital which at last appeared to be adequately funded to become a physical entity. The site itself had little pretension to beauty. The modern, red-brick facility would rise up from a patch of scrubby wasteland, swampy in one corner, with a heavily congested road running immediately behind it. Imran did not give much attention to the building's externals. Once inside, however, the Shaukat Khanum centre was a plate-glassed, slick-floored repository of the latest research and treatment equipment. There were airy waiting rooms with a variety of ethnic artwork on the walls, potted palms and a large reception area which was occasionally flag-strewn to give éclat to ceremonies. Many an equivalent Western hospital would be put to shame by the obvious care and attention that went into making the patient feel welcome there. Imran was clearly quite proud of the place, to which he had given some £200,000 of his own money by late 1993, even if as yet he remained its principal exhibit. As the building progressed, he liked to take potential donors through it, detailing the various amenities. Walking into the lobby, he once waved at a framed photograph someone had left on a desk showing himself sporting a luxuriant bouffant and said, 'And there's Mr Shampoo.' Imran and his board took another significant step forward when, in December 1992, they appointed a new full-time hospital director: David Wood, the former chief medical officer and head of development of a 650-bed facility in Colorado, and as such a man who brought both proven fundraising and clinical skills to the job.

If the hospital was what 'fired Imran up to an almost messianic level', to quote *Today*, it was, perhaps, because he had graphic family experience of Pakistan's generally abject track record in providing even basic cancer care. Everything was now geared to this cause. A friend recalls that, for some two years, Imran basically did nothing but 'raise money through a never-ending round of auctions and dinners, and travel around the country on goodwill missions'. One could tentatively conclude that what he was really doing was showing the Pakistani public how a retired Test captain could grow old gracefully. It hardly needs adding that he was treated as a sort of secular saint, at least in Lahore, where there were confirmed instances of both men and women fainting away if they saw him. Imran, it's widely agreed, was commendably gracious to his fans. He was also human. A certain tetchiness, occasionally remarked on in English county dressing-rooms, showed itself again when an elderly beggar once approached him outside the gates of his home for a donation: he did not obtain it. It's only fair to raise the possibility that the man's pitch might simply have been unduly persistent, and/or ill-timed. Imran's interviews and speeches around 1993–4 made frequent reference to his personal indifference to money, and it's certainly true that he lived more frugally than at least one of his World Cup-winning colleagues.

For the time being, Imran resisted the temptation of a formal entry into national politics. He did, however, accept an unpaid position as Pakistan's first ever ambassador for tourism. This was an area hitherto under-explored in the country's 45-year modern history. As well as announcing Imran's new, 'critically prestigious' role, the Islamabad government would undertake a vigorous publicity campaign, primarily aimed at the American market, promoting Pakistan as an 'earthly paradise' of combined Eastern and Western charms. If lacking the comic potential of, say, Gateshead's one-time efforts to restyle itself as the 'Venice of the North', this was still something of a stretch. In 1993, Pakistan was not the vacation resort of choice for most Midwesterners.

Imran blamed the relative indifference of the global holidaymaker to date on an irrational fear of Pakistan's cultural traditions. 'I don't want to go to a place where there are a lot of people, such as the south of France, where everybody knows everybody else', he remarked. 'Pakistan has had some bad publicity abroad because we're branded with Muslim fundamentalism and a military dictatorship that leads people to think of suppression.' (This particular association had, indeed, occurred to the US State Department, who put out a recurrent 'travel advisory' in the mid-1990s for any of its citizens planning to visit the region.) 'Yet it is not as if you are beaten with sticks if a woman does not have her legs covered. That is a myth. Pakistanis love tourists, yet ever since the Crusades there has been this fear of Islam. It is always portrayed as an evil religion.' Imran said this, it should be noted, some eight years before the 9/11 attacks on the American homeland.

There was more to a public appearance by Pakistan's new ambassador for tourism than a few scene-setting remarks and the distribution of glossy leaflets, however. Like many successful figures in politics, showbusiness, sport and elsewhere, Imran used a number of techniques for intensifying audience response. He invariably arrived late for meetings and rallies, and when crowd anticipation reached an appropriate level he would suddenly rush in, surrounded by an animated group of baggy-trousered admirers whose presence made Imran seem all the more important to any foreigners in the audience unaware of his fame as a cricketer. In later years, while on the political campaign trail, he often made dramatic entrances, preceded by bands, marching units, kite-flying children, imams and others. At Lahore, in February 1997, crowds could hear the excited screams of Imran's entourage long before he stepped out of a shiny Range Rover to address them. Conversely, he remained the most personally unassuming figure anywhere in Pakistani public life, and still liked to walk around the streets of his home town 'without a big fuss', he told a reporter.

Much of Imran's ambassadorial work went on in London, where he put forward a variety of specific plans to enhance Pakistan's tourism potential. Among these was a proposal to build a resort of 'ten luxury lodges of native mud and brick' in the foothills of Kashmir's Karakorom range. From there, he said, visitors would be 'conveyed with guards into the tribal areas. There would be designated areas for camping, tents with portable showers, and local cooks. It would be the ultimate [destination]. There are bears and snow leopards there and hardly anyone from outside knows about it.' While characteristically full of enthusiasm, Imran proved himself to be not particularly well suited to the more mundane and bureaucratic aspects of his job, which inevitably involved haggling with various government ministers for funds. In 2009, the World Economic Forum Travel and Tourism Competitiviness Index put Pakistan a lowly 73rd on its list of leading holiday destinations, 18 places below India, though somewhat ahead of Zimbabwe.

Although fiercely ambitious to advance Pakistan's fortunes wherever he could, Imran also knew when the time was ripe for inaction. The particular political turbulence in the country from the spring to the autumn of 1993 was a good example. Nawaz Sharif's term as premier was interrupted in April that year, when the state president used his emergency powers to dissolve parliament and appoint Balakh Sher Mazari as the caretaker prime minister. Just 38 days later, Pakistan's Supreme Court revoked the presidential order and reinstated Sharif. He lasted in office another seven weeks before being replaced by a Washington-based, former World Bank official named Moeen Qureshi. Qureshi, too, proved to be something of an evanescent figure on the national political scene and was followed in turn by Benazir Bhutto, whose centre-left Pakistan People's Party swept to power in legislative elections held that October. Pakistan had thus had the services of five administrations in six months. In the midst of this, either Mazari or Qureshi, or possibly both, had offered Imran a post in the cabinet, which he declined.

Thanks to their fondness for building themselves offices of Babylonian opulence, and also to the economic sanctions imposed on Pakistan as a result of its nuclear programme, all of the aforementioned governments operated constantly on the verge of national bankruptcy. By mid-1995, the country was having to 'reschedule' its impressively large foreign debt repayments. A number of domestic groups displayed their concern at the way Pakistan was being governed by organising street demonstrations, several of which turned into riots. It would of course be wrong to claim that the protests were aimed exclusively at the profligacy of the various governments' spending policies. There was also a certain amount of friction between, on the one hand, those who wanted Pakistan to be a democratic and progressive welfare state and, on the other, those who preferred a more narrowly religious interpretation of the 1956 constitution. The overall result was a decade of recurrent civil unrest, punctuated by regular allegations of corruption levelled against all of Pakistan's leading politicians. It was in this climate that Imran declined to throw in his lot with any of the major established parties.

In fact it's arguable that his fundraising drives led more or less naturally to a career in politics without his even consciously knowing it at the time. Imran had also liked a good scrap as a cricketer, and often looked back fondly on the various wars-by-proxy in which he'd risen to fame. There may never have been a more aggressively patriotic player. The eventual outcome was a 'chronological, logical evolution', Omar Kureishi believed. Imran's hospital activities 'showed much the same mixture of idealism, hard-headed economics and controlled polemics [which] would be his stocks-in-trade in the years ahead'. To these earlier themes he soon added a vocal concern about the ruling elites in Pakistan, where 'kickbacks, commissions and outright robbery' were rife. Many of the country's senior military officers, in particular, came to realise the advantages of an entrepreneurial approach to their jobs. In just one example of the many available, an Admiral Mansur ul Haq, the head of the navy from 1994 to 1996, left his post in some haste for the United States, from where the Pakistani government eventually extradited him to face charges of 'gross, wholesale [and] systematic corruption, betrayal, dereliction and grand larceny'. The National Accountability Bureau in Islamabad struck a deal with ul Haq in which, without admitting any wrongdoing, he returned some US$8 million to the state. Imran was not alone in pointing out that this voluntary payment amounted to the equivalent of 1,300 years of the Admiral's salary.

Despite a number of semi-official overtures, Imran resisted the temptation to make a professional cricket comeback. After March 1992 he restricted himself to a few charity matches on behalf of the hospital, and seems to have been sublimely indifferent to the various third-party books, videos and other spin-offs brought out to celebrate his career. The gossip columns, that daily substitute for immortality, now saw a bit less of him than before. He did try his hand at television commentary and occasional interviewing, and soon regretted it. Imran 'literally sweated [his] way through' one live encounter with Jeffrey Archer, who confirmed to me that this had not been a success. 'Imran wasn't a natural on air, because strangely for someone who want[ed] to enter the bear-pit of politics, he's not an extrovert, and if anything rather shy. Frankly, I think his talents would have been wasted on TV.' Another well-placed source added that, in his opinion, Imran's essential problem as an interviewer was that 'he liked to transmit and not to receive'.

For all that, believing 'there [was] enough stuff out there already', Imran apparently never contemplated writing anything further about himself. He did, however, continue to contribute a series of richly opinionated articles to the *Daily Telegraph* and other British outlets. The fussily handwritten copy was always punctually delivered, and not burdened by any undue sense of deference to the host nation. Sunil Gavaskar once advised Imran to tone down his printed remarks, lest the *Telegraph* see fit to cancel the arrangement. One former sports editor recalled that he had once gently suggested that his guest columnist 'revisit' a piece in which he had expressed various reservations about the English county cricket system. Although he had made some 'extremely sound' points, 'it seem[ed] just a bit too partisan to win over any hearts and minds'. Rather than lengthening the article, as had been proposed, Imran decided to make it even shorter, rightly describing it as 'hard-hitting'. Like most of his journalism, it was good stuff, with just that touch of the haphazard which raised it above the level of a full-on rant. The supposedly old-school figure of Colin Cowdrey was just one of those who approved; he considered 'Khan's pieces always intelligent [and] occasionally touching on genius'. By the mid 1990s, Imran's writing was his biggest regular source of income. His few investments, including that in a Lahore supermarket, were thought to have been motivated less by the desire for personal reward than by the opportunity they offered to further provide for his hospital.

The interplay between the Eastern and Western versions of Imran continued to give rise to some good-natured comment about the man the press called, tritely, perhaps, the 'playboy saint'. It's arguable that the struggle to resolve the balance to his own satisfaction had been going on in one form or another ever since he arrived in England in 1971. Imran made no pretence about the fact that he enjoyed aspects of the good life, or at least the opportunity it afforded him to mingle on equal terms with those not normally within the orbit of an Asian-born cricketer. The Marchioness of Worcester remained a close friend. She named a horse after him. He saw something of Mick Jagger and his ilk. The cricket-loving (and Oscar-winning) songwriter Tim Rice remembers an incident from the mid-1990s 'when a near-namesake, and a pal of mine, Tim Wright, took Imran up on a rather vague "we must have lunch sometime" offer. When Wright duly met the great man in the restaurant he discovered that he had thought he was meeting me. A strained meal followed.'

Imran was aware of the fact that mutterings about his social life were 'but part of a larger attack' once again under way by enemies within the Pakistani press. The Karachi-based *Newsline*, for example, would imply that 'the former speedster' was also something of a religious zealot 'with more than a soft corner for the Afghan Taliban [something Imran denies] ... Khan's "self-righteousness and high-flying principles fail to explain the link between his strange fondness for the [clerics] and his passion for all the good things in life which have come from the west",' the paper added, quoting an anonymous source. Two other authors, James Forsyth and Jai Singh, were principally concerned with mustering evidence to portray Imran as a chronic amnesiac when it came to overlooking various 'troubling' aspects of his past life, and deployed some possibly selective facts of their own regarding his 'demagoguery' and 'two-facedness'. The general thrust was that Imran was an irresponsible, serial shagger. In time they even called attention to the fact that he had formed a close relationship with a woman who was 'half Jewish'. Imran himself remarked only that he had been 'brought up in a predominantly female household' and as a result 'like[d] women very much. I find it hard to understand why the English exclude girls from certain places. I've never grasped Women's Lib and the idea of the sexes competing. I think of them as complementing each other ... Pakistanis are much warmer towards their women than the English. They offer them respect and protection.'

Some of Imran's apparent contradictions on the subject were on hand when he joined a three-day shooting party arranged by his friend Syra Vahidy and her husband early in 1994. 'We were up in rural

Pakistan,' says Vahidy, an eminently fair-minded person with no axe to grind. 'And here was Imran, in native costume, accompanied by this German girl [Kristiane Backer]. It was all slightly odd. For the first time since I'd known him he seemed to be profoundly interested in religion and in his roots as a whole. He talked a lot about rediscovering himself. "For too long I was ignorant of my traditions," he said. Imran also took the opportunity to instruct [Backer] on the correct Islamic protocol for a woman, for example that she should always cover her head. In fact he was rather insistent about it. From my experience, he was a completely changed man [in] that he talked not about cricket but about the Almighty's infinite understanding and forgiveness. It was obviously heartfelt stuff, and it was quite a revelation to me. Imran seemed almost to have reinvented himself as a man of God. Of course, he and his girlfriend still slept together at night.'

The way in which 'Imran' and 'ball-tampering' came to be associated in some people's minds was innocuous enough in its particulars, even if the result was long-running and ultimately sensational. It began when the author Ivo Tennant, a well-respected sports correspondent for *The Times* and other publications, quoted Imran in a biography as saying, 'I have occasionally scratched the side and lifted the seam.' Tennant went on to describe a fixture in 1981 when, as we've seen, his subject had applied a bottle top to the ball, which had subsequently 'started to move around a lot'. As generally happens in the cricket publishing world, the book was launched to minimal fanfare and duly enjoyed a small but respectable sale. Imran's admission concerned a now largely forgotten county match 13 years in the past, and amounted to three brief sentences out of a 70,000-word text. I happened to be working for the same publisher at the time, and can confirm that there was no great sense of any dramatic scandal being abroad. It was a perfectly well written book of the sort (and I speak with well-earned humility on the subject) that tends to get politely noticed in the trade before going on to a long and peaceful retirement in the discount bins.

All that changed when, after some early, lesser news comment, an enterprising features editor at the *Mail on Sunday* splashed Imran's 'shocking' *mea culpa* across his paper's front page. According to the publisher's estimate, some six million people would come to read about the 1981 incident over the course of the next 24 hours, which was approximately 5,997,000 more than had initially bought Tennant's book. Reactions to the story were mixed. 'I was deeply disappointed,' a then member of the Pakistani cabinet recalls. 'To say that it all happened a long time ago wasn't enough. Our nation's most illustrious sportsman was guilty of sharp practice. These are the hard facts. They cannot be diluted by the passage of time.' To Imran himself, who resigned his position at the ICC, there seemed to be a double standard at play. Seam-doctoring, he said, was 'as old as the game itself'. Over the years, he had seen 'almost all the great bowlers' do it, 'and very few of them were ever called a cheat'. In an interview published with the *Sun* he went on to imply that 'the biggest names in English cricket', not excluding the late Jim Laker, had been occasional tamperers. In 2008, Imran added, 'All I did was give one instance where I used an object.' In an ideal world, the disclosure should have been the starting-point for a long overdue debate on 'what was and wasn't acceptable practice', and was thus intended more in the way of a public service than as a tabloid headline.

As soon as the press got wind of the story an avalanche of criticism descended. Some of it was of the usual sort that tended to surround Pakistani cricket. Imran's remarks came less than two years since the heated 1992 series in England, when Ian Botham recalls of a break during a one-day international at Lord's (in which Imran himself wasn't playing), 'The umpires took one look at the ball and in no time at all came to the conclusion that it had been tampered with.' Although, as Botham adds, 'we were told not to discuss with anybody what had gone on', the story had promptly become both a front- and back-page lead, and added significantly to the view that 'the Pakis had been at it [ball doctoring] for 30 years', as one distinguished former England batsman said in 2009.

Some of the turmoil also arose because of a particular desire to get at Imran. Chris Lander believed it was a 'classic case of "We build 'em up and we chop 'em down"', or the so-called tall-poppy syndrome. One prominent English sports commentator, speaking to me, perhaps wisely, on condition of anonymity, remarked of the subject of this book, 'Even by today's celebrity standards he was a quite magnificently self-important fellow for someone who happened to be quite good with a bat and ball ... [Imran] reeked of condescension ... You always felt you should back out of his presence as though taking your leave of royalty.' Under the circumstances, a degree of *schadenfreude* at Imran's expense was a fair bet among certain journalists.

Another possibility was that at least some of the criticism came from the fact that, over the last 15 years or so, 'our chubby little chaps had

had the gall to pull the lion's tail, [which] had stirred up a hornet's nest of resentment against them', in General Zia's slightly mixed 1987 metaphor. Imran himself seemed to interpret events in this light when he later remarked to *India Today*, 'There is a lot of racism in [Western] society. Where is this hatred coming from?' It was a fair question, but it still seems a stretch to portray the British media of 1994, as at least one prominent Imran supporter does, as 'irredeemably and institutionally racist'. As in most other areas, the scrupulously open-minded majority coexisted with the perhaps less enlightened fringe still fond of 'Paki' jokes that stereotyped the subcontinentals as swarthy and devious, although occasionally having a good sense of rhythm. It's conceivable that Imran came in for the pounding he did for a variety of reasons, some of them obscurely related to his skin colour. At least on occasion, he seems to have favoured this particular explanation of events. One of Imran's hospital associates, who saw him almost daily in the mid-1990s, thought 'he probably had a much sharper outlook on these things after he left cricket and got out in normal society for a change ... He became a *lot* more aware of what you call civil rights. So yes, it's possible he saw some of the attacks on him and on other Pakistanis as racially motivated.'

Some time after Ivo Tennant's book was published, an unknown party drew Mike Gatting's attention to an unflattering reference in it to himself. The passage in question seemed to imply that Imran had called the former England captain uneducated, an obvious slur both on Gatting and the John Kelly Boys' Technology College of north London. It was a spurious and, perhaps worse, legally reprehensible thing to have said. In time Gatting sued both Tennant and the book's publishers (but not Imran) and won substantial damages. The general feeling was that both the offence and its outcome did little to help an already strained Anglo-Pakistani sporting relationship.

Two factors emerged out of the Tennant affair, which became something of a *cause célèbre* in the book publishing world of 1994. The first was the obviously quite acute sensitivity of various parties to the ball-tampering issue, and its 'racist' subtext. This particular grenade had already once been lobbed in the direction of the British courts, when Sarfraz Nawaz sued Allan Lamb over his claims that Sarfraz had shown him the different methods for lifting the seam while they were team-mates at Northamptonshire; the case was eventually dropped. The second was the potentially equally charged matter of an Englishman's schooling and, by extension, of his perceived slot in the social order.

Two years after Tennant's book was published, both factors combined in one of the more spectacular celebrity feuds of recent times.

In early November 1994, Imran set off on a countrywide tour of Pakistan to raise the final tranche of money for his hospital before it opened its doors. For the next 45 days he travelled the towns and villages, 29 in all, in a sort of Popemobile, alighting to give upwards of a hundred speeches. Imran's basic message combined the key financial appeal with what the *Sunday Times* called 'rousing, quasi-religious sermons attacking feminism, atheists, politicians, "evil" Western values and the "brown sahibs" or those Pakistani elites who aped their former colonial masters'.

Vastly helpful in the whole process was a sort of call-and-response litany that developed between Imran and his audiences. It had started early on in the tour, in a dusty Punjab market square, when some man with a big voice had shouted from the crowd, 'Give them the long handle, Imran', apparently a reference to knocking the established politicians for six. A loud roar had gone up. As soon as he could be heard, Imran shouted back some such remark as 'I'm going to' or 'Let's do it together'. Various other repartee of a cricketing nature followed throughout the remainder of the tour. Such exchanges brought delirium, after which Imran could say more or less anything he chose and still be sure of a warm, materially gratifying response. When all the figures were added up, he had collected the equivalent of £2.5 million, most of it donated in small notes or coins.

One British Sunday newspaper stringer followed Imran on the fundraising trail and thought he resembled another 'aloof but oddly charismatic' figure: the Prince of Wales. 'Both men suffer from arrested development. They have the same sense of destiny and the same identification with the man in the street (whom Imran calls "the masses").' A certain 'humourlessness' and 'addiction to worthy causes' were also qualities they apparently shared. In fact, their core appeal was 'almost identical', although the heir to the throne might perhaps have struggled to demonstrate the correct grip for an in-ducker, as Imran did when a child once marched gravely out of the crowd to present him with an orange for the purpose.

At Lahore, the next stop, there was a predictably large and respectful audience on hand. Wearing a baggy-fitting *kurta hizar* and comfortable white trainers, Imran spoke slowly for the first few minutes, seeming to choose his words carefully. He was there not only to raise money, he said, but to share certain concerns about the state of the world with his fellow citizens. Then, as it appeared to one English observer, a cricket fan and doctor named Chris Leahy, he switched to schoolmaster mode: 'There was a slightly exasperated tone to be heard as he ticked off one looming spiritual crisis after another.' But Imran was lecturing a class that was 'quite obviously thrilled and proud to be there ... At the end there was a tumultous ovation. He was almost like a messiah to them.' Touring the outlying villages, Imran stood up the whole way in his automobile, clearly enjoying the scene as much as the crowds did.

On 29 December 1994, the Shaukat Khanum hospital opened to the public. Standing at a podium between assorted political dignitaries on one side and Imran on the other, a young cancer patient named Sumera Yousaf did the honours. The hospital's services gradually came on line, as scheduled, over the next six months – first the walk-in clinics and pharmacy, followed by the operating rooms, and the remaining outpatient facilities. Even now, the Karachi-based press criticism didn't let up: year after year Imran would open the papers only to see carping editorials about his alleged favouritism towards his home town. The hostility often spilled over from leader pages into news columns: favourable stories, like the opening ceremony, were banished to inside pages, while unfavourable ones, often concerning some minor construction delay, were highlighted on the front page, right-hand column, where thinly veiled, necessarily anonymous allegations of bribery and corruption also did the rounds. The fact is that the ordinary Pakistani citizen of limited means now had access to the sort of critical healthcare treatment previously reserved for what *The Times* called a 'tiny minority composed of the country's military and civilian rulers, or those who had used their influence for personal gain', in so far as there was a distinction between the two. Behind the media venom, it was clear that Imran had accomplished something of longer-term national consequence than even winning the World Cup.

Nor was the whole project brought off in a vacuum. At some stage during his 1994 fundraising tour, Imran became persuaded of the merits of a populist political ideology that came to dominate his life from then on. 'Travelling around like that changed me,' he remarked. 'The most interesting thing was that the really rich people, of the sort I'd been to school with, hardly contributed anything, while thousands of others were lining up to drop a few rupees each into the collecting box. It was my first real contact with the grass-roots, and it came as something of a shock. Essentially, what Pakistan had was a tiny ruling elite sponging off the majority of the citizens, who had nothing.' The 'fun-loving Romeo' regularly taken to task in the *Weekly Standard* and elsewhere was now replaced by the intense, almost fanatical social reformer who would make it his life's mission to campaign to 'reverse the standard government policy of protecting only the top one or two per cent of society and exploiting the rest'.

As transformations go, Imran's wasn't, perhaps, in the Damascene calibre. Despite some churlish press comment, he hadn't exactly been living a life of unremitting frivolity and decadence up until then. His work at UNICEF had been going on for nearly a decade. But it does seem fair to say that there was a marked shift in Imran's priorities, and that this occurred fairly soon after he returned to Lahore from the provinces. A hospital associate with whom Imran worked particularly closely watched with interest as his longtime friend became completely absorbed by the 'sort of radical agenda he'd somehow avoided for 42 years'. The same source adds that he never doubted his colleague's sincerity, although he noted an early 'lack of information'. Imran's basic innocence of organised politics made him a natural prey for yet more 'vicious [and] sustained' attacks in the media. In time he took even more flak as a social campaigner than he had as a cricketer. The overall thesis was that Imran was a dilettante whose only experience of foreign affairs, to quote the *Herald*, 'had been of the kind he conducted in various bedrooms in London or Sydney'. The odds were 'strongly against a sportsman ever successfully becoming a statesman', according to the *Sunday Times*. 'Khan, however,' the paper allowed, 'has long since shown his capacity for uncritical self-belief and an ability to ignore the factional yappings' that invariably greeted a public figure in Pakistan.

Even Imran's detractors agreed that the nation wasn't particularly well served at that time by self-denying, visionary political leaders. Much of what Nawaz Sharif had taught the country to regard as 'prosperity' was, in fact, nothing more than a debt-fuelled illusion. As in so many other policy areas Sharif's rhetoric was impressive, but there was little indication of any strategy for long-term economic growth beyond continued massive borrowing from the Americans, and the associated perks it brought for a privileged few. In 1994, the Pakistani military's net worth was estimated at £12 billion, some five times the total foreign direct investment generated by the Islamabad government. The army owned 15 per cent of the country's land, two-thirds of it concentrated in the hands of the 80 most senior major-generals and generals. Sharif himself seems not to have been personally inconvenienced by the austerity measures he periodically visited on the Pakistani people. While in office, it was revealed that the premier owned a row of luxury flats on London's Park Lane, among other legitimate assets controlled by a company headquartered in the British Virgin Islands.

National elections held after the political crisis of mid-1993 returned Benazir Bhutto (whose own accommodations ran to an ancestral home, complete with private zoo) to power. Bhutto's efforts to modernise Pakistan came, in turn, to be tempered by certain allegations of personal improbity levelled against her and members of her immediate family. According to published reports, the new prime minister smuggled CDs containing uranium enrichment data to North Korea on a 1993 state visit in exchange for various return considerations by Pyongyang. A subsequent *New York Times* report claimed to have unearthed documents relating to a network of Swiss bank accounts maintained by Bhutto and her husband Asif Ali Zardari, whom his wife went on to appoint as Pakistan's Minister for Investments. Though never convicted of a crime, Zardari spent eight years in prison on an assortment of fraud, deception and other charges. A Swiss magistrate later indicted Pakistan's first couple on various counts of money laundering, which involved $13 million in cash and a $200,000 diamond necklace located in a Geneva safe-deposit box. The Polish government then charged Bhutto and Zardari of having awarded themselves a 7.15 per cent sweetener, worth roughly $2 million, from the sale to Pakistan of 8,000 tractors. Authorities in France raised the possibility that the Bhuttos had taken substantial commissions in similarly arranging for Dassault Aviation to replace 12 of their country's air force jets. A Pakistani federal investigation of 1998 concluded that Bhutto 'was clearly responsible for loss to the exchequer [by] misuse of her office' in the matter of the unauthorised purchase of a $2.1 million helicopter. Meanwhile, a Dubai-based bullion dealer named Abdul Razzak Yaqub acknowledged that he had enjoyed an 'exclusive licence' to import more than $500 million in gold into Pakistan in return for various trade concessions, although he denied published charges that he had 'showered the PM in diamonds and other jewellery as a thank you'.

It is, perhaps, only fair to add that both Sharif and the Bhuttos consistently denied any wrongdoing and insisted that the charges against them were 'malicious' and 'politically motivated'. No court ever convicted any of them of a criminal offence. But at a time when the United Nations ranked average Pakistani household income 127th out of 158 countries surveyed, and 55 per cent of her adults were functionally illiterate, it struck some as odd that the media would carry daily reports of the successive prime ministers' offshore funds and Swiss bank accounts. For all the judicial reviews, no Pakistani politician had yet come up with a coherent, anti-corruption populist campaign theme. As Enoch Powell once observed, 'electorates the world over like a tune they can whistle'. Appalled by what he saw around him in the mid-1990s, Imran gave Pakistan that tune. At its core it was a local variation of 'Power to the People'.

Between the socialite and the social crusader, then, Imran defied easy categorisation. These were trying times both for the more gushing feature-page writers and, conversely, for those who were out to get him. One former cricketer rightly draws attention to the 'regal façade' and an obvious affinity for issuing orders, but beneath this was a surprisingly shy, bookish and now 'totally devoted' believer who saw himself 'irrevocably' at the mercy of Allah. Wasim Raja, one of Imran's closest playing colleagues for 15 years, with whom he mildly fell out and made up again 'almost annually', left the best description of this 'rare bird': he was a 'different man at different times ... I knew at least three or four Imrans'.

A good example of what Raja possibly had in mind came in the very early days of 1995. Within a month of opening his cancer hospital, Imran was reportedly enjoying an evening out with his girlfriend Kristiane Backer at Annabel's nightclub in London's Berkeley Square. Although catering to a wide clientele this was not, perhaps, the customary haunt of a born-again Muslim of increasingly radical social views. While on the premises, it's said that Imran fell into a 'long philosophical discussion' on comparative religion with Lady Annabel Goldsmith, 60, after whom the club was named. Sitting beside her was her striking young daughter Jemima. Some two years earlier, Imran had met Kristiane Backer at a dinner party hosted by his then lover Susannah Constantine. The same general pattern apparently repeated itself here. According to at least one account, 'Backer became angry with Imran for flirting with Jemima' and 'gave him an earful' on their return home that night.

Jemima Marcelle Goldsmith had been born on 30 January 1974, in London, where she was brought up mainly by her mother. Between numerous overseas holidays, her home was Ormeley Lodge, a listed Georgian mansion whose grounds were adorned by life-size sculptures of rhinoceroses, gorillas and other exotic fauna, situated on the edge of Richmond Park. Jemima's father, the Anglo-French billionaire financier Sir James Goldsmith, was a man of unorthodox family values. Known for his polyamorous romantic relationships, Goldsmith sired eight known children by four women, three of whom he married. A newspaper profile once referred to him, not wholly approvingly, as 'the Mick Jagger of the asset-stripping world'. Goldsmith was widely credited with having coined the maxim, 'When you marry your mistress, you create a job vacancy', although its true provenance is disputed. In 1963, aged 30, he embarked on a 15-year affair with the former Annabel Vane Tempest-Stewart, who at the time was married to the businessman and club owner Mark Birley. The couple went on to have two illegitimate children, Jemima and her brother Zac. In 1978, Goldsmith and Lady Annabel married 'to formalise [the] offspring ... We didn't do it as a great act of passion,' the bride confided, 'more to make sure that the children's name would be Goldsmith when they went to school'. A third, child, Ben, was born in 1980. Some six months later, Goldsmith moved to New York with his new mistress Laure Boulay, Comtesse de la Meurthe, with whom he had two more children. The rest of his life was largely devoted to a sometimes overlapping enthusiasm for ecology and libertarian politics. In 1994 Goldsmith was elected to represent a French constituency as a member of the European parliament, and subsequently founded the short-lived eurosceptic Referendum Party in Britain. He died in July 1997, aged 64.

Goldsmith's extramarital activities meant that Jemima's was effectively a one-parent family, albeit a rather rarefied one. Like Imran, she grew up in a large, loud, mildly chaotic household, surrounded by two brothers, two half-brothers from her mother's first marriage and a cadre of paternal half-siblings. Tall, lanky and athletic, with a mane of brown hair, she is said by those who know about such things to have shown the 'tomboy toughness' and 'steely self-assurance' that 'came from being considered one of the guys'. Or that's one view. Jemima also seems to have enjoyed being escorted around town by older men, at least one of whom remembers her as 'coy'. Several newspaper reports refer to her as both 'level-headed' and 'diffident'; one well-placed source insists she was 'quite a deep-thinking and brainy girl' who was able to cordon off satisfying her partner's sexual appetite as a necessary part of the courtship ritual – 'you always got the impression she'd rather be curled up with a good book'. In October 1993, Jemima enrolled to study English at the University of Bristol. Again, some disparity exists between the accounts of her time there. One fellow student describes her as of moderate intelligence with a 'rather superficial' approach to literature. 'Jem thought of herself as a great reader, but in my experience it was the sort of reading that involved rather a lot of *Cliffs Notes*.' They may have done the trick, because in short order she went on to become an accomplished, multi-lingual journalist. A second university acquaintance is perhaps closer to the mark when he calls Jemima 'very practical ... she didn't occupy her mind with grand ideas or ultimate meanings. She looked after necessities.'

In early January 1995, Jemima was 20, single, rich and physically quite arresting. 'Long-stemmed and languid' in one profile, she was noted for her 'photogenic hair, model-high cheekbones and a seemingly permanent, knowing half-smile ... The room stopped when she walked in.' Although less than half his age, she was neither intimidated nor awed by Imran.

In later years, even so, there would be a certain amount of sport made in both England and Pakistan of Jemima's alleged shortcomings. Imran's political opponents would conjure up an unflattering picture of an airhead Sloane Ranger whose only practical accomplishment in life had been learning to ride a horse. Jemima's domestic skills were thought to be rudimentary. 'Harrods have got these very clever little meals now that you just pop in the microwave and it's all done for you!' she's said to have enthused to a friend when she was about 17 or 18. Prior to going up to university, Jemima's scholastic record was modest: as a teenager at London's independent Francis Holland school for girls (alma mater to Joan and Jackie Collins) she was more obviously excited by showjumping than academics. A 1995 Sunday newspaper profile, employed to this day by journalists and biographers, described Jemima as a 'total princess', cutting a swathe through the drawing-rooms of Mayfair and Chelsea in a slinky Hervé Léger dress and black silk high-heeled Christian Louboutin shoes. Two or three years later, the pictures of her traipsing around Lahore with her immaculately made-up eyes peering out from under a native headdress would be the focus of much satirical commentary.

On the other hand, Jemima had at least the functional competence of the experienced socialite. She was 'extremely gracious' and 'spoke just as politely to a shop assistant as she did to Princess Margaret', I was told. She was also 'charmingly self-effacing' and 'completely without side'. By all accounts, Imran found himself entranced by Jemima's spirited liveliness and her humour; nor would he have failed to note her being a handsome woman. They already had several friends in common. Although Imran was Muslim and Jemima was part-Jewish, they shared a *noblesse oblige* code of behaviour derived from tradition and a strong sense of honour.

I was at boarding school with two of Jemima's half brothers, Rupert and Robin Birley, and don't remember them as being given over to a life of aristocratic languor. It's true that they made a certain splash on days out when a Mercedes sometimes came to pick them up, with Blitz, the family's Rhodesian Ridgeback, seated up front next to the chauffeur. For all that, both brothers were intelligent and unassuming and duly went on to productive careers. In 1970, on a visit to a private zoo, the 12-year-old Robin was severely mauled by a tiger and left permanently disfigured. Sixteen years later, Rupert, then 30, ventured out into the waters off Togo, West Africa, and was never seen again. The stories are worth mentioning if only to refute the theory of the Karachi *Facts*, and others, that Jemima lived in a 'completely pampered world [where] unpleasant things just didn't happen'.

The relationship with Imran moved rapidly, causing some amused talk among their friends. The press started writing about the affair around Easter of 1995, and it would be fair to say that they, too, were broadly sceptical about the couple's long-term prospects. *The Times* wrote that Jemima was 'a celebrity who was known for her well-knownness', while Imran, by contrast, was a 'titanically serious figure' who was also 22 years her senior. Certainly the eventual outcome came as a surprise to the outside world and, to at least some in Pakistan, as a nasty shock. There was something approaching hysteria among the populist end of the media in both Karachi and Lahore. The state radio presenters who read out the announcement appeared to be commentating on the final stages of the World Cup, and one of them forgot himself and bellowed an anguished 'No-ooo!' live on the air, as though an Englishman had just unfairly taken the last Pakistani wicket.

Both Imran and Jemima were well liked by some, but despised by others. Very few people had a neutral opinion, and even some of those who liked one or both of them individually were perturbed by the idea of them being together. In any event, the couple had their work cut out for them. Writing a century before the fateful meeting at Annabel's, Rudyard Kipling had observed, 'Oh, East is East, and West is West, and never the twain shall meet.' It's become a universal and perhaps somewhat tired aphorism. But it's still true that many of those who have attempted to settle in Pakistan over the years have encountered difficulties when it comes to transplanting themselves into the host society. In the 1980s, the impoverished state went through its own version of a Cultural Revolution. Violent upheavals brought about by General Zia's Islamicisation campaign, and exacerbated by local grievances, included a series of occasional, bloody attacks on British and American interests both in Karachi and the other major cities. Religious tensions were inflamed, and in Multan in July 1988 an Anglican chapel was burnt to the ground, after which crowds took to the streets demanding the removal of 'filth' from their community, the signal for the Western press to make one of its periodic moral flyovers to condemn this apparent breach of hospitality. It was not an entirely isolated lapse. An officially tolerated harassment of at least some Western immigrants, with numerous reported instances of assault, lasted well into the 1990s. It would only be fair to add that, in turn, many expatriate Pakistanis continued to feel themselves less than fully embraced by modern British society.

The challenges of biculturalism had been an obvious theme for Imran himself ever since the day in April 1971 when his mother had packed him off on his first tour of England, with the words, 'Don't bring back a foreign wife.' Mrs Khan had been concerned that an outsider would never come to terms with the unique qualities of Pakistani life. As Imran wrote in his autobiography, 'She felt that to expect a Western girl to adapt to our culture was asking far too much, and that sooner or later the whole thing would break up ... I always assumed that I would follow in the footsteps of my older cousins, three of whom went to Oxbridge and came back to arranged marriages in Pakistan.'

Twenty-four years after Mrs Khan had issued her edict, Imran announced his engagement to Jemima Goldsmith. The initial reaction to the news was everything his mother might have feared. In the words of one Goldsmith family member, 'There was a brief pause, a momentary reflex of disbelief, then the fire storm broke with full fury.'

Overnight, Imran was back on the front pages of all the tabloids. The overall tone of the coverage, both there and in the broadsheets, could be characterised as satirical. In the *Daily Mail*, Nigel Dempster enlightened his readers with the news that 'Jemima will find herself in a back room in Lahore while men in pantaloons sit next door discussing fundamentalism. Culturally, it certainly won't be SW1.' Alluding to the same problem, *Private Eye* ran a picture of Imran and James Goldsmith on its front cover: in the speech bubbles, Imran was saying, 'May I have your daughter's hand?' and his prospective father-in-law was replying, 'Why? Has she stolen something?' Perhaps wisely, Jemima herself reportedly spent most of her time at Ormeley Lodge, away from the press, while paparazzi ringed the estate's perimeter, telephoto lenses at the ready. On one of the few occasions she ventured out, for a shopping trip to Knightsbridge, she was trailed up Brompton Road by a posse of 'reporters, paparazzi and a persistent American tourist, all shout[ing] lewd endearments at her back'. Jemima glanced round once, scowled at the intrusion, then ran for the cover of a passing taxi.

The reaction closer to home was described as 'mixed'. James Goldsmith, for one, was not happy at the news. He complained, at length, to his estranged wife about it, citing Jemima's cultural and religious differences from her fiancé, and demanding that she finish her degree at Bristol before even considering marriage. It's conceivable that the furore reminded him of the events surrounding another inter-faith relationship some 40 years earlier. Then aged 21, Goldsmith had asked a Bolivian tin magnate named Antenor Patiño for permission to marry his daughter Maria, who was 18, and pregnant. Patiño reportedly replied, 'We are not in the habit of marrying Jews.' At that the young couple had eloped, only for Maria to suffer what proved to be a fatal stroke in her seventh month of pregnancy; their daughter, Isabel, was delivered by Caesarean section. (It should be stressed here that, despite an awkward start, Goldsmith fully reconciled himself to Imran, whose 'natural charm [and] intelligence' he enthused about for the rest of his life.) Meanwhile, the various reports, features, editorials and gossip doing the rounds in Pakistan practically paralysed the normal workings of the nation's media. There would be widespread and ongoing references to Jemima's 'Zionism', and a general reaction in the country as a whole that ranged from amusement to stupefaction. (Again, this was in contrast to the 'extremely warm and supportive' Khan family response.) As Imran ruefully acknowledged, 'I suppose if my marriage proved one point, it is that I am not a politician.'

On 16 May 1995, the couple went through a two-minute Islamic wedding ceremony in Paris, where James Goldsmith had a home. The bride wore traditional Pakistani dress and revealed that she had been taking instruction in her husband's religion. Press reports that Jemima now 'spoke Urdu fluently' proved premature, however. Nor had she 'thrown away her wardrobe of couture dresses', 'swor[n] to become a devout Muslim' or 'legally changed her name to Jamila Haiqa', all of which appeared in the press. It was a deliberately low-key, family-only occasion. Belying what *Today* called her reputation as 'the Material Girl of the Sloane set', with an 'extremely healthy acquisitive streak',

Jemima asked that in lieu of wedding presents her friends make a donation to the Shaukat Khanum hospital.

Five weeks later (after a paparazzo had snapped them consummating their marriage on a hotel balcony), Imran and Jemima went through a civil ceremony at Richmond Register Office, followed by a reception at Ormeley Lodge. This was perhaps more in line with what *Today* and others had had in mind. There was evidently a great deal of vintage champagne drunk, though none of it by the groom. Princess Michael of Kent, Elle Macpherson and David Frost were among the guests. Later that summer, the newlyweds left for Pakistan. As usual where Imran was involved, there was an animated group of reporters and photographers waiting for the couple on their arrival at Lahore airport. Although Imran was 'beaming', Jemima looked 'pale and drawn'. For someone who later gave her three least favourite activities as 'flying, having my picture taken and giving interviews', it was a faintly ominous start to married life.

The next few years would be a difficult time for Jemima, in some respects more so than for her husband. Frequently ill and continually homesick, she was also mercilessly targeted by Imran's political enemies. Nor had she ever quite taken to his other great love aside from his family and his hospital. Challenged once to name her three favourite fast bowlers, Jemima replied, 'Um, you've got me. Luckily, Imran retired long before I met him. I'm bored by cricket, [and] frankly I wouldn't know the difference between a fast bowler and a slow one.'

Although no longer representing the BCCP, Imran himself continued to be a significant figure behind the scenes. Despite everything, he still enjoyed the sport – 'the greatest game that man ever devised', he told a reporter – and the pleasure was evident in his schedule. Three years after his retirement, Imran was showing up at Test matches, hosting parties for his favourite players, offering *ad hoc* coaching, writing articles, passing off opinions on this matter and that, doing everything possible, it seemed, not to lose touch with the only real world he'd known between the ages of 18 and 40. With the passage of time he was becoming noticeably mellower towards old opponents, although, as one of them puts it, 'He was perfectly civil, but that was it. With Imran, you always felt you weren't getting so much friendship as friendliness. He'd wave if he saw you, but you could wait a lifetime for him to answer a letter.' Mike Vockins, the long-serving secretary at Worcestershire, remembers an incident when he was on the way to Pakistan as manager of the England 'A' team in November 1995. 'Imran had been spotted at Heathrow by a couple of the players, but he and Jemima were whisked through to the first-class lounge. When we were up in the air I sent a message to first-class via one of the attendants suggesting we might meet up – for old time's sake, and also because I felt that Nasser Hussain might value talking with him about cricket in Pakistan. Imran might have been sleeping, or felt it better to look after his wife, but he declined the offer.' Other old colleagues Imran came across would broadly agree that he was a 'nice bloke', 'very civil' or even 'chummy', but that if you 'look[ed] to him for an emotional commitment, you made a big error'. One particularly well-known former Packer star took some classes in psychology in the 1980s, and now believes that Imran was 'the sort of guy who's not at his best one-to-one ... He's happier playing a role, performing to a sea of undifferentiated faces.'

Of course, just because he'd gone on to other things, it didn't mean that Pakistan's World Cup-winning captain had suddenly become one of those peculiarly sensitive politicians who don't care to dwell too much on their past. Imran had a clear and unshakeable belief in his place somewhere near the top of cricket's hall of fame, a claim that by and large proved more justifiable as time went on. His national team's fortunes did not conspicuously improve in his absence. Wasim's captaincy proved only partly successful, and led to a players' revolt broadly similar to the one against Javed 12 years earlier. The board eventually turned to Imran's old *bête noire* Salim Malik to lead the team. This appointment, too, was not met with universal enthusiasm. A year or two later, three Australian players alleged that Salim had offered them £130,000 each to throw a Test match. According to one English Sunday tabloid, the Pakistan captain unwittingly admitted to them that he could 'fix any game' on a subsequent tour for £50,000. A board of inquiry sitting in Lahore would later hear that an unlicensed bookmaker named Pervez had gone to the Pakistan team hotel with $100,000 concealed in 'his inner garments' to distribute to certain players. The tabloid went on to break the less than sensational news that there was 'heavy illegal betting' going on in subcontinental cricket. The Pakistani board responded by prohibiting the use of mobile phones in their team's dressing-room. An anti-corruption panel later banned Salim and the bowler Ata-ur-Rehman for life.

Overall, cricket's sixth World Cup, hosted jointly by Pakistan, India and Sri Lanka in early 1996, was not one to savour fondly for the ages. The tournament both began and ended in logistical chaos and what

Wisden described as 'regrettable' scenes of mob violence. There were subsequent calls for the arrest of the head of the organising committee, PILCOM, on a charge of wasting public money. Pakistan's selectors began their team's defence of the title by reinstating the 39-year-old Javed in the side. A similar recall for Imran was discussed 'at the highest level', I was told. It would have had a 'strong psychological impact', one of the board recalls. 'Before Khan, captains were seen but rarely heard. He virtually created the modern team boss, but my understanding was that he wanted nothing more to do with politics, at least of the cricket sort.' Imran did, however, appear at the ground for Pakistan's quarter-final tie against India at Bangalore, where Javed recalls seeing him 'chatting away with Wasim Akram' as the team practised. Wasim, who was carrying a side strain, controversially pulled out of the match just before the start, leading conspiracy theorists to speculate that he might have withdrawn as part of a fix. Although there's no evidence to suggest anything of the sort, the reigning world champions went on to lose the tie by 39 runs.

The news was particularly ill received back in Pakistan. One fan reportedly shot his television and then himself, while Wasim was subjected to outrageous insults in sections of the press. Angry crowds demonstrated outside his home, where they burnt his family and him in effigy. Javed then took the opportunity to announce his final retirement; his criticism of the board for having ignored his strategic views throughout the competition was met with a certain official disdain. Sri Lanka went on to beat Australia in the cup final at Lahore. The awards ceremony was marred by a televised shoving match between supporters and opponents of Prime Minister Bhutto, who presented the trophy. In that one brief moment in front of the reviewing stand, the Imran era effectively came to an end. All had not gone well since his retirement, either for the team or himself – the ball-tampering row, ructions with Javed, Wasim and Waqar incarcerated in the West Indies, the allegations against Salim and others, a spate of coups and resignations among the board, ongoing captaincy issues and the final, bitter pill of the World Cup loss to India. But now, Imran told a reporter who asked him about a possible comeback, it was 'all history'.

Jemima Goldsmith's transformation into a Pakistani housewife would long be a topic of amusement among both the press and some of her friends. It was not quite a case, as Nigel Dempster had suggested, of being cooped up in a back room 'while men in pantaloons [sat] next door discussing fundamentalism'. The Khans' compound in Lahore was spacious, tastefully furnished and decidedly opulent by most local standards. There was a high wall between the house and the street. 'Fundamentalism' seems not to have featured on the list of typical dinner-table conversations, which were more likely to be dominated by the latest concerns at the hospital. Even so, Jemima essentially found herself in the position of a young bride sharing a roof with several of her extended family. 'When I went to Pakistan, there were definitely things that I found very, very hard,' she remarked some time later. 'I think, my God, how did I live five years with Imran's whole clan, who I was very close to? I mean, I really liked and respected them, but obviously, they lived very, very differently, and there was his father and his two sisters and their husbands and children, there were 10 children in the house, and kind of a chaotic environment and, you know, I do think, how did I do that?'

According to the Khans' friend Yusuf Salahudin, speaking to the press some years later, Jemima found it relatively easy to adapt to the role expected of a woman in Pakistan. There were 'few or no problems' when it came to such matters as wearing the appropriate dress in public. He praised her dogged and ultimately successful attempts to master Urdu, and to assimilate in other key ways. Even so, certain 'teething issues' remained. 'Every time Jemima came here she would fall ill,' Salahudin recalled. 'She particularly suffered from amoebic dysentery. When she visited [one] April, she was hospitalised for three days.' As the marriage progressed, Jemima began to spend up to four months of every year in London, or on the Goldsmiths' estates in Paris, Spain and Mexico. The whole process must have been grim to someone who so hated flying. While in Lahore, Jemima spent much of her life in purdah, largely hidden from public view, although once an enterprising paparazzo caught a well-shaped ankle on film as it emerged from a chauffeur-driven car. The picture showing the transgression was never published, but pirated copies of it later did a brisk trade on the internet.

Not long into their marriage, the Khans commissioned the building of a seven-bedroomed house in the Margalla hills north of Islamabad. Although not exactly tranquil – a dawn chorus of Rhesus monkeys, jackals and exotic birds could be heard cackling away in the surrounding bush – the property at least afforded Imran and Jemima the privacy that was lacking in Lahore. Several friends who visited the estate described it as a sort of Asian Berghof craning out over Islamabad, with sweeping views of the Himalayan foothills. Unfortunately, due to the familiar construction delays it would be early 2000 before the new home was finally ready to be occupied. For five years Jemima bided her time in the 'chaotic environment' of Lahore, where she was apt to bump into a stray in-law in the corridor if she happened to get up to leave her room at night. Imran was often away at the hospital until late, sometimes returning home only after a protracted official dinner.

'On politics, I'm very interested yet remain fairly neutral,' Imran had written in his first autobiography in 1983. Five years later, in the book's sequel *All Round View*, he revealed a new-found concern for Pakistan's depressing litany of military coups, civil wars, assassinations and institutionalised corruption – and more specifically for the country's appalling healthcare facilities of the sort that had contributed to his mother's early death. Imran's political development also came to include what opponents such as Benazir Bhutto called his 'romantic socialism' and his 'cleverly cynical balancing act' – promising increased national security while simultaneously decrying the traditional military budget – a stance his admirers lauded as a brilliant synthesising of time-honoured patriotic ideology with the social realities of the modern age. 'No matter how naive this may sound, I would like to see disarmament take place, not only between India and Pakistan, but worldwide,' Imran said. 'I see no difference between money made out of arms trading and that which is made through the drug trade. Both are evil.'

Although increasingly free with an opinion, Imran didn't show any personal affinity for politics until well into the 1990s. One of his English county cricket team-mates told me of an incident in the 1980s, after the TCCB introduced random drug tests.

> If your name was pulled out of a hat, you had to go with your team doctor and pee in a jar, which would then be borne off to the authorities. Imran's turn duly came up, and as a result of making a big performance about not wanting to relieve himself in public he was eventually able to submit a specimen which mysteriously contained a high quantity of Harvey's ale, a drink which to my knowledge Immy had never consumed. 'That could have been the end of my political ambitions,' he said, which in 10 years was the only time I'd heard him refer to them.

There is certainly no suggestion that Imran at any stage took performance-enhancing or recreational drugs. This fastidiousness his team-mate remembers would be very much in keeping with his lifelong sense of personal dignity.

In the words of another county colleague, 'The only party Imran showed any interest in joining when I knew him was the one going on at Tramp.' That was perhaps to underestimate his ability to be both platitudinous and aggressively populist, and a deeply ingrained work ethic that was always going to find a new outlet for itself. 'The motivation for politics came from a genuine desire to make social change,' Imran recalled in 2008. 'The reason I thought I would succeed was actually my training from cricket. It made me believe nothing was impossible. As long as you don't give up, you can win from incredible situations. So long as you fought to the last ball, I always believed you could win.'

While fundraising for his hospital, Imran increasingly began to look to the political stage as a means to modernise Pakistan's 'Dickensian' social services and effect other critical public sector reforms. By 1994–5 his speeches dealt with current issues and were delivered before partisan audiences. Even so, a number of colleagues would come to express a mixture of surprise and concern at his eventual career choice. Javed Miandad remarks that he was 'amazed', since Imran 'used to be one to always shun politics and I never thought it would be his calling'. A rather closer friend, Yusuf Salahudin, advised Imran not to get involved. 'Politics in this country is a dirty game and he's altogether too straightforward and honest for it.' Others were more narrowly concerned with Imran's personal safety. The life expectancy of even a well-connected Pakistani lawmaker didn't inspire confidence. In the autumn of 1996, Murtaza Bhutto, the prime minister's younger brother, had come home to Karachi after a long period in exile to contest the leadership of the family party on the twin promise of a 'radically altruistic' welfare programme and 'sweeping' anti-corruption reforms if elected. The exact events that followed on the afternoon of 20 September remain open to dispute. But it's agreed that Murtaza and his aides were driving home from a campaign rally on the outskirts of town when up to 80 police officers opened fire on his convoy. According to witnesses, Murtaza had emerged from his car with his hands raised above his head, at which point the police 'frenziedly' raked the whole party with automatic weapons. The slaughter went on for some six minutes. In the silence that followed, the police are said to have circled the bodies with pistols, administering the *coup de grâce* to

Murtaza and several others with a shot to the back of the neck. In all seven men died in the assault. Although savage even by the notoriously brutal standards of Pakistani politics, it was a not unfamiliar fate for those who challenged the status quo. Several people I spoke to admitted, with good reason, to being worried about Imran's welfare.

'Most fellows who join us [in the National Assembly] either do rather well for themselves or face a sticky end,' Benazir Bhutto remarked in a 2007 overview of Pakistani politics, from which she was again in exile. It was the peculiar tragedy of her life that Bhutto herself came to exemplify both these facts. With certain rare exceptions, Imran professed complete disinterest in his own safety, refused to wear a bullet-proof vest and travelled around the country without security, often at the wheel of an open jeep.

On a more routine note, there were also questions about whether he was temperamentally suited to the job in the first place. Imran was serious, and seemed to calculate everything; Pakistanis tend not to want their leaders to be calculators. He was stiff with people, and could be brusque. One friend assured me that Imran was riotous company in private, but agreed that he could be 'an acquired taste ... He wasn't one to submit to such campaign stupidities as wearing funny hats or driving around the streets in a psychedelic bus.' One of the Vahidys' shooting party adds, 'I saw kids come up to Imran when we were in the hills together, and he would sort of brush them off. That was more than 10 years ago, and I'm sure he's improved with time. But let's just say he's not one of life's natural baby kissers.'

Even so, 21 years in Pakistani representative cricket, 10 of them as his nation's captain, had given Imran a thorough grounding in administrative wrangling. After dealing with the likes of Rafi Naseem and his colleagues at the BCCP, he had little to fear in Islamabad. For obvious reasons, there was also a popular groundswell of support for an Imran candidacy, along with a matching degree of hero-worship among the Lahore press. One 1997 profile simply entitled 'SuperKhan' read much like a cross between Father Alban Butler's *Life of St Francis* and an authorised hagiography of Che Guevara. The panegyric included the now conventional wisdom that Pakistani public life needed 'cleaning up', and added that the 'redeemer of our fortunes on the sports field' was the man to do it.

Imran's steady radicalisation had come about in several phases. As mentioned, he appears to have been singularly taken by the Balochi warlord Sher Mohammad Marri, whom he met in London in 1984.

(The so-called 'Balochi Tiger' had subsequently fallen out with many of his partisans and died alone, in Indian exile, in 1993.) Ten years later, Imran's nationwide hospital fundraiser had first brought home to him the dire financial inequities and out-and-out feudalism of Pakistani rural life. 'I realised then we needed economic policies to help the bottom 40 per cent of society and not the top one or two per cent,' he told me. Here, too, a degree of social anxiety was an important driving force. Identification, perhaps over-identification, with the Pakistani nation gave almost all the leading figures in the state assembly, whatever their background, a sense of pride and belonging, and an object for commitment and mobilisation. Imran was no exception. In later years he was to exhibit some flexibility in his views on multilateral disarmament by continuing to support Pakistan's independent nuclear deterrent (a programme which, according to some estimates, had cost the taxpayer the equivalent of $7 billion between 1976 and 1998), largely as a bulwark against India. In time he was also able to tap into a fashionable, if not entirely unjustified vein of anti-Americanism. 'I look at the US, which has 35 per cent of the world's resources and 4 per cent of the world's population – it's sickening,' Imran told *The Times* in 2006. 'Some people cannot ever have enough material possessions. It's a disturbing way to live your life.'

According to several sources, Imran was also drawn to the charismatic figure of Lieutenant General Hamid Gul, the 60-year-old former head of the Pakistani intelligence agency and a man known for the extremity of his views. Gul, who sported the regulation military moustache and thick black hair worn *en brosse*, had been a leading figure in organising the mujahideen resistance to the Soviet occupation of Afghanistan from 1979 to 1989. As such he's credited with having at least tacitly encouraged the rise of the Taliban, and for having taken a relaxed view of their efforts to support themselves through the sale of opium and black-market weapons. Although the CIA played a full part in the same struggle, Gul subsequently became passionately anti-American, apparently because Washington reneged on its promise to provide the Afghans with further military and economic aid following the Soviet withdrawal, but also due to 'the Pentagon and its Israeli-Zionist accomplices blocking my promotion to army chief of staff'. The general later called the 9/11 attacks on New York City and Washington the work of 'renegade US Air Force elements working with the Jews'. (Gul's name would subsequently surface in connection with the November 2008 bombings in Mumbai, which killed 173 people.)

According to the *Daily Times*, in 2003 Gul went on to declare, 'The Muslim world must stand united to confront the US in its so-called War on Terrorism, which is in reality a war against Muslims. Let's destroy America wherever its troops are trapped.' Speaking a year later, Imran in turn specifically warned the US against attacking on what he called 'the holiest places of Islam', while making it clear he did not condone any physical violence against any other adversary. Imran went on to note in the same interview that the US had signed a civil nuclear deal with India, 'and on the other hand it is threatening Pakistan. This bears ample evidence of its true anti-Islam posture,' he concluded.

In 1996, Pakistan remained in its seemingly perpetual state of *de facto* civil war, or wars, between the civilian and martial rulers on one front and the liberal and religious forces on another. It was neither a democracy, nor a theocracy, nor a permanent military dictatorship. The rapidly growing population ran the gamut from primitive asceticism to decadent vulgarity (although, admittedly, the same could be said of the US). Successive governments had squandered money like a chav Lottery winner, erecting huge municipal palaces and importing gas-guzzling American cars by the thousand for rural areas where there were no roads. Pakistan's most sustained economic growth was to be found in the 'parallel' or 'alternative' sector. This branch included a thriving black market, a large illicit drug industry, and illegal payments to politicians and government officials to ensure state contracts. Not only were such practices commonplace, but those involved in them proceeded with virtual impunity: no one had served a day in prison for tax evasion at any stage in the nation's history, and successful prosecutions for corruption were nearly as rare. As Imran noted, 'If one sets up in business in Pakistan, one has to make allowances in the costings for bribes. It's everywhere ... An ordinary policeman earns a basic pay of 975 rupees [roughly £60] per month, on which he is expected to maintain a family. Unless he's corrupt, it is impossible for him to live decently.' Broader social development indicators reflected long-standing problems in providing basic health and education services. Only a third of all Pakistani children between the ages of six and 13 attended school, a rate below that for Somalia. It was estimated in 1996 that 28 per cent of the population lived below the official poverty line, which was based on the government's assessment of an income sufficient to provide 'minimum life'.

The Bhuttos had created a business dynasty that was known not only for its attempts to deregulate and liberalise the national economy, but for its in-house extravagance and brutality. In October 1996, the tribunal set up to investigate the killing of Murtaza Bhutto found that the assassination could not have taken place 'without approval from the highest level of government'. There had been no shoot-out, as the police had claimed, but 'a clearly co-ordinated [and] premeditated ambush'. The report concluded that the prime minister was 'probably complicit' in her brother's murder. On 5 November, shortly after the tribunal's findings were made public, Benazir Bhutto was dismissed from office by an emergency fiat of the state president. Three months later Nawaz Sharif returned to power when his Pakistan Muslim League won an impressive 91.2 per cent of the votes cast in new legislative elections. One of Sharif's first acts in office was to push through a 'thirteenth amendment' to the constitution, effectively stripping the president of his authority to dissolve parliament. A 'fourteenth amendment' soon followed, making it impossible for MPs to remove a sitting government by a vote of no confidence. As a result there were now no external administrative checks on the prime minister's power. When Pakistan's chief justice Syed Sajjad Ali Shah attempted to vacate the amendments, he too was ousted. The outgoing judge remarked that his country appeared to be in the permanent grip of 'despotic regimes us[ing] extremists and external support to keep democracy at bay'.

It was in this climate that Imran formally launched his Tehreek-e-Insaf (or 'Movement for Justice') party. There were seven founding members. Its essential platform was one of social equality allied to national self-reliance. 'All through Pakistan history, stooges of the past and present colonial masters have led us,' Imran's manifesto read. 'Their contribution has been merely to mortgage our children's future and short change our dignity by making compromises under the guise of the much-abused supreme national interest ... The party will restore the sovereign and inalienable right of the people to choose political and economic options in accordance with our social, cultural and religious values. We are [a] broad-based movement for change whose mission is to create a free society based on justice. We know that renewal is only possible if people are truly free.'

Before long, Imran was roaming Pakistan from one end to another, shaking hands and invading tea houses, cafes, factories, farm buildings and schoolrooms. People greeted the newly declared candidate with a warmth rarely seen even in the subcontinent. An admiring observer wrote of seeing Imran 'walk alongside a fence, hands out, his body swaying backwards so they couldn't smother him [while] the crowd on the other side of the fence grabbed his hands and tried to pull him to them.' There was a particular frenzy among students and young people, many of them female, whom the Tehreek-e-Insaf identified as being 'totally alienated by the existing power structure' – again, one has only to think of Barack Obama in 2008 to get something of the mood. Partially as a result, Imran's party was transformed in the headlines from a lost cause into a viable challenge to the ruling elites. Having initially ignored him, his political opponents felt compelled to go on the attack. Benazir Bhutto began to mock her old Oxford contemporary as a 'me-too' candidate, whose core ideology amounted to 'little more than a few greeting-card pleas for unity and world peace'. If so, they were apparently what a vociferous section of the electorate wanted to hear. An AP writer named Tony Gill followed Imran and Jemima to a rally in Lahore and described the scene there as one of 'churning, burning humanity closing in on the glamorous couple ... There were shouts of "Imran Khan Zyndabad" ["Long Live Imran"] while onlookers hurled either flowers or themselves at his feet.'

Though not a natural orator, Jemima came to play an active part in her husband's inaugural campaign. Gill watched admiringly as she addressed one rally in Islamabad. 'A child placed a garland, the first of many, around her neck ... "Nazuk si hai" ["She is fair"], several spectators observed, while paparazzi encircle[d] her in a cacophony of clicks and flashes. A few places away, Imran seemed to smile at all the attention his young wife was attracting.' Nor was she there merely for her photogenic qualities. 'Benazir Bhutto may speak the language of liberalism and look good on Larry King's sofa,' Jemima later wrote in a typically stinging piece in the *Daily Telegraph*. 'But both her terms in office were marked by incompetence, extra-judicial killings and brazen looting of the treasury. Benazir has always cynically used her gender to manipulate: I loved her answer to David Frost when he asked her how many millions she had in her Swiss bank account. "David, I think that's a very sexist question." A non sequitur, but one that brought the uncomfortable line of questioning to a swift end.'

A colleague regarded Imran and Bhutto as having 'a love–hate relationship', because though each basically disliked the other, each also showed an intense interest in the other and maintained an unrelenting scrutiny of the other's activities and attitudes. That may suggest jealous and obsessive lovers; in fact, there was little love between Imran and the political establishment at any time, especially after he went into his first national campaign in 1997. By and large, the attacks on him fell into two categories: the partisan and the personal. One former Pakistani Test player contacted me in 2007 with what he promised to be a 'sensational revelation' about Imran. It should be noted that the source in question is not universally popular but possessed of an extraordinarily high degree of self-confidence, while being some way short of truly adept at cricket. He did, however, know Imran quite well over a number of years. The story he told me was that Diana, Princess of Wales, had visited Lahore in 1996 while in the throes of a 'steamy affair' with the Pakistani-born heart surgeon Hasnat Khan. Khan himself 'wasn't even in the country, but she came here to bone up on his family culture'. That would fit the known facts, but the player went on to say that Diana was 'desperate to marry Hasnat Khan. When she was in Lahore she sought out Jemima [and] the two women sat up talking through the night about what it took to be the wife of a traditional minded Muslim. Later they went out to the hospital, did the sights together ... Diana later admitted to the doctor's family that she had become very close to Imran at the time. This didn't surprise me. She was a vulnerable young woman alone in Pakistan, you remember. Imran wasn't exactly the choirboy that the voters thought he was. He'd had dozens of affairs, some longer-lived, some shorter. And Diana had all the qualities he prized. How could you be more pukka English than that?' Even so, it's worth repeating that Imran's political rivals would lose few opportunities over the years to exaggerate and exploit his reputation as a lothario, and that there is no concrete evidence that he ever strayed from his wedding vows. Many of the more lurid tales about his social life as a cricketer are, possibly, the fruits of mere gossip-mongering. Once he became a contender for the premiership, real malice came into play.

The attacks continued on several fronts. In time Imran formed a particular mutual antipathy with the Muttahida Qaumi Movement (MQM), a Sindh-based party which was either a crusading force on behalf of southern Pakistan's dispossessed or a loose-knit sectarian rabble of thugs and torturers, depending on your political perspective. In 1992, MQM's leader and founder Altaf Hussain chose self-imposed exile in London rather than face possible trial in a case related to the murder of the outspoken Sindh scholar Hakeem Muhammed Saeed, for which nine other MQM members were sentenced to death. (All nine defendants' convictions were later overturned on appeal.) Imran added that in his opinion some of the bad blood between the MQM and himself was 'an extension of the old Karachi-Lahore rift. Even when I was a successful Test captain, it didn't entirely stop.' The MQM were later to play an active role in the ethnic riots in Karachi of May 2007 in which 47 people died and several hundred more were injured. As a result, Imran was quoted as saying that 'the British government has shown appalling double standards. On the one hand it is fighting a war against terrorism and on the other it has given refuge to the number one terrorist of Pakistan, Mr Hussain.' Hussain, in turn, signalled his intention to present the national assembly in Islamabad with evidence of Imran's 'bad character'. The case continued. In a completely separate and coincidental development, someone set off a bomb in the Shaukat Khanum hospital shortly after Imran first announced the formation of his party. Seven people died and 34 were wounded in the explosion, which some in Pakistan credited to the Indian intelligence services. Imran told me that he had narrowly missed being on the premises, as 'I was due to show a donor around the facilities that morning, but the guy was late.' The Khans then faced more muted, if unexpected criticism when James Goldsmith's lawyer of some 30 years took exception to comments attributed to Jemima in which she questioned Israeli policy towards Palestine. The lawyer resigned his position, remarking that Jemima 'no longer understands what being a Goldsmith means'.

In the summer of 1996, a London court case arising out of the 'ball-tampering' issue overshadowed Imran's attempts to launch himself on the political stage half a world away. The long, tragicomic saga had its roots in the Ivo Tennant biography published in 1994. In it Imran had not only admitted to having once lifted the seam, but then went on to tell both the *Daily Telegraph* and the *Sun* that he was by no means alone: 'the biggest names in English cricket have all been at it,' he confided. Later that spring, Imran gave a perhaps ill-advised interview to *India Today* in which he implied that the ball-doctoring row had been 'blown out of all proportion' because of his skin colour. 'There is a lot of racism here,' he noted. 'How come the noise started when the West Indies and Pakistan began winning matches with their fast bowlers? Australians can get away with anything because they are white ... Look at people such as Lamb and Botham making statements like: "Oh, I never thought much of him anyway and now it's been proven he's a cheat." Where is this hatred coming from?'

Imran later indignantly claimed that he had been misquoted by *India Today*, whose 'shock exclusive' saw him marching incautiously into the minefield of the British class system. Whereas 'educated,

Oxbridge types' such as Christopher Martin-Jenkins, Tony Lewis and Derek Pringle all took a rational view of the tampering debate, the same could not be said of Imran's critics. 'Look at the others: Lamb, Botham, Trueman,' he allegedly said. 'The difference in class and upbringing makes a difference.'

In an attempt to correct the record, Imran wrote to Botham on 6 June 1994, assuring him that he had 'not once called anyone lower class or under class' since he 'didn't believe in the class system'. He went on to remark that he had 'never intended this issue to get personal' and had simply wanted the ICC to 'define what were the acceptable limits of ball-tampering', a practice that 'has gone on ever since the game has been played'. As a goodwill gesture, Imran's letter appears to have been only partially successful. Just two days later, Botham's solicitor Alan Herd replied by saying, 'You have grossly libelled Ian' and demanding a public apology. Imran, in turn, offered to write an open letter to *The Times* to 'clear up any confusions about racist or class slurs', which he felt were largely the result of *India Today* having distorted his original comments. Again, it wasn't enough. On 21 July, Botham instructed Herd to issue a writ of libel to Imran, and Allan Lamb then followed suit. (The third man allegedly smeared, Fred Trueman, told me that he had better things to do with his time than 'sit on my arse waiting for some court' to entertain a defamation charge, which was 'best settled over a pint' – an eminently sane formula, if not a very practical one in Imran's case.)

As Trueman said, 'the entire balls-up' essentially stemmed from events that had taken place in various past England–Pakistan matches, chiefly in 1992, and never been fully resolved. The circumstances were somehow right for a climactic legal shoot-out between the two nations' most talented and charismatic players. Imran, for his part, was reacting not only to Botham's specific complaint but to a swelling chorus of 'condescension and abuse' that had given rise over the years to headlines such as the *Sun*'s 'BLOODY CHEATS'. The Pathan code of honour demanded satisfaction. 'Botham totally over-reacted and took the whole thing too personally,' Imran told me. 'All I was ever trying to do was to start a debate about what ball-tampering really was. The [suit] was completely unnecessary. I'm a man of peace. But I'm going to respond when someone attacks me or attacks the Pakistan team.' It was as if the Imran–Botham feud was a test of nationhood by proxy. In the midst of the more narrowly defined libel proceedings, both the principal parties seemed to be fighting a substitute Test match with their respective countries' virtue at stake. 'Charged' was the word most seasoned cricket watchers used to describe the atmosphere at the time the case finally came to court, where Imran, Botham and Lamb each went into the witness box to air his views on patriotism, race and class, although, to the fascinated observer from the *New York Times*, 'they might as well have exchanged their formal attire for the helmet and chain mail of the medieval jouster'.

The summer of 1996 was an unusually fraught one even by the recent standards of English cricket. At the World Cup, the national team had 'resembled a bad-tempered grandmother attending a teenage rave', according to *Wisden*. 'Unable to comprehend what was happening, on the field or off it, the players just lingered, looking sullen as well as incompetent.' The team then narrowly beat India and were heftily defeated by Pakistan in the English home season. Ray Illingworth's three-year reign as chairman of selectors and all-purpose supremo ended in some disarray. To compound a miserable term, the TCCB fined Illingworth for having brought the game into disrepute by comments he made in his autobiography, and then promptly wound itself up in favour of its replacement, the England and Wales Cricket Board. In an unpromising start for a body which pledged itself to remove factionalism and restore plain-talking, it was to be known by the acronym ECB, the 'and Wales' apparently having died at birth. But the season's principal drama took place over two weeks at the High Court in London, where Imran arrived each morning accompanied by his radiantly pregnant wife. By some mischievous quirk of the legal calendar, the hearing overlapped with the first Test between England and Pakistan at Lord's, with which it shared certain broad and often unintentionally comic characteristics. Pakistan won the match, in the course of which live TV pictures showed Waqar apparently doctoring the ball, by 164 runs.

In his defence, Imran had prudently engaged the services of George Carman, QC, by popular consent the most able, and feared, barrister of his generation. The thrice married, hard-drinking Carman had built up a client list over 40 years at the bar that included the likes of Jeremy Thorpe, Richard Branson, Mohamed Al Fayed, Elton John, Ken Dodd, Tom Cruise and the Yorkshire Ripper's wife Sonia Sutcliffe. It would be fair to say that he favoured a robust cross-examining technique, and could be castratingly rude when the occasion called for it. Carman began his 14 hours' questioning of Ian Botham by asking the former England star if he was a drug-taking liar who cheated on his wife.

Botham admitted to a certain amount of pot use over the years. It would, perhaps, have been hard for him to deny, since he had already spoken of it at some length in a front-page interview in the *Mail on Sunday*. However, Botham assured the court that 'my wife and I have a very successful marriage, thank you'. In a subsequent exchange, Carman read out the unpublished letter that Imran had offered to send to *The Times* two years earlier. After a suitable pause, he then walked slowly to the witness box, leant forward and said, 'In the interests of the great name of cricket and to avoid a blood battle in the courts, and in the interests of good relations between the Pakistani cricket team and the England team, did you not think that Mr Khan made a fair and eminently reasonable proposal?' 'No, I did not,' said Botham.

After three days of largely inconclusive sparring, Carman introduced the first of a series of star witnesses. The former England wicket-keeper Bob Taylor appeared in court to don a pair of red and black Mitre gauntlets that an usher reverentially handed him wrapped in tissue paper inside a blue satin-lined box. 'They will probably bring back memories,' Carman purred. Mr Justice French asked, in more businesslike fashion, 'Do you recognise those gloves?' 'Very well,' replied Taylor. 'I wore them during the incident.'

The 'incident' in question happened during the India Test at The Oval in 1982, when Botham was seen throwing the ball to Taylor who, according to counsel, 'vigorously agitated' it in his palms before returning it. Imran had alleged that this was done to alter the condition of the ball, in match circumstances that had apparently favoured the batsman. (Botham had scored a double century in the Test, managing to dislodge several tiles from the pavilion roof in the process, but took only two wickets.) 'Is there any truth in the extremely grave imputation that you were trying to remove the lacquer off that ball?' asked Charles Gray, QC, counsel for Botham and Lamb. 'None whatsoever,' replied Taylor, who assured the jury he had merely been 'wiping condensation off the surface'. Later in the session, the Warwickshire and England medium-pacer Gladstone Small told the court that he believed seam-picking was common practice among bowlers, although he personally had never done it. Later still Geoff Boycott took strike, flourishing aloft a Reebok cricket boot, with which he hoped to expound on some ball-scuffing procedures. But first the legendary England opener requested three minutes of the court's time in order to make a personal statement about his former Yorkshire colleague Brian Close. Close had earlier appeared as a witness for Botham and Lamb and had replied 'No comment' when asked whether Boycott was an honest man. After heated objections by Charles Gray, the judge intervened to disallow Boycott's impromptu speech. 'It appears this witness's evidence is in danger of getting completely out of control. I think he should now leave the witness stand. You are released,' he said. 'That's a pity,' Boycott replied.

Meanwhile, Imran's lawyers had succeeded in serving subpoenas on both the current England captain Mike Atherton and the team coach David Lloyd. Atherton arrived in court direct from Lord's, where the five-day match with Wasim Akram's Pakistan was scheduled to start the following morning. The final England practice session was cancelled as a result. Sharp-eyed observers didn't miss the point that this meant a former Pakistan captain had at least inadvertently managed to sabotage his nation's opponents on the eve of a Test. Atherton had the impression that the jury were 'totally confused and bored' by the intricacies of reverse swing and ball-tampering, but riveted by the sight of Imran's entourage. 'As I stood in the witness box, with Jemima Khan's big doey eyes looking balefully, first at the jurors and then at me, I feared for Botham and the outcome of the case,' he says. Atherton fared better in court than some. Belying his nickname of 'the Judge', the South African-born, Hampshire and England batsman Robin Smith seemed to be perplexed by some of the legalese during his appearance in the box. 'Jeez, your honour,' he protested. 'I'm only a simple cricketer.'

Charles Gray, for the plaintiffs, then questioned Kathy Botham, who confirmed that Imran's class aspersions had made her and her husband 'furious'. Lyndsey Lamb broadly echoed the sentiment. George Carman declined to cross-examine either woman, but again drew the jury's attention to Imran's offer to put the whole matter to rest by writing to *The Times*. 'There was an opportunity, one might say a golden opportunity, to bury the allegations for ever. Did they take it? Oh no. Why not?' he enquired.

Eight days into the proceedings, Imran took the stand to deny that he had ever called anyone in cricket a cheat. 'Nor have I ever at any stage in my life believed in a class system,' he added, rattling off his answers so rapidly that the judge was more than once forced to implore, 'Please slow down. You are going at fast bowler pace.' 'I don't look at people and what class they belong to,' he insisted. 'I never have. Those kind of comments are against everything in the way I was brought up.' Imran, who swore an oath to Allah on the Koran, giving his full names as Imran Ahmed Khan Niazi, conceded that his proposed open letter might have struck the plaintiffs as something less than a full-scale expression of regret. 'I was not prepared to apologise for something I'd never said. I wasn't going to lie and say I called them this and that, and then grovel for it,' he remarked. It may be that Imran considered the matter overnight, because the next morning he withdrew his defence plea of justification and told the court that, having listened to evidence in the trial, he now accepted that Botham had never tampered with a cricket ball. 'I have heard Ian and I have heard David Gower, and I respect them both. And if they say they were squeezing the ball – fine; they were squeezing the ball,' he said of an incident in the Lord's Test of 1982. For all that, he still had certain technical reservations about his fellow all-rounder's career. Botham had 'not realised his potential', Imran told the court, and had 'blamed everyone else' for the shortcoming. It was 'a shame'. Imran added that both he and Richard Hadlee were older than Botham, but as their world ratings went up, his fell. 'He never fulfilled his promise, I felt ... He [was] a bitter man' who took out his frustrations on the selectors, his opponents, his team-mates, the media, 'everyone but himself', for being 'shunted out of cricket in an undignified way'.

After deliberating overnight, the jury returned a 10–2 majority verdict in Imran's favour. Thanking them for their service, the judge called the proceedings a 'complete exercise in futility'. Each side was required to pay its own costs. Botham and Lamb appealed the decision, but eventually withdrew their claim in 1999, by which time they faced estimated legal bills of £260,000 and £140,000 respectively. Ten years later, the heat of the moment appeared to have given way to a lingering mutual coolness. The normally effusive Botham told me, 'I have nothing to say about Imran Khan. I don't want to give him the time or the publicity.' (Botham had previously remarked, 'I don't suppose Imran and I will ever be sharing a dinner table again, and that's something that doesn't keep me awake at night.') In broadly similar vein, Allan Lamb wrote: 'Many thanks for your enquiry with regards to Khan, but I am not interested in getting involved.' One's tempted to ask whether the whole thing could have been settled out of court as Fred Trueman had suggested. Or, as one star witness speculated, did the highly public and expensive wrangling meet some deeper need to redress years of perceived 'imperial arrogance' on one side and 'chippy resentment' on the other? Perhaps the parties themselves couldn't have resolved such subtleties of motivation. In later years, Imran seemed to incline towards the judge's view of the proceedings. 'It was completely unnecessary and a terrible, draining experience for everyone,' he told me. 'The justice system works in a mysterious way, although I suppose it at least prepared me for a political career.'

If the publicity-shy Jemima had 'loathed' the public exposure of sitting in court, worse was to come. Imran threw himself into the 1997 legislative elections, despite initial opposition from his wife, who reportedly thought him 'crazy' to run, and his own private misgivings about exposing a party that was still only six months old to the charms of the Pakistani democratic cycle. Rather understandably, Jemima seems to have had doubts about the wisdom of seeking to lead a highly visible political life while simultaneously raising a young family: the couple's first son Sulaiman Isa was born on 18 November 1996, and a second, Qasim, followed on 10 April 1999. Jemima told one friend in London that she hated being in the spotlight because she liked to be able 'to shop at Harrods and not be recognised'. Many might have shared her qualms about the stress attendant on Pakistani public life. A 14-hour-a-day gerbil wheel of redrafting some party policy document while being attacked by everyone from the prime minister to Javed Miandad must have tested even Imran's inner reserves. (Jemima did, however, 'enthusiastically endorse' her husband's passion for environmentalism, something of a Goldsmith family *cause célèbre*, and delivered a well-received keynote address to the International Green Network conference at the University of Warwick in July 1997.) At least one close political friend of Imran's came to see him as a sort of chameleon, adapting himself to the different people with whom he talked, 'which must have put him under even more stress every day'. He did this, in the friend's view, not out of cynical pandering, but because of his constant desire to 'avoid personal confrontation, argument and unpleasantness'.

For his first national campaign, Imran and the Tehreek-e-Insaf party declined a merger offer that supposedly would have guaranteed them 30 parliamentary seats, and instead announced a nine-point manifesto linked by a common theme:

Freedom from political, economic, mental slavery
Freedom from injustice
Freedom from poverty
Preedom from unemployment
Freedom from homelessness
Freedom from illiteracy

Freedom to generate wealth
Freedom from fear
Freedom for women

Amidst what a critic in the Pakistan Muslim League characterised as a 'fuzzy agenda of romantic-Maoist mumblings', Imran struck a more militant note by now actively supporting Pakistan's nuclear programme. 'Public testing has to be done to tell India that we have the bomb,' he said. 'My party is clear that we have to show them that we have a deterrent.' International sanctions imposed as a result merely strengthened his conviction. 'Most of us in Pakistan feel that we should not be dependent on development aid. National self-esteem suffers when our leaders have to go begging for money. We have to conduct reforms on our country and stand on our own feet.'

There were moments when the 1997 campaign took an almost surreal turn even by accepted Pakistani political standards. As Jemima later recalled in an article in the *Sunday Telegraph*, 'Imran was widely accused of being part of a Zionist conspiracy because of his marriage to a person with a Jewish father and a Jewish maiden name.' In subsequent developments, 'A mob of crazed mullahs insisted that my citizenship be revoked, and that I be thrown out of the country ... They took out full-page newspaper ads, inciting people to riot outside our home. Bearded fundos took to the streets with placards bearing my name (misspelt) and the word "infidel".' A blurred photocopy apparently showing a cheque for £40 million, supposedly from James Goldsmith to fund Imran's party, appeared in a number of Karachi-area newspapers. It little mattered that the document in question was a crude forgery. Meanwhile, Nawaz Sharif and his Pakistan Muslim League issued a list of 'Six questions for Tehreek-e-Insaf convener Mr Khan', which accused him of having hired a London advertising agency and of once being an international playboy, among other apparent abuses of the Election Commission rules. The Bhuttos in turn had issues with the fledgeling party's alleged practice of 'doctoring television footage and photographs to make the size of their meetings look big'.

Not surprisingly, the attacks eventually took their toll on the Khans' marriage, particularly coming at a time when Jemima was reportedly already suffering from a combination of lingering culture shock and post-natal depression. 'Because I was taking on the corrupt elite, my wife became a soft target,' Imran says. 'She was accused of insane things ... Zionism ... being part of a Jewish conspiracy to take over Pakistan. I thought it was so absurd I didn't even take it seriously, but it had a big impact on her.'

The Tehreek-e-Insaf's charges of unsportsmanlike play weren't, therefore, merely the fulminations of a poor loser. Apart from the personal vitriol, there were some curious events on the election day itself, including a case where a busload of Imran supporters presented themselves at a polling station in Lahore, only to be told that the officials there were 'too busy' to accommodate them. When the would-be voters returned an hour later, as directed, they found the building closed. Fraud, of course, is known to happen in Pakistan; but it does seem some particularly strange occurrences took place that Monday, 3 February. According to the official 12-man International Progress Organisation (IPO) team sent to monitor the elections, 'the results cannot be considered free and fair because of violent interference in the voting procedures, intimidation of the electorate [and] administrative mishandling throughout.' Among the stories cited by the IPO was that of a Muhammad Haneef, a polling agent in Karachi 'who [was] abducted with three others (who managed to escape) by members of an armed faction. He was severely beaten and died. The delegation of the IPO inspected the dead body in the Abbasi Shahid hospital and spoke to the medical staff ... It was reported to the delegation that Pakistani security forces who were present in and around polling stations did not prevent widespread kidnappings, coercions and violent assaults.'

Having said all that, Imran and the Tehreek-e-Insaf fared particularly poorly in their first full public examination. The party failed to win a single seat out of the 207 available. By most official counts they secured between 130,000 and 160,000 votes, or approximately one per cent of the 19.3 million strong popular ballot. For purposes of comparison, this put the Tehreek-e-Insaf somewhat below the 2.2 per cent figure enjoyed by James Goldsmith's Referendum Party at the British general election held three months later, and in danger of rubbing shoulders with the likes of the Natural Law Alliance, whose manifesto favoured a daily regime of levitation, at the same contest.

Despite scoring a duck at the polls, Imran remained upbeat, remarking, 'We are the fastest growing movement in Pakistan, and the most popular among young people.' It's true that the party's electoral fortunes improved following the state president's 2001 decision to lower the voting age from 21 to 18. But it was also true that the

Tehreek-e-Insaf seemed to many observers to lack not only any nationwide grass-roots organisation, but also any discernible core beliefs. Imran (who had never previously voted) was only rarely willing or able to make specific policy pledges on the burning issue of the Pakistani economy. He could not avoid, of course, answering reporters' frequent questions on the subject, which he usually did with variations of his 'freedom' mantra followed by slightly generic reminders that 'We are Pakistan. We are one!' It wasn't enough. As one otherwise friendly profile in the *Guardian* later remarked, 'Imran's ideas and affiliations since entering politics have swerved and skidded like a rickshaw in a rainstorm.' While he continued to denounce bribery and corruption, he remained 'notably vague' when it came to proposing any substantive reforms. This apparent inability to offer a detailed or even explicit agenda for change (again, possibly with its Obama parallels) was a frequent theme of both domestic and foreign press accounts of the campaign. Five years after the triumph of winning the World Cup, Imran still commanded a wide degree of personal affection bordering on hero-worship. He remained one of the few cricketers whose fame transcended the sport. But as a select list of current or former players would confirm over the years, it didn't necessarily follow that just because you were good on the field you were destined to be successful at anything else, such as politics.*

Imran's electoral prospects suffered another setback just six months later, when a court in California ruled him to be the legal father of five-year-old Tyrian White. Tyrian's mother Sita White was then living and working as a yoga instructor in Beverly Hills. In a statement issued through his lawyer, Imran asserted, 'It's simply not possible for me to travel the world fighting court cases in every country. My work is in politics and with my hospital in Pakistan. As I do not live in California or England, my response is to welcome Ms White to Lahore, where I would be glad to present my side of the story.' Imran's political opponents weren't slow to note this latest instance of what the Pakistan Muslim League called his 'world of moral bankruptcy [where] the smallest hanky-panky gets punished and the major adulterers like himself go scot-free'. Compounding a generally miserable summer, most of which Jemima spent back in England, James Goldsmith died

* As just one example, Ted Dexter, at the height of his glamour as England's captain, stood as the Conservative candidate for Cardiff South East in the 1964 general election. He lost his deposit.

on 18 July; the Khans' friend Princess Diana was killed just over a month later.

'We are facing a multi-crisis,' Imran told an interviewer in 1998, part of a sombre world overview that struck one British critic as 'owing something to Private Frazer, and his catchphrase "We're doomed", in *Dad's Army*'. Imran continued: 'Most of the major institutions have collapsed, and there is no coherent policy or way forward. What remains is a sort of mafia state that depends on bribes and pay-offs for its continued existence. There is a kind of ingrained dishonesty which has become part of the culture ...'

Imran was speaking about politics, but it was a reasonable sketch of Pakistani cricket at the tail end of the millennium. As a result of accusations that Salim Malik had offered his nation's opponents substantial cash inducements to throw matches, and that the Pakistani board allegedly knew all about it, the government set up no fewer than three official inquiries. Imran went before one, telling Justice Malik Mohammad Qayyum that certain of his former Test colleagues had been involved in cheating and 'nefarious financial activities'. 'I'm sure some of the players were in on the betting,' Imran added, before going on to recall the story of the 1990 Austral-Asia Cup Final in Sharjah. The belief that this was all an exclusively Pakistani problem remained deep-rooted, although it later emerged that two Australians, Mark Waugh and Shane Warne, had been approached by an Indian bookmaker known only as 'John', and had given him certain information about the weather and the state of the pitch for a consideration of £2,500 each. Salim Malik subsequently received a life ban, eventually lifted by a court in October 2008, by which time the former Essex and Pakistan batsman was 45.

Following the 1997 election, Imran continued to stump the nation in classic whistle-stop fashion, whether from the rear platform of a train or bus, or in his specially adapted jeep. His message was simple and unrelenting: the government of Nawaz Sharif had centralised power in the hands of a few potentially or actively corrupt, American-backed cronies and 'is borrowing money just to pay off Pakistan's debts ... There is no clear policy to get us out of this mess. We are in a complete crisis.' Imran added that the original idea had been that he and Jemima would campaign together, 'but I had to pull her out of politics to shield her from [the] attacks ... That is when our problems began because we were spending time apart. That then exacerbates the problems of a cross-cultural marriage, and she inevitably missed her friends, family and home more than she might have.' Throughout 1998–9, Imran spent three weeks of each month out of the home engaged in politics and charitable fundraising. Back in Lahore, Jemima was left holding the baby and eventually organising her own non-profit fashion label, which, in the words of the catalogue, 'employ[ed] native Pakistani women to embroider western clothes with delicate eastern handiwork'. After six collections, the label closed in 2001.

Imran's moral ardour for Pakistani national renewal was real, but made him few friends among the established parties. In late 1997, Nawaz Sharif remarked, 'Khan is demonstrating the desperation of a failed conspirator, whose plot to capture power with the help of his [foreign] father-in-law's wealth and intrigues has met with a brick wall.' The prime minister seems not to have been moved by James Goldsmith's recent death, if he was even aware of it. Partly as a result of Sharif's criticisms, the 'bearded fundos', as Jemima would term them, continued sporadically to picket the Khans' family home in the months following the election, and to call for the expulsion of the 'Zionists' and 'scum' within. No wonder, perhaps, that when Imran happened to meet Javed Miandad at a cricket function in 1998, 'he told me by way of personal advice to never get into politics'.

For a start-up party with no parliamentary representation and little cash on hand in the bank, the Tehreek-e-Insaf would appear to have attracted more than its share of attention from its better endowed rivals. One knowledgeable source in Islamabad remarked that when speaking about Imran, Nawaz Sharif 'was so imbued with fury that sometimes the skin on his face seemed to boil'. The prime minister had never been an enthusiastic fan of his nation's most famous son, and was still known to refer to the time when he had been 'biffed around' by the delirious crowds waiting to greet Imran and his team on their return to Lahore airport after beating India in 1987.

Eleven years later, events took another curious turn when Imran and his wife wandered into a shop in Islamabad one day and paid the equivalent of £450 for a boxload of 397 glazed blue bathroom-floor tiles. The vendor apparently assured them that the goods were locally manufactured and had no historical value. Some time afterwards, Jemima attempted to ship the tiles to her mother in London, with the idea that they might eventually add a colourful ethnic touch to Ormeley Lodge. Instead, Customs officials in Lahore impounded the shipment and rapidly determined that the Khans were guilty of the 'serious offence [of] exporting goods of paramount archaeological interest', a crime which in theory carried a penalty under the terms of the Antiquities Act of 1975 of up to seven years in gaol, and/or a fine of 5,000 rupees (£50).

By the time formal charges were laid in January 1999, a pregnant Jemima was safely home in England. 'I'm afraid I scarpered before I could be arrested,' she later revealed, adding that she had good reason to believe that had she not done so she would have given birth to her second child in a Pakistani prison. Imran was left behind to face the leisurely judicial proceedings, which seemed to him 'to go on for ever ... Because I was a national hero and so on, the government couldn't attack me directly, so they did it by harassing my wife. To say it was politically motivated is an understatement. The whole thing was a crass abuse of power.'

According to Imran, a receipt for the tiles in question and subsequent carbon-dating documents were duly presented to the investigating authorities. But officials countered that this was a 'clear case of heinous smuggl[ing] of artefacts prised from their ancestral home', which they apparently came to believe was the 100-domed Shah Jahan mosque in Thatta, Sindh, built around 1647. The pre-trial administrative wrangling went on for most of 1999, making the London High Court proceedings seem pacy by comparison, and proved an unwelcome distraction to a man already stretched by the demands of his hospital and his nationwide political campaigning. Imran's 'forced labour', as he referred to it, was made particularly burdensome by various writs threatening his wife with summary arrest should she ever again set foot in Pakistan. 'Nawaz Sharif wanted her locked up. It was ludicrous. She would never have faced a fair trial,' Imran remarked. On 12 October 1999, the prime minister fell from power in a largely improvised coup led by the army chief of staff Pervez Musharraf. Some three weeks later, Jemima voluntarily returned to Pakistan. 'Under the military rule, we fear no victimisation,' Imran announced, a shade prematurely, perhaps, in the light of longer-term developments, as his veiled wife stood at his side. On 3 April 2000, the Lahore High Court quashed the smuggling charges against the Khans, after an official from the Ministry of Culture and Archaeology came forward to confirm that the tiles 'now appear[ed] to have been made at some time in the last 40 years' rather than in the mid-17th century.

* * *

Even in the midst of dealing with the Pakistani justice system, Imran would still allow himself certain relaxations. He spent much of the late spring and summer of 1999 in England, where he unwound as best he could. He seems to have enjoyed these occasional Western breaks for their own sake, but also because they gave him a social leeway generally speaking denied in Pakistan. Jeffrey Archer remembers Imran hosting a lavish party at Annabel's that May, apparently to celebrate the birth of Qasim Khan. Another friend watched admiringly as the austere Muslim politician supposedly sashayed into a London restaurant with Jemima and a glamorous entourage that included several young women, one of whom 'brayed back and forth with a bloke in a velvet smoking-jacket who I believe was an earl, but who favoured a butch, urban-aggro way of speech'. Not that Imran was ever completely free of the cares of his job, as a *Guardian* journalist sent to interview him noted. 'He seldom sat in the same chair for very long throughout the session. During our two or three hours together he was all over the room and he continued to talk animatedly on the phone on average about once every 10 minutes.'

Imran also took the opportunity to attend several ties of the 1999 World Cup, which again ended poorly for Pakistan. On 31 May he was on hand at the county ground, Northampton, to see his country lose against the odds to Bangladesh. As Ladbrokes had rated Pakistan 33 to 1 on to win, there were inevitable mutterings about the legitimacy of the result. Imran would later recall, 'I went blue in the face persuading everyone that it was a genuine loss.' Three weeks later, Australia beat Pakistan in a cup final that lasted barely four-and-a-quarter hours, roughly half its alloted term, but which seemed to this observer to effectively be over from the moment the Pakistani players padded mournfully on to the field, looking as though their team mascot had just been run over. Again, Imran would be called upon to defend his former colleagues' honour. It had just been another one of those off-days that happen in cricket, he insisted. The soon-to-be deposed Nawaz Sharif appears not to have been similarly convinced. Shortly after the team's return to Pakistan, the prime minister called on the government's accountability bureau to investigate what he called this 'crushing national humiliation'. As a result, Wasim Akram, Salim Malik and Ijaz Ahmed were all briefly suspended; on 13 September, the three players were fully exonerated and reinstated by the board, although eight months later Justice Qayyum's inquiry handed down its own long-term ban on Malik.

On 4 July 1999, President Bill Clinton announced a ceasefire to end the latest Indo-Pakistani clash over Kashmir, the first since the two countries had each successfully detonated a nuclear weapon. Many in Pakistan came to view the peace terms as an unconditional surrender on their part. In particular, the newly appointed army chief of staff appears to have had increasing misgivings about his civilian head of government. 'I had some minor [issues] with Sharif,' General Musharraf confirms. 'Among other things, we fell out about the sackings of two major generals, the appointment of two lieutenant generals, and his request to me to court-martial a journalist for treason. I must say that I was quite amused by the PM's style of working: I never saw him reading or writing anything.'

Three months after Pakistan's withdrawal from the disputed Northern Areas, Nawaz Sharif committed political suicide. In a show of displeasure with his army chiefs, Sharif ordered a commercial airliner carrying General Musharraf, his wife, several generals and 196 civilian passengers to circle over Karachi airport, which he then closed to traffic. After a further series of heated radio exchanges, the plane eventually landed, allegedly with only three minutes of fuel to spare, and Musharraf assumed control of the government. Sharif was put under house arrest, tried by Pakistan's anti-terrorism court, found guilty of hijacking, and ultimately went into exile in Saudi Arabia. 'His was the coup,' his successor later remarked. It was somehow typical of the national cricket board that its current chairman, Mujib ur Rehman, had gone to Sharif's house as the crisis unfolded in order to congratulate the prime minister on 'getting rid of that swine Musharraf'; he, too, suffered a sharp decline in his professional fortunes in the years ahead. After the PM's spokesman had gone on television earlier in the day to announce the mass retirement of Pakistan's chiefs of staff, commando units loyal to Musharraf had scaled the wall of the state broadcasting complex in Islamabad, taken it without resistance, and turned off the power. An hour later, programming resumed with a picture of a pink rose accompanied by martial music. Troops patrolled the streets of all Pakistan's major cities, distributing sweets and sherbet to anti-Sharif protestors. It was all over within a few hours, without loss of life. In a keenly awaited formal judgement on the affair, the nation's Supreme Court later ruled that 'General Pervez Musharraf, Chief of the Army Staff and Chairman Joint Chiefs of Staff Committee, is a holder of [a] constitutional post. His purported arbitrary removal by Sharif in violation of the principle of audi alteram partem was ab initio void and of no legal effect.'

On 6 November 1999, an interviewer asked Imran how long he thought Musharraf's honeymoon with the electorate would last. While welcoming the military takeover in general terms, especially as Musharraf seemed all but incorruptible compared to his predecessor, Imran admitted being mildly concerned that there might conceivably be 'a dispute of some sort' between the new head of state and the judiciary within a period of about six months.

He was a trifle pessimistic. It was June 2000 before the Supreme Court ruled that Musharraf should hold 'free and fair elections [with] adequately represented opposition parties' inside three years – a request the general thought 'most oppressive'.

TEN
All-Rounder

In May 2000, *Vanity Fair* published a profile of 'cricket superstar Imran Khan and his lovely wife Jemima' going about their business in the course of a typical day in Lahore. The magazine did not paint an enticing picture of the couple's current living conditions. The Khans occupied three small rooms in a cramped family home described as having 'grimy sofas' and 'peeling paint'. The water and electricity supply was sporadic, and Jemima and her young sons were plagued by stomach bugs. Imran was reportedly sanguine about his domestic circumstances. 'Struggle is good for you,' he told *Vanity Fair*. 'If people avoid struggle, they decay. Life has been very easy for Jemima. Maybe I'm a Godsend, to make her struggle.'

It would be fair to say that the Khans were not pleased with *Vanity Fair*'s overall depiction of their lifestyle. To Imran, the whole thing was 'overblown' and 'another example of the Western media's negative portrayal of life in a developing country'. Besides, he added in an interview with *The Times*, it was quite wrong to talk about the family living in Lahore when they had since moved to Islamabad, where they occupied a 'seven-bedroom property in one of the city's most exclusive areas'. Imran's comments were echoed by Jemima, by now a convert to Islam, who dismissed the idea that she had any doubts about Pakistan. 'I am perfectly happy with my life out here and very settled,' she assured reporters. 'The problem is that if I say Imran is a very unmaterialistic man and that a life of luxury doesn't matter to him, that gets interpreted as "He forces me to lead a life of misery", and it's not what I'm saying,' Jemima added. As a result of the brouhaha, Imran's animus against at least some of the press became more noticeable, as, in time, did his bitterness and anger at what he felt to be General Musharraf's betrayal of his promise to usher in a new era of accountability to

Pakistani politics. What followed, instead, was two years' relentless succession of austerity drives, bank crashes, riots, bombings, kidnappings, assassinations, suicides and hijackings, which brought Pakistan up to the events of September 2001.

Thanks to a lavish public expenditure programme undertaken by both the Bhutto and Sharif administrations, there were, at least, a few visible fruits to show for Pakistan's national bankruptcy. As state president, General Musharraf was able to enjoy a splendid new residence in Islamabad that *Today* described as 'undecided between Nazi neoclassicism and Las Vegas kitsch'. There were various other, less picturesque schemes involving the digging of cross-country sewer lines and improving the nation's antiquated road and rail infrastructure, but these seemed to be mired in what even Musharraf refers to as 'chronic nepotism and incompetence ... [the] victim of enormous corruption among ministers, bureaucrats and bankers, the last being handpicked by the first because all the major banks were nationalised'.

Politically and economically, then, Pakistan would seem to have been primed for a leader who promised to restore budgetary discipline while pursuing a Utopian-liberal social agenda. But more than four years after its formation, the Tehreek-e-Insaf remained a niche player which consistently attracted less than 3 per cent support in national opinion polls. By 2000, some observers had concluded that the party would never amount to anything more than a one-man show that relied almost exclusively on Imran's personal fame and connections for its survival. Conventional wisdom held it that he should ally himself with one of the established political dynasties, perhaps that of the Bhuttos, if he was serious about aspiring to high office. Benazir Bhutto herself had other ideas; she was sure that her 'lifelong friend' (still only 47 years old) was 'simply too proud' to be party to any back-room compromises. And she believed that sooner or later the country would come to choose between the two Oxford contemporaries as 'a national beacon of hope [after] the despondency of the Musharraf years'.

At the conclusion of a one-day international between Pakistan and Sri Lanka in February 2000, the master of ceremonies announced Imran Khan as the man of the match instead of Wasim Akram. The capacity crowd's roar had rarely subsided throughout the day's play, but at that it welled up to the accompaniment of several dozen firecrackers. It was further proof that, whatever his electoral prospects, 'Khan Saab' remained an icon of Pakistani cricket, as well as being the father figure to many of the current players. When the announcer's mistake was corrected and Wasim came forward to collect his award, he remarked that he 'didn't mind in the least' being called Imran, since he was 'the man responsible for making Pakistan the world force it is today'.

Between commenting on everything from nuclear proliferation to the plight of Sindh's nomadic herdsmen, Imran continued to deliver some typically caustic views on the national sport. Whether published in Pakistan, India or England, his cricket journalism remained unflinchingly opinionated, tending to hammer away at a single point, quite often involving the bungling of a bureaucracy somewhere, and as a rule avoiding the charm and irony of his memoirs. He was not shy about moral judgements. 'Institutional racism' in sport was 'as unacceptable as the hated apartheid regime' had been in South Africa. Nor had he quite yet reconciled himself to the 'inept power elite' still apparently behind Pakistani cricket. In early 2004, Shoaib Akhtar, one of Imran's heirs as the team's prime strike bowler, controversially pulled out of a Test against India with an injury he described, with unusual precision, as a 'slight strain of the eleventh rib'. The Pakistan Cricket Board (PCB) was not impressed with the diagnosis. Following the Test, they called Shoaib in front of a specially convened medical commission to investigate him and four other injured players. Imran, in turn, launched a stinging broadside at the PCB, which was chaired at the time by his old Test colleague Ramiz Raja. 'This is a joke ... a farce ... Nowhere in the world has a medical inquiry of fast bowlers ever been conducted,' he said. Not for the first time, the board 'has made a complete mockery of Pakistani cricket'. In private, Imran advised Shoaib to look into the possibility of suing 'the men in blazers who have questioned your integrity'.

On 28 December 2000, Jemima, her sons, her mother and other members of her family were on a British Airways flight to Nairobi when a mentally deranged Kenyan student broke into the cockpit and attacked the pilot. The jet plunged 10,000 feet and, as with the Musharraf incident a year earlier, was said to be 'only moments' from crashing into the desert below. Jemima, by her own account, stayed calm because of the children, hugged them, and prayed 'like mad' (to whom?) throughout the ordeal. It must have been exquisitely terrifying for a woman who disliked flying under the best of circumstances. Eventually the would-be hijacker was subdued, and the plane landed safely in Nairobi. Imran had not been on the flight himself, but later joined his family at their hotel. His first words to Jemima were,

'Well, baby, I hear you had a little turbulence. You should have flown PIA.'

The story, if true (and it comes from Jemima), was quintessential Imran. There was his typically cool and phlegmatic disregard for mortal fear, even when it was his immediate family who were the ones at risk. Since Imran believed that the date and time of his own death was predetermined, he didn't fret about it. 'If you are involved in the politics of change, you could be bumped off at any moment [and] I've come to terms with that,' he remarked. 'I am a Muslim and I believe my time to go is ordained by my God. Death doesn't scare me in the least.' On top of that, there was his only half-facetious dig at Jemima's electing to fly British Airways when there was a 'perfectly good Pakistani carrier' available. By now, possibly, it's been established that Imran was fiercely patriotic. But he seemed to go beyond that here, implying that his wife, who called herself 'both Pakistani and British', had revealed her true national colours in her choice of airline. It was a small point, but an example, perhaps, of the sort of perceived slight that can cumulatively burn a marriage.

By the time of the BA incident, the Khans had finally taken up residence in their villa in the Himalayan foothills. Oddly enough, several friends and political colleagues who visited Imran in his alpine idyll found him variously 'withdrawn', 'subdued' or even 'depressed'. According to one party supporter, 'While remain[ing] the most open and obliging of men ... while receiving hordes of petitioners, while giving aid to cancer victims, needy friends and down-and-out cricketers, he was never one for loving humanity blindly.' Perhaps Imran was merely reacting to the larger national picture. A further two years of headlong decline had dashed most of the hopes he'd allowed himself at the time of General Musharraf's takeover. With a balance of payments deficit of roughly $6 billion and rising, Pakistan had since reached the stage where it had to rely for its survival on a series of institutionalised loan sharks charging up to 60 per cent annual interest, as no one offering better terms was available. But Imran was, at least, a willing and by all accounts doting host to his daughter Tyrian White in the summer of 2001. The nine-year-old reportedly spent two months staying with him and her putative Anglo-Pakistani family at the Goldsmiths' home in London, before returning to her mother in California.

Irritating and embarrassing as snide Karachi media reports about his love child were to Imran, far more ominous was the direction the government was taking in the build-up to the scheduled 2002 election.

By then President Musharraf at least had the distinction of having held high office over a sustained period with no serious charges of personal corruption against him. In Pakistan, that in itself was an achievement. Similarly, he could, and did, claim credit for modernising a number of the state's archaic administrative functions. Under Musharraf's Local Government Ordinance of 2000–1, elected assemblies replaced the existing colonial arrangement by which a commissioner and a prefect of police ran the various regions much like a personal fiefdom. From now on, power would be devolved into the hands of a network of some 5,000 individual councils, each with a 33 per cent mandatory minimum representation of 'women [and] other minorities'. Indeed, it's arguable that the general did more for grass-roots democracy in Pakistan than any of his highly touted predecessors. In time Musharraf both lowered the national voting age and created 60 new reserved seats for women in the 342-strong National Assembly – not, on the face of it, the initiatives of a 'power-crazed tinpot dictator', as Imran once characterised him.

Still, even over the course of his first two years in office, Pakistan's chief executive (and, as from June 2001, self-appointed president) would elicit a wide range of reactions. In time, Musharraf and his henchmen introduced the country to the full range of characteristic features of Third World military regimes, including, but not limited to, mass arrests and round-ups, interference in the judicial system, and blanket press censorship. Such things tend to polarise opinion. In a departure from her public speaking style, Benazir Bhutto once described the general as 'the fucking stupidest guy on the face of the earth'. President George W. Bush, in contrast, saw him as an 'intellectual engine'. In manner the hyperactive Musharraf was the Energizer Bunny, making it hard for his political opponents, or anyone else, to get a word in edgewise. Time and distance have not conspicuously enhanced his reputation. Anyone making it to the end of Musharraf's memoir *In the Line of Fire* will have encountered a central character who manages to combine platitudes about 'new politics', 'innovative form[s] of popular consultation' and a pledge to carry on 'listening and learning' with a degree of self-regard, if not rampant megalomania, reminiscent of the great comic-opera political monsters of the recent past. 'Mugabe-esque' might be stretching the point too far, but the general's cheerful suspension of the national constitution, among other activities, would surely have brought a receptive gleam to that particular tyrant's eye.

For 53 years, Pakistan had observed the 11th of September as a solemnly unifying public holiday commemorating the anniversary of the death of the state's founder Muhammad Ali Jinnah. The date assumed a new and nationally more divisive significance as from 2001. In the seven years that followed, Islamabad increasingly came to treat the West as 'a sort of giant cash machine', in the words of the *Spectator*, extracting some $12 billion of aid from the US alone. Britain and other nations, along with multilaterals including the World Bank and the International Monetary Fund, donated as much again. Some of this munificence would be used for its intended purpose – preventing terrorism by 'provid[ing] the United States and her allies with certain specific flight corridors, intelligence, travel information and records, [and] internal security data which will serve both our nations' interests, [and] preserve us from the threat of an Indo-American pact,' as Musharraf put it in an emergency television and radio broadcast on 19 September 2001. Far more went into the familiar 'commissions' which lined the pockets of senior Pakistani military and civilian officials, including those at the very highest level of government.*

'Everyone here wanted to help the Americans immediately after 9/11,' Imran told me. 'But they squandered the goodwill. Many of us in Pakistan watched in horror as the US began pounding Afghanistan ... To me, the Taliban were an aberration. Everyone knows that kind of medieval zeal is not what Islam is about. They were an embarrassment to much of the Muslim world, it's true. But that still doesn't make them terrorists.'

It would be quite wrong to claim, as certain critics did, that Imran actively welcomed the 9/11 attacks as somehow representing an overdue lesson in humility for the world's one remaining superpower, if not God's punishment for alleged injustices against Muslims. He made it abundantly clear both at the time and subsequently that he condemned the outrage. But it would be reasonable to say that the struggling Tehreek-e-Insaf party was re-energised at least in part by its initially lonely, principled stand against the excesses of what became the 'war on terror'. As in any war, pressures for conformity against the enemy

* The president failed to mention it, but before coming to his decision to 'unequivocally' support the US, he and his chiefs of staff had first war-gamed the Americans as an adversary. The Pakistani forces would be 'obliterated' in any real-life conflict, they rapidly concluded, a significant factor when it came to forming the country's new strategic alliance.

rose and flourished, at least in the early stages, and the fear of disloyalty deeply influenced Pakistani politics. Zeal for the 'great patriotic cause' appears to have been behind a number of Musharraf's post-9/11 initiatives, such as his withdrawal of funding for some 200 Islamic educational institutions, and a wide range of public-order crackdowns. Imran, by contrast, took the opportunity to flay the United States for what he felt to be its 'unjust and unethical' overreaction to having been 'hit'. On 13 October 2001, denouncing the US-led invasion of Afghanistan, he spoke of a sense of 'helplessness' at the direction the war on terror already seemed to be taking. 'In Pakistan there's a terrible feeling [that] we're no longer in control,' he said. 'It is very difficult to convince the people here that on one side is this huge superpower and on the other are these impoverished women and children in Afghanistan who have already suffered 20 years of war. It's very difficult not to sympathise with them against the United States ... Terrorism is bred where there is hatred and anger, and I'm afraid that when civilians are killed there will be a lot more hatred against America.'

Seven years later, events had done nothing to modify this bleak assessment. 'If my women ... my wife, my family, was hurt by a bomb, or killed, I would pick up a gun,' Imran announced in November 2008. 'To shoot [coalition] forces,' he clarified. 'Innocent people are dying in my country ... The American attitude is shocking. All they want is obedient slaves.'

'Imran seemed to make few allowances for his bride,' an anonymous Goldsmith family source later revealed to several British newspapers. By 2002, 'Jemima had struggled with homesickness, a huge fundraising workload, pregnancy and illness. Married life soon fell short of the ideal. With the cultural differences so extreme, each felt that he or she was the one who had sacrificed more, and the creeping impression that this wasn't appreciated by the other party created a silent but growing hurt.'

After the unusually public honeymoon had come domestic routine, 'immense loyalty and affection ... many good things shared ... but overlaying it all the petty little annoyances of marriage, imperfections noted, and of course the unique charms of moving in with the in-laws for five years'. As well as the background pressures, Jemima had faced the relentless attacks of her husband's opponents and the so-called antiquities smuggling charges of 1998–9. She had at least enjoyed three years of relative success with her eponymous fashion label, which at its peak employed around a thousand Pakistani women. 'The clothes are a bit of both East and West,' Jemima announced, 'because that is how I feel myself.' The business collapsed shortly after 11 September 2001, when orders from New York 'dried up overnight'.

Political matters were not going all that well either. The Tehreek-e-Insaf had fared poorly in the phased Pakistani local government elections held between December 2000 and July 2001. After five years, Imran's party remained either 'frustratingly in chrysalis' or 'a complete joke', depending on which newspaper you read. One Karachi-based media outlet compared its core appeal to that of a 'hermit gibber[ing] in the wilderness'. As low as people's opinion of the ruling elites might be, most of them had not as yet been seduced by Imran's message of change. 'What we've seen in Pakistan in 11 years is that four governments have been dismissed for corruption,' he remarked in June 2002. 'The voters are sick of the same people. They have seen them time and time again. Basically politics has been confined to families and the same families have ruined Pakistan.' Imran evidently saw himself as a bit different – the solitary figure on a shore, shouting out to a flotilla of his countrymen as they slid into the shark-infested waters of another national election. 'I'm unlike all the other candidates,' he insisted. 'The fact that every year I collect millions of rupees from Pakistani people for a charitable project makes me the only politician who can do it, who people believe in. That's what is lacking in Pakistani politics. People do not trust the politicians.'

Perhaps alone, too, of the party leaders contesting the elections scheduled for October 2002, Imran spent much of the preceding summer based in a Georgian mansion in the London suburbs, from where he was able to watch a full season's cricket. Ten years earlier, the journalist Qamar Ahmed had exchanged words with his nation's World Cup-winning captain in the course of a flight between Adelaide and Sydney. 'We nearly came to punching each other until Javed intervened,' Ahmed recalled, the second time that particular trinity had occurred. In June 2002, a more conciliatory Imran walked into the Lord's press box during a break from his television commentary on England's first Test of the summer with India. 'I think he felt embarrassed about what had happened,' says Ahmed. 'He shook hands with me in front of all the pressmen present. It was a big gesture. We're now friends as before.'

Conversely, the 2002 election campaign destroyed the Imran-Musharraf relationship, such as it was. The president began proceedings by announcing a long, and legitimate, list of complaints about Pakistan's 'scelerotic' political process. Having lowered the voting age and raised both the overall number of seats in the National Assembly and those reserved for minorities, Musharraf then decreed that all candidates for the legislature should be university graduates, at a stroke disqualifying some 96 per cent of potential office seekers. This was done, he remarks, 'not only to have better-educated parliamentarians but also to sift out many undesirable politicians', to him a 'vastly popular' initiative that 'gave our bodies a new, younger, more enlightened outlook'.

Less welcome was the general's sanguine acceptance of what the official IPO observers called 'a pervasive atmosphere of bullying, coercion [and] violence directed at opposition candidates and their supporters' that made the 1997 election seem tame by comparison. Musharraf appears not only to have taken a relaxed view of the intimidation and brutality that characterised the campaign, but, in the IPO's words, to have then 'signally failed to protect the integrity of the country's 65,200 polling places', a number of which opened to voters for less than the officially mandated nine hours, or 'allowed the secrecy of the ballot to be compromised', among other irregularities. Despite Musharraf's enfranchising of Pakistan's youth, overall voter turnout was down to 39 per cent as compared to 41.65 per cent in the 1997 contest. A second team of observers sent by the European Union later published its findings about 'the authorities' misuse of state resources in favour of approved political parties [and] the president's imposition of serious restrictions on opposition campaign activities, which clearly ran contrary to the Code of Conduct for Political Parties ... The main televised news broadcast consistently promoted the government's views on election-related activities ... Broadcasts containing dissent or criticism of the authorities were the exception rather than the rule.' The election was followed by six weeks of political paralysis, at the end of which Musharraf appointed 58-year-old Zafarullah Khan Jamali as prime minister. Mr Jamali's Pakistan Muslim League (Q) party enjoyed a less than overwhelming mandate, having won just 25.2 per cent of the popular vote. Musharraf considered his new prime minister 'extremely loyal to me ... his cooperative role was most praiseworthy.'

Home from England, Imran threw himself into his second national campaign, despite being prey, along with his party, to the various 'pre-election administrative contortions', of which more in a moment. In so far as there was a hot-button issue that got him going, it was Pakistan's complicit role in the continuing coalition action in Afghanistan. In so far as there was a reason for his increasing contempt for the state president, it was the 'inept and confused' way in which Musharraf had blundered into a 'ruinous' alliance with the Americans. Unfortunately, at least some of Imran's high-minded stand against this 'senseless slaughter of fellow Muslims' was negated by Jemima's casual admission that she had once read Salman Rushdie's book *Shame* as part of her university English course. It was not a universally popular association. As a result, 'more crazed mullahs allied to [Musharraf] immediately insisted that my citizenship be revoked and that I be run out of the country'. The familiar placards accusing the Khans of being part of a Zionist conspiracy reappeared at Tehreek-e-Insaf election rallies, along with the 'bearded fundos' who made their presence felt outside the gates of the family home in Islamabad. 'They targetted Jemima [and] it rattled her,' Imran noted.

In August, just before announcing the election, the president's powerful principal secretary Tariq Aziz held a series of meetings with the major parties. Aziz had subsequently helped to reinvent the Pakistan Muslim League as an obediently pro-Musharraf group (although a vociferous rump remained loyal to the exiled Nawaz Sharif), by the expedient of allegedly offering the party leadership a guaranteed minimum 80 seats in parliament. It was an unusual use of presidential patronage, yet that very singularity perhaps played to Musharraf's favoured theme: namely, that there was an 'unprecedented national emergency' in the wake of 9/11. The president had already put his authority on the line by staging a referendum in April 2002 which asked coyly whether, 'For the survival of the government system, the establishment of democracy [and] to fulfil the vision of Quaid-e-Azam, you would like to elect General Musharraf as head of state of Pakistan for a further five years?' The result showed a gratifying 98 per cent level of support for the president. Yet when Musharraf's representatives, accompanied by members of the Pakistan intelligence agency, the ISI, later sought to convince Imran to join a pro-government alliance, the so-called 'King's Party', the meeting ended in acrimony. 'The essential proposal was that I join the coalition, which would do Musharraf's bidding once elections were held, and that in return I would be made prime minister.' Imran at first stalled, and then roundly declined the offer when the delegation pressed him for a reply. Colourful language was used. 'You'll never be elected now!' the head of the ISI (political wing) reportedly shouted at him.

On 25 September, Imran addressed a capacity audience waiting for him inside the earthern cricket ground at Kamar Mushani, a small mining community just north of his ancestral home and would-be constituency of Mianwali. Some 6,000 party faithful, equivalent to half the town's adult population, applauded wildly as, dressed in all-white *shalwar kameez,* their leader climbed a flight of steps to sit on a rickety-looking wooden platform erected on the side of the pitch. When the welcome showed no sign of abating, an MC took the microphone to announce that the meeting would not convene unless there was order in the public stands. A moment later Imran himself rose, faced the pavilion and raised his arms in a quieting gesture like that of an umpire remonstrating with an unruly spectator moving in front of the sightscreen. The crowds immediately fell silent. Speaking in his familiar sepulchral tone, Imran then reportedly told them, 'Musharraf was wrong to give support to US troops for their war in Afghanistan. Our country has become a servant of America ... I was made to understand that when the general won the referendum he would begin a clean-up of the system. But it wasn't the case.' After another sustained round of applause, Imran went on to announce that, if elected premier, he would bring about 'police and army reforms' and make a 'heavy investment in education'. While hardly radical in itself, this was followed by the promise to 'weed out the over-staffed government agencies' which continued to do 'little or nothing' on the people's behalf. Judging from the tumultous response, Imran seemed to hit a deep nerve when he spoke of sending the displaced bureaucrats to join graduate students in performing some form of national service 'such [as] teaching poor children in the countryside'.

Back in Mianwali itself, the administrative seat, the newly reconstituted Pakistan Muslim League (Q) party was putting up a strong fight. The PML(Q) candidate, Obaldullah Khan, was a local landlord, alleged to be more than passingly familiar with the drug trade, who had just emerged from nine months in gaol for corruption. Mr Khan's campaign against his near-namesake included a full range of print and broadcast advertisements, among other, less formal outlets, referring to his opponent's 'Jewish wife'. Imran admitted that he faced an uphill struggle to be elected, but insisted that he and the party would carry on regardless. 'I cannot stop now. It's in my blood,' he said.

On election day, 10 October, Imran joined his wife, family and senior colleagues to watch the returns. The early reports were discouraging, as between them the PML(Q) and the Pakistan People's Party

Parliamentarians (PPPP) swept first the south and then the remaining cities. At 2 a.m., Imran went to bed, thinking the worst. When he woke the next morning, the Tehreek-e-Insaf were in 18th place out of an officially recognised 73 parties in the popular count. They eventually polled 229,125 votes, or some 0.8 per cent of the 28 million Pakistanis who cast a ballot. Imran himself was the only one of his party's candidates elected to parliament. Just over a month later he was sworn in to seat NA-71, representing Mianwali, formally agreeing, 'I am a Muslim and believe in the Unity and Oneness of Almighty Allah and the Books of Allah', and that he would bear true faith and allegiance to Pakistan, discharging his duties and performing his functions honestly, to the best of his ability, not allowing his personal interest to influence his official conduct or decisions. It was 16 November 2002; Imran had just turned 50.

The president and his political fixer Tariq Aziz, along with representatives of the ISI, had continued actively to solicit Imran's support up to the moment he took his seat. Once again, the core proposal was that he throw in his lot with the pro-Musharraf PML(Q), in return for which he would be promptly appointed prime minister. An army source close to the president adds that there had been plans 'to then send Mr Khan on a lengthy goodwill tour of western Europe and the US', apparently with the idea of his renegotiating Pakistan's numerous loan agreements – some of whose proceeds went to the treasury, as advertised, and some to an opaque network of powerful 'foundations' controlled by the military. At that point, Musharraf evidently still didn't know what Imran thought of him ('just a total conman and a coward', he found out later), but there was to be no such accommodation. Early in November, the Tehreek-e-Insaf confirmed that the party was 'strictly non-aligned' and would not enter into any alliances or deals. Two days later, Musharraf reportedly told Tariq Aziz that Imran would 'surely agree' to be a roving ambassador if the terms were right for him. It appears to have been another case of wishful thinking on the president's part. On 5 November, Imran's party again put out a statement declaring its independence. Speaking for everyone who has attempted to plumb the depths of the Imran–Musharraf relationship, as well as for that larger group that tries to make sense of Pakistani politics, the army source confessed, 'The General did not understand Khan [or] that he couldn't be seduced.'

When the time came, Imran used his parliamentary vote in favour of Maulana Fazal-ur-Rehman, the Jamiat Ulema-e-Islam party's nominee as premier. It was a not uncontroversial choice. Fazal-ur-Rehman, who enjoyed the nickname 'Mulla Diesel' following allegations that he had been involved in a fuel sale scandal, was the head of a fundamentalist Muslim coalition broadly united by its opposition to the war in Afghanistan. In his capacity as general secretary of the Muttahidah Majlis-e-Amal ('Council of United Action') religious alliance, Fazal-ur-Rehman had previously led a series of anti-Musharraf street demonstrations and threatened the US with a holy war if they continued their 'slaughter' of innocent Muslims.* 'Khan has more than a soft corner for the ousted Taliban,' a senior member of the Tehreek-e-Insaf anonymously told Pakistan's *Newsline*. 'He thinks that the orthodox religious militia did a great service to Afghanistan and Islam before they became a target of the Americans.' When I asked him about it, Imran denied having any particular affection for the Taliban, but by endorsing Fazal-ur-Rehman it seemed to *Newsline*, among others, that he was siding 'against the liberal, democratic and progressive elements in Pakistan society' and instead taking a 'conservative view [on] women, education, fine arts, television and sports'.

While Imran struggled with the intricacies of elective politics, Jemima had busied herself with a number of UNICEF-related activities, including field trips to Kenya, Romania and Bangladesh, and a high-profile role promoting the benefits of the UN's Breastfeeding Manifesto. She eventually completed her BA in English, suspended some seven years earlier, in May 2002. Later that year, Jemima enrolled in a postgraduate course in Middle Eastern studies, specialising in 'Modern Trends in Islam', at the University of London. She had played a full part in her husband's second, personally successful election campaign. The big rallies in and around Mianwali had been packed with crowds who called her name and waved her photograph. Before Imran spoke, he and his wife would materialise onstage in a handsome and carefully arranged tableau, to a roaring welcome. But the constant attacks from other quarters had taken their toll on Jemima, who left Pakistan in early 2003 with the couple's two sons, and would visit the country only sparingly from then on.

* * *

* After another week's haggling, the president then located the moderate Mr Jamali, a sometime hockey administrator who was thought more congenial to himself.

In June 2002, the Pakistan army had launched Operation Kazha Punga in an attempt to root out a cell of al-Qaeda operatives and their families living in the country's rugged North-west Frontier Province. From a tactical point of view, the mission went poorly. A force of 500 soldiers, including elements of the Special Services Group and regular infantry, duly surrounded and entered the al-Qaeda compound, but then came under attack from supposedly pregnant women who pulled automatic weapons from under their clothes. In the ensuing melee ten soldiers lost their lives and the majority of the terrorists escaped into the hills. As President Musharraf recalls, 'The operation was a turning point, because for the first time it highlighted the magnitude and seriousness of the threat against us.'

By January 2003, with the help of American money and hardware, the Pakistan army had formed a helicopter-borne Special Operations Task Force, specifically to 'provide [a] fast-reacting, hard-hitting unit to effectively police the remote areas' and 'impose the will of the elected government'. The Americans then added a fleet of unmanned drones which would fly intelligence-gathering operations 24 hours a day over Pakistan's tribal regions. Over the next year the US made all sorts of proposals to enhance security arrangements in the general area. They wanted to set up radio relay stations in the mountains of Tora Bora; they wanted to dig a tunnel through Peshawar and another parallel to the Khyber Pass; they wanted to deposit heat in underground caverns by setting off a bomb, then draw on the energy later; they saw splendid opportunities for an electrified fence that would run some 130 kilometres (80 miles) from the westernmost fork of the Indus through to the Afghan border. All these glittering prospects would become reality, however, only if Musharraf and his cabinet could be persuaded that ceding a further chunk of Pakistan's sovereignty would be repaid by continuing economic largesse from Washington.

As far as can be ascertained, Imran didn't actively oppose all the American initiatives. In many cases he didn't even know about them. The Pakistani president ensured that few if any of the more grandiose proposals ever came to a parliamentary vote, preferring, instead, to negotiate on a case-by-case basis direct with his country's *de facto* bankers. In time even Musharraf appeared to grow slightly uneasy that 'I [had] given so much ... A number of the demands [on us] were ridiculous and may even have been mischievous.' The US Army Corps of Engineers were ultimately denied the opportunity to build their tunnels or set off their underground bombs, though Musharraf did unhesitatingly agree both to the requested overflight privileges and to the establishment of 'purely logistical' bases in Sindh and Balochistan.

Imran, to the extent that he was aware of them, was unimpressed by these apparent transgressions of Pakistani soil. Even if al-Qaeda was developing an elaborate network of terror cells that, as claimed, stretched from the Horn of Africa to the remote areas of the Hindu Kush, from Kabul to Kansas, what mattered was protecting his nation's territorial integrity. Speaking in November 2008, he recalled the case of a parliamentary colleague who was travelling with his family in two jeeps close to the Afghan border.

> A helicopter gunship comes on top [overhead]. The instructions are that the moment the gunship comes you stop your cars, get out and put your hands up. This is in your homeland, OK? ... So they all did that. They all stopped the cars, got out and put their hands up. The [pilot] came back and bombed them. The guy showed me the pictures. His six-year-old son lost both his legs. His brother gets killed. His brother's son gets killed.

Imran's preference for self-determination in foreign affairs while, as he vainly hoped, a 'competent leader' ushered in much-needed social reforms grew steadily throughout his first five years in the legislature. From the start of his term, it was clear that he saw his duties somewhat differently from the average provincial member of parliament. Like any good MP he worked long hours on behalf of his Mianwali constituents, helping to bring a degree of economic relief to an area known for its extremes of heat and cold, and largely distinguished in terms of infrastructure by its dilapidated Second World War aerodrome, various hockey fields and tombs, and a notorious pre-Partition gaol. Meanwhile he also continued his travels abroad. It's said that he came to be widely acknowledged as the assembly's most expert and experienced spokesman on international affairs, quite apart from his reputation as a globally adept fundraiser. When overseas, Imran consistently sought out heads of state, foreign ministers and party leaders. Some saw him, if only out of curiosity or respect for his former career; but many others had only limited time for a mere member of parliament, a leader of a fringe socio-political group regarded in some quarters as having little if any future. In these years, Imran was often on his own as he travelled the world. Alone, doggedly meeting with anyone who would give him the time, choking back any frustration, always tirelessly hawking the party line, he more than once found himself addressing half-empty press conferences where the questions tended to be concentrated as much on his personal life as on Pakistan's role in the world. Like a bowler relentlessly pegging away on a flat pitch, said *You*, he 'rolled up his sleeves and got on with it'. The analogy wasn't idly chosen: Imran, an ambitious man who wanted to compete with the best, sometimes saw politics as the 'great game' which he, on behalf of his people, still 'passionately' wanted to win. In the meantime, life was an occasionally beguiling, occasionally numbing blend of heated debates on Afghanistan and Kashmir, interminable procedural wrangling, and long, hot afternoons spent on the Standing Committee on Public Accounts.

Cricket itself still played quite a prominent part in Imran's routine. Pakistan suffered the latest of their now seemingly perennial World Cup disappointments in the tournament staged in South Africa in early 2003. Rock bottom likely came in the match against India at Centurion Park, played in front of 20,000 vocally partisan fans and a television audience implausibly estimated at a billion. Largely thanks to Tendulkar scoring 98 from 75 balls, the Indians won by six wickets. The Pakistan board subsequently disposed of eight senior players, including the captain Waqar Younis, Wasim Akram and Saeed Anwar. 'After [that], a lot of my friends asked me to intervene, and despite my commitments in politics I have agreed to help with coaching,' said Imran, speaking at the launch of a network of regional training clinics later that spring. Unfortunately, the much heralded new dawn of Pakistani cricket proved illusory. Twelve months later, after the national team again lost both a one-day and Test series to India, there was to be further upheaval. Javed Miandad lost his job as head coach for the fourth time, Inzamam returned as captain and the PCB's chairman General Tauqir Zia stepped down after questions were raised about the selection of his son Junaid for the national side. There was some further obsessive tinkering by the board with the game's domestic structure, but nothing substantial. 'Departmental cricket, played between corporations, is a joke,' Imran told the newspaper *Dawn*. 'I have contacted the PCB [and] they assured me that this structure will be removed from next year. Who can say what will happen? This is Pakistan, where things change overnight.' Imran also commented on the frequency with which the board altered the names of the various first-class tournaments. 'One doesn't even know which trophy is being played for any more,' he complained.

On 18 December 2002, Imran's cousin Javed Burki, 64, was arrested by the National Accountability Bureau, or NAB, run these days by the army. NAB had long had a civilian equivalent, but had been revamped by President Musharraf, who was said to be not wholly averse to employing it against his political opponents. Burki, the country's former Test captain, was detained in his capacity as chairman of the Pakistan Automobile Corporation, a company that supplied vehicles to the military. There were said to have been delays in the firm's delivery of a fleet of some 3,000 Yasoob trucks. Burki would spend more than six months languishing in a Karachi gaol without formal charges being brought against him. Not surprisingly, he emerged a visibly diminished figure: he could 'barely walk' on his release, according to published reports. Burki's ordeal inevitably put an additional strain on relations between Imran and the Musharraf administration. I was authoritatively told that the whole affair was 'a [case] of personal vindictiveness. The Yasoob lorries had fallen behind track, as such things do, in 1999, yet it was only three years later that [Burki] was dragged away from his home in Islamabad. By a curious coincidence, it happened to be the same month that Imran had publicly refused to do business with the Musharraf coalition. As a result, anyone connected to the Khan family soon grew used to being treated by the government as outcasts, even outlaws.'*

It was a view that might have been shared by Imran's estranged wife, who remained in London, gradually reacquainting herself with what she had once called 'the transient pleasures derived from the high life and nightclubs'. In late 2003, Jemima took out a full-page advertisement in several Pakistani newspapers, declaring, 'It is certainly not true that Imran and I are having difficulties in our marriage. This is a temporary arrangement, and Inshallah [God willing] I will be coming back to Pakistan once my studies are finished and the building of our new farmhouse is complete.' If the overall intention of the exercise had been to put an end to the speculation about the couple's relationship, it appears to have been only partially successful. When a state president also happens to be a military dictator, his political opponents' misfortunes naturally enjoy widespread press coverage. Over the next few months, most of the Islamabad and

---

* I contacted General Musharraf in 2008 to ask him for his side of this story; he declined to comment.

Karachi media duly competed to run increasingly lurid articles about Imran's 'failed' marriage.

None of these problems, however, appeared to impair his legendary self-confidence. On 1 April 2004, India completed their rout of Pakistan in the first Test of the series at Multan. The winning margin of an innings and 52 runs was, for the moment, India's most emphatic victory in their otherwise largely grim 72-year history of cricket away from home. Imran briefly appeared at the ground on the final morning. In what was reported to be an 'action-packed cameo time[d] at exactly six minutes' he criticised the pitch, made various points to Shoaib Akhtar about the position of his leading arm and to Mohammad Sami about his field placings, queried a bat-pad decision against Inzamam, delivered himself of one or two other strictures on Pakistan's technical short-comings, and then left again as quickly as he had come. A fortnight later, the Indians won the Rawalpindi Test by an innings and 131 runs. The veteran commentator Omar Kureishi described the fourth and final day there as 'the blackest in Pakistan's cricket history'. It was the end of Javed's latest tenure as coach; a month later the PCB's chief executive, Ramiz Raja, caved in after barely a year in office and resigned to spend more time with his family.

On the morning of 13 May 2004, Imran's former lover Sita White, or 'Ana-Luisa' as she had taken to calling herself, dropped dead of a pulmonary embolism just before starting her first yoga class of the day at a Los Angeles gym. She was 43. Short of money and a single mother, White had led what was described as a 'druggy and purposeless existence' in California, preoccupied with her decade-long struggle both to extract a larger share of her late father's fortune and provide for her daughter, Tyrian. A court had ruled in her favour in her paternity suit against Imran. White had married twice in recent years, in 1996 to an actor and former 'Marlboro Man', Alan Marshall, and again in 2002 to John Ursich, an Argentinian waiter. At the time of her death she and Ursich were divorcing, with her levelling charges of abuse (which he denied) at her husband, and him accusing her of indulging in a diet of 'nonstop vodka, steroids and cocaine'. The eulogy at White's sparsely attended funeral was delivered by a New Mexico Tech graduate and hedge fund manager named Nicholas Camilleri. He took the opportunity to complain that White's 48-year-old sister Carolina, an ex-model, had boycotted the service and had even gone to court to try and stop it from happening. As an alternative, Carolina announced that she would be holding her own, more exclusive vigil at her Beverly Hills home. Later that night the deceased's body was returned to the police, who had yet to conclude whether or not they were investigating a possible homicide. Camilleri later conjectured that White would have enjoyed the chaotic arrangements following her death. 'She was such a drama queen,' he remarked.

A year or so earlier, White had made a suicide attempt, saying that she had 'had enough of begging for money'. Later, there had been a lengthy hospital stay after an unsuccessful course of cosmetic surgery. Following her recovery, White was introduced to Cameron and Richard Saxby, a married couple who had been involved in numerous lawsuits, including a later disproven case accusing Richard of having inflated the trading prices of stock in one of his companies, an 'electric services' entity called Keystone Energy. In March 1998, Keystone was obliged to 'review' a profit estimate that had doubled its share value overnight. There was some subsequent acrimony of a financial nature between the couple and White regarding the latter's family funds. In a will predating these events, signed on 27 February 2004, White had appointed the Saxbys her executors and, if called upon, 'full and responsible' guardians for Tyrian. At the time she had known the couple for some three weeks. The will further stipulated that none of the following were to have any 'custodial role' in her daughter's life: 'My mother, Elizabeth Kalen De Vazquez, my sister Carolina Teresa White, my brother, Lucas Charles White, my stepmother, Victoria Ann White, also known as Victoria White Ogara, nor Imran Khan.'

A month later, White drafted a letter to the Khans in Islamabad:

> Dear Imran and Jemima,
> I feel the time has come to address the issue of Tyrian's future. I want to make it clear that I have removed myself from the equation. This is not about me, this is not about revenge; it is about justice; justice for Tyrian.
>
> As we have been unable to come to any agreement in the past, I have taken the financial and emotional responsibility for Tyrian's upbringing for the past 11 years. Acknowledgement of your obligation and responsibilities is long overdue.
>
> I am proposing that a trust in the amount of 10 million dollars be established for Tyrian … This proposal is a final offer to bring this issue to a close without legal intervention … I am requesting a response from you within seven days. Should you

> choose not to respond and agree to these terms, the fallout from media intervention in both Pakistan and the UK will be certain and out of my control.

Whether on further reflection or legal advice, White never sent the letter. Seven days before she died, however, she formally removed the Saxbys as Tyrian's guardians and named Jemima as their replacement. Although their fathers had occasionally done business together, the two women had never met. White appears to have been motivated by a genuine desire to, as she put it in the paperwork, 'have the minor enjoy rights of access to both her natural families'. By all accounts, Tyrian and Jemima had taken to one another during the child's periodic visits over the previous three summers. White also told a friend to whom she was close at the end of her life that she regretted having had to sue Imran to establish that he was Tyrian's father, particularly at a time when 'the CIA [were] after me' and floods and a landslide had made her Los Angeles home 'barely habitable'. In a subsequent move, she had had her daughter's name legally changed to Tyrian Jade Britannia Khan White.

Although still not publicly acknowledging paternity, Imran took the opportunity of Sita White's death to issue a statement saying that he and Jemima were prepared to be Tyrian's guardians. The Khans were further said to be ready to fly to Los Angeles 'at a moment's notice'. In the event this step wasn't necessary, as White's sister Carolina successfully petitioned a court for temporary custody of her niece. In time, Imran was said to have come to broadly support this arrangement. According to widely published reports, both he and Jemima continued to 'speak to Tyrian by phone almost weekly' and to send her flowers on her birthday. As of this writing, the now 17-year-old Tyrian remains under her maternal family's care in California. Some misguided critics of Imran have suggested he behaved badly in the whole affair, but this can only have been further evidence of a narrowly partisan political attack.

The timing of these events was particularly acute, as Imran and Jemima were then in the midst of formally ending their marriage. Matters appear to have come to a head for them in the early weeks of 2004. In another emanation of the 'transient pleasures' of nightclubs, Jemima had celebrated her 30th birthday that January with a lavish party at Annabel's. Imran himself wasn't present, but the guest list included the likes of Elle Macpherson, Calvin Klein and Taki, as well as various European pop and film stars. The seemingly ageless but actually 43-year-old Hugh Grant, then basking in the reviews of his role as the bouffant-haired prime minister in *Love Actually*, arrived with Princess Rosario of Bulgaria. Jemima was said to look 'radiant' in what was perhaps one of her less discreet dresses since she had converted to Islam, a low-cut, sequinned number from Yves St Laurent. By the summer of that year she and Grant (a 'huge' cricket fan) were London's most public celebrity item, having rather bizarrely been voted the couple by whom a majority of visitors 'would most like to be shown around the city'.

'I sadly confirm that Jemima and I are divorced,' Imran said in a statement issued from Islamabad on 21 June, the ninth anniversary of the couple's civil wedding ceremony. 'While Jemima tried her best to settle here, my political life made it difficult for her to adapt to life in Pakistan ... This was a mutual decision and is clearly very sad for both of us. My home and my future is in Pakistan.' Contrary to some impressions in the media, a divorce or annulment under Islamic law, although not handed out like coupons for a free pizza, as in the West, is a relatively painless affair that begins with a period of arbitration among the two parties and their families. If that fails, the couple go their separate ways, and the marriage is legally wound up three months later. There is only limited scope for adulterers to be punished by public whippings or any other such chastisement. Under the terms of the Dissolution of Muslim Marriages Act of 1939, a husband can seek 'material redress' if his wife deserts him, but it's generally agreed that in this case Imran waived any claim he might have had to a multi-million-pound pay-off.

Politics and presidential spite, and not Hugh Grant, were responsible for ending his marriage, Imran later insisted. 'Jemima's spirit was broken by personal attacks on her by the Musharraf regime in a bid to sink me,' he said. 'I think she gave up. She thought it was a never-ending struggle and she didn't believe I would make it.' Reports that he was hurt by her high-profile affair with Grant, or anyone else, were 'nonsense', Imran added. Falling back on another cricket analogy, he told a reporter, 'If you lose a match and you've tried your best and fought till the end, you don't actually mind losing. You accept it. It's only if you haven't done your best that you regret it. In this case I don't have any regrets.' There is certainly no evidence that he was any less strong-willed or single-minded in his marriage than was the case in his sports career.

Divorced from his wife, separated from his children and with no party colleagues seated alongside him in parliament, Imran might have struck some as a forlorn figure in mid-term. He responded by immersing himself in both constituency and national affairs, showing a hitherto undiscovered talent for committee work. 'I have never seen this man as focused as he was [that] year,' a Tehreek-e-Insaf organiser told me. 'More than anything else, [Imran] enjoyed presiding over party meetings and listening to the guys' give-and-take. And he [realised] that he was now finally doing the things he had been talking about for years.' That talking had mostly been public. When Imran did speak in private to 'the guys', it was quite often in a curious mixture of the narrowly specific and the sublimely Delphic. As a result it was sometimes up to other people, friends and staff alike, to interpret his wishes. He continued to command intense loyalty. At meetings, among his frequent exit lines were: 'I will handle this' and 'We are all Pakistanis'.

Back in London, Jemima's tabloid reputation as a mantrap was almost certainly undeserved. She seems to have led an only moderately full social life before settling down into the relationship with Grant. There was also a series of highly polished articles appearing under her name in the *Daily Telegraph*. A well-placed source describes the guest list for the average Jemima dinner party as ranging from 'minor European royalty, politicians, academics [and] fun international playboys like Taki right up to fabulously gormless pop stars who talked about Iraq'. It was a crowd Jemima was beginning to enjoy. They, in turn, were evidently fascinated by the inside stories and insights she would dispense about life in Islamabad, which, while challenging, she invariably spoke of with 'respect and nostalgia'.

Imran, for his part, maintained a dignified silence on his divorce. Most of the 'million or so' enquiries on the subject over the next five years were dead-batted away with usually polite, occasionally curt rebuffs about it being nobody else's business. 'Some of the greatest happiness I've ever had was during marriage,' he remarked in 2009. 'And of course the greatest lows were in the marriage, too, because of the peculiar way it went. Once my marriage went – and I've never tried harder in anything to make it work as my marriage – but once it was over you go through a period of sadness and pain, but never do I think about missing it, or living, or going back to it. You know, you just move on.' The general hunch in the press was that the cultural divide had just been too great. James Goldsmith had made the most prescient assessment when, in another of his celebrated quips, he'd allegedly said of

Imran, 'He'll make an excellent first husband.' Better, or inner, reasons for the break-up aren't available to an author, and may not be even to the parties themselves. 'The peculiar way it went' is a suggestive phrase.

In August 1982, Imran had announced: 'I meet people [in England] and feel undercurrents of racism. It doesn't affect me too much because I know England is not my home. But if I had children, I would not want them to grow up here in an atmosphere where there was racism. I've grown up with a lot of pride and I wouldn't want my children ever to have to develop an inferiority complex in a society like this.' Twenty-two years later, Imran's two sons, being raised as Muslims, would find themselves spending nine months of the year in London, with school holidays and half-terms in Pakistan. The timeshare arrangement broadly appeared to suit all parties. 'It's not the situation you would choose for bringing up your kids, and I worry about them constantly, but it works,' Imran says.

For all his stirring pep-talks and political acumen, 'the chairman's specific accomplishments didn't yet look like the stuff of history,' one colleague and journalist confided. 'Will marble tablets read: "He questioned the American adventure in Afghanistan"? Will our grandchildren recall in song and verse: "He deplored inequality"? ... Sadly, it was more a question of the very best of intentions going unfulfilled.' In parliament, Imran followed the mullahs' lead on most domestic issues, declaring himself in favour of traditional religious schools and against such modern frivolities as mixed-sex running races, while talking in general terms about 'rejuvenating' Pakistan. Even some of those most sympathetic to his core anti-corruption message came to the conclusion that he was simply too fickle a politician. 'Imran is essentially a do-gooder, but he has these half-baked ideas, the sort you would pick up at an airport,' says Najam Sethi, both a friend and the editor of Pakistan's *Daily Times*. 'And now he's caught in a no man's land, satisfying neither liberals nor conservatives.' About the one constant factor everyone could agree on was Imran's success as a roving ambassador and fundraiser. On 8 July 2004, he was on hand to collect the Lifetime Achievement award at the annual Asian Jewel gala in London, for 'acting as a figurehead for many international charities and working passionately and extensively' on behalf of his hospital.

Later that autumn, Imran was robbed at gunpoint while driving through the outskirts of Islamabad, according to Tehreek-e-Insaf officials. 'The chairman was proceeding with his maid and two sons, when he was forced to stop abruptly by an overtaking car. Two men with semi-automatic weapons emerged from nearby bushes and relieved the party of their mobile phones, credit cards and a purse. The incident symbolises the complete breakdown of law and order in the country,' said Akbar S. Babar, a party spokesman. A week later, Imran's representatives were back in the High Court, arguing over the terms of the settlement of the 1996 libel action brought by Ian Botham; according to the *Daily Telegraph*, the two parties had 'squabbled about costs' at semi-regular intervals during the previous eight years. From London Imran flew to Washington DC, where he was reportedly 'hauled up and grilled for three hours by US immigration officials', alerted, perhaps, by his recent remarks attributing suicide attacks in central Asia to America's 'ill-conceived and arrogant' policy in the region. A Pakistani travelling in the same party had supposedly remonstrated with the authorities, asking them to respect 'our greatest all-rounder'. There were no cricket fans among the welcoming committee. The semi-shaven, middle-aged man wearing a tan-coloured *shalwar kameez* and carrying a copy of the Koran meant nothing to them except as a potential terrorist. Imran was eventually able to proceed to a charity fundraiser in New York: from there it was on to California and then a dinner party in India where, somewhat improbably, he found himself sitting next to Goldie Hawn. Shortly afterwards, Karachi-based press reports began insisting that he and the 59-year-old actress were an item. Imran angrily blamed the Pakistani intelligence agency for spreading the 'stupid' rumour.

To compound a generally wretched year, Imran could only watch in dismay as the man he now called the 'odious' state president engaged in various increasingly feckless campaigns on behalf of the 'war on terror'. In the early hours of 16 March 2004, Pakistani Frontier Corps forces 2,000 strong surrounded a mud-walled compound in Kalosha in South Waziristan, near the Afghan border, looking for militants. Once again, the soldiers found that they had walked into a trap: a two-week siege followed, at the end of which an estimated 700 men, women and children had died and 50,000 citizens of Kalosha and the surrounding villages had fled after the Pakistani air force bombed their homes. Later in 2004, Musharraf and his army chiefs stationed a garrison of 80,000 troops in South Waziristan. The militants, led by Abdullah Mahsud, a one-legged horseman with a shoulder-length mane of hair flying from his red turban, promptly rode off up the mountain pass and relocated to North Waziristan. Some American legislators were beginning to ask where exactly their roughly $2 billion in annual aid to Pakistan was going. On 2 November 2004, George W. Bush was re-elected US president.

Six months later, on 9 May 2005, *Newsweek* magazine carried a report that US interrogators had desecrated copies of the Koran while questioning prisoners at the Guantanamo Bay naval base. The 300-word story cited sources as saying that investigators looking into abuses at the military gaol had found that American GIs 'placed Korans on toilets, and in at least one case had flushed a holy book down the pan'. Imran lost little time in calling a press conference in Islamabad, in which, flourishing a copy of the magazine, he demanded that President Musharraf secure an official apology for the incident, which was 'a disgrace' and 'an insult to Muslims', who were now themselves 'under attack' from the West. At least 17 people were killed and up to 600 injured when demonstrators then took to the streets in Peshawar, Lahore and other parts of the country to shout anti-US slogans and burn the American flag. In Jalalabad, Afghanistan, two 'foreign missionaries' (an Australian and a Pole, it turned out) were pulverised by a mob of well over 300 citizens running through the town square. Three more people, including an Afghan soldier, were injured in a subsequent pitched battle over possession of the men's dead bodies. It took some five days for the disturbances throughout the region to be fully brought under control.

Imran remained unapologetic, even if he disassociated himself from the violence. 'To throw the Koran in the toilet is the greatest violation of a Muslim's human rights,' he told the *Guardian*. 'Should we close Amnesty and the Red Cross because they bring up violations? When you speak out, people react. Bloodshed is regrettable, but that's not the point.' When I asked him about it in a phone call to Islamabad, Imran's voice, previously unenthused, grew quite heated. 'What I said was, "This article has appeared, and if it's true we're no longer in a war against terror. We're in a war against Islam." That's what I told them in the Assembly ... It's the ultimate insult to our faith,' he boomed. Imran's friend Syra Vahidy met him not long after the incident and recalls, 'All he wanted to do was sit and talk about politics, which basically consisted of a monologue on his part against America.' *Newsweek* subsequently disowned much of its original story. The magazine's Washington bureau chief, Dan Klaidman, said that the apparent errors in its report were 'terribly unfortunate', and he offered his sympathies to the victims of the violence. After a lengthy inquiry, the US Department of Defense was unable to confirm a 'toilet incident, except for one case, a log entry, when a detainee was reported by a guard to be ripping pages out of a Koran and putting [them] in the toilet to stop it up as a protest. But not where we did it.'

Imran took a certain amount of flak as a result both of his original speech and subsequent developments. 'Blood flowed indirectly because of what Khan said,' one Washington newspaper's account opened, and went on to offer the summation: '*Newsweek* lied, people died.' Most editorial judgements were similarly harsh, if not more so. To the *Weekly Standard* he was the 'Khan artist' who continued to 'inveigh against the West by day and enjoy its pleasures by night'. As an overview of Imran's life it was roughly 15 years behind the times, but one perhaps took the magazine's point. A representative blog posted in December 2005 nominated the 'so-called hero' as 'hypocrite of the year ... When the Muslim extremists next decide to riot I'm sure that he'll be giving them some advice on how to throw the Molotov cocktails properly, although I'm not sure if that will involve the use of a bottle top to aid the spin.' There was substantially more in this overall vein on the internet. One anonymous correspondent wrote a 4,000-word exercise in journalistic exasperation, calling Imran a 'fallen star', but ultimately concluding that 'whether or not they agree with him and his policies, people *like* him ... The *Newsweek* saga was the least of it. Imran has committed untold public blunders and flip-flopped around like a newly hooked fish ... Yet even the worst gaffes simply do not outweigh the genuine affection and goodwill millions feel for him. Some political commentators have trouble realising that the public give as much weight to qualities like optimism, honesty, courage, decisiveness and individuality as they do actual achievements.'

In late May 2005, just days after the *Newsweek* riots, Imran was in the United States in his capacity as chairman of the board of the Shaukat Khanum hospital. In a whirlwind tour that took him to Washington DC, New York, Denver and Los Angeles, he raised some $600,000 in 'urgently needed' operating funds, while submitting to an average of 20 interviews and other public events a day. Two months later Imran was again in the US, the country he had once reportedly stigmatised as part of an 'axis of evil' with a ruthless intolerance of all foreign and domestic dissidents. Eluding the official dragnet, he was able to host or attend another series of lucrative fundraisers. On 16 July, Imran was the keynote speaker at the Human Development

Foundation's annual Southern Californian benefit dinner. The HDF describes itself as a non-governmental organisation which 'aim[s] to assist the disenfranchised in Pakistan and elsewhere through education, literacy, infrastructure improvements and micro-loan based business creation projects'. If Imran had any qualms about continuing to tap wealthy American donors to support his various causes, they weren't evident that night in Santa Monica. His speech enjoyed a prolonged standing ovation. The evening then concluded with a two-hour performance by the 84-year-old Pakistani ghazal singer Habib Wali Muhammed and his group, who again brought the audience to its feet with a spirited rendition of the national song, 'Roshan-o-Rakhshan, Nayyar-o-Tabaan, Pakistan rahay'.

As everyone was finally packing up and leaving the hotel, a middle-aged female fan named Adis Lee approached Imran and requested an autograph. He told her he was happy to oblige. As he was signing the proffered piece of paper, Lee asked him if he felt he had made a 'political mistake' in speaking out about the *Newsweek* story.

Imran knocked that one out of the park. 'I'm not talking about politics. I'm talking about decency. It was a foul thing to do. It's a desecration.' At that he affably posed for a picture before walking off into the muggy California night.

While Imran was travelling around raising money, much of the world's attention was centred on the 7/7 terrorist attacks in London. Of the four suicide bombers, three were of Pakistani origin. In response to widespread criticism that he had taken the West's money and done nothing with it, General Musharraf insisted, 'Our … law enforcement agencies have completely shattered al-Qaeda's vertical and horizontal links and deteriorated its communications and propaganda set-up; it no longer has any command structure in Pakistan.' The general then quietly ordered the detention of some 720 Pakistani nationals suspected of terrorist sympathies. It is estimated that he had arrested a total of 3,700 citizens in the six years of his rule to date.

Imran was unimpressed. 'Musharraf is destroying our democracy by using this war on terror,' he said. 'Why did he put so many people behind bars when Pakistan had no connection with the London bombings? In the world's eye Pakistan became a hub of terrorism. And at home, it reinforces the idea that Musharraf is a stooge implementing an American agenda.'

* * *

'After all this time,' the *Weekly Standard* was forced to admit, there were still several mysteries to Imran, 'the aggressively patriotic Pakistani who like[d] to unwind with prolonged stays abroad': the principal one being that he seemed to be several different people. Since 1996, the chief image to emerge had been that of a prodigiously humourless tub-thumper who stormed around with what one writer called his 'permanently hooded eyes and a scowl ... somehow you always felt you were in the presence of an unusually well-groomed scorpion'.

Still, those looking for signs of conventional political airs, or even not-so-conventional, might have been disappointed. This was the same man who in the summer of 2005 hurriedly excused himself from the joys of a *Guardian* interview at the Goldsmiths' mansion in Richmond in order to sit, spellbound, over the fifth day's television coverage of England playing Australia at Old Trafford. Australia's final pair kept out the last 24 balls to save the game. Watching the cricket, Imran came alive. The clouds lifted. 'That was fantastic!' he kept enthusing as he darted back and forth between the interview and the television set. Somewhere under the formidably serious Muslim paladin there was still a flannelled fool struggling to get out. A family friend who happened to be visiting told me that everyone had been 'entranced and engaged' by the sight of the old player as he 'demonstrated various English and Australian bowling techniques' for the benefit of his sons, who, like most of the country, seem to have taken to the sport as a result of that unforgettable series. Two months later, Imran responded to what he perceived to be negative statements emanating from the Pakistani captain and board prior to their home rubber against England. 'Inzamam has said the English start as favourites,' he noted reprovingly. 'The PCB chairman agrees. I don't understand it. Whenever I stepped on the cricket field I always thought we could beat anybody. I would never admit defeat before the match began. They're going to destroy the team by saying it.' Imran then took the opportunity to catch up with some of his former colleagues at an official dinner later that autumn in Lahore. So often defensive and surly in his dealings with the media, he struck at least one veteran correspondent as 'relaxed, witty and incisive' in the company of men who, 'with one or two exceptions, still adored him'.

This was in late September 2005. On Saturday 8 October, an earthquake in northern Pakistan killed 83,000 and injured 75,000; half the victims were children, who were trapped in school buildings. According to some published reports, Imran had been in London at the time, but flew home immediately afterwards. In other accounts he was already on the scene and volunteered for relief work in the worst affected areas, describing it as 'the most severe national crisis' in Pakistan's modern history.

Ten weeks after these events, US missiles were targetted at Osama bin Laden's deputy Ayman al-Zawahiri, who was thought to be visiting one of his wives in the frontier village of Damadola. Part of a vast, primitive plain with irrigated plantations of maize and squash, and populated chiefly by goat herds, the spot can normally be accessed only by the vertiginous hairpin bends of the Malakand Pass. On this occasion the attack missed al-Zawahiri but killed 13 residents, including women and children, in addition to five alleged terrorists. The political repercussions continued long after the explosions had subsided. Imran was one of several National Assembly representatives who seized on the incident. 'This is a civil war in the making,' he said. 'Refugees have been created. Innocent people killed; children left without arms and legs. All under the magic mantra of fighting so-called extremism ... ' General Musharraf subsequently issued a protest to the United States, asking to be better informed the next time they intended bombing his citizens.

Under the circumstances, President Bush's visit to Islamabad over the weekend of 4–5 March 2006 was judged only a mixed success. To mark his arrival a force of some 1,700 Taliban irregulars marched on the north-west garrison town of Miram Shah. The fighting lasted for three days, at the end of which 262 soldiers and civilians had died. After a suicide attack on the Pakistani army position, special forces blew up the town's main Islamic school, which they claimed had been used as a militant base. Not surprisingly, the overall security situation in the region dominated the talks between Musharraf and Bush, who did, nonetheless, find time to visit a heavily policed cricket match. Imran was unable to join them, as the state president had ordered him kept under house arrest for the duration of the visit. Some seven months later, the US launched a missile strike against what was variously described as being a 'theological school' or a 'terrorist camp' in North Waziristan. On that occasion 86 people died. The next day, a suicide bomber blew himself up at a Pakistani army checkpoint, killing 35 soldiers and wounding 60.

Imran's reaction to these events was so archetypal as to impress itself on numerous observers, foreign and domestic. To the *Daily Telegraph*, he was 'a body linguist's dream. Talking about the painfulness of divorce causes him to vanish into the depths of his chair, pulling both sides of his jacket across his chest and pinning them there as if he's on a chilly outfield. [But] get him on the subject of the American and Pakistani army bombing of his homeland and he's on the edge of his seat, arms flailing and eyes blazing.' Back in the National Assembly, a fellow representative watched as Imran rose to join in an already quite lively debate on the tribal areas, 'leaning over the polished wooden desk at a sharp angle', and instantly chopping the air with 'long, bony hands' to call for order.

The colleague, seated nearby, knew what was coming. Even the ruling coalition had admitted to reservations about the specific direction the war on terror now seemed to be taking. Sure enough, Imran launched into a stentorian defence of 'Pakistan's sovereign integrity', paused to decry the 'excesses of foreign intervention' and concluded that 'we are in a war of attrition'. The speech itself was actually not searingly original. But Imran's delivery left no room for doubt as to his passion on the subject. There was real anger in his voice. When I asked him about his views on the matter two years later, he practically shouted down the line, 'People just don't understand what's going on out here. If they did they wouldn't countenance it.'

With the assembly shuttered up for one of its lengthy recesses, Imran took the opportunity to spend several weeks in London. As usual, he took up temporary residence in his former mother-in-law's home. When the *Sunday Times* came to call they found that Imran had 'managed to make a complete mess of the sitting room, with items of underwear and toiletries scattered across the floral sofas and plump cushions, [but] sat serenely in the middle of it all, smiling as his sons' bickering over the playstation in the next room threatened to escalate into violence'. While he was in London, there would be seven or eight requests a day for him to address think tanks, attend charity dinners and give interviews. He accepted the last indiscriminately, even ones where the journalist seemed to be less interested in Pakistani self-determination than in his sex life. One broadsheet reporter was promised a full 60 minutes of Imran's time in which to talk about 'the world situation' over refreshments at Ormeley Lodge. He arrived to find that an elegant tea service had been laid out among piles of 'sporting paraphernalia, dumb-bells and gym socks'. Imran courteously began the proceedings by announcing that they would not be interrupted 'except for phone calls that simply can't wait'. During the hour, there were five such calls, three of them on matters sufficiently complicated that, as the writer puts it, 'it was essential to talk at length'. It wasn't an untypical

Imran performance. Trying to cram everything in, 'he would hurl himself from place to place ... More than once I saw him literally run the few steps from a doorway in the [Goldsmiths'] house to a car waiting at the curb.' The relay would then be taken up by a driver named Abdul Qadeer (not to be confused with his late-1980s 'VIP courier'), who often took Imran to and from Heathrow. For the outgoing trip Qadeer knew to be sitting at the door with the motor running, as there was no time to spare – 'for a 4.15 plane, he left at 3.15' – and Imran then spent the journey 'snap[ping] out a series of instructions on the phone in breakneck English or Urdu'.

When Imran looked back on his life, he made a distinction between the 'humble sinner' who had gone around the world playing cricket and bedding an unfeasible number of women, and his current incarnation as the defender of his country's sovereignty and honour. Although he sometimes spoke as though they were, the two roles weren't mutually exclusive. Wounded national pride was at the heart of the controversy that brought the Oval Test between England and Pakistan to an abrupt conclusion late that August. Midway through the fourth afternoon of the match, Darrell Hair, the senior of the two umpires, ruled that the tourists had illegally tampered with the ball while in the field. The Pakistani team professed their innocence, but Hair, in consultation with his colleague Billy Doctrove, awarded five penalty runs to England – a public indication that the visitors were guilty of cheating. Pakistan declined to leave their dressing-room after the tea interval, and the officials awarded the match to England. (The tourists did eventually emerge on to the field of play some 20 minutes later, but by then it was the umpires themselves who refused to continue, declaring the game to be over.) It was the first forfeited Test in international cricket's 129-year history. In the media frenzy that followed it emerged that Hair, amid accusations that he was somehow biased against Asians, if not racist *per se*, had offered to resign from the ICC's elite panel of umpires in return for a $500,000 pay-off. This latter detail quickly became a mini-scandal of its own. Watching the whole fiasco unfold, it was possible to see how wars begin: in a steady spiral of mutual recriminations, a dispute that had started out being about the shape of a cricket ball ended up in a furious debate about whether or not the umpires' ruling was inherently 'anti-Muslim'.

Imran, who may have been put in mind of his own occasional differences of opinion with match officials, told *The Times*, 'Pakistan lost out and so did cricket. The captain, Inzamam, said he made the protest for his country, but if I were him I would have done it by going out and winning the game. In my career,' he repeated, 'I saw many great bowlers pulling at the seam of the ball. People used to do it openly, but within limits. The only time tampering became a big issue was after Pakistan mastered reverse swing and the English couldn't play it.' Imran later backed away from comments appearing under his name in Pakistan's *Nation* newspaper referring to Darrell Hair as a 'mini Hitler'. 'I didn't quite say that,' he clarified. 'They take down my column over the phone, so it was misreported. I was talking about all those guys who behave like little dictators when they put on their white coat.' Asked a year or two later about Hair, Imran described him as 'a fundamentalist kind of umpire'.

Two months after the Oval Test, Pakistan arrived in India to take part in the ten-nation ICC Champions Trophy. Inzamam was still sitting out a four-match ban for bringing the game into disrepute. His long-term deputy Younis Khan at first declined to take the job, brusquely telling a press conference he refused to be a 'dummy captain', but then changed his mind after another PCB reshuffle. The board had already removed Imran's colleague Zaheer Abbas as team manager. The Pakistan new ball pair of Shoaib Akhtar and Mohammad Asif were then sent home after testing positive for drugs, although both were subsequently reinstated on appeal. Australia beat the West Indies by eight wickets in the tournament final. Surveying these events, Imran was broadly sympathetic to his near namesake. 'Khan has always struck me as a reasonable, easygoing guy,' he said. 'While I don't condone his public outburst, the Pakistan team management had it coming. If anyone had treated me as shabbily as they have Younis, I would have punched a member of the team's think tank.'

Pakistan's turbulent and chaotic political development took another of its cyclical turns in the spring of 2007, following the state president's decision to suspend Iftikhar Muhammad Chaudhry, the Chief Justice, on charges that he had misused his office for personal gain. In a show of his displeasure with the legal profession as a whole, General Musharraf would later remove or arrest 69 more judges. According to Imran and a number of his fellow legislators, Chaudhry's real offence had been to issue various edicts against police abuse, torture and other civil rights infractions while also blocking a series of questionable land-development schemes sponsored by senior army personnel. Apparently concerned that the Supreme Court would rule against his eligibility for a second term in office on the grounds that no active military officer could also serve as president, Musharraf placed Chaudhry under house arrest on 9 March.

The next day, a series of demonstrations and strikes took place throughout the country. Most of the opposition was initially led by bar associations and rights groups seeking to bring Pakistan under the rule of law. But the protests soon evolved into a pro-democracy movement with broad support across the country. Two days of violence in Karachi left 47 people dead and brought pitched battles to the streets of the commercial capital. In an indignant response to his critics, General Musharraf remarked that he was operating in a 'difficult international situation'. Imran and others believed that he had overlaid that situation with false mystique and black-box hocus-pocus, claiming a high-minded purpose for his work where there was really just a dictator's low cunning. The government then imposed press censorship and forbade live TV broadcasts. It would be hard to exaggerate Imran's fury as he used a series of public rallies in Islamabad and Lahore to denounce the 'failed' and 'petty' tyrant whose nation, with its armed militants and tribal no-go areas, finally appeared to be stumbling towards the nightmare scenario of a failed state. In the midst of the various lobbies, parades and riots, the deposed Chief Justice, a solemn 58-year-old man with a ponderous speaking style, was able to leave the confines of his home and embark on a combined nationwide lecture tour and royal progress, which was enthusiastically received. On 20 July, the Supreme Court bench hearing his case reinstated Chaudhry to his former position: a 'glorious day' for Imran, who rather boldly then made a public call for the 'destruction' of dictatorships that ignored the rule of law.

Running as a sub-plot to the national crisis was Imran's own increasingly bitter feud with the MQM and its exiled leader Altaf Hussain. At least some of the long-standing dispute embodied the intense civic rivalry between Karachi and Lahore, although regional and cultural differences were exacerbated by some choice, personally contemptuous remarks on both sides. Imran remained vocally adamant that Hussain and his chief lieutenants were out-and-out terrorists who should be on trial in Pakistan rather than enjoying the hospitality of the British government. For their part, the MQM issued a statement calling Imran a raving lunatic who was 'unfit to hold public office'. Addressing a press conference, the MQM's parliamentary leader Dr Farooq Sattar said that he was filing a motion to have the member for Mianwali disqualified under the provisions of the

Constitution and Public Representation Act of 1976 'which says that no person involved in extra-marital affairs can contest elections in Pakistan'.

On 25 May, a small but nonetheless animated group reportedly gathered in the street outside the MQM offices in Karachi. As police officers stood by, they eventually succeeded in setting fire to a life-size effigy of Imran, recognisable by its bouffant hair, while chanting various minatory slogans. In the coming weeks, each side in the affair took to the airwaves to claim that the other one was fundamentally corrupt. It was a familiar tactic, as Pakistani parties have frequently used selective morality to target and discredit political opponents. Early in June, MQM activists took their case to the offices of the state radio network in Karachi. After giving an interview denouncing Imran, the party's zonal organiser Siraj Rajput purportedly joined colleagues outside the studio's front door to air such slogans as 'Down with Khan' and 'Shameful Khan, Fornicator with Women'. A Faisal Sabzwari added that the former national cricket captain had 'cruelly destroyed the career of many youths belonging to Karachi, and people had not forgotten it' – a partial reading, at best, of Imran's tenure. His colleague Haider Rizvi said, 'Mr Khan is levelling allegations against the leader of a party which rules the hearts of millions of people. Mr Khan has avoided a DNA test after he lost the case against Sita White ... He is a disgusting example for the Muslims of the country and the world ... Imran Khan has lost his sanity after frequent failures in his political life. He is suffering from Altaf-phobia as he has crossed all limits of ethics and decency while criticising Altaf Hussain, who has conquered the hearts of tens of millions of people around the globe.' Mr Rizvi added that the MQM high command had 'tried to cool the sentiments of our people [but] if Khan does not stop attacking us our efforts may not be fruitful if he visits the metropolis of Karachi'.

When Imran later attempted to fly out of Lahore for Karachi and thence to file a complaint against Altaf Hussain in London, the police reportedly turned him back at the airport. Three more days of house arrest followed. Imran was, however, able to call a press conference at which he stated, 'General Musharraf and Altaf Hussain are using fascist tactics ... The general has once again proved that he wants to ensure one man's rule in the country, but he should remember that the nation will never allow him to prolong his forced regime.' In time Imran's attitude to both his chief political opponents would come to reach the level of a pure and honest personal hatred rarely seen outside marriage. On

5 September, the Election Commission of Pakistan unanimously rejected the disqualification charges brought against the Tehreek-e-Insaf chairman. 'The references made on the grounds of immoral practices are dismissed,' the five-man panel said. Imran's party colleague Shahid Zulifqar welcomed the ruling, but warned that the Pakistan intelligence agencies 'have chalked out a plan to kill the chairman', and that in such an event 'severe crises [would] grip the nation and Musharraf and Hussain will be responsible'. By mid-2007, the whole country appeared to be near the abyss, said *The Times*, 'with the rupee in freefall, among other financial indicators, leav[ing] a society characterised by abysmal poverty, systemic bribery, municipal corruption and tribal gangs squaring off against one another in the hills.'

And the army. Everywhere. In July 2007, Musharraf sent in troops to the Red Mosque, located just 2.5 kilometres (1½ miles) from the president's palace in the centre of Islamabad. Maulana Abdul Rashid Ghazi and Maulana Abdul Aziz Ghazi, the two brothers who ran the mosque, had taken to sending out emissaries to 're-educate' any women not wearing the veil, and threatened to declare full-scale civil war if the government did not adopt Sharia law. In the subsequent three-day siege, an estimated 250 mosque dwellers were killed, along with 10 soldiers. One Ghazi brother was shot and the other was captured while trying to escape dressed as a girl. Imran called the event a 'massacre' and poured scorn on the president's use of the term 'collateral damage' in describing the civilian deaths. It was a 'callous Americanism'. Back in London, Imran told George Galloway in an interview for *The Real Deal* that Musharraf was a 'genocidal tyrant' who 'will be out very soon'. There was some muted talk in the National Assembly about issuing articles of impeachment against the president. Although playing a full part in the debate, Imran was apparently able to break off to attend Elizabeth Hurley and Arun Nayar's sumptuous wedding reception in Judhpur, India, where he was pictured, in the words of one unfriendly website, 'clad in an elegant tux, mingling with gorgeous, ballgown-clad lovelies, examining a bottle of wine held up for his scrutiny'.

While much of the Pakistani nation as a whole was busy protesting the dismissal of their Chief Justice, their cricket team briskly stepped off a cliff. The side's long line of World Cup disasters reached its leaden nadir with their three-wicket loss to Ireland's part-timers in the match played at Kingston, Jamaica, on 17 March – St Patrick's Day. But even that debacle would be eclipsed just hours later by the death of Pakistan's

Indian-born, South Africa-domiciled, but English coach Bob Woolmer, at the age of 58. They had already been burning effigies of him on the streets of Karachi before the news filtered through on the evening of 18 March. Four days later, the Jamaican police declared that Woolmer had been strangled, and quite possibly poisoned as well. From this point on, the plot thickened rapidly. According to the AP, Woolmer had been about to blow the whistle on 'rampant illegal betting and match-fixing' on the part of his charges. The Pakistani players came under official suspicion, and the furore added significantly to the country's already dangerously combustible mood. 'I feel Bob was bumped off,' said Sarfraz Nawaz, not a man to ignore a controversy when he saw one. 'It was the betting mafia. [Woolmer] must have seen how the Pakistan team went about its business. You could see it from the body language that something was amiss.' Eight months later, the official Jamaican inquest into the case recorded an open verdict, the foreman of the jury announcing that there were 'far too many inconsistencies' to say definitely whether Woolmer was murdered or died from natural causes.

To Imran, among others, the 'whole tragic saga' of what happened in Kingston blended in with the long-running anti-Asian prejudice of much of the cricket establishment to create a perfect storm of lies and innuendo. Or that was the gist of his public comments on the case. And it wasn't just the usual, 'colonial' suspects who were engaged in a seemingly never-ending conspiracy to do the Third World down. Imran was notably indignant that 'the entire Pakistan team was subjected to fingerprinting, DNA tests and wild allegations', but on turf well beyond that when it came to Sarfraz, whom he recommended the PCB sue for possible defamation. (The board declined to pursue the case.) Whatever its deeper significance, the affair marked a new low in the long, accident-prone history of Pakistani cricket. Following the team's early departure from the World Cup, Imran again signalled his willingness to 'sit down with the chairman of the PCB and see what we can do to bring the nation out of this latest crisis'. In the weeks ahead, he was able to break off from affairs of state long enough to criticise Inzamam's captaincy, comment on the urgent need for new specialist batting and bowling coaches, and once again denounce Pakistan's domestic cricket structure. By now most of his public statements on the game amounted to a basket of small, overlapping complaints about both the administrators and players under-performing. In a CricInfo poll published that April, Imran himself was voted the sport's greatest ever all-rounder.

* * *

On 4 October 2007, General Musharraf issued a National Reconciliation Ordinance that provided an amnesty from prosecution for all those who had served in government between 1988 and 1999. The unprecedented goodwill gesture was chiefly aimed at the exiled Benazir Bhutto, who in turn agreed that her parliamentary party would not oppose the general's bid for reappointment. Two days later, Musharraf was duly awarded a second five-year term in office by a lopsided vote of the National Assembly and four provincial councils. Imran was one of 85 state legislators to show their displeasure by promptly resigning their seats. On 18 October, Bhutto returned in triumph to Karachi, where her homecoming motorcade was bombed, some said by al-Qaeda, at a cost of 140 lives and 450 injuries. Imran was unmoved. 'Bhutto has only herself to blame,' he wrote in the *Daily Telegraph*. 'By making a deal with Musharraf's government – a deal brokered by the British as well as the Americans – she was trying to get herself off the corruption charges ... I don't know how Benazir has the nerve to say that those killed in the bomb blasts sacrificed their lives for the sake of democracy in Pakistan ... I could have warned her that her life would be in danger if she returned here but I doubt she would have listened. But I can tell her this: it is not going to get any easier for her. Whenever she goes out campaigning in public, her life is going to be threatened. It is different for me, because I am not perceived as an American stooge, or a supporter of the war on terror.'

On the afternoon of 3 November, just as much of Pakistan was sitting down to watch coverage of their cricket team's one-day international against India in Delhi, the nation's television screens went black. Troops commandeered the state and private broadcasting stations and managed to dismantle much of the country's phone and internet connections to the outside world. Musharraf, it emerged, had staged what amounted to a second coup by suspending the constitution and declaring a state of emergency. Once again, the general's principal target was the senior judiciary, who had been expected to declare his recent reappointment illegal. After their chambers had been raided by the army, seven of the high court's 11 judges, including Iftikhar Chaudhry, were locked up and the remainder dismissed from office. Three weeks later, Nawaz Sharif, the prime minister deposed by Musharraf's 1999 coup, finally returned to Pakistan in an arrangement brokered by the US State Department. Sharif had originally gone into exile in Saudi Arabia, but later moved to London, where he occupied a small flat in a Victorian mansion block opposite Selfridges store. Eight years after the event, he remained vocally bitter at having been 'shot out of office', although there was nothing unique about that: no civilian government in Pakistan history had ever completed its tenure. Musharraf then paused to announce that parliamentary elections would be held sometime in early or mid January, or, as was eventually the case, the third week of February, before sending in troops to quell a revolt led by an Islamist disc jockey named Maulana Fazlullah in Swat, a mountain valley once popular as a holiday resort, whose mutinous atmosphere Imran now compared to pre-civil war East Pakistan: 297 killed.

After abruptly resigning his parliamentary seat, Imran took his protest underground by giving a series of stridently anti-Musharraf interviews from what was described as an 'undisclosed location outside Lahore'. 'The police have ransacked my home and ill-treated my family members,' he told the journalist Zahid Hussain. 'Our aim is to continue the struggle and mobilise the youth of the country from behind the scenes. This move of Musharraf's will ignite militancy and extremism.' As several commentators noted, it was hard to dislike Imran in full flow. He was a born performer. But the crimes he pointed out about the Musharraf regime rang horribly true. He remarked that the general (who only now relinquished his army post) had engineered a 'Soviet-style coup' by 'locking up thousands of activists, imposing mass censorship [and] appointing a long-time crony as chief justice'. Imran himself played the small, humble man in this villainous conspiracy against the people. He felt for the impoverished and illiterate masses, he told reporters, and lambasted 'foreign and domestic tyrants [who] have destroyed our supreme court, every institution in the land and [are] doing business with crooks and criminals. Musharraf is going to sacrifice 160 million Pakistanis as if they were sheep ... He is worse than the Shah of Iran.' The stage was now set for a climactic showdown between the military hardman and the sports icon whom just five years earlier he had wanted as his prime minister.

Imran initially eluded the dragnet that accounted for some 3,000 other anti-government activists overnight, by 'climbing out of a window and jumping over the back wall of my family's house in Lahore when the cops burst in at 1.30 in the morning'. (He later told me that a sympathetic policeman had tipped him off when to expect their visit.) After that he spent 11 days moving between various cousins' houses and avoiding his cell phone. On 14 November, a picture of a somewhat haggard-looking Imran appeared on the front page of the London *Independent* under the headline 'MY LIFE IS IN DANGER'. The following day he broke cover to address a meeting at Lahore's Punjab University, with the intention of launching a 'young people's mass movement for freedom'. At the rally Imran was himself captured by students from the Jamaat-i-Islami political party, who held him in the nearby Centre for High Energy Physics for an hour and a half, and then handed him over to police at the university gates. In custody, he was charged under the Anti-Terrorism Act with inciting violence, calling for civil disobedience and spreading hatred. 'Most of the university audience had stood and applauded wildly when he first appeared,' Imran's friend Naeem-ul-Haque told me. 'Unfortunately, a small minority of them had been bribed, and it was that group that called the authorities.' Something of a tug-of-war had then ensued. The mob of students surrounding Imran had quickly become a mini-riot, with one group yelling for him to be allowed to finish his speech, and another group yelling the opposite, as Imran himself maintained a Zen-like calm at the centre of the storm. According to Naeem-ul-Haque, 'While waiting for the law, the fanatics pushed their prisoner into a nearby room, where some of them took the opportunity to rough him up a bit.' Imran was apparently undeterred, 'and even managed to deliver a short lecture to the goon squad when they finally arrived to take him away'.

At that Imran was driven across town to Kot Lakhpat prison, before being transferred overnight to a cell at Dera Ghazi Khan gaol in southern Punjab. It was among the very bleakest outposts of a penal system not known for its enlightenment. Looking understandably wan, Imran arrived at the prison gates in handcuffs and was admitted as a 'B-class' inmate, which essentially meant solitary confinement. 'I then made the mistake of saying that I wouldn't eat or drink anything while I was in captivity,' he told me. 'After 50 hours of this, I could hardly stand up.' The deputy superintendant of the gaol, a Mr Bakhsh, later questioned the extent of Imran's hunger strike, telling journalists, 'Khan had bread, eggs and fruit to eat every day for breakfast.' When two of Imran's middle-aged sisters arrived to visit him, they were reportedly manhandled, kicked and spat on by the guards.

Back in London, Jemima called in the couple's two children and told them that their father had been arrested and 'might be executed' as a terrorist. She and her younger son then joined a crowd of several hundred protesters which had formed outside Pakistan's High Commission. Eight-year-old Qasim Khan held up a picture of Imran with the words 'FREE MY ABA' [father]. Other such rallies took place in Washington DC, Madrid, Paris, Sydney and, somewhat improbably, Lodz, in

Poland. On 21 November, six days after the citizens' arrest at Punjab University, the state president magnanimously agreed to release 'our friend Imran Khan [and] all others held under the interim security provisions'. The BBC speculated that the gesture came about partly because the detention of the nation's greatest sporting hero was 'making waves internationally and causing embarrassment for the government'. By then even the American public had been exposed to a week of banner headlines and editorial comment on the subject. Like most of the overseas media in the cricket-playing world, the UK broadsheets treated the president's proclamation as an event to rank alongside the liberation of Nelson Mandela, with almost audible church bells and cannon fire. The domestic Pakistani reaction was more muted, although Imran was able to convene a rushed press conference to elaborate on his future political plans. Looking gaunt, unshaven, but impressively composed, he told reporters that both his party and that of Nawaz Sharif would be boycotting the scheduled January elections. 'I feel that even the filing of nomination papers amounts to a betrayal of the judiciary ... For 11 years I've been saying there can be no democracy or prosperity in Pakistan without an independent justice system. My whole philosophy is based on that ... This is the nation's supreme moment of truth,' Imran concluded.

According to this reading of events, Musharraf had now become little more than a 'classic tinpot fascist', propped up by corrupt foreign interests, who was 'clearly out [to] silence if not destroy his opponents'. If so, the president appears to have been curiously indulgent of a whole series of well-publicised protest meetings and rallies that took place even before his lifting of the state of emergency. On 1 December, Imran was able to address an overflow audience at the Lahore Press Club, where he again elaborated on his decision not to engage in the upcoming elections, 'a rigged poll which will please [only] those really leading the country, George W. Bush and his stooges at the Pentagon'. Two days later, he had nothing to say about the Americans, but otherwise repeated his main thesis. 'Musharraf has painted himself into a corner. He will get out of it only if we dignify this whole fiasco ... I won't ... I'm just not going to be part of it ... If you know something is a fraud, you should not take part. By participating, you legitimise the process.' A week later, Imran was indignant that both Benazir Bhutto and Nawaz Sharif had decided to contest the elections after all, the latter after apparently reneging on a prior agreement. 'It's a complete case of betrayal,' he thundered. 'They say the emergency rule is illegal and yet [they are] legitimising the whole process.' On 14 December, Imran told reporters, 'All [Bhutto] wants is power sharing to get her off the corruption charges against her ... Nawaz has been lured into the same trap. I think he's going to be discredited and decimated by massive vote rigging. He's going to take the biggest blow in the polls.' With both Pakistan's former premiers seeming to turn their backs on the All Parties Democratic Movement's decision of 24 November to 'rigorously boycott' the election, Imran was looking to some observers like an increasingly forlorn and isolated figure. 'Nobody likes him now but the people,' a Lahore newspaper commented.

Pakistan's 41-day state of crisis came to an end on 15 December, after the president had taken the opportunity to announce a series of six constitutional amendments that protected him from future prosecution. On 27 December, Benazir Bhutto was assassinated in a suicide attack in Rawalpindi, just as Imran had feared. Musharraf condemned the killing and once again placed the nation on a state of what he called 'red alert', with partial censorship re-imposed and demonstrations dispersed by club-wielding police. After hurried consultations, the elections were re-scheduled for 18 February 2008. A total of 517 people died in Pakistan as a result of terrorist or anti-terrorist activity in the first seven weeks of the new year.

Imran spent at least some of this uniquely turbulent period not in Pakistan, but in India, where he provided television analysis of his country's 1–0 loss in the latest Test series. He was to comment that the result could have been 3–0 to the tourists had their fast bowler Shoaib Akhtar 'applied himself', a remark that failed to impress Akhtar. On 29 December, two days after Benazir Bhutto's death, a somewhat unfortunate photograph of Imran wearing a pair of snug blue swimming trunks and relaxing on a sunlounger appeared in various outlets, with captions like 'Khan chills out in Mumbai'. Since being released from prison he had spent almost all of his working time continuing his attempt to drum up a boycott of the election. 'People have lost faith in Musharraf,' Imran told an Indian press conference. 'Who will now dare to address a political rally? Who will come to attend the rally? Nobody is safe in Pakistan.'

Indeed, there seemed to be a growing consensus that the president's record since mid-2002 had been a model of serial deviousness, disingenuity and political desperation, and had shown a towering contempt for the Pakistani voter. Nor was Musharraf quite as warmly embraced by his supporters in the war on terror as had once been the case; there is reliably said to have been 'fury' at the State Department when the Islamabad government announced a ceasefire with the Taliban in the frontier region, on the pretext of 'ensuring the integrity' of the forthcoming election. The truce was signed on the militants' side by the bin Ladenite commander Beitullah Mehsud, whom Musharraf had publicly blamed for Benazir Bhutto's death. Imran, for all that, was to take a certain amount of grief for what was variously described as his 'perverse' or 'churlish' decision to sit out one of his country's relatively rare spasms of democracy. To Bhutto's supporter Salman Taseer, the incoming governor of Punjab, 'Khan uses his foreign contacts, or actually his ex-wife's contacts, to come on CNN ... Every time he got the chance to make a decision he, without any doubt, made the wrong decision. He fights with every person; he takes pot shots at almost everyone. He hasn't left anyone in Pakistan alone. The drama of him tearing up his [nomination] papers was just ridiculous.' Demonstrators were occasionally to be seen milling around outside Imran's office in Islamabad. Sometimes they shouted that they were there to arrest him, and once, reportedly, to kill him, but quite often all they wanted was for him to accompany them to the president's palace and seize power. Even more than was the case with other Pakistani politicians, people seemed to either love or hate him. 'He wasn't one to excite tepid feelings,' Bhutto herself had once remarked. By 2008 Imran's cuttings file was a similarly bipolar collection comprising, on the one hand, pieces in which he held forth about the state of the world, and on the other, tabloid tales of his late-night misadventures. To *The Times* he was 'basically shy', to Pakistan's *Daily Times*, 'a bit of a peacock'.

As Imran went around in the early weeks of 2008 conducting his non-campaign, he seemed to become, if possible, even more fixated on Musharraf. The president's malign influence was everywhere, from destroying the judiciary to failing to prevent the fall in wheat prices on the global commodity markets. When Ricky Ponting's Australians began to have second thoughts about touring Pakistan in the spring, Imran blamed the head of state for that, too. 'Musharraf blindly follows the US in the war against terror and we are paying the price,' he told the AP. 'Because of him we are now at a stage where no one is ready to play cricket here.'* Even in 2006, it had seemed to an old playing

---

* After a series of concerns had been raised about the performance of match officials such as Steve Bucknor and Darrell Hair, the PCB now announced that it was considering scrapping Imran's hard-won system of appointing 'neutral' umpires in favour of those considered the best at the job. A full revolution on the subject had brought the board in a circle.

colleague of Imran's that 'he was a bit stuck' on the subject of the president, while *Today* found the relationship 'strangely symbiotic, [with] Musharraf taking the part of the great white whale to Khan's Ahab'.

With nothing currently to play for in Pakistan itself, Imran then left for another tour to drum up funds and support in the United States. For 11 or 12 days he bounced around the east coast with just one companion, an American Tehreek-e-Insaf organiser named Ali Zaidi, for the most part relying on local train services or budget rental cars to get about. The overall impression was some way removed from the popular image of a 'sporting Maharajah', to use *Newsweek*'s phrase. Imran told any US journalists willing to listen that Musharraf was a tyrant and a thug, and that all would be well again with Pakistan given a period of 'political stability'. Asked by the *Wall Street Journal* whether he aspired to run the country himself, Imran replied, 'It's not a question of aspirations. I know, God willing, one day I am going to succeed. And that's not very far away. I know that the people in Pakistan perceive me as probably the most credible leader.' During the tour Imran also attended meetings at the Centre for Strategic and International Studies, the National Press Club and Amnesty International, and even managed to secure an audience with Harry Reid, the Majority Leader of the US Senate. Ali Zaidi told me that the two of them had decided to forego meeting with anyone in the Bush administration 'as they are all on their way out'. Regrettably, Barack Obama was not available. A well-placed source added that Imran's meeting with Reid had in essence consisted of 'little more than a few glassy-eyed pleasantries' on the Nevada senator's part, followed by a bland joint statement. Reid was, however, personally 'quite impressed by Imran, who he seemed to think had been an international croquet star in his previous career'. One or two other Washington luminaries were apparently struck by the spectacle of a distinguished overseas politician travelling around the country carrying his own luggage, something of a novelty in a society whose elected representatives would wear togas if they felt they could get away with it. On his way home to Pakistan, Imran made a brief stop in London, where he joined Jemima and a small group of supporters standing in the rain in Whitehall to protest against a state visit by Pervez Musharraf. Musharraf waved cheerfully to the crowd as his car sped past them into Downing Street.

While they were in America, I managed to make contact with Imran and Ali Zaidi, and ultimately with a number of their non-travelling colleagues. The exchanges that followed weren't without their frustrations. At one point Zaidi (who went on to describe Imran as 'the most determined man I've ever met') rang me back late at night from a sleeper train travelling somewhere on the eastern seaboard, and a male American voice could be heard shouting at him in the background to 'turn the fucking phone off'. A second Tehreek-e-Insaf organiser explained that Imran felt there was 'too much shit' going on in the current Pakistani election, and that his strategy was therefore to 'let the rats fight among themselves' and 'regroup in 2009'. Somewhat later, a third party official contacted me and drew my attention to a mysterious Gospel of Barnabas (published in al-Madinah, and also in Leicester) as a key text in helping to explain some of the 'logical fallacies of Christianity', before going on to chat affably about the state of English cricket. I was aware, throughout my conversations with the three men, that they shared a deep and unaffected respect for Imran. 'It is perfectly possible history will judge the chairman as a most significant world leader,' one of them told me.

Although I'd been warned several times that 'the chairman' now rarely spoke about his past life, Imran himself proved to be an engaging interviewee and conversational all-rounder who slid smoothly from reminiscing fondly about his time at Oxford to denouncing the foreign policy of 'the Bush and Blair regimes'. The only difficulty lay in establishing contact with him in the first place. In addition to the strain of trying to mobilise 'Pakistan's only genuinely democratic political movement' while simultaneously running a major cancer hospital and organising long-haul visits to and from his young sons, it now emerged that the sense of timing Imran had shown in abundance when he was at the crease was less pronounced in his civilian life. Even after agreeing a mutually convenient time to speak, a caller was apt to receive one of three responses, according to the vagaries both of Imran's schedule and the Pakistani phone system.

The first, with a robotic voice intoning: 'Sorry. This number is powered off.'

The second, after a loud and highly animated exchange in Urdu could be heard going on for some moments in the background, culminating in a noise like that of a phone being repeatedly banged against a wall: 'The chairman is unavailable. Try later.'

The third, with Imran himself answering on the first ring: 'OK, go.'

No matter how early he started, the day was 'never long enough' for all the private meetings that party officials had requested, for all the phone calls that had to be made or answered. Each time Imran's assistant appeared in the doorway of the inner sanctum, more and more pages of the pad he held in his hand would be filled with urgent appeals for a moment of the Leader's time. The party was starting a nationwide campaign to provide subsidised bread to the poor. There were hospital fundraisers at which he had to put in appearances. An affiliated diagnostic centre was under construction in Karachi. That, too, needed money. In his spare time, Imran was supervising the building of Namal Technical College on 2.5 hectares (6 acres) of desert outside Mianwali as a joint venture with the University of Bradford, of which he was chancellor. So it seems reasonable to say, as he often did, that he was 'quite busy'. Even when he eventually got back to his new hilltop farm outside Islamabad, after his standard 12-hour day, there was rarely a night in which his mobile didn't ring at least once. Likewise in other houses in far-flung Pakistani towns, in the homes of provincial party workers and donors, a phone would ring in the early-morning darkness and a man, jolted out of sleep, would reach groggily for the receiver to hear the Leader's voice on the line. 'It's round the clock stuff,' Imran told me cheerfully.

On 6 February 2008, police turned back a small group of Tehreek-e-Insaf officials after they had flown in from Islamabad to address a rally in Karachi. The Sindh home minister Akhtar Zamin explained that Imran and his party were not welcome in his province because they were 'going around disrupting the upcoming elections and creating apathy ... If Khan does not want to participate it is fine, but he should not incite other people to do so. He will be free to visit Sindh after the polls have closed,' Mr Zamin announced. Three days later Jemima was, however, able to fly to Pakistan and to conduct an interview with the state president. Musharraf apparently assured her that he would act as a 'father figure' to the country's new prime minister, while expressing relief that 'I won't have to see him for weeks'. He reportedly then went on to describe the twice sacked Chief Justice Chaudhry as 'the dregs' and 'the scum of the earth'. (The president's office later complained that many of his remarks had been 'wilfully misrepresented [by] Mrs Khan'.) Back in London later in the month, Jemima was twice photographed leaving her car on her way in to restaurants without first having taken the precaution of donning any underwear. The editorial writer in the *Daily Times* wasn't impressed. 'What was she doing in Pakistan with that demure dupatta on her head, penning sanctimonious articles about her great conversion to Islam? It didn't take the same woman long to throw off the hijab and cavort in skimpy bikinis on French beaches with her man of the moment,' the paper concluded, harshly describing Jemima as a 'serial protester'.

In the election of 18 February the Bhuttos' PPP and Nawaz Sharif's PML (N) parties won a combined total of 168 seats, against 42 for the pro-Musharraf PML(Q). The president graciously announced that he accepted the result, and 'emphasis[ed] the need for harmonious coalition in the interest of peaceful governance'. He went on to blame the media as the main cause of his fall in popularity. Imran wasn't entirely satisfied, telling a news conference on 22 February that Musharraf should step down immediately and branding a speech by US Secretary of State Condoleezza Rice congratulating the Pakistani people on their free and fair elections as an 'intolerable interference in the internal affairs of the country'.*

A month later, the Bhuttos' supporter Yousaf Raza Gilani was sworn in as Pakistan's 26th prime minister. Mr Gilani, a former speaker of the National Assembly, had previously spent five years in gaol after being convicted of putting some 600 of his friends and constituents on the government payroll. After protracted discussions with his coalition partners, he and the president were eventually to free most of the judges arrested under the November 2007 state of emergency. Imran continued his dogged campaigning on the issue up to the end (and a year later, would still be calling – ultimately successfully – for the reinstatement of Chief Justice Chaudhry), walking at the head of a 'lawyers' march' on Islamabad on 9 March.

As a result of all these factors, the Tehreek-e-Insaf had maintained its independence but lost its representation in parliament. The journalist Karan Thapar asked Imran whether he regretted boycotting the election, as 'had you contested, you'd be a minister and your political career would get a boost, which it badly needs'. There was an understandable touch of asperity in his reply. 'I'm not in politics for my own career,' he told her. 'The Almighty has been kind to me and I have everything I want. I came in for a movement for justice ... For 11 years, my party was clamouring all over the place and no one paid any attention. But for the first time in history a chief justice takes a stand against a dicta-

* A member of President Musharraf's staff who had lived in London for several years in the 1960s and acquired a taste for British satire told me that, 'The way [Imran] carried on always reminded one a bit of the Peter Cook sketch about Greta Garbo going around the place shouting through a megaphone,"I want to be alone".'

tor and I had to stand with him.' Just as the new administration was being sworn in Imran was forced to leave Islamabad hurriedly and fly to Lahore, where his father, Ikramullah Khan, died on 20 March.

The Tehreek-e-Insaf party may have been a lonely one, but it was principled; and ambitious. In the spring of 2008, Imran continued to call for the removal of Musharraf and the repudiation of 'all US influence' in the region. A State Department briefing claiming that the Federally Administered Tribal Areas of Pakistan could lay claim to be 'the most prolific terrorist zone anywhere in the world' (the London, Madrid and Bali bombings all having been planned there) was 'total arrogance on [Washington's] part', Imran countered. 'We should shun the American dictation,' he announced at a press conference after a two-day party central executive committee meeting. 'This is intolerable ... A gross intrusion.' Imran wasn't finished yet: Musharraf was 'loathed', he remarked elsewhere, and this was largely due to his 'connivance' with the 'puppetmaster Bush'. Indeed, he was relentless on the subject. If Imran came across an inquisitive reporter, born in Mumbai, say, long after the foundation of modern Pakistan, he would deliver a short – or not so short – lecture on the history of American post-war meddling in the area from the formation of SEATO through to Washington's involvement in the 2008 elections, with descants on the likes of Messrs Bush and Rumsfeld. At least there was little mystery about what he believed in and wanted to do, as only the thinnest space appears between the Imran who made public statements and the man who engaged in exchanges with other politicians, between what he told press conferences and what he whispered to a party co-worker. As a Pakistani journalist familiar with both men remarked, 'forthrightness was one of Khan's most outstanding traits. Both he and Musharraf were apt to speak their minds.'

In the summer, Imran was back in London to raise money for the party, and to complain about the Americans. 'The United States is pounding the tribal areas, and innocent people are dying. There are no morals in this war,' he told the *Independent*. Imran also addressed a seminar on Indo-Pakistani relations as a last-minute replacement for Tariq Ali. He was 'doggedly on-track', according to his friend Syra Vahidy. 'I didn't speak with him after the session because he was surrounded by so many adoring fans, mostly women.' In July, Imran was back to chiding the 'US-led invasion of Afghanistan' in a series of interviews, at least some of which dwelt on his past life more than he might have wished. Later in the month he did agree to appear in a charity cricket match organised by Jemima's brothers, and enjoyed stands with both his sons. It was his first even semi-competitive appearance in some 10 years. 'I couldn't walk for days afterwards,' he admitted.

While Imran recuperated, Musharraf was facing the final curtain in Islamabad. He maintained his formidable sang-froid to the end. When the president boasted at the Labour Day celebrations on 1 May that Pakistan was more 'nationally productive' than at any time since 1999, the new prime minister, standing next to him, was seen apparently shaking with laughter. If nothing else, however, the regime was quite good at manufacturing propaganda: many overseas commentators bought Musharraf's line. Then, on 18 August, the president announced that he was resigning rather than face impeachment charges drawn up by the governing coalition. In a defiant speech, he said that he had believed it was his destiny to save Pakistan, helped by God, and that he had prevented it from becoming a terrorist state. 'I leave myself in the hands of the people,' he concluded. At that, Musharraf inspected a guard of honour outside his white palace in Islamabad, stepped into a black limousine and left for an undisclosed location. In Karachi, lawyers danced in jubilation.

Three weeks later, Pakistan's parliament elected a new head of state to replace caretaker president Muhammad Sumroo. The man with his finger on the country's nuclear trigger emerged as Asif Ali Zardari, the widower of Benazir Bhutto. As well as being linked both to the death of his brother-in-law Murtaza and to the oligarchic looting of the Pakistani exchequer – although formally cleared of all charges – Zardari now faced questions about the state of his mental health. In a corruption case brought against him by the Musharraf government, Zardari's own lawyers told a London court in 2007 that he had suffered from dementia, depression and other psychological problems. They claimed that he was traumatised as a result of years spent in various Pakistani prisons, where he had reportedly been tortured on the orders of his political opponents. In Pakistan, Zardari had long been known as anything from Mr Ten Percent to Mr Thirty Percent, and his alleged corruption was widely regarded as the reason for the early demise of the family dynasty's two governments. In interviews, he described his ascent to power as 'revenge' for his wife's killing.

Musharraf's departure from the scene brought no immediate relief to the vast majority of the Pakistani people, who were now witnessing both rampant inflation and the collapse of their currency. Even as

Zardari assumed office, a bomb blast claimed at least 22 lives in Peshawar. On 3 September, gunmen attempted to assassinate the new prime minister as he passed by in his motorcade. A fortnight later, another explosion, this time at the Mariott Hotel in Islamabad, killed 45 and left 200 injured. Most reports blamed the outrages on either al-Qaeda or 'Talibanised sectors of the Pakistani armed forces' impatient for control of the country's remote frontier provinces. Zardari did, however, take certain steps towards ending his country's time-honoured role as a client state of the Western allies. On 4 September 2008, US special forces launched a six-hour combined air-ground assault to destroy terrorist sanctuaries in the tribal areas. The unanimous reaction of Pakistan's newly seated parliament was to call on its government to repel any future such raids with military force. Pakistan's army chief, General Ashfaq Kayani, agreed, declaring that his country's territorial integrity 'would be defended at all costs'. When the US military attempted another ground attack 12 days later, employing armed helicopters, it was forced to retreat after coming under sustained fire from Pakistan's army. The next day, the president's office in Islamabad issued a press release announcing its policy on US incursions: 'The orders are clear ... open fire.'

Ironically, Imran himself, after waging a dogged and sometimes lonely campaign over several years for Musharraf's departure, was apparently unenthused by many of these developments. When I asked him about the president's exit, he told me that Pakistan's ruling elite 'will always protect themselves ... It's very much business as usual here. One guy will obligingly scratch the other guy's back.' Seeming to confirm this thesis, Asif Ali Zardari announced late in 2008 that he had no objection to his predecessor as president 'put[ting] his feet up in Pakistan'. Musharraf took him at his word by moving into a luxury villa, complete with a swimming pool and strawberry bed, in the suburbs of Islamabad. It was a depressing scenario for anyone who had fought as long and passionately for justice as Imran had, although it's just possible that there might have been deeper, psychological factors that contributed to his dark mood. An admiring friend told me, 'When Immy begins to feel pleasantly relaxed or playfully enjoying, I think, some danger sign goes up, some inner commandment says no, and he falls back on his constantly replenished list of problems to solve.'

* * *

Compared with certain other Pakistani international cricketers of his era, characterised by Omar Kureishi as being 'all gold medallions and mediocrity', Imran (who, after all, had actually won the World Cup) was practically an ascetic. And certainly by the standards of Islamabad's political class, few of whom took their call for national self-sacrifice too personally, he struck even his most vocal critics as being almost excessively frugal: when he travelled abroad he took 'one battered suitcase' with him, which, as mentioned, he carried himself. Even so, as he often said, he had to make a living. Anyone thinking that Imran merely waited around for rupees to fall into his lap would have only a partial understanding of the man. Now that he had taken himself out of the National Assembly his main forum was the world's television and radio studios, where he held forth on everything from Pakistan's literacy rate to the state of her fast bowling. As Imran remarked to the *Independent* in November 2008, he could earn enough in 30 days' work as a TV sports pundit 'to run my kitchen for the rest of the year'. Most, but not all, of the money came from contracts in India.

As a broadcaster, Imran had all the natural equipment: lucidity, expertise, an eye for visual detail and a mouth that moved as fast as his mind. He wasn't shy of expressing an opinion. Anyone he thought guilty of under-performing, be it a callow debutant or a wizened pro like Inzamam, could expect a tongue-lashing of regal proportions. An informal poll conducted by *Cricket Lore* magazine rated him the game's fourth most popular celebrity commentator – qualified fame, perhaps, but better than unqualified obscurity. One passing concern raised by a number of respondents was that Imran could occasionally seem uncharacteristically obsequious towards an older retired player such as Ian Chappell, 'behav[ing] as a favourite nephew might towards a rich and ailing uncle who had hinted there might be something rather good for him in his will'.* About the only other criticism that could be levelled against his microphone technique was that it was sometimes prone to a certain dour humourlessness: he wasn't one to josh around about streakers or chocolate cakes. 'We had Imran up in the Channel 4 box a few years back,' Mark Nicholas recalled in 2009. 'Technical insights were good, but otherwise there wasn't much aptitude. Dermot Reeve took the piss out of him during an interview, doing an impression of the great

* The phrase was metaphorical: Imran had no financial expectation of Mr Chappell, who continues to enjoy rude good health.

man that seemed disrespectful and he didn't take kindly to. Actually Dermot holds him in great affection, but it went over badly and Imran never came back.'

The troubled history of Pakistan's national sport had taken another abrupt turn in April 2008, when the PCB banned their team's strike bowler Shoaib Akhtar for five years after finding him guilty of repeated breaches of discipline. The board had already imposed a two-year probation on Akhtar after he hit his colleague Mohammad Asif with a bat before the start of a Twenty20 World Cup match. Imran came down firmly on the side of the player. Apparently the problem was once again due to Musharraf, whose personal appointee as chairman of the PCB, Nasim Ashraf, a US-trained medical doctor with little or no previous experience of sports administration, had turned that body 'into a sort of banana republic'. Ashraf left his post that August, on the same day that Musharraf announced his own resignation; the Lahore High Court later suspended Shoaib's ban pending a final resolution, but upheld a fine against him of 7 million rupees. Imran expressed cautious optimism (perhaps wisely, in the light of subsequent developments) about Allen Stanford's so-called 'bash, dash and dazzle' version of the game, but reminded interviewers that there would always be a place for the unexpurgated five-day Test, with its unique emphasis not only on fitness and skill, but on 'discipline, intelligence and character'. Sadly, there seemed to be little immediate prospect of Pakistan hosting any more Tests themselves after the events of March 2009, when gunmen opened fire on Sri Lanka's touring team in Lahore, killing eight people, six of them policemen, and putting cricket back on the world's front pages for all the wrong reasons.

Politically, Imran admitted to being 'in the wilderness' after the events of 2007–8. It in no way deterred him. The most significant aspect of his first 18 months as an ex-MP wasn't so much what he said as the sheer frequency with which he appeared in print or on the air. Imran seems to have been a believer in the theory that providing years of accessibility to influential newsmen is like having money in the bank, allowing the prudent depositor to obtain shelter, or at least a fair hearing, on rainy days. Even for a man not always at his happiest talking to the media, that still held true. None of the lower arts of politics caps the ability to win favourable coverage, and the nation's former cricket captain was a past master of the art. He was everywhere: enthusing about Barack Obama to a Press Club audience in Paris, whistle-stopping back through America, empathising with victims of the fire that devastated Rawalpindi's Ghakkan Plaza in December 2008, embracing the Pakistani nuclear physicist A.Q. Khan (alleged, by some, to have sold weapons technology to North Korea), or going door to door on the dusty streets of Peshawar in his latest recruitment drive for the party. As of mid-2009, the Tehreek-e-Insaf had some 26,000 members worldwide and, Imran reiterated, was thus 'the fastest growing popular movement in Pakistan'. To him, there was a strong correlation between politics and religion, both essentially being about personal liberation. 'The greatest impact of turning to God for me was that I lost all fear of human beings ... Since this is a transitory world where we prepare for the eternal one, I broke out of the self-imposed prisons such as the phobia of growing old, materialism, ego, what people say and so on ... Faith frees you, it drives away your fears – fear of dying, fear of losing your wealth, fear of humiliation; all of that goes ... God willing, everything passes. We will prevail ...'

The words were vintage Imran, even if, to some, they had lost the kind of power they once had. He'd connected millions of Pakistanis with a common political language – the key word being justice, both for themselves and the nation – but after 13 years he seemed to be repeating himself, as was the case in a year's end speech he gave to party workers on 27 December 2008. The Tehreek-e-Insaf would become a major political force 'within the next six months', Imran insisted, before roundly condemning the 'base' Zardari administration, much as he had its predecessor, for 'enslaving the judiciary'. Nor was the goal of Pakistani economic self-sufficiency any closer to hand than it had been under Musharraf. In the spring of 2009, Zardari was seeking oil concessions from Saudi Arabia, a £2 billion loan from the World Bank and the IMF, and a £500 million credit line from Britain's Department for Overseas Development. Indeed, no international capital reserve seemed entirely free of Pakistan's attention, at a time when their head of state enjoyed a personal fortune estimated at between £2.5 billion and £6 billion.

This should have been the moment for a figure of national unity to emerge. But Imran's political balancing act – giving rein to a consistent and obviously deep-felt moral disgust with the rhetoric of power, while going out of his way to assure Western leaders, journalists and financial benefactors that he was a man they could do business with – appeared to be only partly successful. He couldn't seem to entirely satisfy either world. Imran remained a much treasured national icon, but one who was also apparently destined to be one of those essential voices of dissent primarily heard from the political sidelines. A stubborn man by nature, he was, perhaps, well suited to play the role of a sort of 'bouffant prophet', to quote one former cricket colleague (which, again, is in no way to deny his unwavering sincerity and devotion to the cause), booming down his twin messages of imminent disaster for the elites, and popular vindication for the party, from his hilltop eyrie. 'I have absolutely no doubt that we will succeed in either the next election – or the next election after that,' Imran again declared in 2009. An interviewer from the *Independent* asked him if he was looking for another wife to stand by him in the long struggle. 'Not really,' Imran said. 'No. The main reason which affected my [first] marriage was my political life and commitments. Couldn't give it enough time. I am so overstretched ... So a wife is not something that is on my agenda right now. Whether it will ever be ... I don't even know that.'

To accuse Imran of persistence would be like accusing Stalin of show trials or Bill Clinton of priapism. It's the very heart and essence of his being. Some people think both his message and his speaking style a shade on the monotonous side, but no one doubts his resilience or his personal fortitude. Although he's taken to sometimes wearing a bullet-proof vest when appearing in public because of what happened to Benazir Bhutto, 'It won't do you any good if they blow you up,' he acknowledges blandly. 'It doesn't matter what precautions you take, they prepare accordingly. Benazir had security. Her brother had two wagon loads of commandos. Not one moved. All of them were shot dead.'

If personally unassuming, he was also the head of a large, hierarchical organisation. An advance-ticket seller at Lord's assured me that he had once taken a call in which an imperious woman's voice had ordered '"Two seats for Sardar Khan, please." Sardar Khan, indeed. The next day I looked up and saw a familiar face at the window. I said, "Oh, hello Immy. How've you been keeping?" We chatted away. Smashing bloke. Very down to earth. He wasn't any "Sardar Khan" to me.'

For her readers on the *Daily Telegraph*, Elizabeth Grice described the middle-aged Imran as 'lean and deeply creased, but still recognisable as the leonine figure of old'. The Jaggeresque haircut survived (the result, according to the journalist Khalid Hasan, of some discreet transplant surgery), which along with the bespoke Savile Row suits contributed to a sleeker personal style than might have been thought from some of his public remarks of late. At first glance, he could have been taken for someone who made a living on the entrepreneurial fringes of the pop-music industry. It was when he took off his sunglasses and propped them up in his hair that you noticed the dark eyes and intense face that looked as though it had its worries. When he smiled, which he did rarely, it was an 'electrifying experience', even the unsentimental General Zia had once allowed; 'the space all around him was physically brightened.' Imran's voice was a slow, rich, full-bodied instrument that sounded as though it had spent years marinating in port. One journalist wrote that he spoke 'in the measured tones of someone used to being listened to'. Overall, at 56, he remained quite a formidable proposition.

The reaction to Imran's stubborness, or principled intransigence, at least among non-partisan voters, was mixed. Karachi's *Friday Times* ran a regular feature satirising him as 'Im the Dim', while by mid-2009 he was able to enjoy an unusually well-designed and continually refreshed website dedicated to his activities. Called 'Khan Artist', it was a paean to Imran's alleged shallowness and hypocrisy. (The authors of the site might well have benefited from the services of a good fact-checker.) Elsewhere the conventional wisdom was that after 13 years and three elections Imran remained a political outsider (a description he might not have shunned), whose enormous fame had never quite converted into the constantly predicted national breakthrough. Thus, said *Today*, the reason he attracted even such support as he did was 'simply down to his residual glory as Asia's greatest ever sportsman'. But a funny thing happened whenever Imran addressed a rally or even a spontaneous public meeting, as he did in the main square in Peshawar on a cold December evening in 2008. On that occasion he spoke for no more than six minutes, employed few rhetorical flourishes, and other than appealing for more recruits to the Tehreek-e-Insaf, said little of substance. Several thousand spectators cheered him wildly, and a cursory glance around the audience, most of whom were in their teens or twenties, suggested that they were there to do something more than merely salute a cricketer who had retired nearly two decades earlier. It was the searingly obvious moral conviction that came through, and the equally unmistakable dedication to the job in hand. During the evening's follow-up speeches, which lasted an hour and three-quarters, Imran politely declined a seat and stood to one side in the steady rain, frequently waving his cap, nodding and clapping enthusiastically. When he finally left the scene there was a long roar of appreciation from the crowd, which went on for more than 20 minutes after he was no longer there to enjoy it. President Zardari had never been cheered like this.

Though politics was Imran's consuming passion, it still wasn't his whole being. Seeing his sons' interest in the game, he laid them out a cricket pitch at his 14-hectare (35-acre) mountainside farm, where he enjoyed the 'crystal clear days and cold, still nights', sometimes broken by the sound of jackals. The place was about as good a refuge as he could hope for from the thunderous events of recent years in Pakistan. A journalist once asked Imran a rather leading question about his social life, and after a pause he responded: 'It's basically just me and my boys up there on top of the plateau, which I like to call my paradise.' *Then* he smiled.

Career Highlights

Full name Imran Khan Niazi
Born 5 October 1952, Lahore, Punjab
Current age 56 years
Major teams Pakistan, Lahore, Worcestershire, Oxford University, Sussex, New South Wales
Batting Right-hand bat
Bowling Right-arm fast
Relations Cousin Javed Burki, Cousin Majid Khan
Children Sulaiman, Qasim

LANDMARKS

Test debut: England v Pakistan, Birmingham, 3–8 June 1971
Final Test: Pakistan v Sri Lanka, Faisalabad, 2–7 January 1992
ODI debut: England v Pakistan, Nottingham, 31 August 1974
Final ODI: England v Pakistan, Melbourne, 25 March 1992
Best Test match batting: 136, Pakistan v Australia, Adelaide, 19 January 1990
Best Test match bowling: 14 for 116, Pakistan v Sri Lanka, Lahore, 22 March 1982
First-class career: 1969/70–1991/92

BATTING AND FIELDING

	M	I	NO	Runs	HS	Av	100	50	Ct	St
Tests	88	126	25	3807	136	37.69	6	18	28	0
ODIs	175	151	40	3709	102*	33.41	1	19	36	0
First-class	382	582	99	17771	170	36.79	30	93	117	0

BOWLING

	M	I	Runs	Wkts	BBI	BBM	Av	Econ	SR	5w	10w
Tests	88	142	8258	362	8/58	14/116	22.81	2.54	53.7	23	6
ODIs	175	153	4844	182	6/14	6/14	26.61	3.89	40.9	1	0
First-class	382	–	28726	1287	8/34	–	22.32	2.63	50.8	70	13

TEST MATCH HUNDREDS

Runs	4s	6s	SR	Pos	Opp	Venue	Start Date
136	10	0	37.67	5	v Australia	Adelaide	19 Jan 1990
135*	14	5	58.69	8	v India	Madras	3 Feb 1987
123	13	0	61.80	7	v West Indies	Lahore	24 Nov 1980
118	11	1	58.70	6	v England	The Oval	6 Aug 1987
117	9	5	96.69	7	v India	Faisalabad	3 Jan 1983
109*	17	1	74.65	6	v India	Karachi	15 Nov 1989

10-WICKET MATCHES

Overs	Mdns	Runs	Wkts	Econ	Av	SR	Opp	Venue	Start Date
52.2	11	116	14	2.21	8.28	22.4	v Sri Lanka	Lahore	22 Mar 1982
45.7	9	165	12	2.69	13.75	30.5	v Australia	Sydney	14 Jan 1977
32.2	10	79	11	2.44	7.18	17.6	v India	Karachi	23 Dec 1982
37.2	2	121	11	3.24	11.00	20.3	v West Indies	Georgetown	2 Apr 1988
55.5	15	180	11	3.22	16.36	30.4	v India	Faisalabad	3 Jan 1983
38.1	8	77	10	2.01	7.70	22.9	v England	Leeds	2 Jul 1987

TEST CAREER SUMMARY – BATTING

	Period	M	I	NO	Runs	HS	Av	100	50	0
v Australia	1976–1990	18	28	5	862	136	37.47	1	5	2
v England	1971–1987	12	17	3	500	118	35.71	1	2	2
v India	1978–1989	23	29	8	1091	135*	51.95	3	3	0
v New Zealand	1976–1989	7	9	3	308	71	51.33	0	3	0
v Sri Lanka	1982–1992	10	10	1	271	93*	30.11	0	2	2
v West Indies	1977–1990	18	33	5	775	123	27.67	1	3	2
in Australia	1976–1990	13	23	3	733	136	36.65	1	4	2
in England	1971–1987	12	17	3	500	118	35.71	1	2	2
in India	1979–1987	10	15	3	478	135*	39.83	1	2	0
in New Zealand	1979–1989	4	5	2	203	71	67.66	0	2	0
in Pakistan	1976–1992	38	47	13	1540	123	45.29	3	8	3
in Sri Lanka	1986–1986	3	4	0	48	33	12.00	0	0	1
in West Indies	1977–1988	8	15	1	305	47	21.78	0	0	0

TEST CAREER SUMMARY – BOWLING

	Period	M	I	Runs	Wkts	BBI	BBM	Av	Econ	SR	5w	10w
v Australia	1976–1990	18	29	1598	64	6/63	12/165	24.96	2.40	62.4	3	1
v England	1971–1987	12	19	1158	47	7/40	10/77	24.63	2.38	62.1	4	1
v India	1978–1989	23	38	2260	94	8/60	11/79	24.04	2.67	54.0	6	2
v New Zealand	1976–1989	7	13	874	31	5/106	6/109	28.19	2.39	70.6	1	0
v Sri Lanka	1982–1992	10	14	673	46	8/58	14/116	14.63	2.25	38.8	3	1
v West Indies	1977–1990	18	29	1695	80	7/80	11/121	21.18	2.91	43.6	6	1
in Australia	1976–1990	13	20	1283	45	6/63	12/165	28.51	2.53	67.5	3	1
in England	1971–1987	12	19	1158	47	7/40	10/77	24.63	2.38	62.1	4	1
in India	1979–1987	10	15	757	27	5/63	9/130	28.03	2.74	61.2	2	0
in New Zealand	1979–1989	4	7	453	17	5/106	6/109	26.64	2.11	75.4	1	0
in Pakistan	1976–1992	38	59	3131	163	8/58	14/116	19.20	2.44	47.0	10	3
in Sri Lanka	1986–1986	3	6	270	15	4/69	6/125	18.00	2.32	46.4	0	0
in West Indies	1977–1988	8	16	1206	48	7/80	11/121	25.12	3.29	45.7	3	1

Bibliography

Abbas, Zaheer with Foot, David, *Zed,* Kingswood, Surrey: World's Work, 1983

Atherton, Mike, *Opening Up,* London: Hodder and Stoughton, 2003

Botham, Ian, *My Autobiography,* London: CollinsWillow, 1994

Hadlee, Richard, *Rhythm and Swing,* London: Souvenir Press, 1989

Khan, Imran, *Imran: The Autobiography,* London: Pelham Books, 1983

Khan, Imran, *All Round View,* London: Chatto & Windus, 1988

Khan, Imran, *Indus Journey,* London: Chatto & Windus, 1990

Mason, Ronald, *Sing all a Green Willow,* London: Epworth Press, 1967

Miandad, Javed, *Cutting Edge,* Karachi: Oxford University Press, 2003

Musharraf, Pervez, *In the Line of Fire,* New York: Free Press, 2006

Noman, Omar, *Pride and Passion,* Karachi: Oxford University Press, 1998

Sandford, Christopher, *Tom Graveney,* London: Witherby, 1992

Sobers, Garry, *My Autobiography,* London: Headline, 2002

Tennant, Ivo, *Imran Khan,* London: Witherby, 1994

Wisden Cricketers' Almanack, 1972–2009

Sources and Chapter Notes

Author's note: Endnotes are a necessary evil in a book like this. The following pages show at least the formal interviews, conversations and/or other source material mined in the three years beginning in May 2006. While Imran Khan and I spoke on a number of occasions, our main interviews took place on 9 June, 7 September and 26 November 2008. He had no editorial control over the book. As well as those listed, I also spoke to a number of people who prefer not to be named. Where sources asked for anonymity – often, but not always, citing some difference of opinion with Imran dating from his cricket days – every effort was made to get them to go on the record. Where this wasn't possible, I've used the words 'a colleague' or 'a critic', etc., as appropriate. Once or twice, I've resorted to the formula of an alias. (The reader should be assured that every fact stated in the book has been sourced, and for obvious reasons corroborated to the very fullest extent possible, before publication.) No acknowledgement thus appears of the help, encouragement and kindness I got from a number of quarters, some of them, as they say, household names. The unusually volatile exchange rate for the Pakistani rupee against both sterling and the US dollar has been adjusted throughout the text to reflect its value at the time.

CHAPTER ONE

For an overview of Pakistani Test cricket I relied on my own memory and occasional commentary and/or journalism on the matches, and more pertinently on reports appearing in the *Daily Mail,* the *Daily Telegraph, Dawn, The Times* and *Wisden,* and the late and much missed *Cricketer International,* among many other such periodicals. It's a pleasure, too, to acknowledge both the CricketArchive website and Omar

Noman's magisterial history of Pakistan's national game, *Pride and Passion*, as sources. I also made use of previously published articles that appeared in the (Karachi) *Star*, the *Globe* and the *New York Times*, as well as in Javed Miandad's memoir *Cutting Edge;* the last, albeit labouring under its author's note of offended pride, is particularly vivid.

Imran Khan's quotes beginning 'Pakistan's cricketers are treated like Islam ... and 'Too much is at the whim of powerful individuals ...' are from Ivo Tennant's admirable *Imran Khan* and Imran's *The Autobiography*, respectively.

CHAPTER TWO

For events from 1952 to 1973 I'm grateful both to the subject of the book and to two of his relatives who enlightened me on his family background, as well as to others who spoke to me of Imran's experience in growing up in the newly minted Pakistan, notably Naeem-ul-Haque, Antao Hassan, the late Omar Kureishi, Haroun Rashid and Yusuf Salahudin. My hero (I admit it) and friend, the former England stumper John Murray, recalled the colourful circumstances of the International XI's tour of Pakistan of March 1971, which first brought Imran to national attention. Simon Porter at Oxford University CC and Mark Newton at Worcestershire CCC were invaluable in helping piece together Imran's time at those two clubs; I'm particularly grateful to the latter for his hospitality. It's perhaps a small public service, too, finally to put Imran's correct birth date on record: 5 October 1952, not 25 November 1952 as given by *Wisden*, among others.

As well as the above, primary sources included Qamar Ahmed, the late Les Ames, Fareshteh Aslam, Dickie Bird, Judy Flanders, George Galloway, Tom Graveney, Asif Iqbal, Vic Marks, the late Wasim Raja, Dicky Rutnagur, Mike Selvey, Fred Titmus. I should particularly acknowledge the exceptionally patient and helpful Rev. Mike Vockins. Basil D'Oliveira, an inspirational cricketer now, sadly, not in the best of health, gave me his views on Imran and a great number of other subjects in the course of a long and memorable lunch in Worcester at Christmas 1989.

Imran Khan's quotes beginning 'Once when I was thirteen ...', 'The English team was thought to be invincible ...', the former very slightly amended in light of what he told me, are both from his book *All Round View;* Imran's quotes beginning 'I would sprint ...', 'I was by far the best batsman; I saw myself as the next Bradman ...', 'Pakistan is the only country in the world ...' and '... sat talking about me ...' are all from *The Autobiography;* Imran's quote 'The Niazis continued to think ...' is from his *Indus Journey.* The 'One of the first English words I learned ...' quote is from Zaheer Abbas's *Zed.* The 'On [that] tour I developed a strict routine ...' quote is from Javed Miandad's *Cutting Edge.* Simon Jenkins's 'In no other ...' quote appeared in the *Guardian* of 11 January 2008. The story of the adolescent Imran punching a heckler appears in Ivo Tennant's *Imran Khan.*

CHAPTER THREE

Interviews and/or taped conversations, some conducted at the time of my earlier biographies, took place with Qamar Ahmed, Jeffrey Archer, Johnny Barclay, Richie Benaud, Dickie Bird, Geoff Boycott, Mike Brearley, the late Denis Compton, Dar, Ted Dexter, the late and irreplaceable Godfrey Evans, Tony Gill, Antao Hassan, the late Reg Hayter, Alastair Hignell, Asif Iqbal, Javed Kureishi, the late Chris Lander, Neil Lenham, Vic Marks, John Murray, Mark Nicholas, the late Kerry Packer, Paul Parker, Tony Pigott, the late Harold Pinter, Nigel Popplewell, Derek Pringle, Abdul Qadeer, the late Wasim Raja, Tim Rice, Mike Selvey, Fred Titmus, Rev. Mike Vockins and Ali Zaidi. Imran himself spoke to me about this phase of his career in our interview of 9 June 2008. It was a particular pleasure to revisit the County Ground, Hove (my thanks to Hugh Griffiths of Sussex CCC), where I first watched county cricket while incarcerated at a local prep school 40 years ago.

Imran Khan's quotes beginning 'My overall performance on the tour ...', 'I was bullied into bowling medium pace ...', '... a general lack of resolve ...' and '... a major feature of Packer cricket ...' are from *All Round View.* His quotes beginning 'I've always hated taking a beating ...', 'I had to sleep on Glenn Turner's floor ...', '... greeted me with a mixture of hostility, surprise and amusement ...' and 'For the first time in my life ...' are all from *The Autobiography.* Imran's quote beginning 'I was thought to have a superior attitude ...' and the sentence beginning 'If Javed told Imran it was eleven o'clock ...' are both from Ivo Tennant's *Imran Khan.* Javed Miandad's quote beginning '... the combination of pace, guile and reverse swing ...' appears in *Cutting Edge,* as does the alleged story about Qamar Ahmed.

CHAPTER FOUR

Imran's early years at Sussex and the roller-coaster of his post-Packer, pre-captaincy Test career were recalled by, among others, Fareshteh Aslam, Trevor Bailey, Johnny Barclay, Richie Benaud, Dar, Dave Davies, Gus Farley, Judy Flanders, Tony Gill, David Gower, Hugh Griffiths, Antao Hassan, Alastair Hignell, Asif Iqbal, Chris Kelly, the late Chris Lander, Vic Marks, Jonathan Mermagen, Linda Morris, Mark Nicholas, Paul Parker, Tony Pigott, Nigel Popplewell, Derek Pringle, Abdul Qadeer, the late Wasim Raja, Dicky Rutnagur, Yusuf Salahudin, Mike Selvey, the late Peter Smith. I'm also grateful to the source, anonymous but then well placed, at the Pakistan cricket board. Imran's friend Syra Vahidy was also more than generous with her time, contacts and recollections; it was one of the book's major pleasures to meet her in London.

For secondary source material I should acknowledge the British Library, *Chronicles*, CricInfo, Cricket Archive, the Public Record Office, the *Daily Mail, Daily Telegraph, Dawn, The Times, Today* and *Wisden*.

Imran's quotes beginning '[Arnold Long was an] extremely affable man ...' and '... [the selectors] thought our regular first eleven ...' are from *The Autobiography,* in the latter case slightly amended by what Imran told me. A small number of quotes attributed here to Imran, among them those beginning '... cricket fever engulfed ...' and '... everything went overboard ...' are an amalgam of lines from *The Autobiography* and my own interviews of Imran, and I hope faithfully convey the language and spirit of both sources. Imran's quote beginning 'My father insisted that we ...' is from *All Round View;* his quote beginning 'Once, when I went out to bat ...' is from the *Sunday Times* of 1 October 2006. Javed Miandad's quotes beginning '... a plot played out by a handful of players ...' and 'I came to believe ...' are both from *Cutting Edge.* The quote beginning 'his wider appeal ...' is from Omar Noman's *Pride and Passion.*

CHAPTER FIVE

I was semi-gainfully employed as a cricket writer and occasional broadcaster in the period 1979–83, and so am to blame for at least some of the match reports here. *Wisden* and CricketArchive were both invaluable in adding the flesh of exact dates and scores to the bones of personal memory. The late John Arlott, while not one to exude millions of volts of synthetic charm, was a kind, generous, slightly papal senior colleague who introduced me to several of the leading players of the time. I'm also grateful to the late Brian Johnston, Peter Baxter of the BBC, who gave me a brief on-air trial in 1982, Tony Lewis and Neil Durden-Smith. Phil Oppenheim and John Derrick also gave me a cricket job of sorts on the late *London Evening Globe* before both went on to greater things; I'm grateful.

Imran's double life as an English county pro and Pakistan's inspirational Test captain was crisply brought home by, among others, Jeffrey Archer, Fareshteh Aslam, Trevor Bailey, Richie Benaud, Dickie Bird, Geoff Boycott, Mike Brearley, Dar, Ted Dexter, the late Godfrey Evans, Judy Flanders, Tony Gill, David Gower, Naeem-ul-Haque, Antao Hassan, the late Len Hutton, Asif Iqbal, Vic Marks, Jonathan Mermagen, Linda Morris, John Murray, Mark Nicholas, Paul Parker, Derek Pringle, the late Wasim Raja, Mike Selvey, the late Peter Smith. I'm also grateful for his help to my old headmaster Dennis Silk, a former distinguished chairman of the TCCB and president of MCC.

Imran's quotes beginning 'Sussex said that the rules applied …', 'Our first wicket fell…' and 'I admire Ian …' are from *The Autobiography;* his quote beginning 'On paper a 2–1 defeat …' is an amalgam of that source and my own interview of Imran. Imran's quotes beginning 'When I reached the age of thirty …' and '… cricket [was] a job …' are from *All Round View.* Javed Miandad's quotes beginning '… when I received word …', 'When Imran became the captain …' and '… whom he ignored for the first two Tests …' are all from *Cutting Edge.* Imran's quote beginning 'if I was written about …' and the peerless description of Emma Sergeant's 'dreamy, pre-Raphaelite beauty …' are both from Ivo Tennant's *Imran Khan.* Ian Botham's quotes beginning 'I could see that the quarter-seam …' and 'If Constant made a mistake …' are from Botham's *My Autobiography* and *The Botham Report* (CollinsWillow, 1997), respectively. Air Marshal Nur Khan's quote beginning 'Imran's name was suggested …' appears in Omar Noman's *Pride and Passion.*

CHAPTER SIX

The events of 1984–6 were vividly recalled by, among others, Qamar Ahmed, Jeffrey Archer, Fareshteh Aslam, Johnny Barclay, Richie Benaud, Dickie Bird, Geoff Boycott, Dar, Dave Davies, Ted Dexter, George Galloway, Tony Gill, David Gower, Naeem-ul-Haque, Debbie Harris, the late Reg Hayter, Alastair Hignell, the late Len Hutton, the late Chris Lander, Neil Lenham, Vic Marks, Tahir Nawaz, Mark Nicholas, Paul Parker, Tony Pigott, the late Harold Pinter, Nigel Popplewell, Derek Pringle, the late Wasim Raja, Dicky Rutnagur, Mike Selvey, Alex Stacey. Jonathan Mermagen, probably Imran's closest British friend, very kindly answered all my questions in a lengthy phone interview. Imran himself spoke to me about this phase of his career in our conversation of 7 September 2008. I visited Draycott Avenue and a number of the other haunts associated with him in London.

For secondary sources I should credit *Chronicles*, CricketArchive, *the Cricketer International* (and its benevolent former czar, my friend Peter Perchard), the *Daily Express, Daily Mail*, the *Observer, Daily Telegraph, The Times* and *Wisden*. Medical insight into Imran's various injuries was provided by the initially elusive but eventually welcoming Dr Wallace Hodges; I'm grateful. A small number of Steve Waugh's quotes come from his book *Out of My Comfort Zone* (Viking, 2005). My own memory is to blame for some of the accounts of the English county circuit.

Imran Khan's quotes beginning 'I was extremely depressed …', 'a small-minded, self-righteous man …' and 'The hostility was unrelenting …' are all from *All Round View*. Emma Sergeant's quotes beginning 'The things that mattered to him didn't matter …' and 'Imran saw the shattering end …' are from Ivo Tennant's *Imran Khan*. Javed Miandad's quotes beginning 'I had the choice of continuing …' and '… the whole team was there …' are from *Cutting Edge*. The Omar Noman quote beginning 'Meaningless hundreds …' is from his book *Pride and Passion*, which I again recommend to anyone with an interest in either Pakistani international cricket or politics, in so far as there's a difference between the two.

I again made use of a source, who prefers anonymity, with first-hand knowledge of the Pakistan board.

CHAPTER SEVEN

Primary sources included Aslam Anwar, Jeffrey Archer, Fareshteh Aslam, Johnny Barclay, Dickie Bird, Geoff Boycott, Melinda Cooksey, Dar, Ted Dexter, Judy Flanders, George Galloway, Tony Gill, David Gower, Janet Harris, Sarah Jones, the late Chris Lander, Neil Lenham, Jonathan Mermagen, Linda Morris, Mark Nicholas, Paul Parker, Peter Perchard, Tony Pigott, Nigel Popplewell, Derek Pringle, Abdul Qadeer, the late Wasim Raja, Waris Sharif, Jonathan Taylor, Ali Zaidi.

The umpire David Constant, something of a linchpin for this chapter, declined my offer to speak; Constant's former colleague Dickie Bird, however, went on the record at length; he told me that both Imran and his team had been 'a joy' to officiate. I'm grateful both to him and to the source at UNICEF. My former wife Cat Sinclair, who died prematurely in 2007, was an invaluable co-collator of material on the 1987 summer Test series. She is missed.

Imran Khan's quotes beginning 'We were treated with disdain ...' and 'By drawing the series ...' are both from *All Round View*. Imran's quote beginning 'It was just legalised begging ...', Charles Glass's quote beginning 'He sees a class of people ...' and Mark Shand's quote beginning 'I always thought he was a proper sort of captain ...' are all from Ivo Tennant's *Imran Khan;* I'm grateful to Ivo, at one time my fellow worker on the Victor Gollancz chain gang, for his input. Javed Miandad's quotes beginning 'Before the Bangalore Test ...', 'There is some controversy ...', 'Our team donated ...' and 'The board asked me to continue ...' are from *Cutting Edge*. Iqbal Qasim's quote beginning 'I was never sure why ...' and Wasim Akram's quote beginning 'It almost seemed natural ...' are both included in Omar Noman's *Pride and Passion*. Ian Botham's quote beginning 'At the end of the over, Imran came across ...' is from Botham's *My Autobiography*.

CHAPTER EIGHT

A number of well-placed sources put their recollections of Imran in 1990–2 at my disposal. Among them were Qamar Ahmed, Aslam Anwar, Jeffrey Archer, Fareshteh Aslam, Richie Benaud, Dickie Bird, Geoff Boycott, the late Denis Compton, Dar, Ted Dexter, Judy Flanders, Tony Gill, David Gower, Javed Kureishi, Vic Marks, John Murray, Mark Nicholas, Tim Rice, Dicky Rutnagur, the late Peter Smith, Jonathan Taylor. Very nearly every British, Pakistani and other cricket-playing national news organisation extensively covered the World Cup final of 25 March 1992; I should particularly acknowledge the *Cricketer International* of that May, and also the DVD version produced by FSH Marketing (www.cricketvideo.com). Derek Pringle and a colleague in the England team who prefers not to be named both provided the all-important insider account.

Imran Khan's quote beginning 'Overnight, I became a star ...' is from Imran's *The Autobiography*. Javed Miandad's quotes beginning 'In the first Test …', 'It was enough to make us feel …' and 'I wrote pieces where I thought …' are from *Cutting Edge*. Kate Muir's quote relating to 'Gazza, the Beatles and President Kennedy …' is from Ivo Tennant's *Imran Khan*. Ian Botham's quote beginning 'On one side it was so badly …' is from Botham's *My Autobiography*. Mushtaq Ahmed's quote beginning 'We discussed Graeme Hick …' is from Lawrence Booth's book *Cricket, Lovely Cricket?* (Yellow Jersey Press, 2008); I'm grateful to Vicky Fleming for the gift. Kristiane Backer's quote suggesting that 'London has always stood for respect …' can be found on her website www.kristianebacker.com.

Finally, I should thank both the source at the Shaukat Khanum Memorial Cancer Hospital and the party familiar with the workings of the office of the Pakistani prime minister. I did not personally interview Nawaz Sharif.

CHAPTER NINE

'I changed my life; too many people fail to do that' (or close variants of the theme), Imran says. Help in recalling his conversion from bachelor cricketer into a family man and politician came from, among others, Aslam Anwar, Dar, George Galloway, Alix Gibb, Jock Given, Antao Hassan, Tahir Nawaz, the late Harold Pinter, Abdul Qadeer, Haroun Rashid. Imran himself spoke to me about this phase of his life in our interview of 26 November 2008. I'm also grateful to the source familiar with some of the doings of the Goldsmith family, and to the former professional colleague of Imran's who spoke to me about the Princess of Wales; the reader should of course make up his or her own mind about the stories cited.

Other primary sources included Qamar Ahmed, Dave Davies, Tony Gill, Naeem-ul-Haque, Sarah Jones, the late Chris Lander, Jonathan Mermagen, Waris Sharif, Syra Vahidy. Research revealed that HM Courts Service had erased the official transcript of Ian Botham and Allan Lamb's 1996 proceedings against Imran Khan, but a full and sometimes verbatim account was given in most UK broadsheets, notably the *Daily Telegraph*. I also consulted the British Library, *Chronicles*, CricInfo, the *Daily Mail*, *Dawn* and the Public Record Office.

Imran Khan's quote beginning 'No matter how naïve this may sound …' is from *All Round View*. His quotes beginning 'I don't want to go to a place …' and 'The motivation for politics …' are from Ivo

Tennant's *Imran Khan* and a CNN interview of March 2008, respectively. Mike Atherton's quote beginning 'As I stood in the witness box …' is from his book *Opening Up*.

It's a pleasure both to confirm that Ian Botham declined a formal interview, and to have spoken to him and Lady Botham on the phone.

CHAPTER TEN

Parting comment from: Aslam Anwar, Jeffrey Archer, Fareshteh Aslam, Geoff Boycott, Dar, Dave Davies, Judy Flanders, George Galloway, Tony Gill, Naeem-ul-Haque, Janet Harris, Antao Hassan, Asif Iqbal, Chris Kelly, Javed Kureishi, the late Chris Lander, Jonathan Mermagen, Abdul Mirza, John Murray, Tahir Nawaz, Mark Nicholas, Abdul Qadeer, the late Wasim Raja, Jonathan Taylor, Ali Zaidi. I also spoke to a number of sources who, citing a healthy respect for the volatile and personally adventurous world of Pakistani politics, made it a condition to do so anonymously. Wherever this was humanly possible, their remarks were independently corroborated. Further details of the Tehreek-e-Insaf party can be found at www.insaf.pk. A full account of Sita White's death, and its aftermath, appears in *Vanity Fair* of September 2004, which I combined with other, first-hand sources in my own treatment.

Imran Khan's quotes beginning 'If my women …', 'A helicopter gunship comes on top …' and 'Not really …' are all from the *Independent* of 2 November 2008; his quote beginning 'Some of the greatest happiness I've ever had …' is from an undated but obviously recent online interview he gave to CNN. Imran's quote beginning 'This is a civil war in the making …' is from the *Daily Telegraph* of 9 December 2008; the reference to him being 'a body linguist's dream' is very slightly amended from the same source. The scene of Imran Khan campaigning in Kamar Mushani is drawn in part from an unbylined report that appeared on Buzzle.com of 26 September 2002. The reference to the Pakistani state being 'a sort of giant cash machine …', though not a unique observation, appeared in an eloquent piece in the *Spectator* of 15 November 2008. A small number of quotes attributed to Imran in this chapter are slightly adapted, in the light of what he told me, from a report on, and interview with, him that appeared in the *Daily Telegraph* of 12 November 2008. I should also acknowledge the occasional quote from former president Musharraf's book *In the Line of Fire*, a gripping first-hand account of modern Pakistani politics, if not one burdened by excessive self-doubt on the author's part.

Although Imran Khan co-operated with the writing of this book, I should again stress that he neither sought nor received any editorial control over it. I am solely to blame for the contents.

Index